John Letcher of Virginia

SOUTHERN HISTORICAL PUBLICATIONS NO. 11

JOHN LETCHER OF VIRGINIA

The Story of Virginia's Civil War Governor

by F. N. Boney

UNIVERSITY OF ALABAMA PRESS

UNIVERSITY, ALABAMA

Table of Contents

Introduction

The recently concluded Civil War Centennial has brought forth a host of new books about America's greatest tragedy. Military affairs have received the most attention, particularly in Virginia, while many less dramatic but equally vital events on the home front remain obscure.

Gradually the upper echelons of Confederate political leadership are being thoroughly examined, but the task is by no means completed. John Letcher, governor of Virginia from 1860 through 1863, is one of the significant leaders of the Confederacy who is still virtually unknown. The little that has been written about him —two articles by Professor William Gleason Bean are most valuable—treats parts of his prewar career. This study, covering Letcher's entire life with emphasis on his governorship, attempts to fill an obvious gap in American history. For the first time, Letcher's lengthy career is examined in detail: early development as a local Virginia politician during the Jacksonian era, maturity as an influential congressman in the rising sectionalism of the 1850's, the crucial governorship, and finally a gradual fading away in the postwar period.

Letcher's story is only a fragment of the epic of the transformation of the United States from a weak, uncertain confederation into a powerful, confident nation. The emergence of the colossus of the New World is a spectacular and critical event in world history, full of grandeur and suffering, idealism and disillusionment. To trace the course of Letcher's life is to follow one

small current in a torrential flood—but a significant one, for
Letcher was not only a leader but also in many ways a typical
American of his time.

Many persons have helped me on this project. Professor William Gleason Bean, pinpointed the way to several fruitful manuscript collections. Professor James A. Rawley, of the University
of Nebraska, suggested many valuable improvements, and Professor
Edward Younger, of the University of Virginia, furnished overall
guidance and encouragement. General John S. Letcher gave me
free access to his grandfather's private papers—a valuable (indeed
indispensable!) collection never before thoroughly exploited. My
wife's services as a patient reader and incisive critic have also been
essential. Miss Anne Freudenberg, assistant curator of manuscripts,
Alderman Library, University of Virginia, Mr. William M. E.
Rachal of the Virginia Historical Society, and Mr. John W.
Dudley, assistant archivist, Virginia State Library, have all been
more than helpful on many occasions. The cooperation of per-
sonnel at other libraries and depositories must also be acknowledged
—especially the good people of the Filson Club, the Library of
Congress, the Henry E. Huntington Library, the University of
North Carolina Library, the Wisconsin State Historical Society,
the McCormick Library at Washington and Lee University, the
Historical Society of Pennsylvania, and the National Archives.
Finally, I wish to thank the University of Georgia, Washington
State University, and the American Association for State and Local
History for generous research grants that have made it possible for
me to complete this work.

Thanks are also due the editors of the following journals, who
have kindly granted permission for the use in this biography of
material first presented in their publications: *Lincoln Herald,
Revue Historique de Bordeaux et du département de la Gironde,
Civil War History, The Virginia Magazine of History and Biography, The Connecticut Historical Society Bulletin, The Mississippi Quarterly,* and *The Filson Club History Quarterly.*

                                                        F. N. BONEY

Pullman, Washington
May 1, 1966

John Letcher of Virginia

CHAPTER 1

Birth of a Politician

In 1834, at the age of twenty—one, John Letcher knew at last exactly what he wanted to do in life. Politics would be his career, his calling. And with an enthusiasm that was not untypical of young Americans in the Jacksonian Era, he hailed the decision in his diary with some lines from Lord Byron:

> My epitaph shall be my name alone,
> If that with honour fail to crown my day,
> Oh! may no other fame my deeds repay,
> *That,* only *that,* shall single out the spot,
> By *that* remembered, or with that forgot.[1]

Honor! "Honesty" would probably have been a better word, for young Letcher was truly a son of the middle class, little influenced by aristocratic romanticism. Physically and spiritually, his roots went deep into the wellsprings of the American heritage. His forebears had been among the yeomen who had poured generations of sweat and blood into the seemingly limitless land. The Welsh, English, Scotch—Irish past of the Letcher family was distant and vague in time and memory; the Virginia past was real and immediate. The family had moved slowly westward and finally entered the beautiful Valley of Virginia (the Shenandoah Valley), an area settled principally by people of Scotch—Irish and German descent.

John Letcher's father, William Houston Letcher, was born

in 1781 on a farm near Lexington, Rockbridge County. Beginning his adult life as a manual laborer, he gradually worked his way into the middle class. As proprietor of a general store in Lexington, he bought and sold everything from cattle to shingles, and he was also active as a builder and real estate speculator. Thus, the yeoman's son became, by his own effort, a typical nineteenth-century small town businessman. In 1810 he married Elizabeth Davidson, the Scotch—Irish daughter of another sturdy yeoman family, and on March 29, 1813, their first child, John, was born.

John and his brothers Sam and William, and their sister Mary, all grew up in a large, comfortable home in Lexington. Their childhood was happy and vigorous, and all but William lived through the diseases and epidemics that frequently struck. However, their life was complicated by the rigid code of belief and conduct that was imposed by their devout Methodist parents. Mary submitted willingly to religious orthodoxy, but John and Sam, each in his own way, rejected the family religion.[2]

The town of Lexington, surrounded by the rolling farmlands of the Valley of Virginia, was the commercial, political, cultural, intellectual, social, and judicial locus of the countryside. Washington College stood on the highest hill, and by 1839 the Virginia Military Institute would evolve from the local state arsenal. The Franklin Society and Library Company had been sponsoring speeches and debates since the turn of the century. Yet, despite these traces of cosmopolitanism and progress, this little town with fewer than 900 inhabitants remained much like the Valley— isolated, provincial, tradition—bound, dominated by conservative and puritanical brands of Protestantism.[3]

By 1832, 19—year—old John Letcher was restless, dissatisfied, and highly uncertain of his future. He had received the usual early education at an old field school, showing much ability but little ambition. He had already abandoned the orthodox Methodist God of his father, and was considering moving West.

The home ties were strained but not broken. Even in his most rebellious moods, young John admired and respected his father and tried to follow his suggestions, if not always his commands. When his father recommended a higher education at

Washington College, John consented, but without enthusiasm. His pursuit of learning was equally unenthusiastic. A casual interest in local and national politics served as a convenient excuse for ignoring his academic responsibilities. By the end of the year, John Letcher's collegiate career had ended—and so had his father's patience.

A self–made man, William Letcher was eager to give his sons a good start in life, but John's lack of effort baffled and frustrated him. There were other small colleges in Virginia, such as Randolph–Macon and Hampden–Sydney, where a lazy youngster could have a second chance, but was this the right answer? His son was at the first crossroads of his life. The next few years would set the pattern for his future. A conscientious father had to provide the correct guidance. A mistake at this crucial point could be disastrous.

William Letcher chose not to coddle his sons. John was told bluntly that he was "now a man" and would have to earn his own living. From now on he was to be on his own—except that his father would see that he obtained a job as a carpenter's apprentice and would allow him to continue to live at home. Otherwise, John was to shift for himself.

Thus technically—but only technically—John Letcher followed in his father's footsteps, beginning his career as a laborer. A few months of carpentry did wonders. The dreaminess and uncertainty began to fade as he finally—perhaps desperately—began to think seriously of the future. His interest in politics had continued to grow, and it was now almost an obsession. Incentive and ambition came at last in full measure, never to depart. John Letcher, having weathered the first major crisis of his life, set his future course permanently. The tall, lanky, rather awkward young carpenter's apprentice with the straightforward, gregarious personality embarked on a political career that was to span four decades.[4]

He prepared for his new career by compiling detailed notes on the problems and personalities of politics in 1834. Certainly this was a time of excitement, even confusion, as the forces of nationalism, liberalism, and democracy surged forward under the banner of Andrew Jackson. In Virginia and throughout the nation the mass movement that had swept Jackson to victory in 1828 had lost its cohesiveness as deep doctrinal divisions came to the surface. John C. Calhoun was popular with many Virginians, and the substitution of New Yorker Martin Van Buren for him as vice president in 1832 had caused much dissatisfaction in the state. Jackson's head–on collision with the South Carolina nullifiers had driven many strict states' righters, such as John Tyler, Abel P. Upshur, and Thomas Walker Gilmer, out of the ranks of the Jacksonian Democracy. And the President's relentless war on the Second Bank of the United States had brought other factions into opposition. Thus by 1834, the Virginia Democracy was still strong—and still factionalized. The rising opposition coalesced into the Whig Party and even captured the General Assembly and the governorship, but this victory was brief. The Whigs proved to be as deeply divided as their rivals, and the Democrats temporarily recaptured the assembly in 1835.[5]

In this age of fierce partisan politics, a man was forced to pick sides. John Letcher did not hesitate. His father had been as ardent in his loyalty to the Democratic Party as in his devotion to the Methodist Church—a relationship that was more than coincidental and far from unique. The concept of a liberal capitalistic system particularly appealed to this self–made man, who was a perfect example of a class of men Daniel Webster had once described as rural capitalists and village entrepreneurs, men who often served as shock troops in the Jacksonian crusade.[6]

John Letcher's Methodism had yielded to skepticism, and a portion of this skepticism now spilled over into his political thinking. He was a dedicated, often fiery Democrat, but even in his earliest, most idealistic years in the party he never abandoned himself to blind partisanship. At this time his moderation was far more evident in his private conversations and correspondence than in his public utterances, but it was nonetheless real and basic to his political character.

Letcher continued his preparation by writing to great and near–great politicians, seeking their opinions on every conceivable issue. He pored over the columns of Thomas Ritchie's *Richmond Enquirer,* the principal Democratic paper in Virginia, and frequently studied Francis Preston Blair's Washington *Globe* as well. He also joined the Franklin Society, participated regularly in its political and intellectual discussions, and often used its fine little library. Finally, he became the friend and political protégé of the town's leading Democrat, James McDowell. A veteran of the Virginia House of Delegates, the talented and ambitious Mc-Dowell was already well known in western Virginia. In 1843 he would gain the governorship, and would then serve in the House of Representatives from 1846 to 1851, the year of his death.[7]

As a Democrat, Letcher needed all of the practical training in politics he could get: Rockbridge County was Whig territory. The small farmers of the Valley were overwhelmingly Democratic—the invincible Tenth Legion of the Virginia Democracy —but the little trading center of Lexington and its surrounding county stubbornly supported the Whigs. Richmond, Petersburg, Norfolk, Lynchburg, Fredericksburg, Winchester, Staunton—virtually every town and city with significant business activity— evidenced similar Whig inclinations. Lexington was a western town, beyond the Blue Ridge Mountains, situated on the North River, a tributary of the James River. Any internal improvement projects that might turn this water system into a practical highway to eastern markets was welcome. Inclined to be more nationalistic than his eastern neighbors, the average Lexingtonian was unlikely to oppose Henry Clay's proposal to do such jobs with federal funds.[8]

The minority Democrats waged an uphill battle in Rockbridge County. McDowell was their leader, but his ambitions carried him far afield. While this put a strain on the local organization, it did allow Letcher and other young politicos to gain valuable experience. McDowell, pleased with his young protégé's aggressiveness and competence, became truly fond of Letcher and looked upon him as virtually a member of his own family. Over the years he came to depend more often on his ambitious aide to attend to his interests in Rockbridge County while he maneuvered for the governorship.

During his early years of political apprenticeship, Letcher was also greatly influenced by another local Democratic leader, Wil-

liam Taylor, McDowell's brother–in–law, who had been commonwealth attorney for Rockbridge County for almost two decades, and who later was to serve in Congress from 1843 until his
death in 1846, when McDowell would take his place. It was primarily Taylor who convinced Letcher that the profession of law
was the firmest foundation for the risky game of politics. In the
fall of 1836, at the age of twenty–three, Letcher entered Taylor's
law office as a clerk and began preparing for his second, supple-
mentary career. He continued to read extensively, referring as
often to Blackstone's *Commentaries* as to Ritchie's *Enquirer* or
Blair's *Globe* until he received his license to practice law on April
26, 1839.[9]

Nevertheless, Letcher remained in the thick of the political wars.
Like many other Virginia Democrats, he had no enthusiasm
for Van Buren's presidential ambitions in 1836. He was particularly concerned over Van Buren's past support of the enfranchise-
ment of free Negroes in New York. In April, 1836, Letcher wrote
his congressman, Robert Craig, detailing his opposition. Craig
assured Letcher that the "Little Magician" was safe on the sensitive issue of slavery and rated him the best candidate available.
Nevertheless, Letcher continued to look critically into Van Buren's
past. Suspecting that the New Yorker had not wholeheartedly
supported the cause in the War of 1812, he wrote Peter V. Daniel,
newly appointed U. S. district judge and longtime power in the
Virginia Democracy. Like Craig, Daniel defended Van Buren's
record and labelled him the best presidential bet. The old pros
proved to be right, of course, and Van Buren swept to victory
over divided Whig opposition in the election of 1836. To Letcher,
however, as to many other Democrats, Van Buren was a pale
imitation of the mighty Jackson. However, as a loyal party man,
the young Virginian supported the new President throughout his
stormy administration.[10]

During this period, Letcher's political activities broadened
into a new field. He began to contribute political articles to Democratic newspapers such as the Fincastle *Democrat* and even the
influential *Richmond Enquirer*. He showed a genuine aptitude

for using the pen as a political sword—or hatchet. His journalistic talents soon would be given a free rein.

When not politicking, Letcher diligently pursued his legal studies. He also began to handle some routine Rockbridge County land sales and debt collections for Taylor's law office. His main clients were James McDowell and Senator Thomas Hart Benton of Missouri, McDowell's brother–in–law.[11]

Despite a relentless desire to succeed in law and politics, Letcher by no means ignored the social side of life. He became one of a small group of young Lexingtonians determined that the puritanical atmosphere of the Valley would not suppress their right to pursue happiness. Lively, inquisitive, iconoclastic, this close–knit group loved a lilting song, a witty conversation, a care-free game of chance or a lively party, and indicated no prejudice against tobacco, bourbon whiskey, or the pretty girls of the Valley. This small band of brothers included Francis H. Smith, first super-intendent of Virginia Military Institute, and J. L. T. Preston, a professor there for over 40 years; William Taylor's two sons, Dr. James McDowell Taylor, Letcher's lifelong physician, and Robert J. Taylor, first a lawyer and later a Presbyterian minister; John B. Lyle, the proprietor of a small and unprofitable bookstore; and John Warren Grigsby, a cynical and moody young man who served as American consul at Bordeaux, France, in the 1840's, married well in Kentucky, and ultimately found glory as a fighting Confederate colonel. Maturity and matrimony eventually tamed their restless spirits, but the ties of friendship held firm.[12]

Letcher led an active social life, but when the political storm clouds gathered, he abandoned everything but the business at hand. Such an occasion was the county election for the House of Delegates in May, 1838. The Democrats were uncommonly optimistic. In the 1837 election they had been able to gain one of the county's two seats for James McDowell. Now they hoped to smash the Whigs by winning both seats. They renominated McDowell and selected as his running mate their most promising neophyte—John Letcher.

McDowell was after much bigger political game and only reluctantly consented on March 1 to run again against the Whig tide in Rockbridge. He remained in Richmond, where the General Assembly was in session, and turned the entire campaign over to Letcher, who worked furiously to marshal the forces of the local Democracy against the well–organized and confident Whigs.

This, however, was not to be a Democratic year. The Panic of 1837 and the ensuing depression caught the Democrats in office in Washington, and Van Buren's proposal to shift government funds from selected state banks to federal treasuries scattered throughout the nation caused deep rumblings within the party. Senators William Cabell Rives of Virginia and Nathaniel P. Tallmadge of New York favored continuing to deposit federal funds in state banks, and, branding Van Buren's subtreasury plan a threat to states' rights—another national bank in disguise—they formed a conservative faction within the Democracy. At the other end of the party's broad political spectrum, "Old Bullion" Benton of Missouri led the "hard money" men in support of the subtreasury system.

The Democrats were caught in another of their periodic crises of unity, and the results were quickly felt on the state level. The strain was severe in Virginia where Rives' conservatives soon became a powerful and restless faction. James McDowell emerged as the leader of the party regulars, those who followed the Benton-Van Buren line, whereas Thomas Ritchie, the elder statesman of the Virginia Democracy, opposed the subtreasury system and thus tended to lean toward the conservatives. He refused to pick sides, however, and instead worked frantically to close the widening breach. Suffering the usual fate of the conciliator, he caught brickbats from both factions.

The inherently factionalized Whigs were quick to exploit their opponents' difficulties. In Virginia, they won the spring elections, gaining control of the House of Delegates for four long years. In Rockbridge County, the campaign was heated, centering mainly on the issue of a national bank versus the subtreasury system, but the McDowell–Letcher ticket was doomed. The Whig candidates, Alfred Leyburn and Charles P. Dorman, won by a large margin.[13]

Letcher sulked bitterly, blaming Ritchie and Rives for the

disaster. The situation in Rockbridge seemed hopeless. One great disadvantage was the Whig partisanship of Lexington's only news-paper, the *Gazette*. As each election approached, the *Gazette* saturated the area with Whig propaganda, and the Democrats were unable to launch an effective counterattack.

McDowell decided to establish a rival Democratic paper in Lexington. He had no more time for local operations—his Rock-bridge defeat in 1838 had been a serious blow—and he put Letcher in charge of the new journal—the Lexington *Valley Star*. The first issue of the *Valley Star* appeared in February, 1839, hailing strict constitutional construction and states' rights as its basic political faith. This was part of the orthodox Virginia heritage, a conservative Jeffersonian formula for state–federal relations.

Editor Letcher a conservative? The Rockbridge Whigs would have hooted at the idea. To them Letcher was a radical —a left wing Democrat—a Locofoco. Letcher did not completely disagree with this evaluation. He considered himself not a con-servative but a crusader, a descendant of Jefferson, a follower of Jackson, and an heir to the future. Within the generally conserva-tive context of Virginia politics, young Letcher was a liberal.[14]

Letcher's partisan *Valley Star* quickly outlined its political philosophy. Virginia needed an efficient public school system. Van Buren's subtreasury system was sound, and hard money was the only really reliable form of currency. A paper money system oppressed the working man. Resurrection of the national bank was unthinkable. State banks should not be depositories for fed-eral or state funds, and they should be carefully supervised by the state government. All corporations should be watched closely and not granted special privileges. Monopolies should be destroyed. Free trade was wholesome; tariffs were unacceptable. Henry Clay's plan to distribute the proceeds from the sale of public lands among the states was dangerous because it would empty the treasury and thus lead to higher tariffs; it would also violate state sovereignty. Abolition was anathema. The federal government should not finance internal improvement projects.

Internal improvements by state governments, however, were definitely desirable. Like most western Virginians, Letcher was eager to improve the inadequate transportation facilities that linked his area with the eastern seaboard. The *Valley Star* doubted the feasibility of the James River and Kanawha Canal Company project, whose terminus remained far below the junction of the North River and the James River; but, under the circumstances, this effort was better for western Virginia than no internal improvements at all.

The *Valley Star* vigorously supported James McDowell's effort to win Virginia's vacant seat in the Senate, defending as best it could his politically unwise call for emancipation in the general assembly in 1831. In the wake of Nat Turner's Rebellion, many Virginians had seriously debated the future of slavery at that time, but by 1839 opposition to emancipation was growing rapidly in the state, and the cotton South was firmly committed to the continuation and expansion of the use of slave labor. McDowell was neither the first nor the last Virginia politician to be damaged by this sensitive, fluid issue; Letcher, too, would soon experience this fate. McDowell's bid for the Senate failed, as the legislature was too disrupted by intraparty squabbles to give anyone a majority vote. Finally, in 1841, Rives' Conservatives formally joined the Whigs, and Rives himself filled the vacancy. McDowell's efforts to win the governorship came to nothing.[15]

By the end of its first year, the *Valley Star* was firmly established. The Whiggish hue of Rockbridge County was a handicap, to be sure, but the new publication was read throughout the Democratic Valley. Letcher knew party stalwarts in every section of the Valley, and he marshaled them into an informal but effective regional news service. These men sometimes contributed long articles under pseudonyms, and they also solicited new readers.[16]

The free–swinging, hard–hitting *Valley Star* was a success. In Rockbridge, the applause of the Democrats was drowned out by the outraged howls of the Whigs. The *Gazette,* shorn of its monopoly status, led the assault on this brash young editor who had unleashed a relentless attack on all things Whiggish:

> Blinded by party venom, our neighbor certainly cannot see half an inch beyond his glowing proboscis . . . Did you ever see, dear reader, a certain gaunt, long-legged, long necked bird called, we

believe, a "Fly-up-the-creek", or more expressively a "King-Fisher",
from its rare cunning and famous luck in catching innocent little
minnows—perched upon an old dead tree overhanging some bab-
bling brook, and look askant, with fierce eye and watery mouth,
upon the fat little minnows darting about in the water below—now
glancing their silver sides to the sun and now, in wanton joy of the
hearts leaping up into the air? See! how he plunges suddenly into
the water, seizes that poor little minnow, gulps it down, and flies
back, with exulting chattering, to the old dead tree! If you have
seen all this, kind reader, as we frequently have in our fishing days,
you have seen a living picture of our neighbor of the Star. Woe
betide the poor minnow of a Whig who dares show his head above
the water, within reach of his beak. He pounces down upon him,
seizes him in his bill, gulps him down, and fills the air with his
noisy cries—"Forgery! Forgery! Forgery!" "A base forgery." "An
infamous forgery—A WHIG FORGERY—Murder! Murder! Murder!"[17]

Democratic leaders throughout the state cheered Letcher's
success. In neighboring Botetourt County the Democrats were
anxious for him to buy the controlling interest in the Fincastle
Democrat for $850.00 and continue his partisan efforts there.
They painted a rosy picture of a future that would culminate in
election to Congress. Thomas Ritchie advised him to accept the
editorship of a Lynchburg newspaper that would provide a broad-
er audience for his writings. Letcher preferred to remain in Lexington, however, dividing his time between a budding law practice
in William Taylor's office and his editorial duties for the *Valley
Star*.

Law and journalism were for Letcher not ends in themselves, but means to the end of acquiring political power and
prestige. Frequent correspondence with Congressman Robert
Craig gave Letcher access to accurate information about the
Washington scene, while association with McDowell and other
seasoned campaigners, as well as his journalistic activities, kept
him in touch with the intricacies of state politics. And locally, his
activities as a county politician and a lawyer made him familiar
with grass roots feeling and with the machinations of Rockbridge's
numerous courthouse cliques. As the decade of the 1830's ended,
Letcher was no longer an obscure novice in law, in journalism—
or in politics.[18]

CHAPTER 2

Maturity

By 1840 a newly confident and relentlessly ambitious Letcher was ready to launch out on his own, and the next six years would see him reach full maturity. A new political decade had dawned, and the Democracy was in deep trouble. Van Buren was not Jackson; the people simply would not follow him as they had followed "Old Hickory". Also, the Van Buren administration was fatally handicapped by a severe and persistent depression. The Democrats' laissez–faire economic policy precluded their taking drastic action, and the people's cries for relief went unheeded. The Whigs took advantage of the situation. Borrowing a leaf from the opposition's book, they gave the party standard to another warrior-hero, William Henry Harrison of Ohio, and unleashed a ballyhoo campaign unprecedented in American politics.

The Van Buren–Harrison campaign was bitterly fought throughout the nation. In Virginia, a crucial legislative canvass complicated matters. The various phases of the great struggle for power were never entirely separate in the state, but, since the House of Delegates election was scheduled for April, more than six months before the presidential contest, most of the early efforts by both local parties were devoted to the state election.[1]

On March 9, the Rockbridge Democrats rallied at Lexington. After a rousing speech by McDowell, they nominated John Letcher and John Brockenbrough as candidates for the House of

Delegates. These two young lawyers were not always to be allies,
but in 1840 they fought side by side for a common victory. Mc-
Dowell in campaigning vigorously for Letcher, who was by now
his associate rather than his protégé, set the tone of the campaign
by attacking the Whigs as a social class. Letcher followed this
lead, appealing for the votes of the working classes and lashing
out at the Whigs in numerous speeches throughout the county,
in the *Valley Star,* and in a special pamphlet issued a few days
before the balloting. As usual, his platform leaned toward "Loco-
focoism". He also supported Secretary of War Joel R. Poinsett's
controversial plan for incorporating the militia of the states into
the national army, a scheme opposed by most ardent states'
righters.[2]

The Whigs concentrated their fire on Letcher, a "briefless
attorney and political adventurer",[3] and on election day the Whig
candidates, Dorman and Leyburn, emerged as the victors. Though
beaten again, Letcher had reason not to be discouraged: the
spirited Democratic campaign had narrowed the traditional victory
margin of the Whigs. From Washington, Congressman Robert
Craig sent encouraging news: "Your Democratic friends in the
House (and many of them seem to have their eyes upon you) say
you have done nobly . . . ." The Whigs retained a thin edge in the
legislature, but Letcher's star continued to rise even in defeat.[4]

Led by McDowell, the Rockbridge Democrats continued
their aggressive tactics in the presidential canvass. Despite reassur-
ances from Senator Benton and others, Letcher was still unfavor-
ably disposed toward Van Buren, but as a loyal party man, he
campaigned vigorously for the "Little Magician". He had already
studied Van Buren's career critically in 1836, but now he restudied
this subject, giving emphasis to the man's virtues rather than his
deficiencies. Democratic Congressman Aaron Vanderpool of New
York and Van Buren himself furnished the favorable information
Letcher needed to champion the cause in the *Valley Star.*

Letcher spent still more of his time looking into the career
of Harrison, and after careful research, assisted by Robert Craig
and other Democratic congressmen, he published a series of blistering attacks in the *Valley Star.* Harrison was described as a

Federalist backed by abolitionists, and the quality of his general-
ship at Tippecanoe was called into question. His voting record in
the Ohio legislature was criticized, with particular emphasis on
any issue related—however remotely—to the increasingly sensitive
subject of slavery. Letcher sought to substantiate a rumor that
Harrison had been involved in plans to overthrow the government
of Colombia while he was the U. S. minister there, but a lack of
concrete evidence kept him from printing this accusation. Finally,
in keeping with the general tone of this heated campaign, the
Valley Star also questioned the propriety of Harrison's personal
life.[5]

Letcher's efforts were not confined to the *Valley Star*. Invitations for him to speak came from many parts of the western
section of the state and from Richmond, and Letcher filled as
many of these requests as he could, especially in the Valley and
adjoining counties. On occasion, he also engaged in formal debates with Whig partisans. Though he was not an eloquent orator,
his dry and prosaic delivery was bolstered by an impressive mass
of facts and statistics, and on balance he was an effective stump
speaker.[6]

During the campaign Letcher worked closely with Mc-
Dowell, state Senator William "Extra Billy" Smith, Thomas
Ritchie, and other Democratic leaders, but, as usual, his main
efforts were concentrated in Rockbridge County. The Lexington
Whigs were well organized, confident, and even contemptuous
of the opposition. One wrote a comrade that he "would as leave
be bit by any other quadruped as a rabid Locofoco".[7] They ridi-
culed Van Buren as effeminate and foppish, his administration
as extravagant and corrupt. The Democrats fought desperately
to turn the Whig tide in Rockbridge—and as usual, they failed.
The Whigs retained their mastery of the county by a count of
639 to 535. However, the Democrats again carried the Valley
by a large margin. The defection of Rives' Conservatives to the
Whigs was a serious blow, and the Democrats barely carried the
state. However, the election indicated that the Old Dominion's
days of political suzerainty were clearly over—and Harrison was
in the White House.[8]

Letcher was too preoccupied with a personal matter to worry much about defeat. During the campaign he had met Miss Susan Holt of neighboring Augusta County and fallen deeply in love. Letcher was neither handsome nor dashing. He was tall and thin, and his movements often seemed slightly awkward and un-coordinated, but not quite clumsy. His rough–hewn features were topped by an unruly thatch of rapidly thinning sandy hair. Though his complexion was basically pale, his face was always florid (his "proboscis" *did* glow slightly—a physical characteristic that his opponents never failed to exploit!). And yet the young politician was not a dull fellow. Friendly and open–hearted, quick to laugh, thick–skinned, nimble of wit—he was lively enough to brighten any gathering, discreet enough to avoid openly flouting the puritanical code of the Valley. What he may have lacked in refinement he more than made up for in goodwill, optimism, and sincerity. Even the Whigs of Rockbridge had to admit that John Letcher was a pretty good fellow—between elections. And if a young lady was not too bored by politics, she might find him quite attractive, especially in informal, natural situations when he was most at ease.

Susan Holt did find him attractive, and friends expected a marriage late in 1841. However, Letcher discovered that court-ship was as uncertain as politics, and more than once the romance seemed to founder. Discouraged and confused, at times he was tempted to end the whole affair, but he could not put the young lady from Augusta County out of his mind—and the erratic court-ship continued.[9]

Politics was still his main profession, however, and despite a recurrent inflammation of the throat and lungs, he actively backed McDowell's continuing efforts to win higher political ground. The epic defeat in the presidential election of 1840 had shaken the confidence of Democrats everywhere; even the mighty Tenth Legion of the Valley was dispirited. Letcher, McDowell, and other Democrats were on the defensive and spoke less often of what they favored than of what they opposed—a national bank, protective tariffs, the distribution of the proceeds of public land sales, internal improvements by the federal government, abolition of slavery. They fought a holding action, hoping to take advantage of any mistakes the Whigs might make.

During this period of Democratic disarray, the sudden retirement of Congressman Robert Craig gave the Whigs a golden opportunity. They quickly nominated their best man, Alexander H. H. Stuart of Staunton, to oppose McDowell, Craig's logical successor. The disheartened Democrats could not be rallied, and Stuart won a stunning victory in the very heartland of the Virginia Democracy.[10]

Letcher continued to edit the *Valley Star* until October of 1841. Partisan warfare between his journal and the Whig *Gazette* slackened soon after the presidential election. The congressional election early in 1841 caused some friction, but generally passions had cooled. In June, Letcher did criticize new Congressman Stuart's support of John Quincy Adams' crusade against the "gag rule", which automatically tabled all abolition petitions sent to the House of Representatives. Stuart counseled the South not to make the abolitionists martyrs by restricting their right to petition, but by this time southerners were too emotionally committed to their peculiar institution to see the wisdom of his advice.[11]

By 1842, Letcher was devoting most of his energy to his growing and lucrative law practice. A man contemplating marriage had to think of the future. He continued to buy and sell land and collect debts for McDowell, Benton, and others, but was also active in the courts, where he was gaining a reputation as a skillful, thorough lawyer. Although he had temporarily abandoned active politics, Letcher followed closely the swift and dramatic flow of events in Washington.[12]

He was delighted to see the Whigs' 1840 triumph turn to dust. President Harrison died a month after taking office, and avid states' righter John Tyler took his place. Soon the nationalists and the states' righters within the party began to feud. Clay and his followers controlled both houses of Congress, but President Tyler decimated their legislative program with repeated vetoes, splitting the party further. By 1842, Tyler had been read out of the party and was beginning to lean on states' rights Democrats for support. In Virginia, the Whigs quickly felt the effects of the

confusion in Washington. Led by Thomas Ritchie, the rejuvenated
Democrats quickly gained revenge for 1840 by sweeping the state
elections of 1842. Tyler, Upshur, and Henry A. Wise could not
even hold the eastern states' rights Whigs together, and defections
in the more nationalistic western counties were even more numerous. The Democracy gained control of the state legislature, thus
ending four years of Whig dominance.

Even in its darkest hours the Whig party could count on
Rockbridge County, and McDowell's attempt to regain his seat
in the House of Delegates failed. Letcher supported his friend
but did not campaign actively. He was more useful when Mc-
Dowell made another bid for the governorship later in the year.
Since the new Democratic legislature was to elect the new governor, lobbying would be more effective than campaigning. Letcher
went to Richmond just before the balloting to champion Mc-
Dowell. He had influence with a few Valley legislators, but the
master wire–puller in Richmond was Ritchie. On the eve of the
election, Letcher conferred with Ritchie and then wrote Senator
Benton, confidently predicting victory for McDowell. Two days
later the legislature elected James McDowell Virginia's thirty-
seventh governor.[13]

Letcher returned to his law practice, but he did not neglect
his political homework. With Robert Craig's old congressional seat
filled by a Whig, his best source of inside information from Washington was gone. Letcher broadened the scope of his inquiries,
seeking speeches, documents, and general information from a host
of prominent politicians, including John C. Calhoun. In May,
1842, the Carolinian answered a routine inquiry with a ringing
defense of the Resolutions of 1798, the *Valley Star's* basic creed.

Letcher was not impressed. He felt that Calhoun had been
far too inconsistent in the course of his political career. He simply
distrusted this man who had deserted Jackson and flirted with
the Whig enemy, and he refused to support ex–Whig R. M. T.
Hunter's movement in 1843 to make Calhoun president and mold
the Virginia Democracy into a rigidly states' rights, pro–slavery
party. Late in 1843, he stated his position to Governor McDowell:

If our friends [the Virginia Democratic convention in February,

1844] choose Van Buren, or either of those spoken of for the place [the presidential nomination]—always excepting Calhoun, I will spare no exertions to secure their sweep. If it fall upon Calhoun, I may possibly vote for him, but as at present advised shall do nothing more.[14]

The Virginia Democracy was splitting again. Hunter's Calhounites, a coalition of longtime conservative Democrats and former Tyler Whigs, had most of their strength in the eastern section of the state. The Van Buren regulars were strongest west of the Blue Ridge Mountains. Letcher sided with McDowell, Ritchie, Thomas Jefferson Randolph, George C. Dromgoole and the majority of the Democrats to support Van Buren. He was certain that most state Democrats would back the "Little Magician" again, but in September, 1843, he spotted danger and warned Ritchie and Van Buren. He feared that the Calhounites possessed a letter from Jackson stressing the advantages of annexing Texas. He predicted that if Van Buren did not back annexation, the Calhounites would release Jackson's letter in time to ruin Van Buren's chances for the nomination. Despite these warnings, Van Buren remained silent on Texas. Virginia and the entire South strongly favored annexation; the stage was set for a stormy and dramatic nominating convention.

Early in 1844, Calhoun withdrew from contention, and the Virginia Democrats who assembled at Richmond in February harmoniously nominated Van Buren. Letcher was absent. Van Buren's nomination was so certain that he decided to spare himself the arduous winter journey on the primitive road to Richmond.

Suddenly, late in March, the political scene changed abruptly. A letter from Jackson favoring annexation was published— Letcher's warning had been accurate—and, in April, Van Buren and Clay came out strongly against immediate annexation. The Virginia Democracy, equally strong for annexation but already committed to Van Buren, was thrown into confusion. The nominating convention reassembled long enough to repudiate its pledge to Van Buren, and, in May, the Virginia delegation went to the national convention in Baltimore supporting Lewis Cass of Michigan, an annexationist. Soon darkhorse James K. Polk, a Jackson protégé and an ardent expansionist, made his move. The Virginia

delegation quickly mounted his bandwagon, which rolled to victory on the ninth ballot. Letcher, with his longtime reservations
about Van Buren and his desire for the annexation of Texas, enthusiastically hailed the convention's decision.[15]

Despite his efforts to concentrate on the practice of law,
Letcher had performed many political chores in 1843. At the beginning of the year, the enemy's leading state newspaper, the
Richmond Whig, unleashed a prolonged attack on Governor Mc-
Dowell's emancipation stand in 1831. Letcher quickly hit back
with a guest editorial in the *Valley Star* which was reprinted in
Ritchie's *Enquirer* on January 10. Defending McDowell from
this type of attack was nothing new for Letcher, but this time
he added a new wrinkle. He pointed out that in 1832 the editor
of the *Whig,* John Hampden Pleasants, had been a more vocal
emancipationist than McDowell. Pleasants was out of town for
several weeks, and Letcher thus centered his criticism on the real
enemy, acting editor Alexander Moseley. Letcher publicly labeled
Moseley a "political madman and wretched demagogue"—after
privately calling him "a slandering dog"—and condemned him
for trying to create east–west dissension which could lead to a
division of the state.[16]

The *Whig* lashed back at the *Enquirer,* not at the *Valley Star.*
A bitter war of words followed between W. F. Ritchie, Thomas
Ritchie's second son, and Pleasants, who by now had returned
to the helm of the *Whig.* A duel was narrowly averted. Letcher
was immensely relieved when the dispute stopped short of blood-
shed. His practical, bourgeois mind rejected the romantic concept of the *code duelo.* As an editor, he had had more than his
share of public disputes with Whigs, and more than once he had
been tempted to rap the editor of the *Gazette* on his pale proboscis.
However, Letcher's fundamental moderation always prevailed,
and he never resorted to violence. Though quite serious about
his politics, he was no fanatic. He was usually able to prevent
political arguments from harming personal relations.

Though this particular dispute stopped short of a duel, bad
feeling remained. Three years later, with the senior Ritchie in
Washington editing a Polk publication and his two sons editing

the *Enquirer,* Thomas Ritchie Jr. clashed with Pleasants. Pleasants was accused of abolitionism again, and this time the renewed dispute ran its deadly course. Young Ritchie, an experienced and bloodthirsty duelist, killed Pleasants in one of the most savage *affaires d'honneur* in Richmond's history.[17]

In the middle of March, 1843, Letcher embarked on another political mission. Encouraged by McDowell, he tried to gain the Democratic congressional nomination from his area of the Valley. Bedridden for weeks with a severe case of "inflammatory rheumatism", he had to work fast to corral delegates to the nominating convention, which met at Harrisonburg on March 31. Letcher was popular, but there was a general feeling that at 30 he was still too young and inexperienced. William Taylor, his older but less ambitious law associate, won the nomination. With the mighty Tenth Legion recovered from the debacle of 1841, Whig incumbent Stuart resigned, and the Whigs conceded the election.[18]

Disappointed, but still not discouraged, Letcher simply postponed his congressional aspirations. By April, he was in the midst of an even more important campaign. His patient courtship of 20-year–old Susan Holt was approaching a climax. Finally, the young lady consented, and her guardian—a good Democrat—gave his approval. On May 14, 1843, a long, happy, and fruitful marriage began.

Letcher had reached another milestone in his life. Henceforth, whatever his political fortunes, he always found support and encouragement at home. Susan Letcher was a devoted wife, a commendable housekeeper, and a loving mother. Of the Letchers' eleven children, seven grew to maturity in an informal, middle-class household full of laughter and activity. John Letcher never mourned the loss of his bachelorhood; his only regret was that his political and legal activities often took him away from his growing family.[19]

By 1843 the population of Lexington exceeded 1,200 and the proud little town had been formally incorporated. Letcher was elected one of its seven trustees early in 1844, a presidential election year. Honoring his 1843 pledge to "spare no exertions",

Letcher lightened his legal work load and returned to the grueling political routine he had followed in the 1840 campaign.

In the spring elections, the Whigs rallied all over the state for an attempt to regain control of the House of Delegates. In Rockbridge County they were even more powerful than usual, and the Democrats under Letcher conceded. Despite encouragement from Governor McDowell, they did not formally oppose the Whig incumbents. The Whigs swept Rockbridge as expected, but they also carried enough of the rest of Virginia to gain a slender majority in the House of Delegates. In 1845 the Democrats, reinforced by a large number of Whigs who resented the Clayites' opposition to the annexation of Texas, regained control of the legislature and also swept the congressional elections. The victory of 1845 established Democratic dominance in Virginia for the remainder of the antebellum period; however, in the summer of 1844 the trend still seemed to favor the Whigs, and the Democrats frantically prepared for the crucial presidential election in November.

The battle between Polk and Clay was heated and often scurrilous. Under Letcher's direction, the Rockbridge Democrats came to life and joined the ranks of the Tenth Legion of the Valley. The Whigs, too, were eager, and well organized in a network of clubs which interlaced Rockbridge County and spread throughout the Valley and the rest of the state. Back at the helm of the *Valley Star,* Letcher again lashed out at all things Whiggish. Across the paper's masthead danced a new motto, "Polk and Dallas", a slight variation of the *Enquirer's* "Polk and Texas". Again Letcher was deluged with invitations to address party rallies all over the Valley and in other sections of the state. As always, he filled as many speaking engagements as possible. Again, too, he participated in formal debates. He still relied on a thorough understanding of the issues to compensate for his lack of eloquence, and this time issues counted.

Unlike Harrison, Clay was a candidate with a clear record and a firm platform; thus the Whigs put little stress on ballyhoo tactics. In this relatively rational environment, Letcher more than held his own as the fine points of tariffs, a national bank, and especially Texas annexation were discussed. When the showdown finally came, both sides were exhausted. As usual, Rockbridge went Whig, but Polk carried the Valley, the state, and the nation. With political passions spent, Letcher again left the *Valley Star* and returned to his law practice.[20]

Letcher's first child had been born in October, in the midst of the campaign. Little William Houston Letcher was a sickly infant, and local doctors could do little but watch the gradual ebb of life. By mid–spring, the hopeless struggle had ended. Letcher was stunned. He sought solace not in religion—at heart he had abandoned orthodox Christianity—but in work. He submerged himself in his law practice.[21]

But his thoughts were never far from politics. Congressman William Taylor kept him informed of events in Washington, where the Polk administration was drifting rapidly toward war with Mexico over the annexation of Texas and was playing a dangerous game of brinkmanship with Britain over the disputed Oregon territory. Letcher also closely followed political events in Virginia, where a heavy influx of states' rightists and Texas Whigs had changed the Democratic Party. The old Jacksonian spirit was being replaced by a more conservative, states' rights, pro–Southern, pro–slavery outlook. Thomas Ritchie, the grand old man of the party, was losing his power to the new breed, often ex–Whigs like R. M. T. Hunter, Henry A. Wise, and William O. Goode. Letcher would never be entirely at ease with these former opponents.

On the local level, Letcher remained active and planned to succeed the aging Taylor in Congress. In Rockbridge he continued to be a vigorous minority leader. Then in June, 1845, he openly supported Samuel McDowell Moore, a Rockbridge Whig, against George Baylor, an Augusta County Democrat, in a race for the Virginia Senate. Oldtimers were aghast. John Letcher support a Whig! And only a few days after participating in a ceremony commemorating the death of "Old Hickory" himself? Fantastic! Yet the reason was obvious. Moore favored the extension of the James River and Kanawha Canal along the James River as far as the tributary North River, which ran through Rockbridge but not Augusta County. Baylor opposed any extension of the canal.

If the canal was extended and some improvements were made

on the lower part of the North River, Lexington and all Rockbridge could use barge transportation all the way to Richmond
and the coast. Agrarian Rockbridge would at last have adequate
access to eastern markets and production facilities; the economy
of the area would quicken overnight. On this issue Letcher was a
Rockbridger first and a Democrat second, a westerner favoring
internal improvements, but a Jacksonian insisting that the state,
not the federal government, do the job.[22]

Letcher looked toward Congress. Fifty–seven–year–old William
Taylor was ailing. When Taylor died in Washington in January,
1846, Letcher immediately traveled throughout the Valley again
seeking the congressional nomination. Most Democratic leaders
felt that at the age of 32 he was still too young. Besides, James
McDowell had just completed his governorship and was after the
same position. Letcher, realizing that he could not defeat Mc-
Dowell's bid for the nomination, quietly withdrew from contention. McDowell won the nomination and easily overwhelmed half-
hearted Whig opposition in a special election. More determined
than ever to reach Congress, Letcher, undiscouraged, waited for
his next chance. As the aging McDowell's logical successor, he
could afford to wait a little longer. He was a prominent state
Democrat and relatively well known on the national level. Even
in distant Texas, second cousin Sam Houston recognized his potential and wrote an encouraging letter. A lucrative law practice
allowed Letcher to purchase several slaves as house servants. Then,
in February, 1846, his wife gave birth to a healthy girl, Elizabeth
Stuart Letcher.[23]

The past six years had brought happiness and tragedy, triumph
and failure. Yet, in retrospect, this had been a successful, productive period. Letcher had matured as a lawyer, as a politician,
and as a man. His course was charted, and the future appeared
bright. Growing friction between eastern and western Virginia
would soon reach a peak, creating challenge and opportunity
for the ambitious Lexingtonian. The next few years would prove
decisive.

CHAPTER 3

Virginia Liberal

Hostility between eastern and western Virginia was deeply rooted in the history of the state. At the Convention of 1829–1830, the westerners were restless, but their disorganized efforts failed to achieve their prime objective—the white population basis of representation in the legislature. The suffrage was broadened, a strong judicial system was created, and other minor reforms were instituted, but the eastern minority retained control over the dominant legislative branch of the government.

By the 1840's, east–west friction was at its peak. The people of the west—the Blue Ridge was the dividing line—generally favored a free public school system, but the east wanted only stronger state support for the University of Virginia, an institution dominated by easterners. The west cried out for internal improvements by the state, but the east did little to fulfill this demand. Above all, slavery widened the breach between the two sections. By 1840, approximately 87 per cent of the state's 475,000 slaves lived east of the Blue Ridge Mountains, while approximately 55 per cent of the white population of 895,000 lived in the west. This unequal distribution of slave labor created significant economic differences between the two sections. The west was populated largely by small farmers and mechanics; the east stressed large-scale plantations. By 1846 all of these differences had produced acute friction.[1]

Like every other prominent Virginia politician, Letcher became deeply involved in this sectional struggle for power within the state. He had always supported his native west, was thoroughly familiar with its grievances, and entered the controversy without hesitation. Still a staunch Jacksonian, he could not tolerate the undemocratic spectacle of rule by the minority east, and he knew that a strong pro–western stand would enhance his popularity in the Valley and further his congressional ambitions.

As soon as the presidential election of 1844 was over, Letcher used the *Valley Star* to attack the remaining property qualifications for voting and to demand the white basis of representation in the legislature. The Constitution of 1830 was inadequate; therefore, the only solution was a constitutional convention to shape a democratic government for Virginia. The east must stop stalling and make a choice—either real reform or a division of the state with the Blue Ridge as the new border! This was not the first time a westerner had threatened the east with separation, nor would it be the last. Separation would eventually come, but the circumstances would be greatly modified, and John Letcher would find himself in a quite different situation.[2]

The *Valley Star,* the *Gazette* and the people of western Virginia, both Democrats and Whigs, wanted reform. By 1847 the agitation was approaching a climax. Legislative delay in authorizing appropriations for continuing the canal up the James River from Lynchburg past the mouth of the North River to Buchanan greatly increased restlessness and dissatisfaction in Rockbridge County. Letcher, though active in the reform movement, was primarily concerned with his lucrative law practice, but in February, 1847, he was temporarily—and fatefully—diverted.[3]

The Franklin Society began to discuss the west's grievances in its weekly meetings. From February 6 to April 24 the members debated the question: "Should the people of western Virginia delay any longer in taking steps to bring about the division of the State?" Letcher, an active member of the society, was a participant in this discussion which was to be of great importance to his political future.

Slavery, an institution which westerners directly associated with eastern political dominance, became the primary issue. The discussions concentrated on the advisability of gradual abolishment of slavery west of the Blue Ridge, with secondary emphasis on the possibility of a division of the state along the same boundary. Five speakers, all of them slaveholders, dominated the platform. Two natives of the Tidewater, Judge John W. Brockenbrough, Letcher's running mate in 1840, and Colonel Francis H. Smith of V.M.I., Letcher's old friend, opposed any form of abolition. Dr. Henry Ruffner, President of Washington College, Samuel McDowell Moore, and Letcher advocated gradual emancipation and a division of the state.

Letcher made three formal speeches during the debate, in which he labeled slavery a great social and political evil, but, significantly, stressed primarily the legislative neglect which the west suffered at the hands of the east. Letcher was anything but a champion of abolition, having opposed it consistently in the *Valley Star*. He had seen how McDowell had been plagued after his call for emancipation in 1831, and he knew that the South was firmly committed to its peculiar institution. Nevertheless, in order to gain a tactical advantage in a debate on western rights, he made the glaring strategic error of advocating emancipation in Virginia in 1847. He compounded his error when the debate reached a climax with Dr. Ruffner's main address on February 27.[4]

This speech was pragmatic, not idealistic. Ruffner lashed out at both northern abolitionists and southern nullifiers. The Negro was "black vomit", a curse on the land. Slavery distorted the economic and social life of the community. It drove away worthy whites, encouraged laziness and careless farming, and discouraged manufacturing and public education. Through a gradual but relentless system of emancipation and colonization, both the Negro and slavery could be banished forever from western Virginia.

Ruffner's speech had a tremendous impact on his audience. A year later, rising opposition to his proposals forced Ruffner to resign from Washington College, but some members of the immediate audience were so favorably impressed that, on September 1, they formally petitioned Ruffner to write a pamphlet based upon his speech. Ruffner complied, and the famous *Ruffner Pamphlet* was born.

Letcher, one of eleven who signed the petition, planned to use the *Ruffner Pamphlet* as another temporary weapon in his western arsenal. Like the threat of dividing the state at the Blue Ridge, it would be a useful device for frightening reform out of the stubborn east. Virginia politicians had frequently exploited the sensitive issue of abolition for selfish purposes before; why not use it again in a good cause? The theory was logical, but the practical application was clumsy. Letcher foolishly took a public stand for emancipation. The *Ruffner Pamphlet* became a weapon, true enough, but it was soon in the hands of Letcher's opposition, and it inflicted many grievous wounds.[5]

In January, 1848, law and politics were briefly forgotten with the arrival of a new son, Samuel Houston Letcher. Both mother and child were sick for weeks, and Letcher, remembering the tragic death of his first born, stayed close to home until the crisis passed. Young Sam gained strength rapidly and lived to fight for the Confederacy.[6]

By this time Letcher's law practice was expanding rapidly; consequently, he formed a partnership with David P. Curry, a personal friend and a staunch Whig. Basically a moderate, Letcher always drew a sharp distinction between politics and personalities, and among his other Whig friends were James B. Dorman of Lexington and ex-Congressman "Sandy" Stuart, who was often a friendly rival in the courts of the Valley. One of Letcher's closest friends was James D. Davidson, dean of the Rockbridge legal corps, a poet and a political chameleon. Other close friends were James G. Paxton, an influential Rockbridge Democrat, and lawyer John Echols of nearby Monroe County.[7]

Since 1848 was a presidential election year, Letcher could not ignore politics for long and, in May, served as a delegate to the Democratic nominating convention in Baltimore. He favored James Buchanan of Pennsylvania for the nomination, but accepted Lewis Cass enthusiastically and returned to Lexington ready for battle.

Now an official presidential elector, Letcher campaigned en-

ergetically throughout the Valley for the Democratic ticket. He
was no longer interested in local political positions, and any canvassing for Cass that he undertook at this time in his own congressional district would indirectly contribute to his own advancement.
Always frank, he made no particular effort to conceal his strategy.[8]
In October, a Lexington Whig described Letcher's plans in a
letter to William Cabell Rives:

> Mr. Letcher the Democratic Elector has just returned from a
> protracted visit to the Tenth Legion, and boasts that Rockingham
> will give Cass 1700 majority, and that Shenandoah will give him
> 1300. Mr. L. is looking forward to the time when he hopes to
> represent this district in Congress, and some think that he will not
> suffer Ex. Gov. McDowell to be elected again without a contest.
> This being the case he is very much in the habit of praising the
> Democracy of the Tenth Legion, and of magnifying their strength,
> but whether they can or will give the majority indicated "nous
> verrons."[9]

This campaign, particularly in Rockbridge, was turbulent, but
the superbly organized and entrenched Whigs carried the county
for their candidate, Zachary Taylor, by a count of 665 to 501.
Cass swept the valley, barely won the state, and only narrowly
lost the national election. The Democracy's relatively poor showing in Virginia was the result of the continuing and widening
split between R. M. T. Hunter's southern rights faction and
Thomas Ritchie's old Jacksonian wing of the party.

Acquisition of vast new territories from Mexico had stimulated
the controversy over the expansion of slavery and increased sectional hostility. Southern rights sentiments surged in Virginia.
With the masterful Ritchie in Washington editing a Polk newspaper, the Hunterites were able to exploit the new situation and
expand their power within the party. By 1850, the Jacksonians
had shifted to a moderate southern rights position, but the Virginia Democracy remained divided.[10]

Letcher's attention still focused on the Valley. In January, 1849,
he tentatively decided to try again for his district's congressional
nomination. At 36, though still handicapped by his relative youth,
he wrote confidently to his Whig friend "Sandy" Stuart:

> I am satisfied that I will not be allowed to have a single handed

race, with any one. There are several in the District who desire the office, and they are fearful, if I should get in, that I would be inclined to hold on to the place.[11]

The last traces of the political alliance between Letcher and James McDowell had disappeared, and although still a personal friend of the entire McDowell family, Letcher was out to get his former mentor's seat in Congress. Privately labeling McDowell a "half Whig", he maneuvered quickly but cautiously. However, just as in 1846, McDowell's prestige was too great, forcing Letcher to withdraw quietly, still determined someday to replace the aging and ailing incumbent.[12]

Meanwhile the law firm of Letcher and Curry prospered. Everything from debt collection and land sales to trials in the federal district court in Staunton kept Letcher constantly in action. Economically and socially Letcher was firmly entrenched in the upper strata of the southern middle class by 1850. He was able to purchase several additional young Negro women and one Negro man as house servants for his steadily growing family. A second healthy son, Andrew Holt Letcher, was born on March 15.[13]

Letcher did little campaigning in the spring elections of 1849 but was delighted to see the Democrats retain control of the assembly and win all but one of Virginia's congressional seats. He watched closely when the legislators discussed internal improvements, particularly extension of the James River and Kanawha Canal and improvement of the navigability of the North River. In 1847 he had strongly urged improvement of the North River from Lexington to the James River; now, in 1850, he was appointed a commissioner of the North River Navigation Company, an organization seeking funds for this project. Letcher also championed other local improvements, such as macadamized roads, to help end Rockbridge's traditional isolation.[14]

Like most western Virginians, he was vitally interested in reform of the state constitution. He had long demanded that the west be given its rightful share of political power. He plunged quickly back into politics when the assembly, early in 1850, finally yielded to western pressure and authorized a state—wide plebiscite in April to decide whether or not to call a constitutional convention later in the year. The legislators were careful to establish a mixed system of representation for the proposed convention which would preserve the minority east's traditional margin of power. Nevertheless, the Valley, if not the Trans–Allegheny, responded enthusiastically to this chance to reform the Constitution of 1830.[15]

This particular struggle was not the usual Whig–Democrat clash, but rather a battle between reformers and conservatives, and Letcher found himself cooperating with many of his traditional Whig enemies. He was one of the leaders of the reform forces in the Valley, where the overwhelming majority of the people favored reform.

The April plebiscite was a clear mandate for a convention not only in the Valley but also throughout most of the state. Letcher continued to campaign, now seeking election as a convention delegate from the district composed of Rockbridge, Augusta, and Highland counties. Leading reformers in his district encouraged him. Whigs John D. Imboden and David Fultz of Staunton guaranteed him a healthy majority in Augusta County. Rockbridge and Highland also appeared to be his, but Letcher took no chances and continued to campaign vigorously for himself and other enthusiastic reformers.[16]

He canvassed his district thoroughly. On June 8, in a letter accepting a speaking invitation, he concisely outlined his reform platform:

> For years past, I have asserted and advocated the election of the Governor, Judges, Justices of the peace, Sheriffs, Clerks, Constables directly by the people, for limited terms. I maintain the same doctrine still, and on all suitable occasions, hold myself ready to vindicate it orally or otherwise, to the utmost extent of my feeble abilities. I am the uncompromising foe, of the "life of good behavior tenue" [sic] either for the Judges or other officers; believing as I do that it is Anti Republican, and in direct hostility to the genius and spirit of the age, in which we live. If the people are capable of self government (and who amongst Anti Reformers ever will have the hardihood to say they are not), then it follows, that they are capable of selecting all their officers, who are nothing more or less than mere agents and trustees. In private matters, if we wish an agent, we select one whom we believe trustworthy and competent,

and why cannot we do the same thing in governmental matters?

I am a white basis man, and shall use whatever influence I possess to secure the recognition of this principle, in the new Constitution. The mixed basis is to me objectionable on many grounds; not the least important of which is that it gives to the *minority* the power to control and govern the *majority*. The free white population west of the Blue Ridge, exceeds the free white population on the eastern side of the mountain, something like 100,000, and is it not an outrage, that so large a majority should be controlled by a minority? The white basis gives power to the majority, and it is therefore the sound principle, under a Republican government. The West should use all fair and honorable means to secure the adoption of this principle, and should strenuously insist upon it. If they fail of success, it will after the struggle is over, be time enough to talk about a compromise, and the terms of that compromise we must not surrender in advance. It is better, far better to be defeated in a manly fight, than to give up before a blow is struck.[17]

The effort to elect wholehearted reform delegates to the convention was not as easy as it seemed. Lukewarm reformers such as "Sandy" Stuart were willing—sometimes eager—to dilute reform to the point of impotency. These men, quietly backed by the badly–beaten enemies of reform, were a real threat. Though a minority, they skillfully blurred the issues and probed for an advantage. Failing to persuade all Whigs to oppose reform, they attacked the leading reformers, seeking any weakness or liability.[18]

Letcher had one glaring liability—his advocacy of emancipation in 1847. On May 29, Imboden warned Letcher that he had overheard Stuart and John B. Baldwin plotting to unleash a fully documented attack on his past abolitionism. On June 10, Clement R. Harris, an Augusta Democrat, repeated the warning, adding that the *Staunton Spectator* would soon fire the first salvo. Forewarned, Letcher acted early in July. Trying to avoid the consequences of his only major political blunder, he publicly recanted his anti–slavery stand of 1847. The people of the Valley, knowing he had never been an abolitionist at heart, accepted his recantation, and by the end of the month the opposition gave up its attacks.

With Congressman McDowell ill in Washington, Letcher became the leading reformer in his district. Much in demand as a speaker, he followed a grueling campaign schedule. He also corresponded frequently with other reformers, coordinating strategy and occasionally trying to nudge a hesitant comrade a little more toward a completely democratic position.

The showdown came on August 22, and the favored reformers won all five of the district's convention seats. Letcher led the candidates with 1,939 votes. The other winners were Whigs D. E. Moore, Hugh W. Sheffey, and David Fultz, and Democrat Adam Stephenson, Jr.[19]

The conservatives were bitter in defeat, and the victorious reformers endured a barrage of abuse. Letcher described this reaction in a letter to John H. McCue, a reform Whig from Augusta County:

> These antics here, are the most ill-natured, and abusive rascals, that I have on the list of my acquaintances. They curse Fultz for his views on log rolling, and many of them express doubts as to the fact, whether he will be received in a Convention composed of *white men*. . . .[20]

On October 14, Letcher and 123 other delegates assembled in the House of Delegates Hall of the Capitol, and the Reform Convention of 1850-51 officially began. Eight permanent committees were established, and Letcher was assigned to the important executive committee. Preliminary work on this committee and an unsuccessful attempt to secure the post of clerk of the convention for Charles Chapin, Commissioner in Chancery for 15 years in Rockbridge County, occupied Letcher's attention until the convention adjourned on November 4 to await a complete compilation of the census returns of 1850.[21]

The convention was not scheduled to reassemble until January 6, 1851, giving the reformers over two months to prepare for the final struggle. The General Assembly convened for its regular winter session on December 2, and this session became the stage for many preliminary maneuvers.

As usual, the sensitive matter of internal improvements for the west was on the agenda. The North River Navigation Company, which was financed by local subscriptions and matching state funds, was running short of capital. The company had been created to make the North River navigable for barges from Lexington to the canal on the James, but the job was far from completed. Some Rockbridgers wanted to abandon the whole project; others favored obtaining more local and state funds to finish the job.

As a commissioner of the company, Letcher favored carrying on, but as a delegate to the convention he opposed any additional requests for state funds while the larger issue of constitutional reform remained unsettled. To gain real reform the west would need all the eastern goodwill it could find; therefore, traditional western demands for internal improvements should be postponed. Letcher's view prevailed, and the western legislators said little about internal improvements. The assembly was unnaturally harmonious.[22]

Many loyal reformers were outraged when the legislators placed conservative, erratic John M. Daniel of the Richmond *Examiner* on the Council of State. Letcher said nothing. He knew that this, too, was part of the reformers' grand strategy, a cynical—and successful—plot to insure the destruction of the antiquated council by making the unpopular Daniel a member.[23]

The reformers encountered other problems during the convention intermission. Richmond was basically conservative, and many reformers favored moving the convention to a more hospitable environment—for example, Staunton or Winchester. Realizing the impossibility of such an action, Letcher and most of the other experienced reformers advocated, instead, saturating Richmond with propaganda through a new, weekly newspaper which would champion reform in general and the white basis of representation in particular.

Early in December, Daniel Woodson, recently retired co–editor of the Lynchburg *Republican,* went to Lexington and discussed this possibility at length with Letcher and left stimulated by the Lexingtonian's enthusiasm. Letcher and other reformers began to organize support for the proposed organ, and Letcher and his friend Curry both made several trips to the capital during the month to obtain more support among western members of the assembly.

Woodson received enough backing to assemble the required staff and equipment, and the first issue of the Richmond *Republican Advocate* appeared on January 7, 1851, the day after the convention reconvened. Convinced that this reform newspaper "must and will succeed", Letcher wanted the *Advocate* to become a permanent voice for the movement at the state capital. On January 8, he was among the leaders of a western caucus that assessed every reformer $10 for support of the new journal. He also sent sample issues to friends all over the west, seeking additional subscribers. The *Advocate* survived the convention period and thus performed its primary propaganda function, but when the delegates departed, it was left stranded in a hostile environment. It quickly withered and died, disappointing Letcher, who had hoped for a permanent propaganda foothold in Richmond.[24]

The last session of the reform convention began its work without delay with Letcher, though harassed by requests for favors from constituents, in the thick of the fight. As a member of the executive committee, he fought passionately for more democracy in the executive branch of the state government. The committee formally recommended the popular election of a governor for a four–year term, election of a few other executive officers, creation of the elective office of lieutenant governor, and abolishment of the Council of State. The convention approved these recommendations virtually without change, but Letcher felt it necessary to file a minority report in which he demanded that the state treasurer, auditor, and register also be elected by the people, and that the governor serve for only two years. The convention ignored this report.[25]

Outwardly, Letcher took this defeat calmly, but he was actually furious at reform committeemen John T. Anderson of Botetourt County and Samuel McCamant of Grayson County, fellow westerners who had done nothing to help him resist the majority report. In a letter to Curry, Letcher bitterly described Anderson's "contribution" to the cause: "He made no reply [to the majority report] but sat like a stupid ass as he is, in perfect silence until we dispersed."[26]

From the first, questions having to do with the Negro and slavery figured prominently in the convention's deliberations, lurking in men's minds even when other matters were under discussion. Early in January, for example, widespread rumors of an alleged—

and probably non—existent—slave plot to poison white folk sent a tremor through the convention. Such rumors were not uncommon in the antebellum South, but Letcher was shaken nonetheless. His own slaves were well treated and completely trustworthy; at least they *seemed* reliable—but then so had Nat Turner! Letcher seems to have spent several restless nights haunted by the vision of bloody insurrection in Lexington, and he confessed to Curry that "So horrible a thing would drive me to madness".[27]

Thinking that Virginia's 54,000 free Negroes comprised a potential cadre for "so horrible a thing", Letcher advocated shipping them all back to Africa. To facilitate this involuntary "folk movement", he and eighty—six other members of the convention formally endorsed a measure, then being considered in Congress, that would have established a steamship line between western Africa and the United States. He also served on a temporary committee studying constitutional protection for the slave interests in Virginia.

Despite recurring attacks of rheumatism during February, Letcher gradually emerged as one of western Virginia's staunchest champions at the convention. In the seemingly endless debates he was always in the front ranks of the west, complaining about the lack of internal improvements, recalling past attempts to halt the James River and Kanawha Canal at Lynchburg, demanding more representation for western counties and opposing any consolidation of these counties, and generally waving the banner of "western rights". He also instructed Curry and other reformers in the west to organize local mass meetings whenever the conservatives in the convention needed prodding from the grass roots. Letcher was unwilling to speak of compromise until a battle for total victory had been fought.[28]

The high point of his efforts was a lengthy, belligerent speech on March 14. Characteristically using complicated statistics, he lashed out at the hated mixed basis of representation. It was unfair and unrepublican and, therefore, unconstitutional—a violation of the Virginia Bill of Rights. The white basis of representation was the only just and democratic solution. It had worked in other southern states without endangering slave property; it would work the same way in Virginia. In the long run, all property could only be secured by fair play, and never by injustice. If the east refused to give the west its majority right of control, then the time for separation was at hand.

This threat jarred the delegates, and Letcher continued to hammer away. Since slave property was not taxed equally with other property, the west paid *more* than its fair share of taxes, while receiving *less* than its fair share of internal improvements. After declaring his contentment with the Federal Union, Letcher concluded by describing the eastern delegates as men having "but one idea in their heads, and that is negro–ology. [Laughter.] They can never see beyond it; and to their peculiar notions respecting its perpetuation, everything else must be made to conform".[29]

This speech enraged the easterners, but it was only one of many dealing with the representation question. By mid–February this key problem had deadlocked the convention: neither the east nor the west would yield, it seemed. March came and went. April came and went. Tempers were rising on both sides. Despite a barrage of dire threats and pessimistic predictions, experienced politicians, including Letcher, knew in May (if not before) that the main fight was an honorable draw—that the time for compromise was fast approaching. The important figures at the convention had never been quite as angry as the newspaper reports indicated; much of their fury had been for the "benefit" of the home folks.

Early in May the deadlock was broken. A host of proposals and their accompanying objections and revisions were brushed aside, and a committee of four easterners and four westerners was appointed to find a compromise solution. Letcher and George W. Summers of Kanawha County, the key members of the western half of the committee, were largely responsible for the committee's final recommendations.[30]

Basically, the committee proposed a House of Delegates composed of 82 westerners and 68 easterners, and a Senate made up of 20 westerners and 30 easterners. This system of divided power was to remain until 1865 when the legislature was to reapportion the representation in both houses. At that time, if a new basis of apportionment could not be agreed on, the whole matter was to be submitted to the electorate, which would choose whether representation would be based entirely on the number of qualified voters, or based on the number of whites plus the amount of taxes paid to the state. Thus, the committee recommended postponing the sectional showdown until 1865, but since the issue would obviously be decided by a state–wide plebiscite—the legislature was never able to agree on apportionment—the more populous west was assured of victory in 1865.

Letcher favored this deferred victory, as did most other westerners, but the convention rejected the committee's proposals by the scant margin of 55 to 54. The easterners could not accept the prospect of western domination, even if delayed for fourteen years.

The convention was deadlocked again until Samuel Chilton of Facquier County, a member of the compromise committee, presented a viable plan. His suggestion was that the committee's original plan be adopted, but with the added provision that, if the legislature of 1865 failed to find a solution, the people could make a final choice among four different bases of representation: (1) the number of qualified voters, the suffrage basis (2) the total white population, the white basis (3) the amount of taxes paid, the taxation basis (4) the white population and the amount of taxes paid, the mixed basis. Chilton's proposal was received without enthusiasm, but the delegates were weary and anxious to go home, and it was accepted by a count of 55 to 48, and with a few amendments was incorporated into the new constitution by a vote of 51 to 44. The west had finally won—and had only to wait fourteen years for the full fruits of victory.

The convention made other significant changes. The executive branch was not only democratized but also strengthened in relation to the legislative. Two of Letcher's pet projects, the popular election of judges and county officials for limited terms and universal white manhood suffrage, were enacted. The eastern delegates defeated all attempts to change the favorable property tax status of slaves, but this was small consolation for the west's crucial victory on the question of representation.[31]

The easterners gradually realized that they had won a few battles but lost the war. Diehards blamed their own "Janus faced" comrades. The greatest abuse was heaped on the erratic Henry A. Wise of Accomac, who had sided with the east on most minor matters but had supported the west on representation. Richard Ivanhoe Cocke, delegate from Fluvanna County, bitterly described Wise in the closing days of the convention:

> Wise averages about eight to ten speeches a day. He is rapidly losing popularity. People now talk and laugh during his long speeches and he gets furious and vows to talk until doomsday. He is as wild as a march hare and I give you my word that I had rather have a Constitution formed by any ten magistrates in old Fluvanna than one framed after the model of H. A. Wise. The man is doubtless crazy. There is a screw loose some where about his heart or head or both.[32]

Everyone acknowledged Letcher's fine performance in behalf of western rights, especially during the compromise negotiations, in which he displayed great political finesse in guiding the deliberations along lines favorable to western interests. He emerged from the Reform Convention as one of the most popular Democrats in western Virginia, and even his old Whig antagonist, the Lexington *Gazette,* complimented him.

Letcher publicly and privately hailed the new state constitution and traveled throughout the Valley explaining the complexities of the new charter to his constituents. In October, the people of the Valley and every other major section of the state voted overwhelmingly to ratify the new constitution. Letcher's popularity was at a peak, and he quickly turned to larger political game.[33]

As early as March, some eastern delegates to the convention had suggested a compromise: the governorship for the west and the mixed basis of representation for the east. Letcher was quick to see that such a deal would be to the advantage of the east, which was trying to soothe sectional strife at a time when the west was using it as an effective weapon in the convention. Even though he was one of the westerners mentioned for the governorship, he emphatically rejected this *"bare bone,* now thrown to the West".[34]

Letcher was definitely interested in the governorship but not on the east's terms. At the convention he received much Democratic encouragement to run for governor as soon as the new constitutional provision for a popular vote rather than a legislative vote became effective. Reformers of both parties in his home area urged him to seek election to Congress, where he would replace McDowell, whose rapidly failing health eliminated him from contention.

Letcher promised his Democratic supporters that he would not announce his candidacy for Congress until after the party's gubernatorial candidate was selected, so as to remain available until the nomination was actually made. Then, he wisely backed off and quietly studied the fluid situation until the convention ended in August. He plotted his strategy carefully. He would campaign actively for the big prize, the Democratic gubernatorial nomination. Only if this effort failed would he capture the congressional nomination in his district, where he was popular after his performance at the convention. Thus, if failing in his try for the grand prize, he would settle for a virtually certain consolation award.

This practical strategy was wrecked when the date of the congressional nomination convention was moved five days ahead of the state convention. Letcher had to modify his strategy. He could stake everything on the more desirable gubernatorial nomination, declining the earlier congressional nomination which was his for the asking, or he could play it safe and accept the congressional nomination, temporarily abandoning his gubernatorial ambitions. After carefully weighing every possibility, he decided to seize the long coveted Democratic nomination for Congress. [35]

The Democracy of the eleventh congressional district, the heart of the mighty Tenth Legion, eagerly handed Letcher the party standard. Hopelessly outnumbered as usual, the Whigs offered no real resistance, for they were willing to reward Letcher for his convention performance. For the first time in his career, Letcher was a sure winner. Since the plebiscite on the new constitution coincided with the congressional elections, his campaign stressed the importance of ratification of the work of the convention and little else. His own victory was "more than certain".[36]

Letcher won by an overwhelming majority and joined two Whigs and 12 other Democrats in Virginia's congressional delegation. The 38–year–old Lexingtonian had reached a milestone in his career; his political character was set permanently. Over the years his early moderate liberalism had evolved, and by the end of 1851 he had emerged as a moderate conservative. Despite the change, moderation remained the foundation of his political creed.[37]

Maturity and prosperity had calmed much of the restlessness of youth, and experience had tempered idealism with practicality. However, in reality, the times had changed far more than John Letcher. Many of the flaming issues of the past had vanished in the whirl of time. More important, Virginia liberalism had triumphed at the Reform Convention. The attack of the crusaders had overthrown the old order, and now the victors wanted only to preserve the fruits of victory, to conserve the new order.

For the next decade Congressman Letcher's conservatism was accentuated on the national level, as the South struggled desperately to preserve its way of life in a rapidly changing world. American democracy was unable to cope with the rising sectional strife of the 1850's, but Letcher and many other men of moderation and goodwill never gave up their search for an alternative to the coming violence.

CHAPTER 4

Southern Conservative

In December, 1851, Letcher began a congressional career that spanned a critical decade. He was still loyal to what he understood to be the Jeffersonian creed of states' rights, strict constitutional construction, and frugal government. He was determined to defend the rights of the South, but he was equally determined to oppose "radicalism" and "fanaticism" of every kind.

Almost as soon as he took his seat in Congress, Letcher was buried under a landslide of new duties and responsibilities, and the only break in this grueling new routine was an occasional social outing. Much of the new congressman's official time was consumed handling chores for constituents and favor seekers, many of them from other states. Requests for public documents and speeches—the same requests young Letcher had made of his congressman in the 1830's—and pension and bounty claims poured in. Always the realistic politician, Letcher handled them all as a routine part of his new job. He was assigned to the Committee on Public Expenditures, and he quickly became a champion of economy in government.[1]

A basic bourgeois conservatism dominated his every action in Congress. He succinctly expressed his legislative philosophy in a letter in March, 1852, to his friend James D. Davidson:

> The business of Congress is moving on slowly, but not more slowly than comports with the public interest. My own decided conviction

(after a close observation of the sort of business, and the manner of doing it,) is that the less we do, the better for our constituents. Of all the bills that have passed our House I have voted for but *four* I believe.[2]

In an early vote he supported Congress' elaborate reception of the Hungarian freedom fighter, Lajos Kossuth. Throughout the session he fiercely resisted "infamous" proposals to give public lands to railroads in the new states and all other forms of federal aid for internal improvements. Letcher had always rejected such programs as violations of the Constitution, strictly construed, and as threats to the rights of the states; he remained as sternly opposed to the basic tenets of Clay's American system as he had ever been.[3]

The real business of Congress at this time was president—making, and Letcher firmly supported his kinsman and friend Sam Houston, a moderate southerner who favored lessening sectional tensions in every possible way. As early as January, 1851, Houston and Letcher had joined in opposition to a southern convention. A letter from Houston traced the moderate southern path both would follow for the next decade:

. . . let us all, within our appropriate spheres, contribute our utmost exertions to subdue fanaticism and violence, to resist sectional encroachments, to restore kind and harmonious feeling, and to cherish those expansive sentiments of patriotism in which the constitution and the Union originated.[4]

Letcher and most other experienced politicians foresaw the Whigs' nomination of General Winfield Scott, but the Democratic nominee was not so easy to predict. Lewis Cass, Stephen A. Douglas, William L. Marcy, James Buchanan, William O. Butler, and Houston were all possibilities. Early in 1852, Letcher felt that Houston had an excellent chance, but harboring no illusions about his colleagues, he cautioned his friend Davidson: "But such is the trickery and selfish calculating spirit of the politicians that it is not always a safe rule to judge from appearances, or even from what they say."[5]

On the very eve of the Democratic convention in Baltimore, Letcher, although not as optimistic as some of Houston's backers, was still hopeful. The convention finally selected a dark horse, Senator Franklin Pierce, and Letcher, a party regular, joined the overwhelming majority in approving the proceedings. Both nominee and platform supported the Compromise of 1850 as a lasting settlement of sectional antagonism, and Pierce was acceptable to the South. On July 13, Letcher formally pledged his loyalty to Pierce:

> I am entirely satisfied of the soundness of your position on the slavery question, from an examination of your course while in the two Houses of Congress, and will use all honorable effort to secure your election.[6]

Midway through his first session of Congress, the ambitious Lexingtonian, only recently recovered from one of his periodic attacks of fever and rheumatism—and also slightly homesick, dreamed of the future. "Ambitious hopes now and then flash up", he wrote his wife,

> and I calculate the chances of future political and professional distinction. What will be my position this time next year? Shall I be in a situation to promote the interests of my state and country, and by distinguished public service, win a name and reputation, that will be cherished by you and our children, with affectionate pride. For it, I shall struggle, and if energy, industry, and devotion to business can secure it, it will be achieved.[7]

Through steady correspondence with his wife and his friend Davidson, Letcher followed events in Rockbridge County. Davidson also handled some of Letcher's minor court cases and other business details, while Sam Letcher watched over his brother's growing law library and collected a few debts for him. In February, 1852, Letcher gloomily (and somewhat prematurely) predicted the imminent collapse of the North River Navigation Company and other internal improvement projects. The company did complete a series of improvements on the North River from Lexington to the James River and Kanawha Canal, and this new link to eastern markets proved a real boost to the agrarian economy of Rockbridge County. Finally, in 1857, the company sold out at a large loss to the James River and Kanawha Canal Company, but its good works remained to benefit the area.[8]

In July, Letcher's wife bought a young female slave from the estate of James McDowell and then quickly resold the child. Letcher was displeased and embarrassed. Like many southerners, he defended the peculiar institution while shying away from some of its worst features. Late in the month he shared this dilemma with Davidson:

> I regret exceedingly that she bought her, inasmuch as she has been compelled again to dispose of her. I have no fancy for buying and selling that sort of property—never wishing to own more of them than were absolutely necessary for the convenience of my family. But what is done, can't be helped.[9]

Letcher also kept a careful watch on the general political scene in Virginia, for he was still determined to capture the governorship. He strongly opposed John Brockenbrough's attempt to win election to the Court of Appeals on the grounds that his old ally had become too much of a Whig.[10]

Congress finally adjourned on August 31 after weeks of blistering heat, and Letcher gladly left the "corrupt and ungodly City" of Washington and returned to Lexington.[11] Immediately, he joined his partner Curry in their flourishing law practice, which had accumulated a large backlog of work. The presidential election in November was another major chore, as Letcher contributed his usual energy and enthusiasm to the marshaling of the Democracy of the Valley. A sweeping state and national victory rewarded the Democrats for their efforts. Even traditionally Whig Rockbridge County went for Pierce by 1,084 votes to 1,031. Obviously, the new state constitution's provision for universal white manhood suffrage had seriously damaged the Whig cause.[12]

Early in December, the second session of the Thirty–first Congress convened, and Letcher returned to Brown's Hotel, a favorite with southerners, and his Washington residence throughout his congressional career. He still spent much time handling constituents' requests for favors, everything from direct appeals for patronage to hesitant inquiries about free government flower and vegetable seeds. Letcher disliked this practice, but accepted it as an unavoidable duty, an unwholesome sign of the times.[13]

He continued to champion economy in government. Insisting that every legislative technicality be scrupulously observed, he stubbornly fought the wave of appropriation bills which flooded Congress. He used the same tactics in his continuing resistance to land grants for railroads, but he did often tire of the endless debates on trivial subjects. He was not overly impressed with the talents of his colleagues, and he was frequently depressed by the general moral climate of the capital. He openly expressed his dissatisfaction to his old friend John Warren Grigsby:

> Politics is a disgraceful trade, and he who is pursuing an agricultural, or indeed any other honest calling, ought to be content, and would be, if he could only see what we are compelled to see here.[14]

As a newcomer to Congress, Letcher remained in the background. One of his few speeches was a highly effective defense of his Whig friend, outgoing Secretary of the Interior "Sandy" Stuart, who had been unjustly accused of corruption and inefficiency by several Democrats. This spirited defense of a maligned friend was the highlight of this session of Congress for Letcher, who happily returned to Lexington after the inauguration of President Pierce.[15]

As a loyal Democrat, Letcher was determined to support the new President, but as a shrewd judge of men he had his doubts. In a letter to Grigsby he included a frank—and tragically accurate—pen portrait of the nation's new leader:

> . . . a very agreeable gentleman, of fine manners, and handsome conversational talents. While I do not consider him a *great* man, in the popular sense, it can not be denied that he has many of the elements of popularity in his composition. He has an honest face, and an air of frankness and sincerity, that impress all most favourably. Yet despite every thing, I came to the conclusion, that his predominant characteristic is *cunning*. But it is useless to speculate about him. Time will soon test him, and then we shall see of what stuff he is made. My word for it, he has not the nerve of *"Old Hickory."*[16]

Back home, Letcher began to speculate occasionally in Lexington real estate, but, as ever, he was primarily interested in his lucrative law practice. He and his friend Davidson rode from court to court handling litigation of every description. In the summer of 1853, Letcher moved his office to a new one–story, brick building on the town's main street, sharing the occupancy and the rent with Samuel McDowell Moore, but still retaining his partnership with Curry.[17]

Politics was never ignored for long. A Democratic bureaucrat in the Treasury Department kept Letcher informed of events in Washington, and both men were dissatisfied with Virginia's share of federal patronage under Pierce. Letcher was also unhappy with patronage on the state level, bitterly resenting the appointment of easterners to official positions in western Virginia. However, with no opposition for reelection in 1853, the 40–year–old congressman from Lexington eliminated the customary campaign, and on October 15, the arrival of another healthy son, John Davidson Letcher, further brightened his spirits as he prepared to return to Washington.[18]

The Thirty–third Congress, convened with a heavy Democratic majority, was soon entangled in a bitter sectional battle over the Kansas–Nebraska Bill. Pierce, weak and hesitant, favored the measure, and Douglas rammed it through the Senate. Houston of Texas was the only Democratic senator from the South to stand in opposition. Hunter of Virginia was an outspoken supporter of the measure, which shook the Union to its foundations.[19]

In the spring of 1854, the same battle began in the House. Dissatisfied with Pierce's leadership, Letcher did not take a prominent part in the heated debates that followed, but he discussed the situation frankly in a letter to his friend Grigsby.

> The Nebraska Bill has been debated *ad nauseam,* and the result is in great doubt. . . . I have felt rather indifferent to its fate, and though I may yet vote for it, it will be the most reluctant vote I ever expect to give. If the Bill shall become a law I have no idea we shall ever have another slave state admitted into the Union. The only thing that surprises me is that every Northern man, does not vote for it without a moments [sic] hesitation. This is a worse measure for us than the Compromise of 1850—and that was bad enough God knows![20]

In the middle of May, Letcher informed his wife of his final decision:

> We are in the midst of the greatest excitement I have ever wit-

nessed in Congress. . . . I do not feel sufficient concern about the Bill
to whip any person, or to allow any person to whip me. The measure
has but little in it to commend it very warmly to me as a southern
man. I shall however vote for it, but most reluctantly.[21]

Congressman Thomas Hart Benton refought Houston's losing
battle, aided by John S. Millson of Virginia, the only other southern Democrat opposing the bill. The northern Democrats split
evenly. All northern and twelve of nineteen southern Whigs opposed it. The Kansas–Nebraska Bill passed by a narrow margin,
reopening the sectional wounds so patiently and hopefully healed
in 1850.[22]

No longer a novice, Letcher took a more active part in the
daily routine of Congress. He was assigned to the Claims Committee, where he continued his fight for economy in government.
He strongly resisted proposals to reduce the tariffs on special
grades of iron used in railroad construction, and he continued to
oppose every form of federal aid for internal improvements.
He resisted another wave of the future, homestead laws, and sternly warned the western states: "Do not make war upon the old
States by seeking to withdraw their population by donations of the
public lands to those who have no lands".[23]

In July, Letcher, still basically a Jacksonian, opposed granting
Samuel Colt a special patent extension for his famous revolver.
A sharp debate on the influence of congressional lobbyists ensued,
and finally the House appointed a special committee to ascertain
whether lobbyists had been employing improper means to influence legislation. Letcher served as chairman of this committee,
which issued its report on August 3, just before adjournment.
Constantly balked by uncooperative witnesses, this early investigating committee had no real power to compel cooperation. In the
Colt patent extension case, Chairman Letcher and the majority
of the committee issued a report indicating that large amounts
of money had been spent "in getting up costly and extravagant
entertainments, to which ladies and members of Congress and
others were invited with a view of furthering the success of this
measure". The report left no doubt that improper pressure had
been applied in other cases too, but it added that the full truth

could not be dragged from reluctant witnesses. On Letcher's request, the House voted to continue the investigation in its next session, but the committee remained unable to force witnesses to appear and answer pertinent questions. The investigation was finally abandoned in February, 1855.

Letcher and his committee failed to expose fully the sinister lobbying system that operated so effectively in Congress, but new light had been thrown into a previously dark corner of the nation's political world. A faint alarm was sounded, but the system continued to function until it finally exploded in an orgy of corruption in the postwar era.[24]

This was not the first time in this session of Congress that Letcher had spoken against the invisible government of the lobbyists, "a sort of third House". By the end of the session the aggressive Lexingtonian had won a reputation as an exposer of shady deals, a sworn enemy of the unprincipled operators who were, in Letcher's view, destroying the moral fabric of American politics.[25]

Adjournment brought no political holiday: the time for the gubernatorial nominating conventions was approaching in Virginia. The rising sectional strife that was engulfing the nation was felt in Virginia, where the dominant Democratic party remained deeply divided. Thomas Ritchie, the staunch Jacksonian, had retired from politics in 1851, and his moderating influence and organizational abilities were sorely missed. The talented but unstable Henry A. Wise rapidly organized a new southern rights faction within the Democracy. The followers of R. M. T. Hunter had long championed southern rights in clashes with the declining Jacksonians. By 1854 both factions emphasized southern rights—a clear sign of the times in the South. Naturally, each faction reflected the characteristics of its leader, and both Wise and Hunter had shifted their political positions so often that it was difficult to classify either accurately. Both steered a crooked course toward a single unchanging goal: political power. Wise's passionate nature gave his faction a radical tinge, and Hunter's instinctive conservatism and impressive erudition gave his faction a more moderate appearance. By the time of the nominating convention in Staunton, both factions, still fluid, were ready for an initial trial of strength.[26]

Letcher was not impressed with either of these new factions, but the rising sectionalism of the period had destroyed his Jacksonian wing of the party. By 1854 he was virtually a political loner —a dangerous status for an ambitious politician who hoped to become governor. Selecting the least offensive faction, he gradually drifted into the outer ranks of the Hunterites, unenthusiastically but instinctively drawn to the more cautious and moderate wing of the divided party.

As a prominent Virginia Democrat, Letcher attended the nominating convention, planning to stand quietly on the sidelines and watch the battle rage. However, passiveness was never one of his prominent traits, and he was soon bitterly opposing Wise's steamroller tactics. Other old Jacksonians joined the opposition, but Wise swiftly overpowered the Hunterites' candidate, Shelton F. Leake.

The defeated Hunterites closed ranks behind the victor, but Letcher and a few others refused to support Wise actively in his campaign against Thomas S. Flournoy, the Whig–Know–Nothing candidate. Letcher sat out this canvass, not because he sympathized with the rising Know–Nothing movement, but because he disliked Wise. Two months before the convention he had joined Wise, Leake, James A. Seddon, and other leading Democrats in denouncing this new nativist crusade, which was rapidly absorbing the traditional enemy, the Whig party. Letcher's attacks on the Know–Nothings were potent enough to draw howls of protest, and he soon earned the consistent hostility of this new party.[27]

When the second session of the Thirty–third Congress began in December, 1854, Letcher temporarily turned from state politics and buried himself in his congressional duties. He continued to direct the special committee investigating lobbying activities, and was increasingly active in discussions on the floor of the House. His resistance to land grants and reduced duties on railroad iron did not slacken. He denounced Pierre Soulé for his conduct while minister to Spain and opposed any effort to wrest Cuba from Spain by force. President Pierce's veto of harbor improvement appropriations was warmly applauded by Letcher, whose main theme was still economy in government.

Letcher also spoke out on sectional disputes, which flared up constantly. Before returning to Washington he had predicted that efforts would be made to repeal the Fugitive Slave Act and to abolish slavery in the District of Columbia. He was convinced that the slave states had to resist these demands, whatever the consequences, and that the South could afford no more compromises. When the onslaught came, including the demand that slavery be restricted forever to its present boundaries, Letcher sprang to the "defense of the rights, institutions, and honor of the glorious South", declaring that the South could not remain in the Union if such hostile proposals ever became law.[28]

On March 1, Letcher received his license to practice before the United States Supreme Court. Two days later Congress adjourned, and, as usual, Letcher hurried home to Lexington. The joys of being with his family again were dampened when his second daughter, Susan Letcher, died at birth in April.[29]

The May elections brought the grieving Congressman back into action. The gubernatorial battle attracted national attention as a barometer of Democratic strength, but he still refused to support Wise actively. Letcher did conduct a leisurely, almost casual congressional campaign against halfhearted opposition, easily winning re–election. Only a scattering of staunch Know–Nothings actually voted against him.

Wise lost Rockbridge County by 60 votes but won the governorship by a statewide margin of 83,424 to 73,244. The victorious Wise complained of the lukewarm support he had received from the Hunterites. His bitterness toward Letcher and other Democrats who had not even furnished nominal support was intense, and Letcher was destined to feel the sting of his revenge.[30]

For the next six months the practice of law came first; but, when the Thirty-fourth Congress convened early in December, 1855, Letcher returned to the political wars in Washington. The House was now composed of 108 Republicans, 83 Democrats, and 43 Know–Nothings; and partisan warfare flared immediately. For two months a sectional struggle for the speakership raged.

Letcher, now an experienced congressman, was not only a member of the Claims Committee, but also of the powerful Ways and Means Committee. On December 11, he described the tense situation in the House to Davidson:

> We have been day after day voting for a Speaker, and still without a definite result. On the last three ballots today the vote for [Nathaniel P.] Banks, a violent abolitionist and Know-Nothing 107—Richardson [a Democrat from Illinois] 76. Fuller 26 and the balance for one and another. Banks wanted six votes of an election and these I do not think he can get. [Banks eventually won.] It is a most melancholy state of affairs to see a man run for so important an office on *sectional* grounds. So far he has not received a single Southern vote, nor will he receive one if we ballot for months to come. Such a state of things promises nothing for the peace and harmony of the nation, and the stability of the Union. So far we have had but little excitement, but the day is coming, when the bitter waters of sectional strife must break down the barriers that now confine them.[31]

Although Letcher continued to fight a losing battle for government economy and to reaffirm his other previous policies, his main energies were thrown into the rising sectional struggle. On March 13, 1856, he spoke out in the debate on the contested election in Kansas to select a congressional delegate. He strongly supported John W. Whitfield as the legal winner and opposed free–soiler Andrew H. Reeder. He unsuccessfully opposed a congressional investigation on the grounds that it would only aggravate the sensitive issue. Letcher tried to be both southern and moderate, a difficult feat at a time when passion and fanaticism were creeping into the sectional struggle. Even the staunchest moderate was not immune to the tense environment, and, during a bitter debate with Republican Abram Wakeman of New York, Letcher warned:

> So far as the South are concerned . . . if you should have power here, and undertake to pass measures to carry out the principles which you profess, you would find that we had enough spirit to separate from you . . . .[32]

With the Kansas situation deteriorating, Letcher was briefly distracted by events in Virginia. The state Democratic district convention met in Harrisonburg in April to select delegates to the national convention; and this session was actually another round in the struggle for power between Wise and Hunter. The Wise faction backed James Buchanan for President while the Hunterites pushed their own leader. A small Douglas faction was also in competition.

Letcher favored Hunter over the pack, but he knew that Hunter's only chance was as a compromise candidate after Douglas, Buchanan, and Pierce had eliminated each other. Letcher, though never satisfied with Pierce's leadership, preferred Pierce to Douglas or Buchanan mainly because the President had been true to the South in the struggle over Kansas. Letcher's next choice was Douglas, whom he felt he "could fight for . . . with hearty goodwill, and with entire confidence in his success". Last and least came Buchanan. Letcher was convinced that his "federalism", his pro–tariff, pro–Pacific railroad opinions, would seriously handicap Buchanan in the South.

At the Harrisonburg convention, Letcher was one of the leaders of the Hunterites' fruitless efforts to stop the Wise supporters. Using a corps of veteran politicians and newspaper editors from the Valley, which one Wise partisan described as "ticky ass sort of editors and Beer House politicians", he battled vigorously, but the Hunterites were brushed aside, and only Wise supporters were sent as delegates to the national convention in Cincinnati.[33]

Somewhat deflated by the defeat at Harrisonburg, Letcher took his wife on a brief tour of the North, visiting Philadelphia, New York, and Niagara Falls. On returning to Congress he was soon sucked back into the swirling sectional struggle which never seemed to end. In July, he delivered a legalistic and aggressive defense of Brooks' attack on Sumner which concluded with a spirited defense of slavery.[34]

A few weeks later he rose again to defend the South's peculiar institution from the attacks of the Republicans. Finely spun legalisms were combined with numerous historical illustrations in this lengthy, tedious speech. Occasional flashes of emotion broke the monotony. Racial intermarriage was outrageous, he declared, and removal of barriers to miscegenation in northern states was a sinister plot to degrade and defile the white working man. The

Republicans should not seek to exclude slavery from Kansas, and they must stop using their majority power to bring all normal business to a stop in the House. Letcher concluded by reminding his colleagues that "a sectional storm rages wildly" and warning them that "the Union is in imminent danger", threatened by the irresponsibility of the Republican Party.[35]

This was Letcher's longest congressional speech. Although he received many requests for copies, he was unable to rejoice as the Republicans continued to obstruct routine business in Congress. A short extra session called by President Pierce late in August partially broke the legislative log jam by passing a few key bills, particularly a long overdue appropriation for the army. However, all was not going well in Washington, and Letcher gloomily described the situation to Davidson on August 24, six days before the passage of the army bill:

> We have been in session three days endeavouring to pass the Army Appropriations Bill. The indications look very unfavourable for the success of the measure, and I think it pretty certain that we shall again adjourn and leave the Army unprovided for. The Black Republicans avow their purpose to stand out, and I am satisfied they will do so, and hence I am for an adjournment at the earliest practicable moment. The general impression now is that we will close the session on Wednesday or Thursday next.
>
> The Black Republicans have taken the first step towards a Revolution, that may end in a dissolution of the Union. They have exhibited a settled and deliberate purpose to stop the wheels of Government, and in this way accomplished their nefarious purposes. The course of the President in calling an Extra session, may tend, and I hope will tend, to open the eyes of the people of the North, to the consequences of the mad career, of their Representatives. It is to be hoped that reason will yet triumph over folly—That patriotism will yet crush out Treason, and the Republic survive the dangers now impending over it.[36]

The welcomed adjournment sent Letcher hurrying home again, still deeply worried over the continuing sectional struggle, and about steadily increasing government expenditures. The conservative Lexingtonian had been dismayed in August when the members of Congress had voted themselves a husky increase in salary; he had not only opposed the increase but also refused to accept

it—a decision widely applauded in the Valley. At the same time
his constituency, a practical folk, urged him to accept the extra
pay since every other congressman had taken it. After several
weeks of deliberation, Letcher's practical bourgeois instincts
triumphed over his abstract idealism, and he drew his additional
pay from the treasury. Some political opponents labeled the whole
affair a cynical bit of demagogy, but actually Letcher, dedicated
but not doctrinaire, had run true to form. This affair, plus his
untiring fight for economy and integrity in government, won him
great popularity and the nickname "Honest John Letcher, Watch-
dog of the Treasury".[37]

By September, 1856, the campaign for the presidency was in
full swing. The new Republican Party, opposing any expansion of
slavery, picked John C. Frémont as its candidate. The new, unstable Know–Nothings rallied behind former President Millard
Fillmore and the hollow slogan "America for Americans". The
Democracy used compromise and evasion to build a platform supporting the Compromise of 1850 and the Kansas–Nebraska Bill.
Vague and ambiguous language glossed over the touchy question
of exactly when a territory could decide for or against slavery.
James Buchanan, a conservative, "safe" veteran who bore not too
many bruises from the recent sectional fights, was selected to unite
the party—for the moment.

The superbly organized Democrats set their well–oiled machinery into motion all over the nation. In an election in which slavery
and Kansas were the key issues, Buchanan had nothing to fear in
the South, but the Virginia Democracy took nothing for granted.
As usual, Letcher campaigned vigorously. Though "Old Buck" had
not appealed to him as a candidate, Letcher, a party regular who
believed in a unified, national Democracy, did not hesitate to
stand behind this Pennsylvanian who was, after all, a lifelong
Democrat. Letcher had seen enough of the Republicans in Congress to dread the prospect of their success, and he was convinced
that the Know–Nothing movement was a conspiracy to turn the
yeoman masses of the South against slavery. To Letcher, a Democratic defeat would be a catastrophe. Besides, by campaigning for

Buchanan in Virginia, he could cultivate the 1858 nomination for governor, his next major political objective.[38]

Buchanan carried Rockbridge County, the Valley, and the state, and Letcher joined some of his southern colleagues in Washington to prepare for the final session of the Thirty–fourth Congress. Buchanan had won a narrow national victory over the surging Republicans and the fading Know–Nothings, capturing only 45 per cent of the total popular vote even after benefiting from voting irregularities in several key states. The Republicans were on the march, and they would not be docile in Congress.[39]

From the opening day the sectional struggle overshadowed all other congressional activity, and Letcher continued to defend the South and the right of slavery to expand into the territories. He was pleased and relieved when John W. Whitfield was finally recognized as Kansas' official delegate to Congress after months of delay.[40]

Letcher was briefly distracted by the actions of the presidential electors of Virginia. These Wise supporters indirectly recommended to President–elect Buchanan that John B. Floyd be appointed to the cabinet and several other Virginians be given lesser patronage posts. These suggestions were made prior to the electors' official balloting for the presidency, a procedure that bordered on political blackmail. Amid widespread indignation, Letcher fumed, and in a letter to his friend James B. Dorman he commented candidly:

> Their action has been met by a storm of disapprobation, from our own citizens, and from those of other States. Our State has been burlesqued, ridiculed, and sneered at North and South, by all classes of people. Never have I been more mortified, than in hearing Virginia ridiculed for her love of the *"spoils of office"*.[41]

Letcher was worried as well as angry, for it was rumored that the electors' strategy was only part of a master plan that included replacing Hunter with Wise in the Senate and throwing the state gubernatorial nomination to Congressman Charles J. Faulkner in 1858. Letcher was now forewarned that there would be many obstacles on his road to the Governor's Mansion. In a face to face encounter, Faulkner denied any knowledge of a plot, but Letcher was not satisfied. He contacted some of his closest backers in Virginia, but nobody seemed to know what the erratic, unpredictable Wise was planning. The year 1858 remained shrouded in uncertainty.[42]

Soon Letcher was again absorbed in his congressional duties. The report of his special investigating committee was further substantiated when additional revelations of unethical lobbying led to the expulsion of one lawmaker and the resignation of two more. The tide of corruption continued to rise. Letcher continued to fight for strict constitutional construction and government economy, frequently receiving support from conservative northern Democrats. He still opposed high tariffs, not only because he felt they were an unfair burden on the working classes but also because they poured funds into a federal treasury that was struggling desperately to eliminate unmanageable surpluses. The temptation to siphon off surpluses into vast internal improvement projects was obvious. With the Panic of 1857 only six months away, Letcher warned of "an unhealthy condition in the monetary affairs of the country", stressing the growing scarcity of capital and reckless deficit spending by states on elaborate internal improvement projects.[43]

Letcher still did his committee homework, but as an experienced congressman he had much more leisure time. His social life in Washington was no more sectional than his conservatism. Though his Washington residence, Brown's Hotel, catered to southerners, his circle of acquaintances included men from every section of the nation. Though he represented the agrarian masses of the Valley, Letcher was a thorough bourgeois, and he was most at home in the company of businessmen and lawyers, northern or southern. As in the past, Letcher was unaffected, gregarious, and cheerful, and liked nothing better than informal conversation laced with jokes and anecdotes, bourbon and tobacco. He was capable of associating freely and harmoniously with arch Republicans like Thaddeus Stevens, Elihu B. Washburne, and Joshua Giddings. As a southerner, Letcher found some of the views of these men rather obnoxious; as a moderate, he felt that the continuing sectional crisis was exaggerating a few key differences and gradually destroying the traditional flexibility of the American political system.[44]

Early in 1857 Letcher ventured into a business deal with Congressmen John S. Phelps of Missouri and George S. Houston of Alabama and the clerk of the Claims Committee, Abel R. Corbin. They purchased 319,688 square feet of land—officially square 678 —north of the capitol building for $20,779.72. Each of the four partners in this real estate speculation paid $1,025 in cash and signed notes for $4,169.93. All three congressmen continued to vote on appropriations for the extension of the capitol grounds and buildings and other construction projects that directly influenced the value of their nearby land. Letcher's voting record on these appropriations indicated no departure from his customary crusade for economy, but he was clearly involved in a conflict of interest—the one stain on his reputation for honesty and integrity in a Congress sadly deficient in both categories.

The inclusion of Corbin in this speculation was also unfortunate. Corbin was already secretly receiving money from lobbyists and was thus on the threshold of an infamous career of swindling and double–dealing. Later, as a brother–in–law of President Grant, he climaxed his shady career in government by backing Jay Gould's attempt to corner the gold market in 1869.[45]

The Thirty-fourth Congress ended on March 3, and immediately after the inauguration of President Buchanan, Letcher returned to Virginia and another political battle. The Wise and Hunter factions of the Democracy were clashing over Hunter's seat in the Senate, and Letcher began to back Hunter in conversations with key members of the General Assembly. As an effective lobbyist, he also kept Hunter fully informed of political trends in the Valley. By November the opposition was receding, and in December the assembly re–elected Hunter by an overwhelming margin—a blow to Wise's presidential ambitions.[46]

Letcher's own ambitions were constantly encouraged by his friends and allies. Some mentioned the possibility of the speakership of the House or the chairmanship of the powerful Ways and Means Committee, but most were convinced that his chances for the governorship were excellent. Letcher himself was determined

either to win the governorship in 1859 or to retire from politics.
The only major obstacle to his gubernatorial ambition was Wise,
who remained bitterly hostile and completely unpredictable; however, Hunter's victory had weakened Wise's position.[47]

Letcher continued to mix his complex political maneuvers with
a lucrative law practice in partnership with David Curry. In June,
1857, the arrival of another healthy daughter, Margaret Kinney
Letcher, enlarged his family to seven. At the same time he had
to make his fourth stand for election to Congress. This time Whig
John D. Imboden furnished organized resistance, but Letcher was
too strongly entrenched and won by a three to one margin. His
extensive campaigning in this election was largely a successful
effort to drag Rockbridge's Democratic candidates for the House
of Delegates into office on his coat tails.[48]

In December, 1857, the first session of the Thirty–fifth Congress
began. Letcher returned early to Brown's Hotel in order to confer
with his fellow Virginia congressmen on strategy for the battle for
the speakership. The Democrats had regained control of the
House, but the nation was restless. The Panic of 1857 had caused
severe economic dislocations and sent hordes of lobbyists to Washington seeking relief. The Kansas wound continued to fester as
the Lecompton Convention railroaded through a constitution that
established slavery and thus conflicted with the desires of the free-
soil majority. The Buchanan–Douglas split over the Lecompton
Constitution—the beginning of the end of Democratic unity—
came before the end of the month. The atmosphere in Congress
was explosive.

A sectional battle over the speakership was avoided when the
Democrats agreed ahead of time on their candidate. As early as
November, Letcher was rumored to be the choice of the Virginia
delegation, but the Virginians decided to stand as a unit behind
moderate James L. Orr of South Carolina. Dedicated to party
unity, Letcher agreed wholeheartedly. A few southern mavericks
held out for Alexander H. Stephens of Georgia, but he declined
and suggested Letcher. This minor maneuvering in caucus was
settled on the first day of Congress, when Orr was chosen speaker
with solid southern support.[49]

Letcher stood with his southern comrades in the long, bitter
fight over Kansas, but he spoke formally only once—on March
31, 1858, as a member of a special 15–man committee appointed
to study the tense Kansas situation. Speaker Orr had stacked the
committee with pro–Lecompton men, and it was being severely
criticized for not investigating the obviously fraudulent circumstances surrounding the adoption of the Lecompton Constitution.
Letcher defended the committee report, asserting that it had proceeded as far as it was authorized to go and bolstering this contention with a liberal supply of facts and statistics. By April the
House was in an uproar over Kansas and, amid a background of
disorder and a few actual brawls, Senator Douglas' anti–Lecomp-
tonites gained ground rapidly.[50]

Letcher expended most of his energy in this turbulent session
attempting to pass a deficiency appropriations bill, an act honoring earlier financial commitments by the government. As a reliable member of the Ways and Means Committee, he was assigned
the thankless task of pushing this measure through the House. The
bill was quickly entangled in sectional and partisan politics, and
many axes were ground on the Lexingtonian's thick skin. Expensive preparations for a military campaign against Brigham Young's
Mormons who were massively resisting federal—"Gentile"—authority made these overdue appropriations essential, and the
Buchanan administration supported Letcher's efforts. Letcher had
always supported economy programs, but he was equally dedicated
to honoring the government's legitimate commitments. He mas-
tered every complex detail of this financial measure and fought
hard to slip it through the House quickly, but after several defeats,
he settled back for siege operations, relentlessly returning the bill
to the floor after each rejection. For once he was on the receiving
end of vigorous, often picayune criticisms by his customary allies,
the economy advocates. Letcher made little progress until May,
when the seething Kansas situation was somewhat soothed by the
passage of the English Bill, which resubmitted the Lecompton
Constitution to the people of Kansas. With this sectional problem
briefly settled, both houses of Congress finally approved the deficiency appropriations bill.[51]

In the case of the printing deficiency bill, Letcher reverted to his customary stand for economy. Here, too, the bills had been legally authorized, but the prices were ridiculously inflated, and Letcher refused to accept them. After spearheading the opposition which eventually killed this bill, he fought on against rising appropriations and spreading corruption, but his efforts were largely fruitless in the Thirty-fifth Congress. Just before the session ended in June, he did vote to authorize the government to borrow $15,-000,000, but this was simply a case of honoring maturing obligations, not extravagance.[52]

Letcher fiercely attacked a bill authorizing the federal government to regulate steamboats for the safety of passengers. He pointedly warned his fellow southerners that a central government which could regulate water transportation could also forbid boats to transport "the species of property peculiar to the South", a striking illustration of the interrelationship between the reality of slavery and the theory of states' rights.[53]

Unlike many ardent southerners, Letcher was as unenthusiastic about the dashing filibusterer William Walker as he had been about the Ostend Manifesto in 1855. Early in 1858, before the adjournment of Congress, he spoke frankly to Davidson. "I look upon him as no better than a Pirate," he asserted,

> and have no sympathy with him or his marauding. He will receive no "aid and Comfort" from "Old Buck" who will enforce the Neutrality laws as he should do. . . . The peole of this country are too honest to endorse his conduct, or that of any other man, who seeks to despoil a people, who are at peace with us.[54]

In nearly a decade of congressional service Letcher had compiled a satisfactory record. Never the author of significant legislation, he nonetheless gained a reputation as a conscientious, capable legislator, and as a champion of strict construction of the Constitution, states' rights, and government economy. The rising sectional clash had nudged the conservative Virginia a little further to the right, but he refused to forsake his basic moderation and never joined the growing ranks of the secessionists.

By the summer of 1858 Letcher was far more interested in political conditions in Virginia than in his congressional record.

He still had one more session to serve in Congress, but his primary objective for the next 11 months was the Governor's Mansion in Richmond.

CHAPTER 5

The Struggle For Power

The road to the Governor's Mansion was full of pitfalls, and two major challenges had to be met and overcome. First, the Democratic nomination had to be secured—and this would require skillful maneuvering and tireless effort. An even greater effort would be necessary to carry the general election in May, 1859. But John Letcher, now a seasoned veteran of Virginia politics, had waited a decade for the governorship, and this time he would not be denied.

Unrest on the national level complicated the political situation in Virginia. The elderly, inept Buchanan was losing control of both his party and his administration, as the American Democracy split along sectional lines. From the North came reports of passive and even active resistance to the Fugitive Slave Act of 1850, one of the foundation stones of the sectional compromise of that year. In New York, the Republican leader William H. Seward spoke ominously of an "irrepressible conflict", and in Maryland a half-mad fanatic planned a bloody attack on the slave citadel of Virginia. From the South the voices of secession rumbled louder and louder as the nation stumbled blindly toward catastrophe.

As early as 1857, maneuvering for the gubernatorial nomination began within the divided ranks of the Virginia Democracy. This was another crucial round in the continuing struggle between Wise and Hunter for control of the party, and was at first, largely

74

behind—the—scenes. By the middle of 1857 it was obvious that Letcher would be opposed by the Wise faction, which remembered his defection in 1855. The Hunterites gradually began to marshal their forces under the Letcher banner.

By this time Hunter wanted to play down slavery and disunion and take a more moderate southern rights position. Letcher's congressional record during the bitter sectional clashes of the 1850's reflected the exact image he wished to convey. Also, the Lexingtonian was very popular in the western section of the state where Hunter was dangerously weak. Thus, though Letcher had remained in the outer ranks of the Hunterites, he gained their support for the gubernatorial nomination.

There was no shortage of potential opposition. Congressman Charles J. Faulkner was still a distinct threat, and Wise's Attorney General, John Randolph Tucker, was another possibility. In the background lurked a host of other potential candidates, including Secretary of War John B. Floyd, Judge John W. Brockenbrough, Congressmen Henry A. Edmundson, George W. Hopkins and William Smith, and Delegate Augustus A. Chapman of Monroe County.[1]

By November, 1857, the opposition began to snipe at Letcher, clearly the favorite. Though he had repudiated abolitionism and the *Ruffner Pamphlet* in 1850, he could not erase his only major political blunder from the record. The Wise faction was shifting to a more radical southern rights position, and it spearheaded a whispering campaign that questioned Letcher's loyalty to slavery.[2]

Letcher's candidacy became official during the winter, and when Congress adjourned in June, 1858, his enemies attacked him openly. The *Richmond Whig* began the assault, but the *Richmond Enquirer,* edited by the Governor's son, O. Jennings Wise, had joined the onslaught before the end of the month. The whole Wise faction moved into line behind the *Enquirer* and blasted away at Letcher. They continued to emphasize his past abolitionism, but they also criticized his performance at the Reform Convention, particularly his speech attacking the eastern slaveholders and his advocacy of an equal tax on slave and non—slave property.[3]

Before the end of June, criticism became so intense that Letcher wrote a public letter to Hunter's new Richmond newspaper, *The South*, explaining his connection with the *Ruffner Pamphlet* and abolitionism. He frankly admitted that in 1847 he had regarded slavery as a social and political evil but added that since he had then (and still) owned slaves by purchase, rather than by inheritance, he had never considered slavery a moral wrong. He added that in 1850 he had publicly stated that he no longer considered slavery a social and political evil. As to the letter he had signed requesting Ruffner to publish his anti–slavery speech, Letcher said he had considered the speech a calm discussion of the harmful effects of slavery. However, he added, the published version had contained "many things so exceptional that those (with one exception, I believe), who called upon him to publish the speech refused to contribute to the cost of publication". Letcher concluded by bluntly advising those who still did not trust him to vote for someone else.[4]

Letcher's supporters hailed his forthright letter. Congressman Howell Cobb, watching his friend's battle closely, sent his congratulations:

> Your letter is a death blow to all opposition on the score of your former tendency to abolitionism. John Letcher not to be trusted on the slavery question!!—*That will do*—The next thing I expect to hear is that Paul was unsound on the christian [sic] religion.[5]

Anyone familiar with Letcher's congressional record could see the absurdity of accusing him of being "soft" on abolitionism, but Letcher was in the middle of a crucial political campaign, a no–holds–barred struggle for power. Victory came first, not accuracy, and the opposition continued to hammer away on the same theme. The Wise faction was determined to punish Letcher for his failure to support Wise in the previous gubernatorial election and at the same time tarnish the prestige of the Hunterites.[6]

In western Virginia the Ruffners were stirring. The Reverend William H. Ruffner was ready to write a public letter vindicating his father, but Letcher's old friend John Echols was able to dissuade him. But the elder Ruffner did write a public letter to the people of Virginia. Indignantly he declared that he had not exceeded his instructions in writing the *Ruffner Pamphlet*. He demanded that Letcher specify the "exceptional things" added to the pamphlet.

This was a lethal invitation. The prospect of a public dispute over the controversial *Ruffner Pamphlet* frightened the Letcherites, and for once they were slow to advise their candidate. Ruffner's letter could not be ignored, but an open fight had to be avoided. Finally, in mid–July, Letcher resolved this dilemma by having the *Valley Star* declare that he had not meant to question Ruffner's honesty. This indirect apology which did not withdraw the charge of "exceptional things" satisfied Ruffner, who publicly declared that the grounds for the controversy were removed.[7]

Ruffner may have been satisfied, but the Wise followers were not. The *Enquirer* changed its strategy slightly but continued to belabor Letcher. Grudgingly it recognized Letcher's loyalty to slavery and the South, but it added that his old heresy had left an indelible stain. His nomination would give the nation the false impression that Virginia was taking an equivocal stand on slavery at the very time the whole South had to stand firm. The *Enquirer* also claimed that Letcher's nomination would divide the party and lead to defeat in the general election.[8]

During this period Letcher remained in Lexington and quietly organized his campaign. He appealed to friends all over the state to work harder for his candidacy. Reports from the grass roots were encouraging. The *Enquirer's* attacks were rallying the people of the west to his defense, and the Culpeper County area looked safe also. Wise was championing Faulkner of southwest Virginia, but Faulkner himself steadfastly maintained that he was not a candidate. Letcher spoke with cautious confidence: "So far as I have heard, the news is as favourable as I could wish, and all that is necessary is that my friends shall not relax their efforts in my behalf."[9]

Early in July, Letcher visited Rockbridge's Alum Springs, 17 miles northwest of Lexington. His recurrent rheumatism would be eased by several weeks of the murky waters, and, more important, crucial political conferences could be conducted there. By the end of July the holiday was over, and the strategy of the opposition was much clearer. Many rival candidates would be encouraged in the west, Letcher's home territory. This phalanx of candidates—Brockenbrough, Hopkins, Edmundson, Chapman, Tucker, and perhaps others—were to neutralize his western support. Grass roots intrigue and sleight of hand at the convention involving the manipulation of proxy votes and the institution of a two–thirds rule would be the climax, and thus Letcher, clearly the choice of the party's rank and file, would be maneuvered out of the nomination.[10]

While at the Alum Springs, Letcher corresponded with President Buchanan about Senator Douglas' speech on July 9 in Chicago in which the "Little Giant" had continued his attacks on the Lecompton Constitution as a betrayal of popular sovereignty in Kansas. "I am at a loss to understand," he wrote,

> the course of Judge Douglas. It seems to me to be marked neither by wisdom nor policy. Before our adjournment I was informed by two of his friends that he was desirous of securing harmony to the party, and to this end, it was proper that the past should be forgotten. I had hoped on his return home, that such would have been his advice to his followers. Imagine my disappointment therefore on the perusal of his speech . . . Your policy is approved by our political friends here, with scarce an exception. I have heard of but one Democrat in this county who sides with Douglas, in the position he has taken in his Chicago speech.
>
> Judge Douglas will see the blunder he has committed, but I fear it will be discovered too late, to correct it. On my return home I told our friends, that the administration was disposed to deal fairly and justly with him, and that if harmony was not restored, it would be his own fault. And so it has turned out.[11]

The Douglas–Buchanan dispute was tearing the Democratic Party asunder. Letcher advised his fellow southern Democrats to avoid retreating into a narrow, sectional faction or party, and, as usual, he proclaimed moderation a cure for the nation's woes. Optimistically, he predicted a period of sectional reconciliation, and a few weeks later the Republicans scored a stunning victory in the northern congressional elections. His prediction could not have been more wrong, but he was too involved in his own gubernatorial race to spot the storm gathering on the horizon.[12]

His campaign seemed to be going well as the summer ended,

but rumor and counter–rumor created uncertainty. Hunter advised him to say as little as possible in the Tidewater region about his former abolitionism, and predicted that Letcher would not be hurt too badly by his past in that area. Hunter's backing was not particularly enthusiastic, but it was still virtually essential. If he could marshal reasonable support in the east, then victory was certain, as the west, with the exception of the southwest, was friendly.[13]

Some of Letcher's staunchest supporters were worried. His friend Davidson expressed fear of further tricks by the enemy:

> The interests of our friend Letcher have been mixed up lately as the Whigs would have it, with that *"Hottentot"* Dr. Ruffner. I fear it has made some lodgement, and may affect his nomination in a Convention. If L were bold enough, to come out, as a man of the people, in defiance of any Caucus or Convention, he would sweep the state. This would be a bold step for a party man, and probably one of doubtful propriety. . . . Canvasses and Conventions are the curse of the land, and take from the hands of the people, their sovereign right to think and act as they please. A few wire workers—indeed one man—in a Convention, may control the vote of a Sovereign State. It should not be so.[14]

Campaign activities forced Letcher to neglect his law practice, and his income suffered. The Panic of 1857 had lowered the value of his real estate holdings in Washington, but the notes he had signed in this transaction were still due at their original figure, and capital was very scarce. Letcher tried to sell his Washington land at a loss, but he could find no takers. He fell behind in paying off his notes, which were not liquidated until March, 1861.

Hunter's new Richmond paper, *The South,* was also caught in the financial squeeze which was gripping most of the nation. Despite the efforts of the editor Roger Pryor, John Seddon of Fredericksburg, and other Hunter aides to raise additional capital from the party faithful, *The South* joined thousands of other American businesses in bankruptcy in the winter of 1858. This was a blow to Letcher, for *The South* was his only effective voice in the capital city.[15]

Another serious problem was the location of the nominating convention. The Letcherites favored Staunton in the friendly Val-

ley, but the Wise–oriented State Central Committee selected the
more hostile environment of Petersburg. More trouble occurred
in the northwest, a Letcher stronghold. Congressman Sherrard
Clemens, who was working hard for his friend Letcher in this
area, confidently predicted that Judge Brockenbrough would not
accept the nomination. Since the Wise forces were beginning to
shift most of their support toward Brockenbrough, this was welcome news. Clemens and Letcher's brother Sam went to Clarks-
burg to get a direct answer from the Judge about his intentions.
They cornered Brockenbrough in his office and asked for a direct
statement. According to Sam Letcher, Brockenbrough denied
being a Wise puppet and "stated emphatically that he did not
desire to be the nominee".[16]

Clemens seized this statement and exaggerated it. He wrote
letters to the *Richmond Enquirer* and other Democratic newspapers saying Brockenbrough had officially withdrawn from contention. Brockenbrough hurriedly indicated to the *Enquirer* that
he was not campaigning but was definitely available for a draft. A
war of words ensued between O. Jennings Wise of the *Enquirer*
and Clemens, and an affair of honor followed. Wise, an experienced and enthusiastic duelist, severely wounded Clemens, who
hovered near death for the remainder of the year. Fundamentally
practical and moderate, Letcher had always disapproved of duel-
ing, and the news of his friend's injury made him despondent
and melancholy on the eve of the convention. Actually this incident was a political boost for both Letcher and Clemens and a
blow to the prestige of the Wise clan. Clemens recovered slowly,
and he was still hobbling on crutches when he again crossed Letcher's path as Virginia seceded from the Union.[17]

Just before the convention, reports from all over the state were
very encouraging. The Piedmont looked safe; northern Virginia,
even safer. The northwest seemed absolutely secure, and even the
Wise stronghold in southwestern Virginia looked more promising
after John B. Floyd belatedly began to support Letcher. Southside
and the Tidewater, where the Ruffner dispute had been most
damaging, were doubtful despite Hunter's efforts. Richmond was
rather hostile, but some veteran government bureaucrats like

Adjutant General William H. Richardson strongly backed Letcher. The statewide picture clearly indicated victory with the weak areas being more than compensated for by Letcher's overwhelming strength in the west.[18]

The showdown finally came on December 2. The long, bitter, and ultimately bloody canvass had created great tension, and both the Wise and Hunter factions were edgy and quarrelsome as they squeezed into Phoenix Hall in Petersburg. The convention was noisy and disorderly from the beginning, and several delegates reeled drunkenly through their duties. James Barbour, prominent party veteran and bitter anti-Wise partisan from Culpeper, nominated Letcher, and O. Jennings Wise and Nat Harrison of Monroe County led the opposition. The Wise faction nominated four Valley men in an attempt to split Letcher's massive western backing. The Letcherites had made elaborate preparations to defeat this strategy, and so the Wise faction was forced to concentrate all of its support on Brockenbrough. But this failed too: Letcher was the overwhelming choice of the convention delegates. Though the southwest opposed him, and a few Hunterites defected, and the supposedly safe northwest failed to give him a majority, Letcher received solid support from the convention as a whole and was overwhelmingly victorious over the other five candidates. Hunter's Tidewater furnished surprisingly strong support which more than compensated for the weak backing from the northwest. Letcher's vigorous repudiation of the *Ruffner Pamphlet* had cost him some of his northwestern backing, but it had salvaged much more support in the eastern and southern sections of the state. Robert L. Montague of Middlesex County received the nomination for lieutenant governor, as the convention followed the usual practice of giving the ticket sectional balance.

The winner had no time to celebrate. He was still the congressman from Lexington and had to hurry to Washington. He arrived a few days late for the second session of the Thirty–fifth Congress, which had convened on December 6.[19]

The stunning victory of the Republicans in the recent northern congressional elections was a clear repudiation of Buchanan's prosouthern policy in Kansas. Not only the Republicans but also the

Douglas Democrats gained as the breach in the Democracy widened into a chasm. Even in the last session of the old House, the Buchanan Democrats lost control. Early maneuvering for the presidential nomination further confused matters as southerners led a party caucus which took the unprecedented action of removing Douglas from his chairmanship of the Senate Committee on Territories. Moderates like Hunter were beginning to lose control of the restless southern Democrats.[20]

Early in January, before the most bitter battles began, Susan Letcher visited her husband for a few weeks. Letcher frequently complained about the loneliness of Washington without his beloved wife and family, and for awhile life at Brown's Hotel did not seem so drab and monotonous. The Letchers plunged into Washington's social whirl, and for once the congressman from Lexington neglected a little of his legislative homework. This happy interlude was smashed late in January when Letcher was stricken with a severe case of erysipelas (St. Anthony's fire), which caused an extremely painful inflammation of the skin. This disease lasted for more than a week, and Letcher lived for months in constant dread of another attack.[21]

As Congress continued, disaffected Democrats and the Republicans voted down the administration's normal appropriation bills, and the Treasury, already depleted by the depression, cried for funds. By February there was a huge log–jam of rejected appropriation measures, and Letcher despaired of obtaining even minimum funds for normal government operations without an extra session. He still favored economy, but he opposed blatant obstructionism. Heatedly he lashed out at the new anti-Buchanan coalition in the House which was threatening both his Ways and Means Committee's appropriation bills and the South's political power. "I understand that there is an Administration majority here," he said,

> but so far as Lecompton was concerned, so far as this bill is concerned, and so far as other questions that have risen here are concerned, I have ascertained that there is not an Administration majority here; so that there must be an Opposition majority of some sort. What makes it up I do not know, nor does it boot much to inquire. What I desire to do is this: the session is drawing to a close. We

have to pass these appropriation bills for the purpose of keeping
the Government in operation, or a Congress has to come back here
to do it. . . . If that extra session can be avoided; if we can . . . pass
such bills as will keep the Government in operation, is it not the
part of wisdom to do so, and to avoid the inconvenience of an extra
session?[22]

Letcher opposed a homestead bill which passed the House but
not the more conservative Senate. Measures calling for subsidies
for railroads and agricultural colleges and for higher tariffs were
all defeated with Letcher's help, but the votes were very close.
Every year these proposals came nearer to reality as the future
pressed in relentlessly upon the embattled conservatives. Finally,
at the last minute, most of the essential appropriation bills were
passed; the Treasury was saved, but the government operating
budget was drastically reduced. Letcher was relieved to escape
an extra session at a time when he needed every minute for his
own gubernatorial campaign.

His congressional career was finished. His record was solid but
not spectacular, distinguished but not brilliant. He had blazed no
new trails, but he had contributed honesty, moderation, hard
work, and common sense to Congress in a period when all of these
qualities were desperately needed. Despite the rising sectional
crisis, he was complimented by such divergent newspapers as
Horace Greeley's New York *Tribune* and Robert Barnwell Rhett's
Charleston *Mercury*.[23]

Letcher's last session in Congress had been a momentous one,
for here the national Democratic Party completed the last agonies
of disruption. Letcher was well aware of this cleavage, but he
was often distracted by plans for his gubernatorial campaign.
Despite signs of rising opposition in Virginia, he retained his
characteristic optimism. He was very popular in the state, and
he carried the banner of the mighty Virginia Democracy. Nevertheless, trouble was brewing as the moribund Whigs, encouraged
by their foe's national and state schisms, rallied for one final effort.
In February, 1859, they met in convention and nominated states'
righter William L. Goggin of Bedford County for governor and
nationalist Waitman T. Willey of Monongalia County for lieutenant governor. The eastern Whigs were ardent, and most of the

western Whigs under George W. Summers and Francis H. Pierpoint dutifully but unenthusiastically supported the party's ticket.[24]

This gubernatorial battle was watched all over the nation. Meeting in Washington, old line Whigs like Senator John Bell, Senator
John J. Crittenden, and Letcher's friend "Sandy" Stuart envisioned
the Virginia election as the first step in a political comeback under
the banners of conservatism and the Union. In Virginia the re-
surgent Whigs planned their strategy, which Alexander Rives, son
of William Cabell Rives, summarized for a comrade in Lexington:

> Mr. Letcher's course on slavery is a good text to expose their
> hypocrisy on this subject, and a theme, well calculated to prepare
> the way for the next Pres. Election; and to put aside, now and for-
> ever, the unfortunate diversion of the Whigs to the Tom-fooleries
> of Americanism.[25]

Thus the Whigs patterned their campaign along the lines the
Wise faction had already used against Letcher. In the east and the
Valley the *Ruffner Pamphlet* was again the main weapon used
against "Emancipation John". In the northwest he was condemned for not championing internal improvements with sufficient vigor, and was also belabored for representing the party of
slavery in Virginia. The *Richmond Whig* spearheaded the eastern
campaign. It labeled Letcher a traitor to Virginia and her traditions, a man who had injured his own state as much as Joshua
Giddings, Charles Sumner, and other fanatic abolitionists. Exam-
ining the congressional record of "Cunning John", the *Whig* condemned him for opposing pensions for veterans of the War of
1812 and relief for the poor of Washington. At the same time,
he was hit for favoring postal rate increases and accepting a congressional pay raise after voting against it and publicly refusing
to take it. He was also described as an integral part of a corrupt
and spendthrift national administration. A few weeks before the
election, the *Whig* published a letter from prominent Whig John
Minor Botts attacking "Honest John's" speculation in Washington
real estate while voting in Congress on bills which directly influenced the value of his property.

However, the *Whig* saved its heaviest salvos for the abolition
record of "John Ruffner Letcher". It warned that Letcher's elec-

tion would be interpreted in the North as a sign that Virginia was "soft" on the subject of slavery. Letcher was even pictured as fraternally embracing archfiend Joshua Giddings in a fond farewell after the last session of Congress.[26]

In Lexington the *Gazette* attacked more gently, stressing that the *Enquirer's* attacks on Letcher during the fight for the Democratic nomination had created the impression in the North that he was disloyal to slavery. Thus his election would compromise Virginia's strong pro–slavery stand. The *Staunton Spectator,* a powerful Whig journal in the Valley, condemned Letcher for his advocacy of both the division of the state and Ruffnerism in 1847.[27]

The aggressive strategy of the Whigs reached a peak in a pamphlet issued by their State Central Committee in Richmond. This campaign tract criticized Letcher's congressional record and inaccurately labeled him a pro-Know–Nothing, but most of its twenty–nine pages were devoted to a thorough review of his past abolitionism. His conduct in 1847 was examined minutely, and many anti–slavery statements from the *Ruffner Pamphlet* were quoted in full. Letcher's gradual repudiation of abolitionism was investigated with much thoroughness but little objectivity. His Negro–ology speech at the Reform Convention was also stressed. This tract and the *Ruffner Pamphlet* were widely circulated by the Whigs as the election approached.[28]

In the northwest the Whigs wavered. They faced the cheerless prospect of backing an eastern pro–slavery Whig against a western hero who had once opposed slavery but now supported it. Some Trans–Allegheny Whigs openly supported Letcher; many remained neutral. The Wheeling *Intelligencer,* one of their leading newspapers, supported neither candidate but defended Letcher from the attacks of the eastern Whigs. This far western gap in an otherwise solid Whig front would be of crucial importance on election day.

The Whigs were not alone in their lack of unity. All of the wounds suffered by the Democrats in the bitter intraparty battle for the nomination had not healed. The Wise supporters appeared to close ranks behind the victor, but their support was far from wholehearted. Henry A. Wise himself gave Letcher exactly the same support Letcher had given him in the 1855 gubernatorial race—none at all. O. Jennings Wise's *Enquirer* furnished nominal backing but expended most of its energy in a bitter battle of words with the *Richmond Whig*.[29]

Just as in the nomination fight, Letcher and his friends were forced to spend much of their time and energy warding off the opposition's Ruffnerism attacks and reaffirming Letcher's devotion to slavery. The Letcherites effectively pointed out that other staunch southerners like Calhoun and Wise had been inconsistent in regard to slavery over the course of their careers. "Honest John's" congressional reputation for integrity was stressed, and his defense of states' and southern rights in Washington was also emphasized effectively. Actually, both candidates championed slavery and states' rights, and beneath the ballyhoo no great issues were at stake in this bitter Whig–Democrat struggle for power.[30]

The highlight of the campaign was a series of debates between the two candidates. These encounters took place throughout the state but always under the same set of rules. Each man delivered a formal speech, and both followed with a half hour rebuttal. Large crowds witnessed each heated but courteous clash. As usual, Letcher's delivery lacked polish and eloquence, and he almost always overburdened his speeches with statistics and legalistic technicalities. On the other hand, Goggin was an outstanding orator, one of the best stump speakers in the state. Skillfully mixing humorous anecdotes and quick–witted sallies in with his political opinions, Goggin outclassed his stolid opponent. Letcher was more factual, but Goggin was more entertaining. Only before highly partisan audiences of Democrats in the Valley was Letcher able to hold his own in these debates.

Letcher was definitely taking a beating, and soon he rearranged his campaign schedule in order to reduce sharply the number of future verbal encounters with Goggin. Then, in the middle of April, Letcher was forced to cease campaigning altogether. Never fully recovered from his earlier attack of erysipelas, he became seriously ill, and his running mate Montague had to take his place on the hustings. Exhausted, feverish and barely able to talk, Letcher hurried to Brown's Hotel in Washington, where he received special treatments to prevent a recurrence of the dreaded erysipelas. By the end of April, he was strong enough to return to Lexington but still far too sick to re–enter the campaign. He concluded his campaign in the middle of May with a written appeal to the voters in which he prophetically promised to resist any movement of federal troops into Virginia to enforce "unjust, iniquitous and unconstitutional laws, either in Virginia or any other state".[31]

The showdown was scheduled for May 31. During the final week of the canvass, both sides slackened the pace, and the political forecasters went to work. Some enthusiastic Whigs predicted victory, but the experienced politicians in both camps gave the nod to Letcher and disagreed only on the margin of victory. Some felt he would equal or surpass Wise's edge of 10,000 votes in 1855. All over the nation politicians watched this election for an indication of trends which would be significant in the 1860 battle for the presidency.[32]

Election day finally arrived, and a slightly below average turn-out of the Virginia electorate trooped to the polls. Letcher triumphed by a margin of 77,112 to 71,543. At last he had gained the coveted governorship, but his victory was somewhat tarnished. His victory margin of 5,569 votes was only slightly better than half as large of Wise's margin in 1855. His home county of Rockbridge went Whig again, but Letcher tallied hefty majorities in the Valley and the northwest. Eastern Virginia and the Wise stronghold of the southwest went for Goggin.[33]

Undoubtedly the majority of the voters followed traditional party lines, but the striking feature of the contest was the Democracy's sharply reduced margin of victory. Both parties held elaborate post–mortems to analyse this phenomenon.

Wise's hostility had certainly cost Letcher some votes, particularly in the southwest. The half–hearted support of the *Enquirer* and some Wise supporters was no surprise, but the relative inaction of Hunter, his nephew Moscoe R. H. Garnett, and some other key aides was unexpected and very damaging in the east. The passiveness of some other leading Democrats, some overconfident and some hostile, was costly in the east and the south.

Letcher may have been hurt by his close association with the Buchanan administration, which was fast losing popularity in Virginia. Botts' sharp attack on Letcher's real estate speculation in Washington did not enhance the image of "Honest John". Vote-trading in the concurrent congressional elections may have caused some losses, but the Whigs claimed Goggin suffered more than Letcher from this practice. Letcher's poor showing in the debates and his illness in the crucial home stretch of the campaign were significant factors too.

However, the whole picture was not dark. Letcher won in his native west, particularly in the northwest and the northern part of the Valley where his majorities were much greater than Wise's in 1855. His past abolitionism was not too damaging in the Valley and was a real asset in the northwest. His performance at the Reform Convention was remembered, and he was still one of the west's political heroes.[34]

Letcher had only seven months before assuming office, and the rush of events gave him little time to prepare. The birth of Mary Davidson Letcher on September 30, diverted him only briefly from politics. The continuing disintegration of the Democratic Party held his attention. In the South radicals were gaining control, and the old Whigs were reinforced by conservatives and Unionists seeking some organization to resist the rising tide of extremism. The southern congressional elections in 1859 indicated a slight trend toward conservatism, the hallmark of the Democracy's revived opposition. In Virginia the Wise–Hunter breach in the party widened as both men eyed the 1860 presidential nomination, and similar splits plagued the Democracy all over the South.

The northern Democracy fared no better. Douglas was surging ahead as the Buchanan administration foundered amidst charges of inefficiency, corruption, and incompetence. Everywhere the stage was set for the disastrous Charleston Convention.[35]

Then, in October, John Brown struck at Harper's Ferry. The raiders were quickly suppressed, and the slaves did not rebel. Brown was indicted, tried, convicted, and hanged within two weeks. Twin waves of terror and anger swept through the state and the South. Tensions and frustrations accumulated over a

decade of sectional controversy suddenly flooded the land. Even
veteran politicians were surprised—and worried—by the emotionalism and extremism that had sprung up overnight.[36]

Virginia was in turmoil as Letcher prepared to take office. He
had fought hard for the nomination and even harder for election,
and now, at 46, he had reached his primary political objective.
But the dark clouds of disunion and civil war loomed on the
horizon, and Letcher was too much of a realist to ignore them.

At this crucial hour personal tragedy struck. His ten–year–old
son, Andrew Holt Letcher, got a splinter in his hand while playing. Less than a week later lockjaw developed, and within fifteen
hours the little boy was dead. Stunned, Letcher temporarily
drifted into a period of gloom and pessimism. For a brief time his
characteristic optimism left him, as when he discussed politics in
a letter to Hunter early in December. "It really looks to me," he
wrote,

> as if the days of the Republic were numbered. All the indications
> seem to me to point to a dissolution of the Union, and that at an
> early date. There must be a speedy and radical change in Northern
> sentiment, or we cannot remain a united people. They can save the
> Union, and it rests with them to do it. If I am to have a stormy
> administration, so be it, I am prepared for it, and will meet any
> issue that may be tendered promptly and with that decision which
> a Virginia Executive should exhibit. I know what my friends expect
> of me, and they shall not be disappointed.[37]

The storm was coming, and it would smash Letcher's beloved
Virginia. Yet, with a "stormy administration" only weeks away,
the governor–elect was dealt another stunning blow. The dreaded
erysipelas flared up again. Dr. James McDowell Taylor could do
little for his suffering friend, and Letcher returned to Washington
for more special treatments.

The disease responded to treatment, but Letcher found little
else to be cheerful about in the capital. The first session of the
Thirty–sixth Congress was chaotic. The House was locked in a
battle for the speakership which did not end until February. No
party controlled a majority, and a fierce sectional battle raged.
Letcher had witnessed many sectional squabbles in Congress, but

none like this one. The Union could not long survive the bitterness
and hatred boiling over in Congress.

On December 21, Letcher returned to Lexington. A smallpox
epidemic was raging through the Valley, but Letcher worried far
more about the plague of sectionalism that was ravaging Washington. Soon the plague would spread and engulf the nation in a
bloody war. In less than two weeks Letcher would become governor of one of the disintegrating Union's key states. His whole
political life had been a preparation for such a responsibility. The
testing time had come.[38]

CHAPTER 6

Peacetime Governor

On December 31, 1859, Letcher arrived in Richmond in the midst of a turbulent snowstorm, an appropriate omen. War clouds were gathering on the horizon, but that storm would not break for over a year. Letcher's peacetime administration was filled with the tensions of the coming war, and the moderate, conservative Lexingtonian trod a lonely path in opposition to the surging radicalism that led to secession. Routine chores further burdened the new governor, who faced a sterner test than any Virginia chief executive since the time of the Revolutionary War.

Letcher took the oath of office on the day of his arrival and quickly assumed the duties of his relatively lucrative, $5,000–a–year office. For the first few weeks he worked from 8 A.M. to midnight. Many appointments had to be made, and the conscientious new governor carefully examined every application. Numerous applications for pardon, some as long as 100 handwritten pages, also had to be reviewed; Letcher dutifully waded through them, but he issued only a few pardons, hoping to discourage further unjustified pleas.[1]

On January 3, the Letchers moved from the Exchange Hotel into the Governor's Mansion, a stately building that had echoed to the footsteps of the Barbours, Tylers, Randolphs, Nicholases, Tazewells, Robertsons, and McDowells, the Virginia elite. The aristocracy had definitely not monopolized the governorship in re-

cent years, but Letcher was probably the most thoroughly bourgeois chief executive the state had yet known. Still a Jacksonian
at heart, he welcomed visitors from every stratum of southern
society, but he and his family were most at ease with their own
middle class. Tobacco and bourbon whiskey mixed freely with
laughter and songs as the relaxed, informal Letcher household
quickly became a social center in Richmond. Banker C. W. Purcell, lawyer William H. Terrill, and Mayor Joseph Mayo and
their families were the Letchers' most frequent visitors.[2]

Letcher's most important preliminary task was the preparation
of an inaugural address to present to the legislature, then in session. John Brown's raid had left Virginia seething with unrest,
not only from the actual attack but also from the glowing praise
for Brown that poured forth from abolitionists—still a minority
—in the North. The bitter sectional struggle for the speakership
of the House of Representatives also frayed nerves. The Virginia
troops mobilized to stop Brown were still on active duty, and many
localities were organizing their own armed bands. In this tense
period Wise and the radicals made great gains at the expense of
the more moderate Hunterites.

The General Assembly had convened as usual in December and
heard Governor Wise call for large-scale military preparations.
In January Wise was no longer governor, but the executive department was honeycombed with radicals, including Lieutenant
Governor Montague, Attorney General Tucker, Adjutant General
William H. Richardson, and Secretary of the Commonwealth
George W. Munford. The conservative governor kept his own
counsel. Although technically a Hunterite, Letcher had never been
more than a fringe member of that faction, and Hunter's weak
support in the gubernatorial election had cooled his allegiance
even more. Thus not even Hunter and his chief lieutenants knew
exactly what the independent-minded Lexingtonian would say.[3]

The eagerly awaited address came on Saturday, January 7.
Despite literary and organizational weaknesses, it was not lacking
in content. The North, Letcher declared, was responsible for the
current sectional crisis. Yankee attacks on slavery, efforts to restrict
it from the territories, and attempts to nullify the Fugitive Slave

Act had destroyed national harmony, and the damage seemed beyond repair. Yet there was still hope if true conservatives all over the nation would act. A convention of the states under Article Five of the Constitution could solve the problems that threatened the Union; even if such a convention failed in its primary purpose, it could still supervise a peaceful dissolution of the Union. The Virginia legislature should immediately invite all of the states to participate in a national convention, and should also send commissioners to the northern states to ask for repeal of all personal liberty laws. Speed was essential, however, for the southern people would not submit to continued northern aggression or accept a Republican victory in the coming presidential election. Even disunion had to be faced to preserve southern rights.

Letcher concluded by warning Virginia to be prepared for any emergency. He proposed revision of the ineffective militia laws, creation of an efficient military staff, procurement of munitions of war, expansion of the Virginia Military Institute at Lexington, and formation of a brigade of minutemen. This part of Letcher's speech echoed Wise's recommendations of December, indicating the tension and uneasiness throughout Virginia.[4]

The assembly rejected Letcher's two main suggestions—invitations to the states for a national convention and appointment of commissioners to appeal to the North to abolish personal liberty laws. However, the legislators did quickly pass a bill authorizing $500,000 for the purchase and manufacture of arms. The governor appointed his friend Francis H. Smith, superintendent of V. M. I., Colonel P. St. George Cocke of Powhatan County, and George Wythe Randolph, later Confederate secretary of war, to a board charged with carrying out the provisions of this new law. The board swiftly bought $180,000 worth of arms and used the remainder of the appropriation to equip the Richmond Armory as a weapons–making center. Letcher signed the final contract for constructing the arms–making machinery with Joseph R. Anderson's Tredegar Iron Works on August 23.[5]

Meanwhile, Christopher G. Memminger of South Carolina had arrived in Richmond on January 12, hoping to persuade the assembly to join his state in the call for a southern convention.

A month later, two commissioners from Mississippi had come on a similar errand. Faced with the actual prospect of a secession convention, public opinion in Virginia veered sharply back toward moderation. Letcher received all of these Dixie emissaries politely, joined in the round of parties in their honor, but did not help them. He transmitted all of their proposals to the assembly with a distinct lack of enthusiasm. On March 8, the legislators formally rejected the idea of a southern convention, a victory for Letcher and the other Virginia moderates.[6]

During this same period the governor briefly visited Charles Town to speed up proceedings against the last two captive raiders from John Brown's band. A change in presiding judges had delayed the trial of these last two defendants, who were not hanged until March. Despite the delay, Letcher deactivated all state troops, who had been mobilized to stop the raid, by the end of January, keeping a few units on two–hour alert to discourage rescue attempts. He bruskly rejected northern petitions for clemency for the raiders, accurately stating that all Virginians, regardless of party, agreed that hanging was just and necessary. However, he disappointed the radicals in Virginia by not attending the final executions. He certainly approved, but he was determined to remove the whole bloody, emotional affair swiftly from the public view and with the least possible fanfare.[7]

Brown's raid was not easily forgotten, and Virginians were further enraged by the refusal of the governors of Ohio and Iowa to extradite some of Brown's men who had escaped from Harper's Ferry. Throughout February and March, Letcher tried unsuccessfully to bring the fugitives to justice in Virginia. Reporting to the state Senate, he angrily condemned the northern governors for refusing to cooperate. Virginia's rights seemed less and less secure within the Union. "We must meet this spirit of oppression upon the slaveholding States sternly and resolutely", he warned, "and to this end union and harmony is indispensable to success. We must have a united South".[8]

Despite the rising sectional controversy, much of Letcher's time was still devoted to routine duties. Like most chief executives of the period, he failed to allocate his time properly or to delegate minor matters to his assistants; consequently, he was often bogged down in trivia while important matters were postponed. Pardon applications and routine appointments still occupied much of his time, and legal technicalities frequently sent him into time–consuming research in Virginia law codes. Gradually he began to rely more often on Attorney General Tucker for legal opinions, but in many matters he continued to be chief clerk rather than governor. Trivial boundary disputes with North Carolina and Maryland dragged on through most of the year. As an *ex officio* member of the board of commissioners of the Virginia Washington Monument, Letcher corresponded at length with Randolph Rogers, the sculptor who was in Italy working on the project. And the governor spent still more of his valuable time trying to persuade the assembly to appropriate funds for publication of the minutes of the Reform Convention of 1850![9]

In February, the competition between Wise and Hunter grew more heated. Both men wanted the party's presidential nomination, and both fought desperately for control of the Virginia Democracy as the party selected its delegates to the Charleston Convention in a series of district meetings. The Hunterites assumed a more extreme southern rights position. Letcher, still preferring the opportunistic Hunter to the radical Wise, often stayed in his office until midnight discussing politics with party leaders. Early in April, he wrote his old friend and former congressional colleague, George W. Jones of Tennessee, and summarized the political situation in Virginia:

> The Presidential question seems to have absorbed all others. Go where you will, it is the first, and almost the only topic of conversation. We have appointed all our delegates, save in one district, and my predecessor, has been badly beaten. Out of twenty eight delegates appointed Hunter has carried seventeen, and from all the information I have, I think he will carry the district that will appoint tomorrow. Wise's friends take his defeat very badly. The fuss he kicked up over old Brown, gave him an ephemeral popularity, but it died out before, the time for the selection of delegates to Charleston, came around. The expense to which he ran the State, (near $300,000,) has opened the eyes of the people to his carelessness and indifference, in the expenditure of public money, and the reaction

in public sentiment against him, has been without parallel, in the history of any public man of the day.

I suppose now, he will attempt to repudiate the action of the Charleston Convention, should Douglas, be the nominee. Many of his leading and confidential friends here openly avow their purpose, not to sustain Douglas if he shall be nominated, and it is fair to infer, that they speak by the card. We shall see however in due time.[10]

Hunter led the Virginia delegation to Charleston, hoping to grab the presidential nomination by taking a middle ground between the Yancey and Douglas wings of the party. Spurred by Yancey's eloquence, the deep South insisted on positive protection of slavery in the territories through a formal slave code, and Hunter swung toward this position. Letcher watched the convention closely from Richmond. On April 29, the day before the deep South walkout, he candidly appraised his party in a letter to a friend. "I was not very hopeful", he wrote,

> in regard to the Charleston Convention, before it assembled. The proceedings so far, have induced me to fear, that its actions will not prove satisfactory to the Democratic party of the country. Such Marplots as Yancey have no business in our Conventions. They are not Democrats in feeling or principle. They do not desire the success of the Democratic party. They are looking to disunion, and the best means of effecting it. In talking yesterday with Mr. [Bennett M.] Dewitt, Editor of the Virginia Index, he told me he heard Yancey say in this City, last August, that he desired to see Caucuses and National Conventions broken up—that he was a disunionist per se. Such a man has no business in a National Convention, and if he received his deserts he would be put out of it.
>
> This Slave Code proposition has been introduced, for mischievous purposes, and if the Convention adopt it, the Democratic party, will be destroyed. It is directly opposed to the doctrine of Non Intervention, which our party have been advocating and affirming for the last five years, or more. With such leaders as we now have, it is wonderful that the Democratic party has not been destroyed. But is is useless to speculate about these things. The time for speculation has passed.[11]

When the Yanceyites stalked out of the convention and the Virginia delegation stayed, Hunter's chance for the nomination was gone. The Wise radicals hailed the walkout, but the majority of the Virginia Democracy opposed this Dixie extremism, and virtually no Virginia delegates attended the Richmond convention held early in June by deep South delegates. The Hunterites went to the reconvened national convention in Baltimore in mid–June determined to try for reconciliation, preferably by nominating Hunter, but equally determined to side with the deep South if reconciliation efforts failed. When such efforts did fail, the entire Virginia delegation, with the exception of a few Douglas supporters, joined the second southern walkout. This led to a second southern convention which nominated John C. Breckinridge of Kentucky just as the Richmond convention had done.[12]

While the Democratic Party was dying in Baltimore, Letcher was coping with a mass of administrative details in Richmond. The statewide elections held in May had to be verified. The democratic Constitution of 1851 called for more than 4,000 posts to be filled by the will of the electorate, and the governor had to issue an official commission to each successful candidate. Once again the chief executive became the chief clerk, entangled in reams of paper work.

A more important matter further distracted the governor at this time. A syndicate of French capitalists, which had been considering the purchase of the James River and Kanawha Canal for several years, began to negotiate seriously. The state owned most of the stock of this obsolescent and costly internal improvement, and Letcher leaped at the chance to sell this great white elephant to the Frenchmen. Virginians had long dreamed of piercing the great mountain barrier which blocked the Old Dominion from the riches of the American heartland so as to transform sleepy Norfolk into a rival of the great port city of New York. The French organization, Bellot des Minières Brothers and Company, had the capital needed to drive the canal through to the Ohio River system. Monsieur Ernest Bellot des Minières, who owned large tracts of land in western Virginia, served as the syndicate's chief negotiator. Progress was slow, however, and the Frenchmen did not make a definite offer until late in the year.[13]

After a week's vacation in July at White Sulphur Springs with Company F of the Richmond Volunteers, Letcher returned to the Governor's Mansion to find the presidential canvass in full swing.

Efforts to heal the Douglas–Breckinridge breach in the Democracy failed, and hostility between these two factions increased, thus giving the Republicans a golden opportunity on the national level. In Virginia the Constitutional Unionists—Whigs and Know-Nothings with almost no platform but conservatism and the Union —also exploited Democratic disunity. Letcher knew the Democrats were hopelessly divided for the presidential election, but he hoped for reunification later.

The Virginia Democrats were bewildered and despondent. Letcher refused to follow the Hunterites in joining the radical Breckinridge camp. Letcher, convinced that Douglas was the party's legitimate nominee, broke the last tenuous cords which held him on the fringe of the Hunter faction and joined the thin ranks of the Douglas Democrats in Virginia. On August 22, he publicly announced his stand in a letter published in the Richmond newspapers:

> I have purposely avoided committing myself to the support of either Breckinridge or Douglas, in the hope that a compromise would be agreed upon. . . . All hope of an adjustment having now failed, I have no hesitation in declaring that my support will be given to Douglas. . . . The division that has occurred in the Democratic party could have been, and I think ought to have been, avoided. There was no more necessity for a rupture in 1860, than there was in 1856. The division has, however, taken place . . . and it is useless now to enquire into the causes. . . . Such a discussion will not restore union and harmony, but will, of necessity, add to present embarrassments, and will only tend to make certain the election of a sectional candidate to the Presidency, whose success all parties must deplore. I sincerely hope, therefore, that the discussions which now seem unavoidable, between the friends of Breckinridge and Douglas, will be marked by prudence and moderation, and after this struggle has been ended, a spirit of conciliation and compromise will restore union and harmony in our party.[14]

A few days later in Norfolk, Douglas bluntly declared that as president he would feel free to use force against seceding states, but Letcher continued to support him. Universally recognized as a "tower of strength in the State", the governor freely gave his time and advice to the Douglasites. Many Breckinridge supporters, including Secretary of the Commonwealth Munford, had backed

Letcher for the governorship and were now enraged at what they considered his defection. His old friend "Sandy" Stuart encouraged Letcher, for he hoped to entice all of the Douglasites into the ranks of the Constitutional Union Party before election day.[15]

Letcher did not campaign actively in this crucial contest. As the state's chief executive, he felt that he represented all of the people and hence should not play the part of a partisan campaigner. He made no formal speeches and attended no political rallies, but he still managed to indicate his choice quite clearly. Late in October he refused to attend an important political rally in Staunton, but sent an open letter to the meeting which left the opposition wondering just how far the Governor could go and still claim to be avoiding partisan canvassing. "Judge Douglas is my choice of the candidates", he wrote.

> . . . I believe him to be a bold, manly, independent, patriotic States-
> man. He possesses talents of the highest order, and has had very
> large experience in public affairs. He has been faithful and true,
> in the Senate and before his constituents, in demanding the en-
> forcement of all constitutional obligations for the protection of
> the institutions of the South, and he has given our enemies more
> hard blows, and received more in turn, for his devotion to us, than
> any living Statesman of his day. . . . Only four years ago, in Cin-
> cinnati, the Cotton States revolutionists, his most relentless enemies
> of this day, voted for him again and again. . . . If he could be trusted
> and cordially sustained by the South then, I think he can be trusted,
> and ought to be sustained by the South now.[16]

Letcher's repeated championing of Douglas undoubtedly influenced some voters, especially in the west, and even a small shift was crucial in this bitter and very close election. John Bell of Tennessee, the Constitutional Unionist candidate, won a plurality, edging Breckinridge by only 358 votes. Douglas trailed far behind with slightly over 16,000 votes, and Lincoln received only 1,929 ballots, mostly in the northwest. Most of the electorate voted the regular party ticket. Certainly disunion sentiment was weak, for even Breckinridge's basic appeal was "southern rights", not secession.[17]

The presidential election was not the governor's only problem during the latter part of the year. On the Fourth of July he

authorized an artillery salute which cost the state the grand total
of $36.67. Even this routine recognition of the Union was bitterly
criticized by some secessionists. In September, negotiations with
the French capitalists for the sale of the James River and
Kanawha Canal were almost completed, and Letcher called a special session of the General Assembly for January 14 to consider
the Frenchmen's proposals.

Early in October, a visit by the Prince of Wales, later Edward
VII, enlivened Richmond's social season. The prince, traveling as
"Baron Renfro", declined Letcher's invitation to the Governor's
Mansion, naively hoping to stay a few days without being noticed.
Immediately he was plunged into a series of parties and receptions
by the citizens of Richmond, the Letchers included, who almost
overwhelmed the prince with hospitality, exhibiting on a grand
scale the curious American habit of idolizing British royalty. The
grand climax of the uproarious two–day visit came when the in-
spired organist of staid St. Paul's Church delivered a spirited
rendition of "God Save the Queen" while the prince and the
congregation were receiving communion.[18]

Such social interludes were rare for the hard–working governor.
In November and December, he ordered Adjutant General Richardson to apply ahead of time to the War Department for Virginia's 1861 quota of weapons. This special request was officially
based on the danger of "domestic insubordination", and Secretary of War John B. Floyd quickly dispatched the desired weapons
to his fellow Virginians. This incident clearly indicated the
atmosphere of foreboding which engulfed Virginia after Abraham
Lincoln's election. Like Brown's raid, Lincoln's victory was a big
boost for the secessionists. The fickle tides of public opinion began
to flow in their direction again. Most Virginians still preferred to
remain in the Union, but the radicals, led by the fiery Wise, demanded that Virginia close ranks with the seceding states of the
deep South. A less radical and much stronger demand for a
special session of the assembly to examine the current crisis swept
through the state. Like most moderates, Letcher thought time
would calm the public's unrest, but by mid–November he was

forced to advance the opening date of the next assembly from the fourteenth to the seventh of January.[19]

Letcher remained, in his own words, "calm and conservative", but his habitual optimism wavered temporarily in the face of rising anti—northern sentiment in the state. The Union seemed to be disintegrating, and it could only be saved if Lincoln would state his policy frankly and thoroughly. Letcher lamented that the assembly had ignored his call for a convention of all the states in his inaugural speech. He was convinced that a national convention could have resolved the sectional crisis early in 1860, but now he was barely able to resist demands for a state convention —an obvious secession vehicle—and the future looked even bleaker.

The conservatives and moderates lacked organization, public appeal, and a positive program. The vocal, well—organized radicals championed a simple, dramatic panacea, secession. Both sides fought hard, but in the emotionalism and fanaticism of the times, the radicals had a great advantage. Letcher appealed publicly and privately to northerners to show their good faith by repealing the obnoxious personal liberty laws. Any legislation which nullified the Fugitive Slave Act, the foundation stone of the Compromise of 1850 in southern eyes, made the secessionists' propaganda campaign more effective. If these laws were repealed, the radicals would lose some of their most potent ammunition.[20]

At the same time, the governor rejected many requests for an official day of prayer and fasting. Letcher was basically a skeptic, but his main reason for rejecting such requests was to avoid anything which would dramatize the rising tension. However, the pressure increased, and he finally proclaimed his first, but not last, day of prayer on January 4, just before the assembly convened.[21]

Exactly one year after his inaugural address, the governor was again scheduled to speak to the assembly and the people at a time of sectional crisis. Just as a year before, the secessionists were on the march, this time with many new recruits, and again few really knew what the independent—minded governor would say. The secession of South Carolina in December started a chain reaction in the deep South. Lincoln's tragic silence and Buchanan's continued inaction left a political vacuum that was quickly filled by belligerent southern secessionists and radical Republicans in the new Congress, where compromise was more and more unlikely, disunion more and more certain. Late in December, Letcher feared that the Union was doomed, but he still sought a reasonable compromise. By the time he spoke to the assembly on January 7, most Virginians, though faintly hopeful for the Union, favored joining the South if violence erupted, and local military preparations accelerated again all over the state.[22]

Letcher began his address with a general discussion of the dangers of the time, but, significantly, he avoided the lengthy attack on the North which had dominated his 1860 address. Instead, he praised the Union, and his only real sectional attack was leveled exclusively at abolitionist New England, which Letcher felt should be ejected from the Union so that the rest of the states could live together in harmony.

He repeated the two main recommendations he had fruitlessly made to the legislature a year earlier: (1) the assembly should invite all states to attend a national convention for reconciliation, and (2) the assembly should send commissioners throughout the North (except hopeless New England) to work for the repeal of the personal liberty laws. The governor unequivocally opposed the rising secessionist demand for a state convention, stating that the legislature could handle the situation this time just as it had done in 1833 and 1850.

Then Letcher predicted the fruits of disunion. Not two, but four political entities would replace the Old Union. The New York–New England area and the Pacific states would each form a separate nation, and the deep South would form a third entity. The rest of the old Union, the border states, Pennsylvania, New Jersey, and the northwestern states, would be the mighty fourth force that would entice Louisiana, Arkansas, Texas, and Mississippi away from the deep South. Finally this growing giant would wrest Pensacola from the dwindling cotton kingdom, and a rough equilibrium would be established.

Despite the objections of Adjutant General Richardson and Secretary of the Commonwealth Munford, both of whom had

read the speech in advance, Letcher strongly condemned South
Carolina for seceding independently. He proclaimed Virginia's
duty to mediate between the extremes of "passion and reckless-
ness". Lincoln's "house divided" speech and his policy of exclud-
ing slavery from the territories were wrong, but the deep South's
attempt to coerce the border slave states into secession by threatening to tax slaves shipped South for sale was equally unjustified.
As Letcher assessed the situation, a simple six–point plan would
quickly end the sectional crisis:

  (1) Abolish all personal liberty laws
  (2) Protect slavery in the District of Columbia
  (3) Allow slavery free entry into the territories
  (4) Do not interfere with the interstate transportation of slaves
  (5) Punish persons anywhere in the country who incite slave
      insurrections
  (6) Forbid the federal government to appoint anti–slavery men
      to office in the slave states.

Letcher hailed states' rights and the right of secession and
vowed that he would not allow federal troops to pass through
Virginia in order to coerce seceded states. After adding a few
words about funds for V.M.I., sale of the James River and
Kanawha Canal, further reorganization of the militia, enlarge-
ment of the port of Norfolk, and the state debt of over $33,000,-
000, Letcher concluded by pledging his allegiance to Virginia
whatever the future brought.[23]

This address, truly moderate for the times, was cooly received
by the assembly, which reflected the rising secession sentiment
in the state. However, Letcher did receive compliments on his
speech, particularly from the west, where moderation and Unionism were strong. Secessionists bitterly denounced their "tortoise
Governor". His opposition to a convention was decried, and his
vision of a great border confederacy, an idea he had discussed
publicly before his speech, was condemned in fiery language. One
eager secessionist almost gave up:

> The people *are enamored* of this *Union* . . . and I fear we will
> never be able to divorce them. . . . Every contemptible, dirty, sense-
> less demagogue has his own way of saving the country. . . . Letcher

would save us by a middle confederacy, and many small, insignificant satellites have gone to this corrupt, drunken luminary.[24]

The assembly carried out only one of the governor's major recommendations. On January 19, it invited all of the states to send representatives to a Peace Convention in Washington. This convention met from February 4 through February 28, and did not lack distinguished personnel, but the deep southern states, plus Arkansas, Michigan, Minnesota, Wisconsin, California, and Oregon, were not represented.

Nevertheless, after months of pessimism, Letcher's instinctive optimism revived. A visit to Washington early in February allowed him to talk confidentially with old congressional colleagues and delegates to the secret convention, and his optimism increased. Publicly he said little, but he discussed the situation freely in a letter to his friend Davidson. "I know that no effort will be spared", he wrote,

> to impair and weaken any influence I may have at a time like this, when madmen are seeking to overthrow the peace of the country, by overturning its constitution.
>
> I saw Dorman in Washington on Saturday evening. He was in fine spirits and told me he intended to see and confer with Douglas and [Senator John J.] Crittenden about public matters. They are safe men, and both are in great hopes that an adjustment will be effected upon satisfactory grounds. The signs all look well—much more favorable than I supposed when I went to the City. I believe we shall have a settlement upon perfectly fair terms, and in a short time.
>
> Tyler, Rives, Summers and Brockenbrough[25] told me the indications looked very favorable, and this opinion was concurred in by many of my old Congressional acquaintances, with whom I conferred, while there. I think I can venture to say, that all will yet end well.[26]

But by the end of February the Peace Convention had failed. It might have succeeded if it had been tried early in 1860, when Letcher first suggested it, or it might have failed, but certainly by early 1861 the time for reconciliation and compromise had passed. The catastrophe of civil war was all but inevitable.

The Virginia legislature ignored most of the other suggestions in the governor's address. On January 14, it authorized the election of delegates to a state convention, the political device which had facilitated secession in the deep South and had accelerated the revolutionary surge in 1776. Letcher dutifully, but unenthusiastically, issued the necessary proclamation on the following day.[27]

The radical drift continued as, late in January, the assembly appropriated another $1,000,000 for military defense. Of this total, $800,000 was to be used by an appointed colonel of Virginia ordnance to buy additional arms under the overall supervision of the governor. The remaining $200,000 was slated for coastal and river defenses. Letcher delayed two months before he finally nominated Charles Dimmock as ordnance colonel. The Senate quickly confirmed the appointment, but the governor's tardiness had already seriously handicapped the state's efforts to purchase weapons in the industrial North before the war began. It was not until the firing had begun at Fort Sumter that the governor appointed Andrew Talcott to supervise coastal and river defenses. Letcher moved slowly because he wanted to find the best qualified men and also because he desired to avoid any appearance of urgency which would further encourage radicalism. But his caution contributed to Virginia's general unpreparedness when radicalism finally led to war.[28]

Letcher's opposition to extremism did not prevent him from making modest efforts to bolster Virginia's military power, for even the moderates favored reasonable preparedness in such uncertain times. Once again he asked the federal government for his state's quota of weapons a year in advance. But by this time the southerners had retired from Buchanan's cabinet, and the sympathetic Floyd was no longer secretary of war. Washington had started hoarding its military power more carefully, and the arms were not sent.[29]

In this increasingly tense atmosphere, the secessionists put tremendous pressure on the governor. Lobbyists from the South badgered him constantly, and local radicals gave him no rest. Some advised seizing federal forts and arsenals at once; most demanded a more rapid military buildup. Letcher did discuss the strength of Fort Monroe on the Peninsula, Harper's Ferry arsenal,

Gosport navy yard at Norfolk, and other federal installations, but
he adamantly refused to authorize any direct action.[30]

Letcher made strenuous efforts to recruit United States Army
officers for the growing armed forces of Virginia. He made a few
successful contacts through intermediaries, and some army personnel volunteered without solicitation. The executive office was
deluged with tenders of service, but most of these tenders came
from Virginia civilians, not army regulars.

Letcher's courtship of Major George H. Thomas was typical
of his efforts to recruit army talent. Thomas was a tall, reserved
Virginian from Southampton County, with an admirable service
record. He had been seriously injured in a railroad accident in
January and, assuming that he was permanently disabled, had
applied for the position of V. M. I. superintendent. Thus he became a candidate for recruitment and was enthusiastically recommended by secessionist William Mahone, president of the Norfolk
& Petersburg Railroad. On March 9, a letter from Major William
Gilham of V.M.I., the intermediary, offered Thomas the post of
colonel of Virginia ordnance. Replying directly to Letcher, Thomas
said he did not desire to leave federal service as long as it was
honorable to stay. He added that as long as Virginia stayed in the
Union he would remain in federal service unless required to
perform dishonorable or inhumane duties. He repeated these sentiments to fellow Virginian, Captain Fitzhugh Lee, who was on his
way to join the Virginia forces. However, when Virginia finally
seceded, Thomas—the future "Rock of Chickamauga"—did not
budge, and the South lost a magnificent fighting general.[31]

Letcher also corresponded frequently with a potential intelligence agent in New York City during this period, but this venture
into the cloak–and–dagger world soon foundered on the drab
issue of salary–and–expenses. Routine matters occupied most of
the governor's time early in 1861. Visions of sinister banking conspiracies no longer worried Letcher, who had sizable deposits in
several banks, but he was still enough of an old Jacksonian to react
when several state banks failed to pay interest on state funds deposited in their vaults. He withdrew the state funds from the
offending banks briefly and then returned the funds to the chas-

tised banks—a subtreasury reflex, temporary and tepid. He scolded the guilty banks, but his tone was now that of an irritated accountant, not that of an outraged crusader. In the conservative governor of Virginia there remained none of the young Locofoco who had distrusted all banks and embodied the essence and vitality of Jacksonian Democracy.

The problem of housing the Richmond Public Guard, a volunteer organization dating back to the slave uprising of 1800, became acute when its old quarters in the Richmond Armory were filled with arms—making machinery ordered from Tredegar the previous August. Letcher passed this problem on to the assembly, avoiding additional friction with that sensitive, critical body. He frequently hesitated to exercise strong executive leadership even in periods of extreme emergency. This hesitancy was simply a facet of the South's generally negative political philosophy, which stressed individual, property and states' rights and legal and constitutional technicalities, and discouraged direct, positive action by the government.[32]

By the beginning of February, all routine chores were forgotten as the brief, fiery canvass for delegates to the state convention reached a climax. The election on February 4 was a real test of strength in which the radicals tried to gain control of the convention and carry Virginia out of the Union at once. The governor did not campaign, but he encouraged and advised the moderates, making no secret of his own sentiments. He feared that a flood of fake dispatches from the South on the eve of the election would sweep the excited electorate into a secession stampede, but his uneasiness vanished as the returns began to come in. The moderates scored a clear victory, and Letcher made no effort to hide his delight.[33]

The convention opened in Richmond on February 13 with a plurality of moderates. The staunch, largely—western Unionists and the radicals both had sizable blocks, and both of these factions were capable of exploiting future events to attract wavering moderates. For the first time in months, Letcher was honestly optimistic again. The moderates controlled the convention, and his brainchild, the Peace Convention in Washington, seemed to be making progress. Infuriated by their failure to sweep Virginia into the southern Confederacy that was then forming at Montgomery, the radicals lashed out at "the submissionist, the betrayer of the liberties of the people" in the Governor's Mansion. These passionate attacks soon reached the personal level, and an old piece of gossip was revived with a vengeance. From Lexington, Davidson sounded the warning:

> I have heard some remarks about the free use of whiskey in your office in your Mansion, by your visitors and heard it mentioned by your best friend in this County that he had heard, that you [illegible] at your office, at the Capitol. I have heard these things spoken of before: and you and I have spoken of them together.[34]

Davidson suggested that Letcher remove all whiskey bottles from his reception room and give drinks only to special friends in a private room. He also recommended not serving whiskey to convention delegates. If a delegate took a drink with the governor and later appeared to be drunk at the convention, the gossip would increase.

Letcher was surprised and angry. He had certainly never been a teetotaler, and he did serve whiskey to close friends in his office, but he never mixed bourbon and business. He resented this smear campaign, but he had played the rough—and—tumble game of politics too long to lose his poise. In any event, he became much more cautious with his habitual "hospitality".[35]

He again in February turned to Davidson for help. The Peace Convention had started to bog down, and radicalism was once more on the rise. Letcher's optimism rapidly began to pale. He needed more ammunition to fight the secessionists, and Washington was the place to get it. Without an accurate knowledge of the situation there, he could not fight effectively in Virginia. The key was Abraham Lincoln, still silent, still keeping his own counsel. How could Letcher defend the old Union if the new President-elect would not take a stand? He needed a sign, any indication that the tall, gaunt man from Illinois was willing to compromise. He asked Davidson to sound out the new leadership in Washington. If possible, he was to talk to Mr. Lincoln and draw some sort of policy statement from him. Though something of an eccentric,

Davidson was a skillful lawyer with a nimble mind, and a moderate, thoroughly loyal to Letcher.

He went to Washington late in the month, spoke with many important politicians, and had a long conversation with General Winfield Scott, the elderly Virginian who headed the U. S. Army. On the night of February 25, Davidson went to Willard's Hotel, and, in the midst of a large crowd, he talked briefly with the President–elect. The discussion was informal and half playful, and the noise and interruptions of the crowd caused some confusion. Nevertheless, Davidson's report to Letcher was optimistic. Mr. Lincoln was willing to talk with southerners, and seemed inclined toward a cautious policy that would allow the secessionist impulse to wear itself out peacefully. In Davidson's judgment, Lincoln was decidedly not the ogre imagined by southern newspaper editors.[36]

Encouraged by Davidson's report, Letcher fought on against secessionism. President Lincoln's inaugural address on March 4 gave the radicals a boost. Almost all Virginians—Davidson was an exception—criticized this ambivalent speech, which hinted at coercion in some passages and leaned toward compromise and friendship in others. The radicals demanded immediate secession, but the more moderate, conservative majority refused to be stampeded. Letcher now favored a conference of border states, and, if the demand for secession grew irresistible, a border confederacy. The governor kept Davidson informed of the latest events in the second week of March. "Lincoln's inaugural created quite a sensation here", he wrote,

> The disunionists were wild with joy, and declared, if the Convention did not pass an Ordinance of secession at once the State would be disgraced. They are again sobering down, being pretty well satisfied I think, that the Conservatives intend to think calmly over the whole matter before they announce their conclusion. The tendency now is to a Conference with the other border slaveholding states, accompanying that request with a platform on which Virginia can safely stand. Such a result is by no means agreeable to the ultras [radicals], who declare that a Central Confederacy underlies, this proposition. *It may be so,* and if it prove so, what a slaughtering of politicians we shall have in Virginia!! . . . Let the border states make their own arrangements to suit themselves, and the Cotton States

are bound to come into them and reunite their destiny with them. They know this, and hence the extraordinary effort to coerce the Border States into their plans. They have failed and will continue to fail, and we will in the end have things as we wish. Patience and prudence will work out the result.[37]

Letcher remained "firm and in good spirits" as the radicals continued to make slow but irresistible progress in the convention and the state. By mid–March, rumors that Lincoln planned to abandon Fort Sumter stopped them temporarily. Letcher disdainfully described to Davidson their frantic efforts to flood the convention with secession petitions from the grass roots. "Each day accumulates the evidence", he wrote,

in proof of the conspiracy . . . to break up the Government. I have recently heard that members of Congress and Senators representing Border Slave States, urged and pressed upon the Cotton States, the adoption of the policy which has been carried out by them—assuring them that if they would go out Virginia would follow their lead, and she would draw after her, all the other border states. How sadly have they been mistaken in their calculations. At the polls she has rebuked this policy, and now as the last effort of expiring treason, this system of instructions is resorted to. But it will fail of its purpose. They will be defeated again as they should be. . . . I cannot believe that an all wise and just God, will permit these conspirators, to succeed in overturning the best government, that the wit of man has ever devised. They are doomed to certain and overwhelming defeat. Now mark that prediction.[38]

Despite Letcher's optimistic prediction, the end of the month saw the radical tide sweeping the state. The realization that President Lincoln would not give up Fort Sumter severely weakened the conservative position. Aided by the Richmond press and a noisily partisan gallery, the secessionists gradually gained the upper hand at the convention. Emotionalism and radicalism grew together in an almost unreal atmosphere as the people of Virginia stumbled toward secession and the horror of armed rebellion. Letcher refused to yield, but he could not stem the tide. The longer he resisted, the greater hostility he engendered.

Distrust of the governor was evidenced late in March when it was learned that Bellona Arsenal, a federal installation at Midlothian, just west of Richmond, was preparing to ship some arms to strategic Fort Monroe at the mouth of the James River. Rumors spread that Letcher planned to use the Public Guard to convoy the shipment. The assembly on April 1 ordered the governor either to stop the shipment or to seize the arms when they were moved and pay for them out of the $800,000 that had been appropriated late in January. Actually, this was a routine shipment authorized long before Lincoln took office, but the federal government cancelled it in order to avoid an incident. Letcher had to deny repeatedly the false rumors that he was going to protect the shipment. Stirred by passionate radical propaganda, the people no longer trusted moderation, regardless of where it was found.[39]

On April 1, another moderate convention delegate, Letcher's friend James B. Dorman, recommended submitting the question of secession to a plebiscite, and on April 4 the convention rejected what amounted to a secession motion by a margin of 88 to 45. However, this was to be the last effective show of strength by the conservatives.

On April 12, Confederate batteries opened fire on Fort Sumter, and the next day Virginia reacted. Richmond was immersed in a sea of emotion, and that night huge crowds massed. Rockets exploded, tar barrels blazed, and rebel flags waved as throngs of excited, happy people surged through the streets. O. Jennings Wise, Attorney General Tucker, and other secessionists harangued the multitude. Soon the restless crowds converged on Capitol Square. Several cannons were taken from the arsenal on Cary Street, dragged up to the lawn of the Capitol, and fired in salvos, saluting the end of the months of tension and uncertainty. Thoroughly elated, the crowd trooped to the Governor's Mansion, screaming for a speech.

The governor knew that the cannons that blazed in Charleston harbor and on the capitol lawn signaled the disruption of the American Union. It was a saddened Letcher who stepped out on the front porch to address the enthusiastic throng. Thanking the people for their visit, he pointedly—and legalistically—reminded them that Virginia was still one of the United States. He added that he did not "recognize" the fluttering banners and that there was no need for artillery. Advising the crowd to disperse, he con-

cluded his brief speech by promising not to be found wanting when
Virginia was assailed. This markedly unenthusiastic address was
greeted by a chorus of hissing. The radicals had long had grave
doubts about the reliability of the conservative governor who had
resisted secession so vigorously, and now those doubts were con-
firmed by his lukewarm response to the stirring events at Charleston. After raising a Confederate flag over the Capitol, the crowd
surged off in search of more congenial receptions. As soon as the
area was clear, Letcher had the secession flag quietly removed.[40]

On April 15, President Lincoln's call for 75,000 state militiamen to crush "powerful combinations" ended all doubt about
Virginia's course of action. Virtually all opposition to secession
evaporated. Virginians would not tolerate federal "coercion" under any circumstances. Reluctantly, but without further hesitation, Governor Letcher stopped his fruitless fight for moderation
and prepared to lead his state out of the Union. He bluntly rejected Secretary of War Simon Cameron's request that Virginia
furnish three regiments as her quota of the troops the President
had ordered into action. "I have only to say", he wrote,

> that the militia of Virginia will not be furnished to the powers at
> Washington for any such use or purpose as they have in view. Your
> object is to subjugate the Southern States, and the requisition made
> upon me for such an object—an object in my judgment not within
> the purview of the Constitution or the Act of 1795—will not be com-
> plied with. You have chosen to inaugurate civil war, and having
> done so we will meet you, in a spirit as determined, as the Adminis-
> tration has exhibited towards the South.[41]

Still the governor refused to employ radical tactics. Everything
had to be done in an orderly and legal manner. He had previously frowned upon Wise's efforts to organize local units of "minutemen" outside state jurisdiction, and, on April 16, he resisted
pressure by Wise, John D. Imboden, Oliver Funsten, John and
Alfred Barbour, Richard and Turner Ashby, John A. Harman,
and others to seize federal installations before the convention
formally seceded. The governor adamantly refused to act without
the authorization of the convention. Enraged, Wise and his cohorts
met secretly at the Exchange Hotel and issued march orders without legal authorization. Only after he had conferred with a delega-

tion from the convention the next morning, secession day, did Letcher order the seizure of federal posts.[42]

With this dramatic sequence of events, the first phase of Letcher's administration ended. Despite the efforts of moderates throughout the nation, the sectional clash which had been intensifying for years finally tore the Union asunder. This early period had really required two chief executives, one to carry out the routine, traditional functions of the office, the other to lead the people in unprecedented times. Letcher had been preparing for the first job all of his adult life, and he performed capably if not flawlessly. However, like most other contemporary political leaders, he was totally unprepared for the second task, and, like the others, he failed to find peaceful solutions to truly important problems that demanded his immediate attention. He tried desperately to save the Union, which he loved almost as much as his state and the South, but he was severely hampered by the narrow restrictions of his political code and vision.

The times were not ripe for moderation, and the conservatives' position was probably hopeless. For their efforts they received a war they never wanted. Suddenly they were placed on new scales and judged by new standards. For southerners the past was gone, lost forever. Now each man was to be measured by his contributions to victory in the rebellion. For the next 32 months, John Letcher was to be measured by his contributions as the war governor of Virginia.

CHAPTER 7

Introduction To War

The Civil War began for Virginia on April 17, 1861, the day on which the convention, in secret session, voted to secede. For the next six weeks no major battle was fought in Virginia; neither side was prepared for war. Letcher, swept along by the rush of events, worked frantically. Virginia had to be put on a war footing, and liaison with the other southern states had to be established. The complicated task of integrating the Old Dominion into the nascent Confederacy also challenged the governor's ingenuity and patience. Effective, imaginative leadership was essential during this uncertain time.

Prior to secession, Letcher had refused to begin even a limited mobilization of the state's manpower, for he had not wished to encourage radicalism. Even after the secession vote, he hesitated for several hours until the convention officially authorized action. He then issued a proclamation ordering all of the hastily–organized volunteer units in the state to report their manpower and equipment at once. He and Adjutant General Richardson attempted to estimate volunteer strength on the basis of existing records which were incomplete. Probably no more than 18,500 volunteers were available, and one–third or more of these were unarmed.

Letcher quickly accepted South Carolina's offer to send 2,000 troops to Norfolk. The same offer had been made a few days earlier by secessionist Roger Pryor, but Letcher had bluntly rejected it. Now that Virginia had officially seceded he eagerly accepted, and two fully armed regiments of South Carolinians became the first Confederate troops to reach Virginia. Letcher appealed to the North Carolina and Confederate governments for more military aid at Norfolk. These appeals, too, were quickly answered. He sought additional military supplies while tenaciously retaining what Virginia already possessed, and he defended this policy with unassailable logic: since Virginia was to be a major battleground, she needed a major portion of available battle implements. Despite the state's general unreadiness, caused in part by the governor's moderate prewar policies, Virginia was better prepared for war than most of the Confederate states.[1]

On that same fateful day, April 17, Letcher also ordered state troops to seize the Harper's Ferry arsenal and the Gosport navy yard. Once again, however, he acted only after consulting the convention. He now approved the earlier proposals that Norfolk river pilots refuse to guide federal ships to the safety of open water, and he also sanctioned the destruction of the Willoughby Point lighthouse and other essential channel markers. He condoned the harassment and isolation of Fort Monroe and efforts to stop federal officers from surveying the rivers. His orders seemed to be carried out with lightning speed because Wise and other secessionists had begun these operations on April 16. The radicals hailed Letcher's conversion to direct action, but at the same time they cursed him for his legalistic refusal to act sooner. The bitterness of the pre–secession radical–moderate struggle had by no means vanished, and many radicals still distrusted Letcher.[2]

At Harper's Ferry and Gosport, outnumbered federal forces hurriedly put the torch to their installations and withdrew before the onslaught of eager Virginia volunteers. Demolition efforts were only partially successful at both places. At Gosport, many buildings were destroyed, but vital machinery was hardly scratched; numerous cannons and more than 300,000 pounds of gunpowder were saved, and many scuttled ships, such as the *Merrimac,* were salvaged.

Harper's Ferry arsenal was fired more systematically, but as soon as the federal troops departed, master armorer Armistead Ball led a group of civilians into the inferno and rescued much valuable machinery. Though the heaviest machines could not be carried out, few of them were seriously damaged by the fire. Priceless rifle—making machinery and large stocks of infantry weapons were also rescued. The Virginia war machine desperately needed all of this booty.[3]

Letcher ended secession day as he had started it, following orders from the convention. He wrote Jefferson Davis officially informing him of the convention's desire to unite with the Confederacy. This letter brought Confederate Vice President Alexander H. Stephens to Richmond on April 22, and the convention adopted the Confederate Constitution on April 24, subject to ratification by the people on May 23.

Feverish action continued. On April 18, the aroused citizens of Richmond, on their own initiative, seized the customs house, the post office, and several other federal installations. Letcher quickly dispatched the Public Guard to secure these buildings, and he ordered a strict accounting of all financial plunder.[4]

In the confusion of this period, the first stirrings of disaffection began. On April 19, from 12 to 20 western members of the convention met secretly at Richmond's Powhatan Hotel and initiated the movement which eventually separated the northwest from the rest of the state. Led by John S. Carlile and Sherrard Clemens, the latter still hobbling from the wound he had received while campaigning for his friend Letcher in 1858, this little band formed the nucleus of a movement which organized mass Union meetings and conventions in the northwest. These activities eventually led to the formation of the Unionist Pierpoint government and the new state of West Virginia. At a later date, Letcher would be very bitter about western disaffection; at this time, however, he did not interfere with the meeting or the return to the west of its participants on April 21. Either he was unaware of the meeting or his strict sense of legality prevented him from acting when no law had actually been broken.[5]

However, the governor had not forgotten western Virginia completely. Following the advice of a southern sympathizer in

Baltimore, Letcher, on April 19, warned J. W. Garrett, president of the Baltimore & Ohio Railroad, that the sections of his railway within Virginia would be seized by state troops if federal forces were allowed to use the line to reinforce Washington, Baltimore, or other eastern areas. Garrett would soon learn that Letcher was not bluffing.[6]

By April 20 Letcher had ordered the seizure and identification of all vessels in Virginia waters, pending a decision on treatment of northern and foreign steamships. Soon he ruled that only vessels and cargoes absolutely necessary for defense were to be held. All other ships were to be released, and the state was to pay for any damages incurred and for the time the crews were detained. Once again the governor reasoned legalistically, but the practical result of his decision was to deprive the South of several fine Yankee ships.[7]

Before the day was over, Letcher ordered the V.M.I. cadet corps to report for duty in Richmond. The cadets were mere boys, but they had received formal military training and were able to help drill the raw volunteers pouring into the capital. The governor also reminded the convention that the state government needed additional funds at once, and by the end of the month he was authorized to issue $2,000,000 in treasury notes payable to the bearer and redeemable within one year.[8]

The excitement and confusion which enveloped Virginia after secession did not distort Letcher's strategic judgment. He was convinced that the war would be long and bloody. He had little faith in King Cotton, and opposed the Confederate policy of withholding cotton from foreign markets. He doubted that this would lure Britain or France into an alliance with the South. He favored instead, sending every available bale of cotton to Europe in exchange for essential supplies. Thoroughly bourgeois, Letcher was not enchanted by romantic visions of invincible southern chivalry. Rather, he clearly saw the South's industrial and financial weaknesses caused by its traditional colonial economy. He was equally conscious of the power and resources of the North which hung over Virginia's future like the sword of Damocles.[9]

The hectic pace continued, and *"Pawnee* Sunday", April 21,

was no day of rest for Richmond. Rumors that the federal warship *Pawnee* was coming up the river to bombard the capital
rallied all the troop units in the area to something vaguely re-
sembling combat readiness. Letcher alerted all armed regiments
of volunteers between Richmond and the Blue Ridge and in the
central and southern Valley. The *Pawnee* never appeared, however, and the people returned to the near chaos that had prevailed since April 17.[10]

On the same day Letcher, again following convention instructions, appointed an advisory council to assist him during the
emergency. Early in the war Letcher was one of a small minority
of southern politicians who were fully aware of their military
deficiencies, and he quickly appointed three men to the council.
Desiring seasoned soldiers, he selected his old friend, Colonel
Francis H. Smith of V.M.I., and Captain Matthew Fontaine
Maury, world famous pathfinder of the seas who had resigned
from the U. S. Navy to follow his state. Habitually subservient
to the technicalities of the law, Letcher chose John J. Allen, chief
justice of the Virginia Court of Appeals, as president of the council. The governor had to consult the advisory council, but he did
not have to follow its recommendations. Though the independent-
minded Lexingtonian usually followed the council's advice, he
occasionally ignored its recommendations.[11]

Still concerned about future federal attacks, Letcher concluded
"*Pawnee* Sunday" by ordering all guns at Bellona Arsenal moved
to the Richmond Armory. He also asked the Confederates to turn
over to Virginia all heavy guns they had on order with Virginia
manufacturers, but rebel authorities refused. The next day he
confiscated 500 revolvers intended for Confederate forces, but in
a few days changed his mind and returned the revolvers to Confederate agent R. H. Gayle.[12]

The desperate quest for arms continued with some state agents
still shopping in Washington. Even though many Virginia troops
carried only bowie knives and old muskets without ammunition,
Letcher exported some weapons on April 22. At the behest of
Jefferson Davis and his own council, 3,000 muskets were sent to
pro–southern forces in wavering Maryland. One–third of these

weapons were taken from the Harper's Ferry cache, the rest coming from the arsenal at V.M.I. The Harper's Ferry lot reached General George Hume Steuart in Baltimore on April 24, and the rest came by wagon from Lexington a few days later. Steuart, Garrett of the B. & O., and other southern sympathizers urged Letcher to send Virginia troops to seize the supply and transportation center of Baltimore, but the governor refused to violate Maryland's borders. Some of the Virginia weapons were issued to pro–southern forces, but this limited aid was not sufficient to swing Maryland to the South. Letcher then attempted to gain the prize by diplomacy. On April 29 he sent Judge William W. Crump, one of his chief envoys, to confer with Governor Thomas H. Hicks at Annapolis. Federal troops were already in Maryland, and although Hicks was not hostile, he "shuddered at the idea of collision with the federal power" and refused to join with Virginia. Maryland wavered but remained in the Union.[13]

Failure in Maryland was more than compensated for by the governor's successful efforts to recruit more federal military talent. The convention's new guarantee of no loss of rank for federal recruits was a significant boost, and by April 22 Letcher had scored a crucial victory. On April 18, he had sent David Funsten of Alexandria to interview Lieutenant General Winfield Scott and Colonel Robert E. Lee. Funsten failed to get through to Alexandria, and on April 19 the governor dispatched Judge John Robertson on the same mission.

Letcher had met Scott only once, briefly in a crowd, but in October, 1860, the old general had sent him a long discourse on the state of the nation, and Letcher had interpreted the discourse to be pro–southern. At the same time, Scott had allowed a federal colonel to drill Virginia cavalry. Letcher had assumed the general would follow his state, and when Scott rebuffed Judge Robertson, the governor was stunned.

Letcher and Robertson kept in close contact by telegrams, and on April 21, he ordered his envoy to invite Lee to Richmond. The day before, Lee had resigned from the U. S. Army, planning to retire to civilian life, but Robertson's invitation changed his plans. On April 22, the judge and the newly–retired colonel met in Alexandria and boarded a train for Richmond. Upon arriving, Lee went directly to the Capitol, where Letcher offered him command of the state's land and sea forces with the rank of major general. Lee accepted. At once the governor sent Lee's nomination to the convention, where it was quickly approved. The next day, General Lee began the work which eventually led to fame and glory—and Appomattox.[14]

By April 23, the initial confusion was beginning to abate, and at the first hint of calm, Letcher's legal and constitutional scruples were activated. He spent hours debating whether to impose the tariff of 1857 or the tariff of 1861 on a shipment of foreign tobacco being unloaded at Richmond. He would not, or could not, decide, and finally passed this epic problem on to the all–powerful convention.[15]

On the same day the governor ordered all sheriffs, commissioners of revenue, and telegraph operators to stay at their posts and not volunteer for military service. The convention had already recognized the principle of exempting essential home front personnel from the army; Letcher was simply enforcing the policy. On April 24, he proclaimed that all men making equipment for state forces and all men on special duty for the state were automatically exempt from the army, and in May workers on the James River and Kanawha Canal were included in this category. Frequently he had to act to stop skilled workers from joining up, but his policy was often erratic, and he did not always insist upon removing essential workers from army ranks. Requests for exemptions poured in from all over the state, and the governor wrestled with this complex problem for the rest of his wartime administration.[16]

Letcher's proclamation on April 24 also instructed all volunteers to remain at home until they received specific orders. The main reason for this measure was the severe shortage of arms, ammunition, and other equipment—a problem which would continue to challenge the best efforts of Letcher and the whole Confederacy. Letcher repeatedly told eager volunteer units, both in and out of the state, that they could not be used unless they were completely armed and equipped.[17]

During this same period the governor played host to two federal officers who had been captured attempting to destroy the dry dock at the Gosport navy yard before Virginia troops could occupy it. Captain Horatio G. Wright, of the army engineers, and Captain John Rodgers, of the navy, were received by the Letchers on April 22 and for three days lived on parole at the Governor's Mansion, treated more as guests than as enemies. The Letcher children were delighted with their Yankee visitors, who were always at home and ready for a new game. Governor and Mrs. Letcher were genuinely fond of their parolee guests and unable to accept the fact that they were enemy warriors. The two federals were given their official release on the evening of April 24, and early the next morning Letcher accompanied them to the railroad station.

Many residents of Richmond resented the presence of the enemy in the Governor's Mansion. There was some talk of mobbing the Yankees when they reached the station, but the governor's presence there discouraged such plans. Letcher saw his guests off on the first train to Washington, sending along two of his military aides to assure their safety. Wright wrote from Washington the next day thanking Letcher for his hospitality and expressing a desire to renew their friendship after the war. Letcher would not always treat Yankee prisoners so generously, but the Union captain did not forget the Letchers. Four years later, Major General Horatio G. Wright, Commander, Sixth Corps, Army of the Potomac, was able to repay their kindness.[18]

Such personal incidents were minor ripples in the flood of events. By April 24, the convention had decided officially to take Virginia into the Confederacy. On the same day, Letcher proclaimed a statewide election for May 23 to ratify or reject the convention's April 17 secession ordinance. Actually Virginia had already made her decision; there was no turning back. She had charted a catastrophic course on April 17, and the outcome of the plebiscite on May 23 was a foregone conclusion.[19]

The last days of April passed swiftly. The governor's mail was heavy with requests for commissions in the Virginia forces. A battle—scarred veteran of prewar politics, Letcher tried to make

no distinction between old Democrats and Whigs and more recent
conservatives and radicals in his appointments. He judged each
man solely on his qualifications, rating patriotism and spirit as
on a par with formal military experience. Naturally, he was frequently accused of favoring his old Democratic and moderate
cronies.

By May, discontent had bubbled to the surface. Most competent
observers did not blame Letcher for a few unwise appointments,
realizing that he was swamped with applications for the hundreds
of posts to be filled. But many radicals still distrusted this governor
who had opposed secession until the very last moment, and the
chaotically hurried procedure for making military appointments
was a fertile field for criticism. The convention had briefly adjourned when delegate James P. Holcombe described the tense
situation to another delegate:

> The governor and his council are not very harmonious—the com-
> mander in chief has not been consulted about appointments &
> does not like some—incompetent men have certainly been assigned
> to important points in this region—Ought not the Convention con-
> sidering the threatening aspect of public affairs to be reassembled
> at an earlier day . . . ? Could we accomplish anything by personal
> interview with Letcher? There is profound, increasing and dan-
> gerous distrust of him here—I have not believed it warranted.[20]

Although the Confederate and North Carolina governments
rushed more than 10,000 muskets and other equipment to Virginia, supply remained far short of demand. The inevitable confusion of rapid mobilization left some forces idle, weaponless, and
disgruntled, and Letcher still refused the services of out–of–state
troops unless they were fully armed and equipped. He wanted
General Lee to command all troops in Virginia regardless of who
they were or where they came from. However, faced with the
threat of sudden Yankee invasion, he was less insistent on this
arrangement than were many other southern governors. The convention had previously agreed in principle to overall Confederate
command of troops, and Letcher was soon advising Governor
Isham G. Harris of Tennessee to follow this policy in regard to
Tennessee troops coming into Virginia.[21]

By May the military situation in Virginia was chaotic. No

enemy army threatened, but organizational and administrative problems were creating hopeless confusion. Virginia's military system was baffling enough, with its mixture of unprepared militia, new and understrength volunteer forces, and the nascent, paper-tiger provisional army; but the greatest difficulty was the lack of co-operation between the Virginia forces and the Confederate units that were streaming into the state. Though the alliance of April 25 between Virginia and the Confederacy specified Confederate control of all state forces, it was understood that formal transfer of authority could occur only after the plebiscite of May 23 had officially endorsed secession.

Thus a period of confusion was inevitable. Even General Lee could not control the forces unleashed when the legalistic and individualistic excesses of southern culture nurtured the ambitions, jealousies, and emotions of the commanders of the many miniature armies encamped in the Old Dominion. Thousands of Confederate soldiers were massed in the state, but unity of command did not exist.

Confederate Secretary of War Leroy P. Walker had begun to apply pressure on the Virginia government late in April, but still Letcher stalled. He was reluctant to relinquish power to a new Confederacy with its capital in Montgomery, far away in the deep South. Always a devout believer in states' rights, Letcher faced a dilemma. He wanted massive aid from the Confederate central government, but he instinctively opposed yielding any authority to the Confederacy. Friction rapidly developed between Letcher and high–ranking Confederate officials.[22]

This friction increased dissatisfaction with the Letcher–Lee regime. Some out–of–state troops threatened to go home, and more and more people longed for Jefferson Davis' presence in Richmond. The governor's continued refusal to mobilize volunteers before equipment was available was interpreted by some, particularly old radicals, as a lack of aggressiveness and determination.

By May 7, several out–of–state troop commanders refused to accept the governor's orders, proclaiming they would obey only Confederate authorities. On this same day, Letcher, backed by his council, instructed General Lee to take command of all troops in Virginia, whatever their origin, until the president of the Confederacy ordered otherwise. The next day, in answer to a query of May 6 by Walker, Letcher acknowledged that the alliance of April 25 put the Confederates in charge of all troops; but he added that he (and Lee) would continue to command until the Confederacy actually assumed power. On May 10, Walker yielded and temporarily placed Lee in complete command of military forces in the state.[23]

Meanwhile, the governor continued to recruit military talent, systematizing the process by appointing a joint army–navy committee to list potential recruits who were still in federal service. However, Letcher refused to release the U. S. paymaster captured at Gosport despite the council's warning that his detention might lead to federal retaliation which would cripple his recruiting program in the North. He did, however, allow a Yankee worker caught at Gosport to go home after receiving a personal appeal from the young man's father in New York.[24]

Letcher tried not to overlook any possibilities in the grand rush for military talent. Major General W. S. Harney, a native of Louisiana still in federal service, was approached aggressively. Before dawn on the morning of April 26, the general, while traveling from St. Louis toward Washington and a new assignment, was forcibly removed from a Baltimore & Ohio train at Harper's Ferry and placed under arrest by Virginia troops. This action was taken under orders from the governor, who had not been bluffing about stopping all federal troop movements on the B. & O. Railroad. Harney was sent on parole to Richmond, where he had a long conversation with Letcher and his council. He expressed sympathy for the South, but nothing more. Letcher realized the danger of federal retaliation if an important officer like Harney were detained too long, and the general was allowed to leave for Washington on April 29.[25]

While searching for military talent, Letcher did not overlook his former neighbor, Major Thomas Jonathan Jackson, a professor at V.M.I. He nominated the stern Calvinist for the rank of colonel, but opposition formed quickly. Some Lexingtonians and former V.M.I. cadets felt this rather boring professor, who insisted on conducting an unlawful Sunday school for Negro children, was far too eccentric for an important military command. Despite continuing objections to "Tom Fool", Letcher pushed his candidacy. The convention approved the nomination, and Letcher ordered Lee to put Jackson in command at Harper's Ferry. Thus the governor placed one of the South's greatest soldiers on the firing line, beginning the glorious, tragic journey to Chancellorsville.[26]

Other important matters occupied Letcher's attention during this hectic period. On April 29, the convention expanded the advisory council to five members, adding Lieutenant Governor Montague, *ex officio,* and T. S. Haymond, a former Whig congressman from the turbulent northwest. On May 3, Letcher issued a proclamation calling upon the people to prepare for war and authorizing General Lee to muster as many additional volunteers as necessary.

Letcher had unlimited confidence in Lee, allowing him to run the state's military machine without interference. Lee used his unhindered power fully to accelerate mobilization. Sometimes the governor passed along suggestions and information to Lee, and in the middle of May he requested guard details at storehouses and depots in Richmond to combat frequent sabotage. Periodically Lee sent him résumés of the state's rapidly growing military power. [27]

Letcher issued one of his few military orders on May 5. Alabama troops were speeding to Virginia by rail, and Lee was instructed to send them to Norfolk as soon as possible. Letcher himself hurried to vulnerable Norfolk and inspected the valuable navy yard and its defenses. He attempted to straighten out the tangled administrative affairs at the shipyard, became bogged down in details and technicalities, and failed to establish an effective over–all policy.

Equally worried about the state's other conquest at Harper's Ferry, he ordered Colonel Jackson to remove all usable equipment from that exposed position at once. The governor refused to allow Virginia troops to occupy strategic heights on the Maryland side of the Potomac. Such a move would be militarily sound, but clearly illegal. More important, it would be a political blunder certain to alienate still wavering Maryland.[28]

The governor's work was not all strictly official. Before Virginia seceded, Letcher had received many letters from the North appealing to the Old Dominion to stand fast in the Union. After secession the northern letters became belligerent and threatening. On April 21, a stern warning came from Wisconsin:

> Permit me to say to you that there is a storm gathering in the Northern Horizon which will sweep every Southern Pro Slavery madman from the face of the Earth. Injure a hair of the head of John Minor Botts [who still opposed secession] and we will start such a revolution in your state, which will sweep the bloated pro slavery aristocrats of your State to annihilation.
>
> I see clearly the hand of Providence in all your acts. You are arousing now the last Conservative Element at the North and let John Minor Botts be injured and we will hang Wise upon the same gallows where was executed John Brown and we will not be surprised that your body may yet dangle from the same gibbet and have inscribed upon your tomb stone "Here lies a traitor to his Country who deservedly met his end by disgracing the gallows that gave immortality to the name of John Brown."[29]

The threatening letters from the North continued to arrive, and a week later a New Yorker predicted disaster for the South. "The game of brag is now played out", he wrote,

> we have our foot fairly in, and the greatest misfortune that can now befal [sic] us, is to *have you cave in*. Now my dear Traitor we want a few heads and will in due course have them—my great desire was to avoid the present crisis & the distress and unavoidable expense thereof. I give the administration 2 years to do up the work, Baltimore comes down too easy—Richmond, Charleston & Montgomery ashes will sell for $1 per bushel. We will call for it on our way to Mobile.
>
> New Orleans will be taken care of by the West. . . . We are now put to the trouble and cost of a friendly visit and some of our boys will find with you hospitable graves, but Virginia will have our company until it suits our convenience to quit, by her making atonement [sic] or our going directly over the ashes of Richmond to visit our relatives of South Carolina, where we shall pause long enough to wipe her name from the map of the United States.
>
> You have been grossly deceived by political demagogues. . . . Your

insanity and mean duplicity & folly will have brought the devastation on yourself for which every *Traitor* among you, deserve the halter, (not from us) but from the honest yeomanry of your country, whom your infernal *party politics* have misled. The Almighty God in whose hands we are, is directing the course of events & will work out his end.

Running out of dire prophecies, the passionate New Yorker concluded his letter with a clipping from a recent edition of a New York newspaper. Again the future seemed ominous indeed:

> We have in the Northern cities at least three hundred thousand of the most reckless desperate men on the face of the earth. The Goths and Vandals who sacked Rome . . . were angels compared to these fellows who are known by the generic name of "roughs." Of course they are all in for the war, and the spoils thereof—more particularly the spoils. They have no stake in this world, no hope for the future. They will fight like demons for present enjoyment, and where one is killed twenty more will spring up in his place. . . . The character of the coming campaign will be vindictive, fierce, bloody and merciless beyond parallel in ancient or modern history.[30]

By May the correspondence was dwindling. On May 8, the last warning came from a former Virginian living in Cleveland:

> Let Jeff Davis go to Hell, for as sure as the sun shines water runs, & grass grows, Davis & all his abettors will find a felon's grave. The South (and all that sides with Her) is doomed to total distruction [sic]. God almighty can't save them!! The North North! Why man, in 4 weeks I could raise 500,000 men that would swim through a Sea of Blood, just for the fun of it!!! Words cannot describe the awful demons there is [sic] here. This Letcher is no Phantom. No, it's Real Real!!!! So if you can make peace, do it on any terms. Save the People at any disgrace of Honor—do it or suffer the above.[31]

Letcher filed these unofficial letters from the North with his private correspondence and occasionally showed them to friends, but he never answered them.

Friction with Confederate authorities continued throughout the month, but Letcher remained on friendly terms with most other southern governors. Despite the severe arms shortage, some light artillery was sent to North Carolina and Tennessee. Letcher was determined to try to co–operate with the other southern governors, to meet them a little more than half way whenever possible.

With the danger of a Yankee attack increasing every day, Letcher altered his policy on outside volunteers. Inadequately armed volunteers were still rejected, but by May 9 he was pre- pared to accept reasonably well–armed volunteers from anywhere in the South if they came forward in sufficient numbers. This new policy angered some southern governors who wanted to hoard their own manpower, and Governor Joseph E. Brown of Georgia refused to furnish equipment for volunteer units in his state which planned to fight in Virginia. Despite this clash, Letcher generally worked harmoniously with the southern governors during the early days of the war.[32]

Letcher was still hoping to obtain military hardware from the North, and became more and more incensed at what he consid- ered inadequate support from the Confederacy. By the middle of May, concerned about his lack of liaison with Confederate leaders, he was anxious to confer personally with President Davis about Virginia's role in the war effort. The Confederate government was equally concerned, and within a week it accepted the Virginia convention's invitation to move to Richmond.[33]

Meanwhile, rumblings of discontent grew louder in the north- western section of the state, the area that had swung the guberna- torial election to Letcher in 1859. Opponents of secession were scattered throughout Virginia, but only in the northwest were they numerous enough to be dominant. Letcher received many letters from friends in the area warning of the growing threat of the Unionists.

Letcher was aware of the danger but uncertain of the remedy. After much advice from George W. Summers in the northwest and a lengthy consultation with General Lee, he decided to send arms, but not troops, to the loyalists. The northwest was isolated from the rest of the state; sending troops there would only arouse the Unionists and the neighboring states of Ohio and Pennsylvania. If a race developed to concentrate forces in the northwest, Virginia was sure to lose. She could not spare the troops, and transportation facilities through the Alleghenies were inadequate. The best bet was to send arms and to hope that the loyalists could turn the tide of Unionism without outside interference. Letcher explained his strategy to Summers:

> While this line of policy is suggested by our comparative weakness, and by the difficulty of collecting, in any short time, an organized force in Northwestern Virginia, sufficient to meet a large body of troops coming against us, it is also called for by the distracted and divided state of our own people; and I know of no better way of establishing unity of feeling and of securing a hearty cooperation on the part of all our citizens, in the support of the state, in the position it now occupies, than by placing arms in the hands of the men known to be loyal and true, to be used in their own defense.[34]

Letcher sent William W. Crump, his most trusted troubleshooter, to the northwest with muskets. He also designated the town of Grafton as a concentration point for volunteers. Letcher hoped this would be enough to intimidate the Unionists but not enough to incite an outside attack. The Unionists were not intimidated, however, and on May 13 the first anti–secession convention was held at Wheeling.[35]

On May 11, Letcher issued a proclamation, approved by the convention, prohibiting exportation of general provisions from Virginia to any state still under federal control. Following his council's advice, he signed a $16,000 contract with B. & J. Baker for repair of three Yankee ships scuttled in Norfolk harbor. The contract allocated only $5,000 to refloat the *Merrimac,* but this small investment was the beginning of a revolutionary change in naval technology.[36]

Frequent false alarms accentuated continuing shortages of almost every type of equipment. Telegraph wire became extremely scarce as several emergency lines were hastily constructed, and Letcher began to hoard this vital material. He also hoarded Virginia's precious gunpowder supply, rejecting several Confederate requisitions. The shortage of weapons became so critical that he ordered an official census of all state–owned arms late in the month.[37]

The state's rapidly expanding military forces constantly created new difficulties, and Letcher gave General Lee a free rein. Usually working through his main aide–de–camp, S. Bassett French,

Letcher confined himself to minor, nonstrategic problems. He acted to furnish the troops with better clothing at their own rather than state expense, and declared that all eligible voters in the ranks of the Virginia volunteers could participate in the plebiscite on May 23. There was no question as to how the people, both soldiers and civilians, would vote. Virginia had seceded more than a month ago, and the plebiscite was merely a formal ratification of an accomplished fact. Nevertheless, May 23 marked the end of Virginia's independent experiment in secession and the beginning of Confederate dominance in the Old Dominion.[38]

The period from April 17 to May 23 was one of the most trying in Virginia's history. She was forced to break her old allegiance to the Union and gradually merge with the infant Confederacy, while simultaneously preparing to wage a total war for survival. New problems begged for solutions, and the old experiences and traditions gave no answers. Turmoil and confusion were unavoidable, and Governor Letcher was in the middle of the struggle. Mistakes were made in the headlong rush of events, but the governor furnished the steady, balanced leadership that was needed.

CHAPTER 8

Consolidating The Rebellion

For the next few months the Confederacy gradually assumed control of events in Virginia. As the state's chief executive, Letcher was a key figure in this transfer of power. If he co–operated, the transition period would be relatively smooth; if not, chaos would follow. With large scale warfare beginning in earnest, Letcher's firm leadership was essential for the survival of the Confederacy.

The new Confederate era began for Virginia when Jefferson Davis arrived in Richmond on May 29, but the transformation of dignified old Richmond into a congested, noisy, restless rebel metropolis had already begun, and the citizenry turned out in mass to hail their new war chieftain. Governor Letcher, his advisory council, elderly Mayor Joseph Mayo, and other dignitaries met the president at Petersburg and accompanied him on the final lap of his railroad journey from Montgomery. The train arrived at 7:30 in the morning, but it was greeted at the depot by a large, enthusiastic crowd. Guns boomed and bells peeled as Davis was cheered by throngs of spectators all along the route to the Spotswood Hotel. Only after Davis made a brief speech did the happy crowds disperse.[1]

This hearty welcome did not eliminate friction between the Confederate and Virginia governments. Ratification of secession by plebiscite on May 23 removed the last legal obstacle to transferring state forces to Confederate control. Almost before President Davis could unpack, Letcher suggested a conference to discuss the transfer. He was particularly concerned about the control of the weapons-making machinery from Harper's Ferry and the rank of officers who had quit federal service to join the state's forces and were awaiting transfer to Confederate service. Virginia had promised these men that they would not lose rank by switching from federal to state service, and now Letcher and his council insisted that the Confederacy honor this pledge too.

On June 1, Letcher offered to turn over all state forces and military equipment except the Harper's Ferry machinery to the Confederates. Davis replied the next day. He stated that the Confederate Congress and the Virginia convention had made similar rulings about the rank of officers transferring from federal service. He promised that virtually every officer switching from federal to Virginia to Confederate service would retain his original rank. He added that probably not a single man would lose rank by transfer but that he could not absolutely guarantee this in every case. He concluded by emphasizing the central government's desire to control the rifle-making machinery from Harper's Ferry.[2]

Letcher was not completely satisfied, but arrangements for the transfer continued. The three original members of his council, Allen, Smith, and Maury, formed a committee to confer with Davis on the entire operation. Two days later the committee reported that the Confederate position remained fundamentally unchanged. Davis' refusal to guarantee that every single officer who transferred to Confederate service would retain his old rank displeased Letcher, but he was under great pressure to act quickly. The council recommended an immediate transfer of forces on the Confederacy's terms. Secretary of War Walker reminded him of the state convention's military agreement with the Confederacy, April 25, calling for the transfer of forces. The last legal obstacle, the election on May 23, had been removed, and the Confederates expected co-operation. Even greater pressure came from the enemy. Federal armies were beginning to nibble away on the northern and western areas of the state; it seemed that a military showdown was at hand.[3]

On June 6, Letcher finally transferred to Confederate authority all of the state's armed forces. With one exception, all property and material captured from the United States was turned over to the Confederacy for the duration of the war.

This single exception, the rifle—making machinery from Harper's Ferry, tells a story of its own, a tale of the over—developed concept of states' rights and the picayune legalism that were sinister cancers within the body of the newborn—and already dying—Confederacy. When Virginia volunteers captured Harper's Ferry, Colonel Charles Dimmock, chief of ordnance, took charge of the valuable machinery there. On April 24, Letcher summoned master armorer S. Adams, who had just slipped back to Virginia after an unsuccessful attempt to buy weapons in the North, and ordered him to go to Harper's Ferry and bring the rifle—making machinery to Richmond.

Adams left immediately, but before he could begin his mission Letcher ordered some of the machinery sent on loan to Fayetteville, N. C., where an adequate source of steam power was available. The great bulk of the machinery was then sent to Richmond and installed in the state armory. Rifle production did not begin immediately because some of the machinery needed repairs and skilled labor was scarce. The Confederates were anxious to gain control of the machinery, but Letcher's proclamation of June 6 offered them no encouragement.[4]

Davis, Walker, and Josiah Gorgas, head of Confederate ordnance, pressed for control of the machinery. Their efforts had no noticeable effect on the governor, but the convention was influenced enough by June 29 to order Letcher to turn over the machinery and the armory that housed it to the Confederates for the duration. Gorgas pressured Dimmock for immediate cooperation, but Dimmock refused to act without the governor's approval. Davis and Walker increased their pressure on Letcher, who demanded ironclad assurances that the Confederates would never move the machinery farther South.

Letcher finally yielded, and on July 12 instructed Secretary of the Commonwealth Munford and Attorney General Tucker to transfer both the machinery and the armory. However, the governor insisted that they obtain a guarantee that none of the machinery would be moved from Richmond. He briefed Dimmock and ordered him to compile a complete inventory of everything that was lent to the central government.

This was only the beginning. Dimmock and Gorgas, both Yankee–born rebels, argued incessantly while the inventory was being taken. The future of some uncompleted state ordnance projects caused a dispute between Letcher and Walker, and they also argued over Walker's refusal to guarantee that the machinery would never be sent South. Transferring the responsibility for meeting the armory's payroll created additional friction and confusion.[5]

These endless little disputes caused the whole matter to flare up again, and the Dimmock–Gorgas feud became so heated that on July 25 Letcher again had to order his ordnance chief to transfer the machinery to the Confederates. When, in August, Gorgas tried to carry out a centralization program that called for shipping some of the machinery to the excellent facilities in Fayetteville, Letcher rushed back into the battle with a barrage of legalistic objections.

These additional complications accelerated an administrative summit conference which had started earlier in the month between Gorgas and Colonel Albert T. Bledsoe of Confederate ordnance and Dimmock and Tucker for Virginia. An agreement was finally reached on the last day of August, and the governor signed the final contract transferring the machinery and the armory to the central government on September 2. The Confederate government had its way in this ridiculously long and complex bureaucratic tussle. The whole episode clearly illustrates some of the Confederacy's internal flaws.[6]

Letcher faced numerous other problems as the tempo of the war increased. Late in May and early in June, he launched an investigation to be certain that the Pamunkey Indians were voluntarily working on river defenses. He strongly opposed all efforts to clamp a forced labor system upon the docile redskins and continued to watch over the Tidewater Indians after the Confederates took charge of local defenses. Because of rising costs, he abandoned the emergency practice of keeping the telegraph offices open all the time, and he closely supervised the hurried construction of several new telegraph lines. He also supervised the disposal of captured federal funds. Letcher authorized local officials to open and read the mail of any suspicious persons, and clarified his exemption policy by declaring deputies as well as sheriffs essential home front personnel.[7]

The governor's mail included some complaints about various aspects of Virginia's first, faltering efforts to wage war. A resident of Charles City County protested the construction of a small fortress in the front yard of his riverside home. He was a loyal Virginian, as ready as the next man to sacrifice for the cause, but he felt the destruction of his beautiful front lawn and some of his buildings was carrying warfare too far. He suggested that the fort be moved a short distance down river to the front yard of a Yankee neighbor. Letcher passed this appeal on to General Lee, who ignored it. This trivial incident illustrates how unprepared psychologically many Virginians were for the coming storm.[8]

Early in June, the state's efforts to raise volunteers in the southwest were partially thwarted when Davis imprudently ordered General John B. Floyd to muster an independent brigade in his home area to defend the vital Virginia & Tennessee Railroad. On June 6, Letcher protested, and the next day he objected to the transfer of four state companies to Floyd's command less than a day after all state forces had been placed under Confederate control. Davis agreed that these actions were irregular, but he asked for the governor's cooperation in this emergency. Letcher grumbled, but, putting practical necessity before technical legality, he complied. Floyd continued to recruit in the southwest.[9]

The governor continued to exempt essential workers from military service, and he constantly encouraged railroad construction to close dangerous gaps in the state's rail system. Although the council said he lacked the power, Letcher directed the president of the Richmond, Fredericksburg & Potomac Railroad to build a cross–town connection with the Petersburg Railroad at Richmond. After a year of delay, he finally succeeded in joining the R. F. & P. and Virginia Central Railroad systems at Richmond.

However, he failed to obtain an extension of the Virginia Central from Covington to the Ohio River. Virginia's rail system was the most efficient in the Confederacy, but the demands of modern war were to strain it to the breaking point.[10]

Early in June, the shooting war began in earnest as Union troops occupied fringe areas of the Old Dominion. Letcher pressured Davis for aid, and a week before the first real fight at Big Bethel, he issued a proclamation ordering all remaining inactive volunteers to their rendezvous points. He also called for more volunteers and alerted the militia, theoretically all able–bodied white males from 18 to 45, instructing them to equip themselves as best they could and begin weekly drills.[11]

Hampton Roads, Harper's Ferry, and the railroad junction at Manassas were all threatened by the growing power of the Yankee army, but the loudest alarm sounded in the northwest, where strong federal forces threatened to penetrate all the way to Staunton and isolate the entire northwestern area of the state from the Confederacy. Following the advice of his council, Letcher called out the militia in the endangered area. General Lee sent Brigadier General Robert S. Garnett with reinforcements to this turbulent sector.[12]

Letcher had continued to send agents into the northwest, but on June 10 he decided to see for himself exactly what was going on, hoping that his presence might strengthen the fading rebel elements in the area. He borrowed a pair of pistols from General Lee— previously he had had no use for pistols in his political career—and headed west on June 12, overtaking General Garnett's force at Monterey. On June 14 he issued a proclamation to the people of the northwest, appealing to them to abide by the election of May 23, which had endorsed secession, and hailing state loyalty as the highest political allegiance. He reminded the people that the plebiscite had also approved a constitutional amendment which abolished all special tax privileges for slaveholders—a change Delegate Letcher had unsuccessfully sought at the Reform Convention. Letcher concluded by saying that only cowards and traitors would fail Virginia in her hour of need. He returned to Richmond in a few days. Despite his efforts, the Confederacy's position in the northwest continued to deteriorate rapidly.[13]

By mid–June a number of wartime problems were coming into clearer focus. Virginia had 40,000 volunteers in the field, but General Lee wanted at least 11,000 more. Various supply shortages were already acute, and gunpowder and arms remained scarce. The state had spent over $2,000,000 since the end of April, yet construction of some fortifications was proceeding at a snail's pace. Clashes with the Confederacy continued, but they were not as serious as those in most other southern states. In a report to the convention, Letcher stressed one of the bright spots in this gloomy picture: General Lee was directing the state's military operations. Events in the next few months caused many to question Lee's ability, but Letcher never doubted his greatness. Throughout the war, the thoroughly bourgeois governor was an unwavering champion of the dignified, aristocratic general.[14]

Exactly two months after secession, Letcher presented a résumé of events and his actions since the beginning of the year to a secret session of the convention. He reviewed his efforts to prepare Virginia for war, stressing the prewar arms appropriations and the work done by men he had appointed to secure arms and prepare defenses. He summarized the campaign to recruit top military talent from the federal army, and also emphasized that V.M.I. had been the main source of lieutenants. He mentioned the continuing naval expansion, adding that the *Merrimac* had been raised and was being repaired at Gosport.

Speaking with his customary candor, Letcher said efforts to recruit a 10,000–man provisional army had failed and suggested disbanding the tattered nucleus of this organization. Claiming that great military progress had been made since secession, he gave the primary credit to Lee. The governor then discussed a program that had been severely criticized—his appointment of military officers—saying he had done his best, disregarding past political affiliations and stressing present loyalty to Virginia. He admitted a few unfortunate appointments, the result of military inexperience, particularly in the days before Lee arrived, and promised that these mistakes would be corrected. After continuing with a long, complex discussion of the state's finances, one of his favorite subjects, the governor concluded his report with a ringing appeal for a unified war effort, always his wartime creed.[15]

The convention was a far from friendly audience. Letcher had been severely criticized during several of its secret sessions, and on several occasions Delegate Dorman of Rockbridge County had been hard pressed to defend his friend. Dorman was pleased by the convention's favorable response to Letcher's message, and he hoped that it would soon be made public so that much of the unfair criticism being hurled at the governor could be silenced. The convention showed its new confidence in Letcher by abolishing the advisory council on July 19. The council's activities had decreased noticeably since the transfer of forces the previous month, but its abolishment did increase Letcher's work—load as he continued to struggle with a bewildering multitude of problems.[16]

On June 28, Frederick J. Cridland, British consul in Richmond, complained that British citizens were being forced into southern military units. Letcher rejected the complaint, reminding Cridland that all Virginia forces had been transferred to Confederate control. He added that international law permitted a nation to demand the military services of an alien if the enemy was not the alien's homeland. Cridland's complaints continued, but Letcher stood firm. In August he authorized a routine investigation of the status of aliens during state militia mobilizations, but he ordered no changes. Cridland continued to pester Letcher, and a few aliens actually escaped service in the state militia, but the governor usually ignored the complaints. This minor harassment continued until the middle of 1863, when the Confederate government, increasingly impatient with Britain's policy of non—recognition, expelled the British consul at Richmond.[17]

During the latter part of June, Letcher tackled a new problem. He instructed the railroads to be sure that all persons leaving Richmond had a pass signed by the governor or some other authorized official. Written orders would suffice for military officers. Letcher was concerned about the masses of strangers swarming in and out of Richmond, but southerners, a free, individualistic folk, were unaccustomed to such government regulation. This mild security system and similar systems elsewhere in the Confederacy were not very effective. On the other side of the Potomac River security measures were also crude and inefficient by modern standards.[18]

On the last day of the month, Letcher reminded Secretary of War Walker that the state was meeting its last volunteer troop payroll, and that beginning July 1, the Confederacy would assume this obligation as specified in the transfer of forces agreement. On the same day Letcher received a call for 3,000 men, Virginia's quota of the new 30,000-man reserve army corps. These new recruits were to be armed, trained, and commanded by the Confederates. Hesitating only long enough to borrow seventy—one percussion muskets for his militia, Letcher issued a proclamation on July 4 calling for more volunteers to assemble at Richmond and Staunton. At the same time he disputed the right of the Confederates to organize the force and appoint its officers. Letcher felt that the Confederate Constitution forbade these violations of Virginia's rights. He was a staunch states' righter, and just as legalistic as the average southern lawyer—politician, but he realized that war demanded practical, flexible leadership. After officially protesting, he did not hinder this Confederate project. The absurd dispute over the Harper's Ferry machinery showed that his flexibility was limited, but generally the governor was willing to cooperate with the Confederates and to put necessity before principle for the duration. A similar common sense approach by other southern governors would have greatly strengthened Confederate unity.[19]

The turbulent northwest began once more to distract the governor; another visit to the area was clearly called for, but the press of business and a slight sickness delayed his departure. On July 9, Confederate Adjutant General Samuel Cooper asked him to mobilize the militia of the northcentral area of the state at Manassas Junction. Despite vigorous complaints about earlier militia calls from the affected areas, Letcher assented, and before leaving for the northwest on July 11, he instructed his aides to cooperate with all Confederate militia calls. Shortly thereafter, Secretary of War Walker broadened the call to include all counties north of the James River and east of the Blue Ridge. Letcher's aides immediately prepared the necessary proclamation.

These urgent calls for troops were clearly necessary. Federal pressure was increasing rapidly on three fronts in Virginia. On the Peninsula, Yankee forces had been steadily reinforced ever since the clash at Big Bethel. Near Manassas, troops were massing for a great battle. In the northwest, General Garnett was killed and his little army mauled at Rich Mountain. In this hour of great peril for Virginia, Letcher cooperated wholeheartedly with the Confederates.

The governor reached the Greenbrier River early on July 13 and immediately conferred with officers of Garnett's dispirited army. He discussed setting up a rear–guard defense at Cheat Mountain, but this vague meddling in military strategy was nipped in the bud when a messenger arrived with orders for a general retreat. The governor stayed long enough to receive the bulk of the army on July 14. He then entrained for Richmond.[20]

Letcher reached the capital the following day, worried, exhausted, and physically ill. The strain and tension of the last few months had finally taken their toll, and once again he succumbed to sickness at a crucial time. He signed the proclamation calling up the militia which his aides had prepared in his absence, and then retired to his home for rest and medication, leaving his three aides, S. Bassett French, Richard Catlett and Greenlee Davidson, son of James D. Davidson, and Secretary of the Commonwealth Munford to handle routine executive chores in his absence. By July 18 the governor was back in his office, but he planned to return to the northwestern area of the state on the following day.[21]

He briefly postponed his trip, however, as events moved swiftly toward a climax at Manassas. On July 19, President Davis requested an additional militia call in the Shenandoah County area to free General Joseph Johnston's troops to reinforce Beauregard at Manassas. The militia call of July 15 had stirred up much resentment among many freedom–loving Virginians who felt that the state had already done more than its fair share. Letcher ignored this discontent and complied with Davis' request. Johnston's troops were able to slip away from the Valley and march to Manassas just in time to play a key role in the overwhelming Confederate victory.[22]

During these massive and unpopular militia levies, the governor continued and even expanded the liberal exemption policy originated by the convention. Armament industry workers, bank officials, overseers, essential millers, police in Richmond, Staunton and Fredericksburg, railroad workers, telegraph operators, government workers, doctors, druggists, smiths, cobblers, miners, and even the sexton of a synagogue and a Bible seller were excused from militia service. When Joseph R. Anderson volunteered a battalion of Tredegar workers for temporary field service, Letcher emphatically rejected the offer.

The July militia calls were unproductive in many areas. Too many men were taking advantage of the liberal exemption system, and some areas contained a large percentage of Unionists. By August, Letcher tightened up on exemptions and created special militia boards to examine every person seeking to avoid service. These modifications did nothing to quiet the rising chorus of protests over militia mobilizations.[23]

As the white manpower of the Confederacy was clumsily marshaled for military service, a traditional southern fear became magnified. Would the slaves rise while their masters were away at war and drown the South in innocent blood? Were the women and children at home facing a greater danger than the men on the firing line? Letcher had seen the terrible vision, dreamed the hideous nightmare. Like most southerners, he hesitated to think the unthinkable, but occasionally he had spoken of the horror of "Southern women sacrificed to the brutal passions of the negro", an apparition which lurked in the mind of the old South.

Letcher was quick to act when even the possibility of Negro unrest was revealed. He ordered that only a limited number of volunteers be accepted from the York River area of the Tidewater, a region heavily populated by Negroes. He also ordered the jailing of any Yankee residents in that area who appeared to foment slave unrest or hamper the war effort in any other way. He remained ever alert to the danger of a slave uprising that was never to come.[24]

Letcher also had a more personal worry at this time. Before the war, his eldest son Sam, an adventurous 13–year–old eager to see the world, had gone to Baltimore and shipped out on a freighter. While the ship was still at sea, the war began. The governor feared that the boy would be seized when he returned to Baltimore. The federal authorities might even try to intimidate him through his son. Late in July, Letcher's fears were dispelled when Sam reached Richmond, having landed unmolested at Baltimore and passed uneventfully through Washington on his way home! As the war intensified, such journeys became more difficult, of course, but traffic between the lines never stopped completely.[25]

Letcher was very active in the familiar field of finance. On July 19, he prohibited the acceptance in payment of debt of any bills or notes of merchants or banks in Yankee–held areas of the northwest. At the end of the month, he authorized veteran state auditor Jonathan M. Bennett to issue $7,000,000 in Virginia treasury notes. These notes had been authorized previously by the convention and the assembly, but a shortage of engraving and lithographing equipment had caused a delay. When the equipment was finally available, the auditor sought and received the governor's signal to act. The state banks had already stretched their credit capacities to the limit, and large scale issuance of treasury notes was an attractive alternative. However, this expedient stimulated inflation—a scourge that eventually was to undermine the whole southern economy.[26]

Before the month ended, another clash with the Confederates occurred. Only a few days before the battle at Manassas, Gorgas, frantically seeking more gunpowder, demanded the state powder stored at Lynchburg. Since Virginia had bought this powder before the war, it had not been included in the transfer–of–forces agreement. Dimmock refused to give the powder to his old antagonist, and Letcher told Gorgas to apply directly to him. Gorgas had no time for formalities, and on July 20, on the eve of the battle, Confederate troops under orders from Secretary of War Walker simply seized the gunpowder. The day after the battle Gorgas formally apologized, claiming unconvincingly that he had not known that the powder belonged to Virginia, and adding that the powder had not been used but was safely stored in Richmond awaiting the governor's pleasure. Letcher had made another quick trip to the west during this controversy and when he returned he was partially soothed by the victory at Manassas. Again putting common sense ahead of legalistic indignation, he told Gorgas to keep the powder and to arrange for payment later. Letcher concluded the affair by instructing Gorgas to consult him in the future before taking any more state supplies.[27]

The Manassas victory dangerously increased southern overconfidence, and demands for the demobilization of the state militia poured into the governor's office. Letcher simply passed these letters on to the Confederate secretary of war without comment. Despite increasing grass roots pressure, he was willing to let the Confederates decide the matter. He also tried to coordinate state and Confederate efforts to obtain adequate uniforms for Virginia volunteers.

Late in August, Colonel Blanton Duncan of Kentucky came to Richmond seeking 1,500 muskets. After receiving a requisition from Gorgas, Letcher gave Duncan 1,000 old flintlock muskets. He also appealed to the people of Virginia to donate winter clothing to state troops in the Confederate army. An emergency request by the secretary of war for arms and equipment for an Alabama regiment bivouacked near Richmond was promptly granted by the governor. He also granted Beauregard's request for seven pieces of state artillery and their accompanying equipment, and agreed to furnish Floyd's Confederate brigade with 1,000 reconditioned muskets in exchange for an equal number of old rifles. In response to an appeal from Wilmington, North Carolina, he sent that vital seaport some muskets and one large piece of coastal artillery.[28]

Meanwhile, federal forces in the northwest continued to advance against weak and scattered resistance. On July 28, Davis sent Lee to coordinate rebel forces there. By September Lee was ready to attack federal troops on Cheat Mountain. On September 5, one week before the assault, Letcher sent a letter of encouragement, reiterating his confidence in Lee. On the eve of combat, Lee was too busy to answer at once, and on September 12 his attack on Cheat Mountain failed miserably. A few days later Lee wrote the governor and discussed his failure. He laid most of the blame on a sudden rainstorm and concluded that he must try again. Try again he did in October—and again he failed. Criticism of "Granny Lee" was intense. Lee's prestige was badly tarnished, but Letcher's faith in the general's ability never wavered.[29]

Several more disputes with the Confederates occurred in this period. On September 9, Letcher chided the secretary of war for his slowness in paying some medical, commissary, and quartermaster personnel who had transferred from state to Confederate service. Secretary Walker blamed administrative red tape for the delay, and remarked in passing that only a few Virginia officers had been rejected for Confederate service. The idea of *any* state officers being rejected enraged the governor, but he conceded the Confederacy's legal right of rejection. After mildly disputing Walker's explanation for the delay, Letcher ended the matter by reiterating his desire to co–operate with the central government.

On September 13, the governor complained to Davis about what he considered inadequate Confederate defensive preparations since the transfer of forces—a problem that concerned every southern governor. He listed specific needs all over the state. Davis defended his generals and politely suggested that the governor was not familiar with everything that had been done. Letcher accepted this reply, and, unlike some southern governors, tried not to pester the busy president about local defense unless a real danger existed.

A little later in September, another mild dispute arose over the power of appointing the officers of several Virginia units transferred to Confederate control before they were properly organized. Letcher wanted to appoint the officers; Davis politely but firmly refused his request. Again Letcher accepted the president's verdict without undue controversy. Secretary of State R. M. T. Hunter stirred up a minor dispute over the ownership of some muskets, and again Letcher quietly accepted Davis' ruling.[30]

Thus, Letcher made a sincere effort to alter the political habits of a lifetime, to de–emphasize strict legalism and rigid states' rights doctrines for the duration. One great advantage he had in this largely, but not entirely, successful endeavor was his tremendous confidence in Jefferson Davis. When sickness temporarily disabled the president early in September, Letcher showed no outward sign of concern, but he wrote frankly to his friend Davidson later in the month:

> The President to day for the first time, in three weeks was at his office attending to his public duties. He is rapidly improving, and I hope will soon be well. His loss at this time would be a sad affair to us, and would result in the most serious embarrassments to our cause. We could not supply his place with a man who would enjoy so much of public confidence, and who would be able to render such valuable aid. He is one of the few men, suited to lead and control the great popular movement now in progress.[31]

Letcher's confidence did not extend to Secretary of War Walker. Publicly he said nothing because he feared the fragile unity of the Confederacy would be endangered by open criticism—however justifiable—of high Confederate officials. But on September 14 he privately lashed out at Walker, who had previously sent Davis a confidential letter of resignation, effective September 16. "It is rumored to day", Letcher wrote Davidson:

> that the Secretary of War is about to resign. I hope it is true, as he is universally regarded as utterly unfit for the place. He has but little talent—neither legislative nor executive experience [,] is timid and undecided, even upon the most common questions that arise. I have heard no speculations as to his successor. There is one comfort however,—the change must be an improvement.[32]

President Davis appreciated Letcher's cooperation. Already he was finding some of the other southern governors bitterly opposed to even the mildest direction or regulation by the central government. Nurtured for generations, the states' rights spirit in the South was already beginning to nullify the Confederacy's attempts to wage war, and Davis needed friends wherever he could find them in the governments of the states. Letcher remained basically loyal to Davis, but even his cooperation had limitations.

Late in September Confederate attempts to begin an "aeronautic inspection of the enemy" were grounded by Letcher's refusal to impress sulfuric acid, which was needed to generate hydrogen for an observation balloon. He instinctively disliked impressment as a threat to the traditional right of private property, and he forwarded the Confederacy's request to Attorney General Tucker for a legal opinion, a practice that was becoming more and more frequent. Finally, Letcher bluntly stated that he lacked the power to impress such goods, and the project was abandoned. Hence the only effective balloons in Virginia's sky belonged to the Union army, and they occasionally obtained valuable military information.[33]

Though not interested in balloons, the governor was still anxious to obtain many kinds of equipment, particularly military hardware. He tried to procure arms in France through the same French capitalists who had negotiated to buy the James River and Kanawha Canal just before the war, but his agents made little headway in their poorly coordinated efforts. The arms shortage remained critical. Early in October, another Dimmock–Gorgas battle began over a few Virginia cannons. When Gorgas tried to take this artillery, Letcher angrily protested to the new secretary of war, Judah P. Benjamin of Louisiana. Benjamin apologized profusely, insisting that no insult to Virginia had been intended.[34]

For the last six months Letcher had been completely engrossed in the multiple tasks of his office. Virginia had gradually merged into the Confederacy, and all the while she had been involved in the opening rounds of a ruthless, total war. Governor Letcher guided his people through these perilous times. His leadership was certainly not flawless, but it was more than adequate. His services were indispensable. His energy, determination, patriotism, and practical common sense came to the fore as he successfully completed the first half year of his wartime administration.

The tremendous tension and the relentless pace took their toll on the conscientious governor, but he stayed on the job, relaxing when he could, working when he should. John Lewis Peyton, North Carolina supply agent preparing for a trip to Europe, visited the Governor's Mansion in October to obtain a pass authorizing his departure by rail. He described in detail his brief evening visit:

. . . Letcher, in an elbow chair by the fireside, among a few chosen friends who were mellowing over their pipes and tankard. A glass of "mountain dew," and a whiff of the calumet, put us at once upon the best of terms with the company, and we spent some time amid clouds of smoke, produced by Virginia tobacco, listening to their views on the subject of the war . . . the half military, half political household. . . . Though he had been much in public life, his manners were plain and uncultivated, and somewhat of "the rough and ready" style. He was about sixty years of age [Letcher was only 48 at this time!], and his general appearance recalled the lines of Dryden—

"Of sixty years he seems, and well might last

To sixty more, but that he lives too fast"

He was tall and slender, except in the region of the stomach, where he was unduly developed, at the apparent expense of his shanks, which were very spindling—a peculiar configuration of the masculine form, said to result, in the "tide-water" country of Virginia, from too frequent a use of "peach and honey." His hair was carrotty, and closely cut, standing over his scalp like bristles. Two small kindling gray eyes, deeply set upon either side of a straight nose, gave an expression of animation to his features. His mouth was wide, lips thin, and the general expression of his features coarse but keen![35]

Ancient Virginia and the nascent Confederacy had survived the early days of their uneasy union. The first months of the new era were successful, but the acid test was yet to come. The main political and military dangers lay ahead, and Letcher's greatest trials also lay in the future. His wartime administration had just begun.

CHAPTER 9

The Quickening Pace

The tempo of the war in Virginia increased rapidly after October 1861, reaching a climax with the bloody Peninsula fighting in the spring and summer of 1862. This was the first real test of the whole Confederacy. In Virginia, opposition to the governor's policy of cooperation with the central government intensified, and Letcher faced the first major test of his wartime administration.

Letcher visited the strategic Hampton Roads area twice in October. Late in the month he stood on Sewell's Point, five miles north of Norfolk at the mouth of the James River, and watched the maneuvers of the growing Yankee fleet. Then he went to Norfolk and spent four days reviewing troops. He was impressed by the training and morale of the men, and the disquieting image of Union power off Sewell's Point faded somewhat. The hostile Richmond *Examiner* accused the governor of doing nothing but eating hogfish and drinking whiskey while in Norfolk, but Letcher felt that his presence boosted the troops' morale.

At the end of the month he journeyed to Centreville, in Fairfax County, where General Joseph Johnston's troops were entrenched. Ever since First Manassas, a shortage of regimental flags had worried the general. During that chaotic battle, the lack of flags had made it difficult to tell friend from foe. Johnston had asked the southern governors to provide their states' regiments with appropriate banners. Generally his appeal had been ignored, but Letcher had made immediate arrangements to produce 38 Virginia flags. Letcher carried these banners with him to Centreville, and he personally presented one to each Virginia regiment at a formal review.

This review was rather chaotic. A clumsy drill session ended when the troops broke ranks and crowded around the governor. The men were pleased to see Letcher, and several drunken warriors showed their delight by firing their muskets into the air. This interlude was almost a comedy, but once again Letcher had blazed the trail of cooperation with the Confederates. He was the only governor to furnish a single flag, and Johnston had to have the rest of the regimental flags made himself.[1]

The governor returned to Richmond to find his three–year–old daughter, Mary Davidson Letcher, desperately ill with diphtheria. Medical treatments failed, and the little girl died on November 11. Running true to form, the *Examiner* picked this time to increase its attacks on the governor, and finally, toward the end of the month, Letcher's brother Sam, a lieutenant colonel of Virginia volunteers, publicly labeled Editor John M. Daniel "a mendacious slanderer and coward". Daniel was already under bond to keep the peace, so no duel followed, but the *Examiner* continued to criticize Letcher—and just about everyone else—frequently.[2]

The demands of the hour forced Letcher to keep to business. On November 18, he gave the reassembled convention his first résumé of the state's war effort since June 17. Criticism of Virginia's policies, particularly by Virginians in Confederate service, was one reason for the summary. Also, the convention, presided over by Lieutenant Governor Montague in recent sessions, was preparing to disband permanently. Criticism of Letcher in the convention had slackened considerably, and he tactfully stressed the convention's positive actions in his defense of the state's war effort. Letcher hardly mentioned his own contributions. He singled out Dimmock and the state's financial officials led by Jonathan M. Bennett for special praise, and he added that Virginia had spent $6,000,000 on the war since secession.

Letcher criticized the Confederates for rejecting the services of several Virginia officers during the transfer of forces. He added that these men were still receiving state pay and retaining their state rank. Thus Virginia kept her pledge that federal officers joining state forces would not suffer loss of rank.

The governor then appealed to the convention to remedy at once the growing evils of extortion and speculation, i.e., buying essential goods at their source and selling them to consumers for exorbitant prices. All over the South ruthless war profiteers were practicing this buy–cheap, sell–dear technique to reap inflated profits at the expense of the rebel war effort. Bourgeois Letcher certainly did not object to legitimate profits, but he wanted to prevent the new mania for speculation from undermining the southern economy.

He reminded the convention that salt was selling for $20 a sack while a Virginia volunteer received only $11 a month. He called for quick action even before the legislature met but made no specific proposals. What could he say? Any direct, statewide attack on speculation would be a revolutionary challenge to the traditional, laissez–faire economic system, and Letcher and his people were not yet prepared to abandon the golden past, the very cause they fought for. This was not the only time the governor tried to combat profiteering and inflation, but these menaces were never checked in the Confederacy.[3]

The convention applauded Letcher's report, but he had no time for bows. He continued to send state muskets to friends in need: 1,000 to General Humphrey Marshall in Kentucky, 500 to the state of South Carolina, and then more to John C. Breckinridge's First Kentucky Brigade in Tennessee. He occasionally complained about weak spots in Confederate defenses in Virginia but usually accepted Confederate explanations without further protests.[4]

The problem of mobilizing militia units for specific threats required constant attention. Confederate General J. B. Magruder's frequent, panicky calls for militia in the Peninsula area became a special problem. During the last half of 1861, Union pressure had gradually increased at Fort Monroe on the tip of the Peninsula and on the nearby waters. As early as June, Magruder had mobilized all the militia on the Peninsula without notifying the governor. Only with his own militia call–up of July 15 did Letcher realize the extent of the earlier Peninsula mobilization. Magruder defended his action and requested that the Peninsula militia be retained under his command. Letcher was far from pleased with Magruder's conduct but allowed him to keep the militia.

By October, Magruder was again nervous, and asked the governor for additional militia for the defense of Williamsburg and Yorktown. By December, the general was desperate, and Letcher approved another militia call–up. However, he quickly changed his mind when Secretary of War Benjamin informed him that the Peninsula was not in immediate danger.

Despite Magruder's erratic performance, Letcher was determined to cooperate with legitimate Confederate requests for militia. On December 11, he yielded to pressure from Magruder and calmer rebel commanders and instructed all colonels of Virginia militia to obey mobilization orders by any Confederate general. Thus he voluntarily relinquished his primary control over the state militia, an almost unheard of act of cooperation by a southern governor. Responding in his usual fashion, Magruder alerted all militia south of the James River to be prepared to march to Jamestown or Williamsburg on a day's notice. McClellan's Union army did not land on the Peninsula until the next spring, but Magruder still imagined a Yankee behind every ripple in the water.[5]

The running battle between Dimmock and Gorgas flared up again late in the year. This time Dimmock, always supersensitive to any real or imagined Confederate infringement on his authority, was aroused when First Lieutenant Briscoe G. Baldwin of Gorgas' command took some state muskets stored in the Confederate–controlled armory in Richmond in order to obtain spare parts for repair work. As usual, the dispute became more and more heated and complicated as it developed. By December, everyone involved was short–tempered and irritable. Until the middle of the month Dimmock and Baldwin did most of the fighting, but then a letter from young Baldwin brought Letcher into the thick of the fray. The letter decried the governor's pettiness,

saying that only "the most morbidly sensitive or persistently suspicious" could believe that the Confederates meant to "injure
Virginia, or insult her executive".

The younger brother of John B. Baldwin, veteran Whig from
Augusta County, should have known that this approach would
not gain the cooperation of the governor. Letcher carried the
issue directly to Secretary of War Benjamin, who characteristically
tried to drown the fight in a flood of soothing words and vague
generalities. But this time Letcher would not be placated, and he
continued to press the evasive Benjamin for a settlement. This
picayune dispute dragged on for months before it was buried in
the rush of events. A less high handed procedure by the Confederates would have avoided the whole clash, for the governor
was always willing to cooperate when treated with respect.[6]

On December 2, Letcher reported to the newly–convened
General Assembly, meeting for the first time since April 4. After a
brief speech on the righteousness of Virginia's cause, he declared
that the war must continue until the independence of the Confederacy was firmly established, but admitted he had no idea
how long this might take. Calling for total war, Letcher championed an invasion of the North to awaken the Yankees to the
reality of battle. He had privately advocated an invasion of Maryland in November, and he was to repeat his call for an offensive
into the North many times in the future.

Continuing his report, Letcher warned of the danger of inflation. This time he suggested a partial remedy: some restrictions
on the mass of small note currency being issued by cities and corporations, and the outlawing of such issues by individuals. He
also recommended that niter and gunpowder production be stimulated, but he did not say in what manner this should be accomplished. The status of the state's twelve–month volunteers, aid to
neighboring states, disloyalty in the northwest, and state schools
and state institutions were all mentioned in this long, disjointed
address.[7]

On the same day, Letcher conferred with his old friend and
former adviser, General Francis H. Smith, and made plans to
reopen V.M.I. at the first of the year in Lexington. Davis sug-

gested that the reopened Institute accept some non–Virginians and train them as officers for the Confederate army. Letcher agreed that a few, perhaps 50, outsiders should be accepted if the Confederates would pay $425 yearly tuition for each of these special students. V.M.I. reopened on schedule in January, and 53 Confederate officer–candidates were included in the total enrollment of approximately 250 cadets.[8]

By the end of the year, Letcher's health was completely restored, and he continued his busy schedule. His $5,000 a year salary was rapidly shrinking in real value as inflation swept through the South, hitting hardest metropolitan areas like Richmond. Letcher had prospered before the war, but he had invested most of his liquid capital in his large, well–furnished home in Lexington and his real estate speculation in Washington. He had paid off the last note due on his Washington property just before the war started, but in 1862 this valuable property was seized for non–payment of taxes. Dorman, Davidson, and other friends knew that Letcher was going into debt in wartime Richmond, and some of them suggested that he run for the Confederate Senate at the first opportunity. Letcher was noncommittal, but he remembered this advice.[9]

Letcher persuaded his friend Dorman to run for the state Senate where he needed a dependable ally, but Dorman began his campaign too late and lost. In the last two months of the year, Davidson made four separate trips to the northwest for the governor and sent elaborate reports to Letcher on general conditions both there and in the Valley. Letcher's personal prestige remained untarnished in the Valley, but the situation in the northwest was continuing to deteriorate rapidly. By mid–December Letcher and Davidson agreed that conditions were bad, almost hopeless, in the northwestern area, and they feared that the Valley might soon be under assault.[10]

Letcher supported another former member of his advisory council, Captain Matthew Fontaine Maury. Maury recommended constructing a fleet of small, steam–powered gunboats to drive the Union fleet out of the South's coastal waters, and in December the Confederate Congress adopted Maury's plan. However, shortages and bureaucratic red tape delayed construction, and the success of the large ironclad *Virginia,* formerly the *Merrimac,* ended the whole scheme. Letcher was still anxious to close the gaps in the state's rail network, and he continued to champion the fireproofing of all state warehouses. Despite several destructive fires, nothing was done by the legislature, and mysterious fires continued to break out, particularly in Richmond.[11]

On January 6, the governor turned briefly from the practical to the theoretical. He sent a long, complex communication to the General Assembly which was loaded with southern political clichés. After a short justification of secession, he devoted most of his message to a detailed summary of President Abraham Lincoln's violations of the United States Constitution. Letcher bitterly condemned Lincoln and compared him to George III. Some of the constitutional violations he mentioned were reasonably accurate. However, many were fantastically farfetched and more clearly reflected the South's over–developed concept of legality and strict constitutionality than Lincoln's broad and logical exercise of wartime executive leadership. Letcher concluded this rambling discourse with his customary appeal to Virginians to fight on until the Confederacy had won its independence.[12]

The next day Letcher again appealed to the General Assembly to prevent wartime profiteering. As usual, he was short on remedies, but he did recommend copying Georgia's new anti–speculation law, an act which was never effectively enforced. The assembly took no action. On January 18, the governor ordered all state offices closed in mourning for the death of John Tyler, and a week later he briefly harassed Joseph Johnston, the commanding general in Virginia, about some missing state muskets. At the same time, he received a letter from an old political ally in the Valley who complained that the practice of ignoring prewar politics in making wartime appointments was alienating some Democrats. However, he added that the governor had gained in popularity since the beginning of the war.[13]

Routine business was suddenly eclipsed by a crisis which threatened to cost the South the services of General Thomas Jonathan Jackson. General Johnston had assigned Jackson to the Valley, and Jackson immediately initiated the rapid, daring maneuvers that were to become his trademark. Letcher fully supported his former neighbor and ignored all criticism of Jackson's strategy, including a complaint from his own brother serving under Jackson. He also dispatched several shipments of rifles and cannons.

Early in January, Jackson succeeded in pushing the Yankee forces out of the Valley. He then stationed the bulk of his 11,000-man army at Winchester, but left Brigadier General W. W. Loring's command at the western salient of Romney to serve as an advanced guard in case the federals attacked again. Loring and his officers felt dangerously exposed at this post, and they protested Jackson's strategy directly to Secretary of War Benjamin. On January 30, Benjamin ordered Jackson to pull Loring's troops back to Winchester. This was inexcusable civilian meddling in military affairs, but the Davis administration played this dangerous game frequently.

Jackson was infuriated. He obeyed the order, but he also sent his resignation to Benjamin on January 31. The same day he wrote to the governor, protesting Benjamin's interference and requesting recall to duty at V.M.I. Letcher sprang into action. He cornered Benjamin in the War Department and demanded to know the whole story. Benjamin's soothing pleasantries had no effect on the angry governor, and finally the secretary promised not to interfere with Jackson again. Somewhat pacified, Letcher turned to leave, but overheard one of Benjamin's aides mumble that Jackson was crazy. Letcher exploded. He administered a tongue lashing to the entire Confederate War Department and concluded by saying that if Jackson was crazy, he hoped some of his insanity would rub off on Mr. Benjamin and his bureaucrats.

After talking with his old friend J. L. T. Preston, a colonel on Jackson's staff, Letcher journeyed to Winchester to appeal directly to the general's state patriotism. General Johnston, ex-congressman Alexander R. Boteler, and others also urged Jackson to stay on duty. Jackson went into solitude, prayed for guidance, and on February 6, he agreed *not* to resign. Whereupon Letcher pressured the battered Benjamin to tear up the general's resignation. Davis had given Benjamin his full support, but they were

156 JOHN LETCHER OF VIRGINIA

both glad to end the squabble by rejecting Jackson's resignation. Nevertheless, they rebuked Jackson and Johnston, and transferred and promoted Loring. Thus Letcher and a few others redeemed the Davis administration's bungling, and Jackson stayed in the field, ready for his destiny.[14]

During this clash with the Confederates, Letcher tried to persuade the sluggish legislature to field more troops and organize more reserve forces. Having no organized block of supporters in the assembly, he lacked effective liaison with its most influential leaders. Publicly, the governor and the assembly seemed in harmony, but beneath the surface lay much friction, some of it going back to the prewar clash between the moderates and the radicals. Privately, Letcher expressed his dissatisfaction in a letter to another Rockbridge County friend, businessman William Weaver:

> The dilatory action of our Legislature, in providing troops to replace those now in the field, has given me great concern. A Bill should have been passed the first week of the session, but instead of this, we are in the last thirty days of the session, and nothing has yet been done. The people will not put up with this trifling much longer, and they ought not to do it. If the war is to be successfully conducted on our side, we must move with more expedition. In war times what ever is to be done, must be done promptly. Delays are ruinous, as I fear we may sooner or later ascertain to our cost. I hope however for the best.[15]

A few days later he repeated his complaint to General Smith: "The Legislature", he wrote,

> has done nothing yet towards raising the required number of troops to supply an army after the expiration of the terms of service of the volunteers now in the field. This is one of the bad signs of the times. It exhibits a criminal indifference, that cannot be too severely condemned. I have done all I could to stimulate them to action, but without effect.[16]

Letcher formally requested action on February 5, but the lawmakers seemed more interested in getting previously mobilized state militiamen released from active service and returned to normal inactive duty in their home counties. Finally, on February 8, the assembly ordered all white males from 18 to 45 years of age to enroll at least in their regular county militia group.

The governor attended a Confederate cabinet meeting on February 10 and agreed to keep pressuring the assembly to mobilize the state's manpower. On the same day the assembly granted the governor the power to draft militiamen to meet a locality's unfilled quota of volunteers. Only constant prodding by Letcher, coupled with the fall of Fort Henry on the Tennessee River and other Confederate defeats, coaxed the Virginia legislators into this forceful, virtually revolutionary preview of Confederate conscription in April. Letcher quickly pressed his advantage and suggested the formation in the cities of home guard units composed of all white males 16 to 18 and 45 to 60 years old. A few weeks later the assembly complied, lowering the maximum age to 55.[17]

At the behest of the secretary of war, Letcher again appealed to the legislature to field more state troops. On his own initiative, he also recommended the organization of an independent, state-controlled army of 10,000 men, a force to be recruited in addition to regular Confederate quotas. Though he tried not to pester the Confederates unduly, Letcher was worried about the defense of his state. A small Virginia army would, he said, insure the state against any defensive oversights by the central government. The assembly eventually authorized the Virginia State Line in May.[18]

Minor clashes with the Confederates continued, and rumors of spies, sabotage, slave insurrections, and other sinister conspiracies were rampant in Richmond. The wary governor watched carefully for any sign of trouble in the restless, overcrowded capital.

In the middle of February, the assembly directed Letcher to organize county exemption boards similar to the militia boards he had created in August. These new boards were far too lenient with their friends and neighbors, but Attorney General Tucker ordered them to tighten up their procedures.[19]

On February 22, the birthday of the father of the old Union, Governor Letcher attended the second formal inauguration of President Davis, a ceremony which officially marked the transition of the Confederate government from provisional to permanent status. Davis delayed appointing his cabinet for several weeks while he tried unsuccessfully to persuade the Senate to retain the unpopular Benjamin as secretary of war. At length, he placed

George W. Randolph in charge of the War Department and made Benjamin secretary of state. Briefly, the rebel government had drifted along without a cabinet, causing much uneasiness. During this period Letcher was concerned but for the sake of unity said nothing publicly. However, on March 3, he freely expressed his feelings to his friend General Smith:

> There seems to me to be a great want of judgment [,] energy, and practical wisdom in the management of our affairs. Loring's forces are withdrawn from Winchester, at the time they are most needed at that point, and this is followed by an order directing Tennessee troops to return to their own State. Then again [General Benjamin] Huger's command [at Norfolk] is weakened by ordering the remnant of [General Henry A.] Wise's Brigade to Manassas, and sending other portions of his command to North Carolina. I confess I do not understand such military movements as these. They may perhaps be all right, but if so, the people remain to be convinced of it.
>
> Our situation at this time is not pleasant, nor can I see that our prospects are encouraging. The lines seem to me to be drawing closer and closer, and I see none of the evidences of that energy, activity, and wisdom which is necessary to save us. Still we must bear the ills that are upon us, and fight it out. It is better to die than be subjugated. I hope never to survive the day, that Virginia is over run by these vandals.
>
> We have no cabinet as yet. The reason why, I do not understand. It is a subject of much street talk, but every body seems to be in the dark. If Benjamin and [Secretary of the Navy Stephen R.] Mallory are retained, we are a doomed people. The public sentiment of the country is against them, and the President ought to dismiss them without hesitation.[20]

By this time a desire to send guerrilla fighters into the federal-occupied northwest was spreading through the state. On March 27, the assembly authorized the governor to organize ten or more such units composed of refugees from the northwest. Bitter over the fate of that section and fearful for the exposed Valley, Letcher enthusiastically organized the guerrillas, euphemistically designated rangers. He issued commissions to agents and sent them behind the Union lines to recruit their companies, whereupon civilians and Confederate commanders in the west began to complain: the new rangers were actually robbers, plundering Unionists, Confederates, and neutrals with complete impartiality. What they lacked in patriotism they made up in aggressiveness. One group, the self–styled "Dixie Boys", specialized in stealing horses and cattle of every loyalty and soon became famous—or rather infamous—in the northwest.

On April 9, General Lee recommended disbanding the rangers, who were harassing the Confederates almost as much as the Yankees. Letcher consulted Attorney General Tucker, who declared that the governor lacked the authority to do so. Letcher hesitated until August, then assigned all of these bushwackers to the nascent Virginia State Line, the state's private little army. Despite much criticism, Letcher continued to support the concept of guerrilla warfare well into 1863.[21]

By March, routine problems were overshadowed by the ominous Union preparations for an offensive. Prodded by President Lincoln, the cautious McClellan finally set the powerful Army of the Potomac into motion, and Virginia braced for the coming holocaust. On March 1, Davis proclaimed martial law in the Richmond area and arrested John Minor Botts and some others suspected of disaffection. Letcher accepted this as a necessary emergency act, while protesting the harshness of General Benjamin Huger's martial law regime in Norfolk, which Davis and Lee soon modified.

On March 8, Benjamin requested 40,000 Virginia militiamen, and Letcher mobilized the entire state militia—everyone from 18 to 45, technically designated the first class of militia. He then declared that the mobilized militiamen could enlist in an already active field company if they wished. On March 12, he again granted Confederate generals authority to organize militia in their areas of command. The mobilization call was repeated almost a week later, and Letcher ordered vacancies in state volunteer companies in the field filled with newly activated militiamen and new units formed with the remaining militiamen.

The mobilization was confusing and not totally effective, particularly in the western areas where many took to the woods at the first sound of duty's call. All over the state others avoided service through numerous escape hatches in the militia laws. Some simply bought a substitute. Less affluent citizens obtained certificates of physical disability from certain doctors for modest fees of five and ten dollars. Letcher tried to plug some of the legal loopholes, and finally 30,000 Virginians were actually mustered. This was only 75 per cent of the state's quota, but, nevertheless, Letcher had cooperated fully, and the new troops were of great value to General Johnston as he prepared for the Union onslaught.[22]

Letcher's wholehearted cooperation with the central government brought more and more criticism from the people of Virginia. The legislature, which had been in continuous session since early December, reflected this growing hostility and even intensified it. The lawmakers began to examine some of the governor's policies, demanding all executive records on special problems, such as the endless disputes with the Confederates over their use of state property. Letcher's March mobilization was vigorously attacked in secret sessions of the assembly.

The governor responded to this rising, often bitter opposition by exercising his executive powers with more caution and restraint during the rest of his administration, and thus his efforts to cooperate with the Confederacy lost some of their vitality. Letcher still tried to lead his people along the path he had chosen, but his pace slackened somewhat. He could not ignore the will of the people or their representatives in the assembly. By April, the wary assembly had pressured the governor into an official proclamation that prolonged its life past the normal deadline.[23]

Certainly the times were not normal as McClellan's powerful army landed on the tip of the Peninsula and began its slow, ominous march toward Richmond. Letcher reacted vigorously. He offered the Confederates some old brass artillery for the city's defense, and he ordered all state volunteers who had finished their hitches to report back to their old units at once. He ruled that they were members of the state militia as soon as they finished their volunteer service and hence mobilized along with the rest of the militia.

The governor also alerted the home guard units, ordering them to prepare to serve under Confederate General Henry A. Wise.

Even though 100,000 Union troops were on the march less than 60 miles from Richmond, this order raised a storm of protest which, as usual, was spearheaded by the legislature. Technically, Letcher had exceeded his authority, since home guardsmen were legally required to serve only in the immediate environment of their city. After the customary conference with Attorney General Tucker, Letcher rescinded the order. After this rebuff, he refused to allow home guardsmen to come under Confederate control for more than a month unless they volunteered for four years of active duty—an unlikely prospect, to say the least. This time the harassed governor quickly retreated when challenged for ignoring the strict construction of a state law during an emergency.[24]

During this dangerous period, some emergency plans were formulated for the evacuation of Richmond if Johnston could not stop McClellan. The city's exposed position caused some to advocate moving further South even if the federal offensive was stopped. Letcher opposed evacuation for any reason, and he made it clear that he and the state militia would not desert their homeland. His firm stand was one factor in the Confederacy's decision to remain in Richmond.

As tension mounted, Letcher on May 6 made several recommendations to the assembly: remove all slaves from areas threatened by the federals, pay bounties to increase production of essential goods, restrict the speed of trains in order to reduce wear and tear on scarce equipment, be strict with exemptions, and champion an invasion of Maryland. Letcher also bitterly condemned the Confederates' failure to fortify the land and river approaches to Richmond adequately, and he requested state funds to do the job.

Five Union gunboats were on their way to test the capital's river defenses. The citizens of Richmond were excited and apprehensive, and Letcher nervously waited. He had little confidence in the obstructions placed in the river, and he thought that the only way to stop the onrushing armored monsters was to board and capture them before they could do too much damage. The showdown came on May 15, when the gunboats were repulsed by artillery at Drewry's Bluff, seven miles below Richmond.

Despite its failure, this naval attack lit a fuse under everyone. The legislature appropriated $200,000 for the defense of Richmond, and Letcher ordered the formation of a new city defense battalion composed of almost every white male not already mobilized in the home guard. The worker's battalion from the Tredegar Works was called out, and volunteers were sought to relieve penitentiary and bridge guards for combat service.

All state banks which had state funds on deposit had already evacuated the city, and Letcher deposited all public funds in an old iron safe in the treasury office even though some state offices had already moved to Lynchburg. The assembly granted the governor the power to impress materials and labor to stimulate the production of scarce lead and saltpeter and, as previously mentioned, authorized the Virginia State Line.[25]

The climax of Confederate preparations for the Yankee offensive came on April 16, when the Congress passed the first conscription act. Letcher thought this a big mistake as he favored a volunteer system with the state mobilizing or drafting militia to fill any gaps. He failed to appreciate the central government's overall manpower problems, and he probably did not realize that many states would not employ any kind of draft to supplement their volunteers. As a staunch states' righter, he considered the conscription act "the most alarming stride towards consolidation that has ever occurred". Letcher considered the new law unconstitutional, but, unlike many of his fellow southern legalists, he was willing to go along with it for the sake of unity. After victory, he would be the first to challenge it in the courts. This was his stand in a flurry of correspondence between the rebel governors, and his opinion doubtless encouraged some other governors to accept this revolutionary law. Once again the governor's common sense and flexibility, stimulated by the immediate Yankee threat, triumphed over his states' rights heritage. Once again he cooperated with the Confederacy at a crucial point in the war. He ordered state officials to enforce the conscription act, and only in the case of the V.M.I. cadets did he defy it. Conscription was never very effective in the South, for many states, particularly Georgia and

North Carolina, resisted it vigorously, and only a few followed Virginia's example of wholehearted cooperation.[26]

While administrative wheels turned slowly, two powerful armies maneuvered for a showdown near Richmond. On May 16, Letcher conformed with Davis' call for a day of prayer for victory by closing all state offices. Richmond waited uneasily for the battle that would decide its fate, and on the eve of combat, May 30, Letcher visited Johnston's army. Only two days after the savage but indecisive battle of Seven Pines, the governor was demanding the return of two horses commandeered by the Confederate forces. He also presented his kinsman J. E. B. Stuart a sword for his daring ride around McClellan's army. More important, he permitted local state officials—jailers, constables, and sheriffs—to assist the Confederates in their usual roundup of stragglers and deserters. General Lee replaced the wounded Johnston, regrouped his army, and attacked on June 25. After seven days of bloody battle, McClellan was driven back to his fleet, and Richmond was saved.[27]

Letcher frequently visited the army during its fight to defend Richmond, but at the height of the Seven Days' Battle he was briefly angered by Confederate actions in western Virginia. General Harry Heth made an independent troop call which expressly nullified all exemptions granted by county exemption boards. On June 27, Letcher mildly protested to the new secretary of war, George W. Randolph. The troop call was quickly revoked, and Heth was transferred to Chattanooga. The governor was further irritated when he discovered that some of the gun–stock machinery from the Harper's Ferry loot had been removed from Richmond for safekeeping. Since the contract transferring this machinery had recognized the Confederacy's right to remove the machinery if it was in danger, Letcher had no legal grounds for complaint, and he contented himself with a few routine protests.[28]

While the blue and gray armies were still locked in combat near Richmond, Letcher issued a proclamation calling for recruits for the new Virginia State Line. He had recommended this state force to the assembly in February, but the lawmakers did not act until May. This delay was only one instance of the continuing struggle for dominance between the executive and legislative branches of the state government. The assembly had become so hostile to Letcher that it did not even consult him about the proposed Line. Instead, the legislators held several lengthy discussions with Davis before finally authorizing it. Recruits for the Line had to be ineligible for Confederate conscription, and Letcher directed his recruiting effort primarily toward loyal Virginians in federal—controlled areas of the state.

From the beginning, volunteers for the Line were scarce. In August, Letcher tried to increase the manpower of the Line with militia calls in the southwest, but these calls bore little fruit. Inflation and greedy merchants pushed the price of supplies so high that the Line could not afford adequate clothing and equipment. Inevitably, Confederate and Line officers clashed over these scarce supplies, recruits, strategy, and countless other details. By late September, even the Line's commander, John B. Floyd, saw the hopelessness of the situation and advised Letcher to transfer the Line to Confederate service. The governor, absorbed in technical details of the operation of the Line, postponed any broad policy decision. Once again he was acting more like a chief clerk than a chief executive.

In September, the Confederate government raised the maximum draft age to 45. The Line still took men over the old limit of 35, but Letcher continued to recruit primarily in federal—controlled areas with the permission of Confederate authorities. Other southern states did not always notice the details, and they watched with interest as Letcher seemingly attempted to recruit some draft-eligible men into an independent state army. This was a dangerous example to set in a nascent nation which desperately needed central planning and coordination.

The main mission of Floyd's little army was to protect vital salt works in the southwestern tip of the state, but its history was short and inglorious. At its peak the Line never numbered over 3,600 men, and it drained more than $1,300,000 from the state treasury. Its military contribution to the Confederate cause was negligible. The Virginia State Line was another example of the insanity of divided effort in modern war, but Letcher stubbornly refused to disband it. Floyd complained several times that the governor's meddling was handicapping operations. Finally the assembly abolished the Line in February, 1863, despite accurate warnings from Letcher that the disbanded troops of the Line would disappear with all of their valuable equipment before the Confederate army could absorb them.[29]

The frenzied pace of May and June had taken its toll on the governor. He was exhausted and again plagued by a series of brief illnesses. Fearing one of the serious sicknesses which so often hit at crucial moments, Letcher went to Lexington early in July for a week of "lime stone water and relaxation". In his absence, the executive department was run by his two most trusted assistants, Munford and French.

Letcher had another motive for his visit to the Valley. He wanted to test the political winds, having decided to run for the Confederate Congress in 1863 if his prospects looked favorable. The visit was generally encouraging. His efforts to prod the people into cooperation with the Confederates and a more vigorous war effort had alienated some, but he still seemed popular with the majority. Both his health and his ambition had been revitalized by the time he returned to Richmond.[30]

Almost at once the reinvigorated governor proposed a new and dangerous state policy. On July 28, he asked Secretary of War Randolph to turn over to Virginia authorities some prisoners of war from the northwestern section of the state. He wanted state courts to try these prisoners for treason! He also requested that several captured federal officers be turned over to the state to stand trial for inciting slave revolts.

The Confederate authorities were highly reluctant to comply with his requests. As early as May, Letcher had urged retaliation if any state ranger officers captured while recruiting behind federal lines were hanged. His new proposals went much further. Trying captured soldiers for offenses that carried the death penalty in Virginia law would surely bring retaliation from an enraged Union, which could interpret a "rebel" to be a "traitor" too. Carried to their illogical conclusion, Letcher's proposals meant raising the black flag of no quarter over the fields of Virginia.

The Confederates quickly decided that captured Union troops organized by Francis H. Pierpoint's puppet government in northwestern Virginia would not be handed over to state courts for treason trials. Letcher accepted this verdict, but he continued to request that a few Union officers be handed over to Virginia justice for inciting slave insurrections. Davis had recently denounced some Union officers as "murderers and robbers", and thus he was not in a good position to refute Letcher's charges of criminal conduct. Davis stalled. On September 11, Secretary of War Randolph told Letcher that specific charges against specific offenders would be necessary. Gradually and gently Letcher's proposal was rejected. Finally, only one man, a Virginia civilian who had helped invading Yankees, was handed over to state justice. Letcher's fantastically strict interpretation of two state laws was vetoed by cooler Confederate heads, and a terrible Pandora's box remained sealed.[31]

By August the Peninsula campaign had ended in a southern victory, and federal military pressure in other areas of the state had eased. Letcher had contributed to military success by continuing to support the Confederates. Rising opposition in Virginia to any infringement on traditional rights and privileges had forced him to act with a little more caution, but his cooperation had still been vigorous enough to be significant, and perhaps even decisive.

CHAPTER 10

The Acid Test

For the next half year Letcher worked ceaselessly to fulfill his responsibilities, which became more complex as the war unleashed its full destructive power on the state. New problems evolved, and past experiences furnished no guide. Indeed, custom and tradition were positive handicaps which the governor would have to abandon if he was to lead effectively.

Routine business claimed much of Letcher's time in the latter part of 1862. By August, requests for military discharges were as numerous as exemption petitions had been earlier in the year. Hiring out black convicts to the Tredegar factory involved much bookwork and frequent disputes over wages. The plight of the northwest still distracted the governor, and he always kept Davis informed of the latest facts and rumors about the area. Despite the press of business, Letcher loaned General Jackson his most trusted aide, S. Bassett French, at the end of August.[1]

Inflation continued to surge ahead, and neither the state nor Confederate governments took effective action. On August 16, Auditor J. M. Bennett warned Letcher that the state treasury was all but empty, and Letcher ordered the issuance of more treasury notes—hardly a measure likely to stabilize the currency. Letcher's own fixed income continued to shrink in the inflationary spiral. His only real help came from friends in Rockbridge County, who periodically sent him large amounts of food. He paid for all of it, but Rockbridge prices were far lower than Richmond prices, and he achieved a real, almost essential saving.[2]

The inept, quarrelsome Confederate Congress did nothing to bolster the southern economy. Letcher had never hesitated to criticize the federal Congress in the 1850's, and he was even less hesitant to condemn the southern Congress. As usual, his strongest attacks were delivered in private letters to friends. "Congress is in session", he wrote Weaver late in August, "but I am sorry to say, there is but little harmony and unity of action. The whole time so far has been spent in wrangling, not very creditable either to their intellects or their patriotism. So far they have done nothing practicable or valuable".[3]

On the other hand, when Congress did discuss forceful action, Letcher's states' rights instincts were likely to be offended. In September, he confided his concern to General Smith. "It is amazing", he wrote,

> that those who commenced a war for the maintenance of State Rights should so soon have become forgetful of the doctrine. It is now contended in Congress by some of the Cotton State men, that the Confederate government, has the power to conscript all the civil officers of the States, from the Governor down. Strange as this may sound in your ears, it is yet gravely and vehemently insisted upon. If such a doctrine were carried into practice, the State governments would be destroyed, and all State lines obliterated. We should be reduced to a military despotism, and so far as State Rights were concerned, we would be worse off than before the Revolution began —bad as that was.[4]

By the end of August, battlefield reports dominated the news. Lee's Army of Northern Virginia and the Army of the Potomac, now under the inept John Pope, were maneuvering for another trial of strength. On August 27, there were rumors of another great rebel victory with Jackson and Stuart surrounding the federals and Lee preparing to finish them. In a few days the triumph of Second Manassas was being hailed in Richmond. More rumors clouded the details, but the Union army was clearly in headlong retreat. On September 2, Davis wrote Letcher confirming the victory and emphasizing "the brighter prospects for our cause".[5]

Even this brilliant victory could not obscure another major

problem, the shortage of salt. The blockade had cut off outside supplies, and federal troops had occupied some salt–producing areas. The vital salt works in southwestern Virginia were still intact but very vulnerable. Galloping inflation accentuated the shortage among the masses, and the situation became critical as the time for salting meat approached. Early in August the governor visited the salt works in the southwest, and on August 19 he called a special session of the assembly which had adjourned in May.

The legislators reconvened on September 15 and, after hearing the governor suggest that the state build its own salt works, they passed a law on October 1 which made Letcher a virtual salt czar in Virginia. He was empowered to do anything necessary and proper to secure possession, production, and distribution of sufficient salt for the state. He could impress any property necessary for salt production, and could take control of any railroad or canal to ship needed salt so long as he did not interfere with Confederate army shipments. He could also set the price of salt.

Earlier, in May, Letcher had been granted extraordinary powers to stimulate the production of lead and saltpeter, but he had not used these powers extensively. Now, as salt czar, he again hesitated to use his broad powers, despite the emergency. A lifelong democrat, he could not bring himself to exercise dictatorial powers, regardless of the justification. Previous attacks on his strong executive leadership had increased his natural caution and conservatism, and he would not act decisively.

As early as June, he had toyed with the idea of seizing uncooperative salt works, but now that he had the authority he continued to hesitate. On October 10, he issued a proclamation outlining his salt policy. Out-of-state contracts would be voided if Virginia did not receive enough salt. Uncooperative works would be seized by the state, and salt shipments would have top civilian priority. A small army of state salt agents would supervise the purchase and distribution of salt in Virginia, and a ceiling price would be set. The courts were to have no jurisdiction over any of these actions.

Letcher, Judge William W. Crump, and George W. Munford

took a train to the southwest to implement the program. Using the train as a moving office and hotel, the governor struggled with his toughest executive problem. Late in October, Munford wrote his wife of Letcher's fight with the greedy salt producers:

> . . . the Governor is as firm as a rock and hard to be moved when he puts his foot down. He has . . . Back Bone. If the salt dealers don't come to terms pretty soon he will seize the whole concern and work the operations for the State.[6]

Letcher negotiated at length with the producers, seeking in vain to establish a fair price ceiling. Soon after the negotiations began, Letcher asked Attorney General Tucker if, as governor, he had the power to impress salt. Tucker answered affirmatively, but Letcher once again failed to act decisively. Before the month ended he did succeed in contracting for 500,000 bushels of salt at the reasonable price of $2.33 per bushel, but this was only a fraction of the state's needs. The shortage was still critical.

The governor's reluctance to use his full powers in this emergency doomed the whole program to certain, if gradual, failure. The elaborate state bureaucracy created to carry out the salt program was hopelessly enmeshed in its own red tape. Even if it had been efficient, it would have had little chance to succeed under Letcher's weak leadership. Having failed to compel the producers to co—operate, Letcher buried himself in the technical problems and routine paperwork of this new state agency. Once again the chief executive became the chief clerk.

The price of salt continued to rise. Letters of protest poured into the governor's office. The people were not interested in the legal principles or the administrative procedures involved in the salt program. They wanted salt, enough for their basic needs at a price they could afford to pay.[7]

Despite the public outcry, Letcher did not change his conservative policy. The threat of impressment was used effectively in December to squeeze some 2,000 bushels of salt out of the producers at $2.75 per bushel, but this was a special requisition for the Virginia State Line. Even in this case, Letcher timidly asked the attorney general to verify once again his power to impress.

Generally, the governor continued to avoid the forceful action necessary to make the program work effectively.

The stumbling program was further hampered by inadequate and poorly administered transportation by rail and wagon. Even Letcher's first large purchase of salt in October was largely wasted, owing to difficulties of distribution. Union military offenses also hurt the program, and by the end of the year Saltville was the only major salt–producing area still operating in the state.

The timid salt czar faced another touchy problem. Other Confederate states had contracts with salt works in Virginia. In his proclamation of October 10, Letcher had reserved the right to void out–of–state contracts if the shortage of salt became critical in Virginia. When transportation mixups and bureaucratic red tape delayed some salt shipments to other rebel states, a storm of protest arose. Howell Cobb reminded his friend Letcher that Georgians were defending Virginia and that some Georgians had invested operating capital in several Virginia salt works. He appealed to Letcher's sense of justice not to restrict shipments to Georgia. Governor Brown of Georgia also inquired about Virginia's new salt regulations, and Governor Zebulon Vance of North Carolina bitterly complained of delays in salt shipments to his state.

Letcher was irritated, for he prided himself on his cooperation with other southern states. Convinced of the necessity of Confederate unity, he promised to honor out-of-state contracts. This doubtless helped rebel unity, but it did nothing to alleviate the salt shortage in Virginia. The governor also honored all previous contracts between the salt producers and counties and cities in the state. This not only put further limits on the amount of salt available to the central state agency, but also complicated the administration of the new system.

Gradually the state's salt program came to a near standstill. The governor hesitated to impress needed salt at reasonable prices, and he refused to seize any uncooperative production facilities. In addition, the whole cumbersome system was poorly administered, tangled in reams of red tape. Inefficient administration invited corruption and favoritism, and some state officials received salt outside the regular channels of distribution. Early in 1863 the assembly finally intervened. It authorized the seizure of some salt works by the state, transferred most of the salt czar's duties to the Board of Public Works, and appointed a Superintendent of the Salt Works under the board with a salary equal to the governor's. Letcher retained the power to mobilize militia for impressment duties.

The superintendent and the board proved no more efficient than the governor, and the salt program continued to founder. It took the board over three months to impress any works, and the distribution system remained inefficient. Whatever new vitality the board brought to the problem was diluted by Letcher's continued opposition to impressment. Several times he stymied the board's efforts to impress by refusing to call out the necessary militia. Letcher's failure to remedy the salt shortage in Virginia was only a part of his and the Confederacy's larger failure to halt the inflation which ravaged the entire South.[8]

Letcher's home front difficulties were overshadowed by military events in September, 1862. He had been calling for an invasion of the North for months. Now his wish was fulfilled as Lee's army marched confidently into Maryland. Letcher cooperated with Confederate efforts to reap a harvest of deserters and potential conscripts in the liberated areas of Virginia by ordering all state military and police forces in these sections to help enforce the Confederate conscription act.

By the middle of the month a battle was pending near Antietam Creek. Rumors of victory began racing through Richmond. Letcher had visited the army frequently, and had complete confidence in Lee and his troops. When President Davis proclaimed a victory celebration on September 18, Letcher quickly closed all state offices for the day. A week later he discussed the battle in a letter to General Smith. "General Lee's campaign has been a most brilliant one", he wrote,

and has completely silenced the slanders, and croakings of his enemies. He has proved himself as I always believed he would do, the great military man of the age, and has shown, that he was better able to lead our noble army in the field, than any man we have.

God grant that the same success may attend him hereafter, and that each day may add something to his high and well deserved reputation. I feel perfectly satisfied, that all will work out right, so long as he has charge of the army.[9]

Throughout the South, Antietam was hailed as another glorious Confederate victory. Actually it was a defeat. Lee's invasion had been repulsed, the chances for foreign intervention were greatly reduced, and the way was cleared for President Lincoln's powerful Emancipation Proclamation. Antietam was the beginning of the end for the Confederacy.

News from Maryland did not reduce minor but constant friction between the state and central governments over a few Virginia officers who were demoted when they transferred to Confederate service. As usual, Dimmock made matters worse. Recently promoted to general of Virginia ordnance, he harassed the Confederates even more than usual. During the Maryland campaign, the Confederates became so exasperated with Dimmock that they placed him under arrest. Letcher sent a routine protest to Secretary of War Randolph, and Dimmock was released with apologies. The new general immediately returned to his fanatic defense of Virginia's real and imagined rights.[10]

On September 27, opposition to Letcher's earlier militia calls flared up again. Echoing grass roots sentiments, the House of Delegates demanded to know the governor's authority for the August 30 muster—one of the calls he had issued in the southwest to bolster the Virginia State Line. Letcher presented the house a legal and practical justification which left little room for argument; nevertheless, the delegates' warning was clear. Letcher continued to move cautiously while at the same time trying to cooperate fully with the Confederates. This was a virtually impossible bit of political juggling which antagonized many Virginians and left the Confederates unsatisfied as well.[11]

Letcher's position was rendered even more difficult in October, when the assembly authorized him to requisition slave labor for work on fortifications when President Davis requested such aid. Once again Letcher had to do the dirty, but essential, work, and the hostile assembly, which had granted him the authority to act, could sit back and criticize him. As usual, however, Letcher was willing to risk his political popularity for the cause.

On October 11, he was given his first chance. Three weeks after the heralded "victory" at Antietam, Davis requested 4,500 slaves to build fortifications around Richmond. Letcher acted at once to fill the requisition. The most difficult task was to apportion the slave draft fairly among the affected counties, and Letcher relied on the Confederate corps of engineers to calculate all quotas. This first slave draft—an obvious violation of traditional property rights—was bitterly resented by many planters. Resistance developed quickly, and by late November only 2,757 slaves had been furnished by the 14 designated counties.[12]

This same basic pattern of resistance continued in future requisitions. The presiding justice of a county often frustrated a draft by insisting that the law be carried out to the letter. This often involved so much red tape that the requisition was effectively blocked. Sometimes a county or city flatly refused to cooperate. In these cases the governor threatened impressment, but, as in the salt program, he was almost always bluffing. His own conservative credo and incessant harassment and criticism kept him from using his ultimate powers. The slave requisition system was not the complete failure in Virginia that it was in Florida and the Carolinas, but it filled on the average only a little over a half of each quota.

In the following months, Davis requested thousands of slaves, and Letcher always issued the necessary requisitions. Each slave mobilization lasted only 60 days, so periodic calls were necessary to keep the slave labor force intact. Davis had complete confidence in Letcher's efforts. He accepted the governor's suggestions about reducing quotas in some counties, and he even abandoned one call when Letcher said no slaves were available.[13]

Resistance grew with each new draft, and some complaints were justified. Inevitably, some counties were hit much harder than others. The same sort of inequity occurred within counties, with some planters repeatedly being required to furnish slaves and others bearing little or none of the burden. Some drafted slaves were overworked or underfed, and others ran away or were captured by federal forces. Occasionally skilled slave laborers were snatched from their essential industrial jobs and forced to dig trenches. Such mistakes were inevitable in the general confusion, but they greatly stimulated popular resistance to the entire program.[14]

As usual, the General Assembly became the focal point of dissatisfaction, and the legislators were quick to lash out at Letcher. The governor was not immune to such pressure, and by September, 1863, his efforts to fill draft quotas had slackened. At that time the city of Richmond flatly refused to meet its quota of 300 slaves. Letcher threatened impressment to no avail. He then threatened to seize all of the slaves of the members of the Hustings Court, but again he was ignored. The Confederates encouraged Letcher to use force, but he still hesitated. By the end of October, nothing had been done and the city had successfully defied the state. Just as in the salt program, Letcher failed to use his powers to the hilt in an emergency.[15]

Despite the rising criticism, Letcher received many compliments on his efforts. Late in 1862, Matthew Fontaine Maury, his former adviser, wrote from Charleston, South Carolina, and complimented him on his administration. Maury said that the very Carolinians who had once cursed him for opposing secession were now praising his wartime administration. Roger Pryor, another opponent of Letcher's prewar moderation, also hailed the governor for his wartime leadership. On October 26, the birth of a healthy girl, Virginia Lee Letcher, further cheered the governor, and he was even more delighted when General Lee became the child's godfather.[16]

By this time the governor was receiving many complaints about unfair prices paid for goods impressed by the Confederate army. On October 27, a Valley miller complained that he had received only eight dollars per barrel for impressed flour. Letcher immediately filed a formal complaint with Secretary of War Randolph. He felt that a price of eight dollars a barrel in the Valley was inadequate when flour was selling in Richmond for twenty dollars a barrel. He wanted to fight inflation, to be sure, but not solely at the expense of the farmers and millers of the Valley.

Letcher believed that improvement of the state's transportation facilities would cure inflation without recourse to price regulation. Once essential goods could be transported to market easily and cheaply, he thought, the law of supply and demand would keep prices down. By stressing inadequate transportation facilities, Letcher pinpointed one of the key weaknesses of the Confederacy. He knew that there was no real shortage of food in the agrarian South. But his belief that inflation in the Confederacy was caused solely by inadequate distribution was a naive oversimplification of the problem. This conservative faith in the viability of laissez-faire economics during a period of total war was shared by many southerners, who did not realize that all America had entered a new economic age.[17]

An endless stream of requests and petitions poured into the governor's office. Farmers wanted help in getting their crops to market. Some areas wanted greater security against slave revolts, but Danville wanted greater security from undisciplined Confederate troops, who were ignoring the authorities and threatening to tear down the town jail. Other citizens demanded more salt, or the discharge of an essential worker from the army, or less impressment and regulation, or as trivial a thing as a letter of introduction. Every day brought something new by way of a request or demand.

The governor's old friends were quick to seek favors, and Letcher seldom disappointed them. "Sandy" Stuart successfully petitioned Letcher to allow his brother to make some whiskey for treatment of the insane at the Staunton asylum; a mild prohibition had been instituted to conserve vital grain supplies, and the governor's consent was necessary to manufacture this fiery medicine. Robert Taylor, Letcher's lifelong friend from Lexington, requested a transfer from Fredericksburg medical service to the Confederate hospital in his home town, and Letcher immediately got Secretary of War Seddon to issue the necessary orders.[18]

In mid–November, the governor once again appealed to the people of Virginia to furnish clothing to their troops for the winter season. Shoes and underclothes were particularly scarce among the troops. The state treasury was beginning to discover large numbers of forged checks, but Letcher left this problem in the capable hands of Auditor Bennett. On December 4, the eve of Lee's victory at Fredericksburg, Letcher exhorted all Virginians to cooperate with the Confederates. Specifically, he asked them to help round up deserters, requisition slave labor, conscript troops, gather supplies, and fight extortion. Always concerned about Richmond's defenses, the governor fruitlessly urged the Confederates to arm all industrial workers in the capital. He wanted every plant in Richmond to copy Tredegar's workers' battalion.[19]

Letcher had no doubt that Lee's army could stop the invading Union forces. Late in November, he expressed his confidence to his friend Weaver:

> Tomorrow I expect to visit General Lee's army at Fredericksburg, and spend a day or two with them. I do not suppose that I can be of service to them, otherwise, than by showing that I feel an interest in the cause, and in them personally. I go to give them my countenance, and to assure them that I feel interested for them in this hour of threatened attack, by our enemies. . . . We have had cloudy, cool and disagreeable weather for some days, and the prospect is now that it will continue sometime longer. It is hard upon our soldiers, but they do not appear to mind it. A Regiment arrived here this evening on the way to Fredericksburg, and they were singing as merrily as crickets. Such an army as we have never before entered the field. They submit cheerfully to every privation without a murmur, and perform all their duties with a cheerfulness and promptitude, never surpassed. Such an army cannot be whipped, and the people they represent can never be subjugated.[20]

Letcher's confidence in the army did not blind him to harsh reality in foreign affairs. "The indications from abroad", he confided to Weaver,

> show no signs of interference on the part of European nations, to put an end to the war, either by recognizing us as an independent nation, or in any other way. We must therefore rely upon ourselves and fight it out. We will be in the end successful, but the struggle may be protracted for months—perhaps years.[21]

After the overwhelming victory at Fredericksburg on December 13, politics and elections were again main topics of discussion. The strategy and speculation were reminiscent of the prewar political battles, and once again Letcher's name was frequently mentioned. The governor did not conceal his ambition to step into the Confederate House of Representatives when he completed his current term of office. Some politicians unfamiliar with Letcher's habitual frankness thought he was really angling for the Confederate Senate, but everyone knew that he was just as ambitious as ever, quite unwilling to retire from politics.[22]

Letcher's address to the newly convened General Assembly early in January could not avoid political overtones, but it was primarily a direct, factual report by Virginia's wartime governor. He proudly reviewed the South's military achievements. He declared that the division of the Union was permanent, but he quickly added that the current division of Virginia was only temporary. He stated that Virginia could never assent to the existence of the illegally created state of West Virginia, and that this area had to be returned to the Old Dominion. As usual, Letcher called for southern unity and a postponement of all internal disputes for the duration of the war.

The governor condemned Yankee vandalism, an element of modern war he would soon experience personally. He defended his earlier proposal to treat federal troops who violated state laws as criminals rather than prisoners of war, but he did not dwell on this sensitive issue. He examined the state's financial condition in great detail, estimating that the war had cost Virginia over $7,000,000. He predicted that expenses for the fiscal year ending on September 1, 1863, would reach the staggering total of $17,691,763.49! Letcher also discussed at length the difficulties of having been a salt czar.

He recommended a few changes in the state's slave impressment law, and most of his suggestions were incorporated into law in March. He also attacked speculators and extortioners. Warming to his subject, he equated speculators with drunkards, adulterers, fornicators and other undesirable but less colorful personages. He repeated President Davis' appeal to the states to suppress speculation, and he movingly described the effect of this economic blight on the families of soldiers in the field. As ever, his proposed remedies were vague, but he did recommend increasing taxes to deprive manufacturers of excessive wartime profits. Letcher concluded his address with a passing reference to the Zarvona affair.[23]

This affair had been brewing ever since the early days of the war. Richard Thomas was a Marylander, a graduate of West Point, and a southern undercover agent with the code name of Zarvona. Soon after the war started, Zarvona volunteered his services to Virginia, and Letcher authorized him to raise a regiment. In the middle of June, 1861, Captain George N. Hollins of the Confederate navy suggested a daring plan for capturing the steamship *St. Nicholas* and then surprising and seizing the mighty warship *Pawnee*. Secretary of the Navy Mallory was uninterested, but he gave Hollins permission to talk to Letcher. The governor approved of the plan, and furnished $1,000 in state funds, together with the adventurous Zarvona, to help carry it out.

Zarvona went to Baltimore to purchase weapons and prepare for this daring coup. Soon Hollins and some two dozen accomplices, including a son of Matthew Fontaine Maury, joined him. On June 28, Zarvona, disguised as a woman, and his accomplices, disguised as mechanics, boarded the *St. Nicholas* as it was leaving on a routine run to Washington. In mid–voyage, the conspirators threw off their disguises and captured the vessel. Most of the passengers were southern sympathizers, and it was not difficult to subdue the surprised crew.

The rebel–controlled *St. Nicholas* was unable to locate the *Pawnee,* which had been warned of danger, so she headed for Virginia. Along the way she stopped three times to capture small Yankee vessels, and all four vessels reached Virginia safely. The *St. Nicholas* was eventually converted into a Confederate gunboat.

Hollins and his men returned to the Confederate navy, and Zarvona reported to Letcher in Richmond. The governor was delighted with his success and nominated him for a colonelcy in the Virginia volunteers. The convention approved the nomination. Letcher then approved a repeat performance by the reckless Marylander.

Early in July, Zarvona returned to Baltimore. On July 8, he donned his female costume again and boarded the steamship *Mary Washington* with several disguised accomplices. This time, however, the federal authorities were ready, and Zarvona and his men were quickly captured. The authorities imprisoned Zarvona at Fort McHenry while they debated his fate. He was treated as a pirate, but Letcher warned the prison officials that instant and equal retaliation would follow Zarvona's hanging. The treatment of the prisoner temporarily improved.

Before the end of the year, Zarvona was transferred to the more secure Fort Lafayette in New York harbor. After an unsuccessful and near fatal attempt to escape, he was placed in solitary confinement for three months. By 1862, his health and morale were shattered. Federal authorities ignored his protests, and his appeals to Letcher and the Confederates seemed no more successful. He was no closer to a formal trial than on the day of his capture. He began to lose touch with reality, and his jailers treated him as a sick, harmless eccentric, more to be pitied than punished.

Letcher had not abandoned Zarvona, but his efforts to prod the Confederate War Department into action were fruitless. By the fall of 1862, Letcher was receiving complaints of similar federal treatment of Virginia civilians, but his protests still brought no response from the Confederates. Disgusted, he decided to take independent action, and on December 29 he ordered that two Union officers and five enlisted men captured by the State Line be placed in solitary confinement in the state penitentiary in retaliation for the treatment of Zarvona. At the same time he ordered two federal officers from northwestern Virginia imprisoned in retaliation for another similar incident.

This last incident involved two Virginia officers who had organized an irregular band, a guerrilla company, in Jackson County under the authority of Letcher's proclamation on June 14 exhorting the people of the northwest to remain loyal to the Old Dominion. These two officers, Captain Daniel Dusky and Lieutenant Jacob Vanner, had raided the town of Ripley and rifled the mails, seeking information about federal troop movements. A superior federal force had trapped their little band in Ripley and forced them to surrender. Dusky and Vanner were taken to Wheeling, convicted of robbing the mails, and sentenced to four years in the Washington penitentiary.

The general question of treatment of partisan raiders enlivened the Dusky–Vanner case. Although the federals soon accepted these captured raiders as prisoners of war, Dusky and Vanner remained in the penitentiary. As in the Zarvona affair, Letcher's appeals for action by the Confederates were fruitless. By September, 1862, Letcher was so angry and frustrated that he suggested to Secretary of War Randolph that two captive federal officers from northwestern Virginia be executed if Dusky and Vanner were not released. This irrational proposal was ignored by the Confederates. Finally, in December, Letcher imprisoned two other officers captured by the State Line.

Despairing of any assistance from the Confederates, Letcher wrote directly to President Lincoln on January 2. After a few paragraphs devoted to recent history, Virginia style, Letcher came to the point—the fate of Zarvona, Dusky, and Vanner. He briefly reviewed their wartime misadventures and strongly protested their treatment as criminals instead of as legitimate prisoners of war. He outlined in detail the retaliatory measures he had ordered, warning that this retaliation would only end with the release or exchange of the three captives.

On January 7, Judge Crump delivered Letcher's letter to Fort Monroe under a flag of truce. Lincoln never answered the letter, which was published in many southern newspapers, but within a few months the three Virginia captives were released. Zarvona, back in Virginia by May, was broken in body and spirit. Letcher gave him $4,290 in back pay, and the once dashing colonel disappeared into obscurity. Dusky and Vanner were in Richmond late in June, and Letcher gave Dusky $100 so he could return to his home. All of the federal hostages were exchanged as soon as their Confederate counterparts returned to the Old Dominion. Except for Zarvona, none of the various prisoners was much the worse for wear at the time of the exchange.[24]

Meanwhile the war continued. On January 7, Secretary of War Seddon asked Letcher to call out the remaining militia in the counties near the Carolina border. The Carolina coast was vulnerable, and Letcher and the Confederates feared that a strong amphibious attack upon Wilmington might succeed. Not only would the South lose another strategic seaport, but a vital north–south railroad link would be severed. As usual, Letcher cooperated and called out the militia in 14 southside counties and the cities of Petersburg and Lynchburg. By this time Confederate conscription was taking able–bodied men up to 45 years of age, gradually whittling away militia strength. At Seddon's suggestion, the militia call was limited to the 40–to–45–year–old bracket. The response to the call was meager, and by March only 80 militiamen were available—though far from ready—for combat. Fortunately, they were not needed. Union attacks on Wilmington did not begin until December and did not succeed until early in 1865.[25]

From August, 1862, through the first weeks of 1863, Governor Letcher wrestled with many problems, some relatively familiar and some brand new. He continued to cooperate with the Confederates, but his traditional respect for individual and property rights and popular opinion accelerated an executive caution which had begun to develop in the earlier phases of his wartime administration. He hesitated to use his powers to the hilt in the face of rising opposition. This resistance was centered in the General Assembly, which was determined to gain power at the expense of the executive branch of the state government.

Letcher's brief career as salt czar illustrated his growing caution, and it also demonstrated his tendency to bog down in administrative red tape, a weakness common to many of his generation. Neither he nor the Confederate leaders had the practical experience or the political flexibility necessary to control the inflation that was rampaging through the South.

Yet despite his growing timidity, Letcher was still a forceful leader on many occasions, far more forceful than many other Confederate governors. Despite increasing dissatisfaction among the people, he was able to carry through, at least partially, many essential programs. His successes outnumbered his failures, and old Virginia held firm in the Confederate ranks as some other southern states began to waver.

CHAPTER 11

Denouement

The final year of Letcher's wartime administration was ushered in by the Emancipation Proclamation, an edict that increased the bitterness on both sides. Letcher continued to co-operate with the Confederates in their efforts to smash Yankee assaults against both the Confederacy and the very fabric of southern civilization. His main opposition continued to come from an unfriendly, jealous General Assembly, which reflected the growing dissatisfaction among the people of Virginia. Despite unending harassment and criticism, the governor stuck to his post.

In mid-January, Letcher was enraged to learn of Union General R. H. Milroy's "Freedom to the Slaves" proclamation, a local echo of Lincoln's sweeping, revolutionary edict. His old desire to punish Union officers for inciting slave insurrections was rekindled, and he immediately addressed the assembly, denouncing Lincoln and Milroy and reminding the legislators that President Davis had promised to hand over to the state any captured federal officers who had tried to enforce the Emancipation Proclamation. Letcher suggested streamlining this procedure by amending state law to allow any circuit court to try such offenders swiftly. Letcher's suggestion was merely a reflection of the bitter reaction that swept through the Confederacy. The South's most sensitive nerve had been prodded, and a tremor of anger and fear shook the land. War was altering the very fabric of southern society, and the people were helpless and frustrated in the face of events beyond their control or comprehension.[1]

A few days later, Letcher was attacked from a new direction in Richmond. Confederate Congressman Reuben Davis of Mississippi accused him of having obstructed the business of Congress by placing a heavy guard around the Capitol and preventing clerks from entering the building late at night. Letcher defended himself in a detailed letter to the speaker of the house, Thomas S. Bocock, a fellow Virginia congressman in the 1850's. Letcher reminded the speaker that the state had willingly allowed the Confederate legislature to use the Capitol, had spent over $6,000 in alterations and improvements, and was supplying gas, wood, and coal free of charge. He stated that he had made no public protest when the Confederates had charged additional repairs to the state without even asking the governor's permission. He explained that a guard was posted to protect irreplaceable state records and that clerks could come and go freely until 11 o'clock in the evening.

Congressman Davis' complaint was just one more discordant note from the vocal but inept Confederate Congress. Actually, Letcher had leaned over backwards to be helpful. His refusal to authorize the addition of a clumsy portico to Mr. Jefferson's Capitol had irritated a few rebel politicos, but generally he had done everything possible to facilitate their work. His reward was Congressman Davis' criticism.[2]

Later in the month, Letcher repeatedly warned the assembly of the dilapidated condition of the state's rail network. He suggested that slaves working on the railroads or in salt, lead, saltpeter, or iron production be more fully protected from Confederate slave requisitions. He also condemned unwarranted seizures of state railroad iron by the Confederates. Quartermaster General Abraham C. Myers had taken a large amount of iron earmarked for Virginia's railroads and used it in the construction of a line connecting Greensboro and Danville. This short line, which was not completed until the spring of 1864, was vital for the rebel war effort, but Letcher, who saw only his own state's disintegrating rail system, felt that Myers was abusing his power and taking advantage of Virginia's cooperative attitude. The assembly, ignor-

ing the governor's many complaints and warnings, enacted no new
railroad laws.[3]

Letcher rejected suggestions that Virginia buy a warship in
Europe and conduct a private war on northern commerce. However, by the end of January he was worried enough about the
state's credit rating abroad to recommend to the assembly that
Virginia buy cotton and ship it to England to meet interest pay-
ments on state bonds owned by Britishers. The assembly ignored
this suggestion, which had, in turn, ignored the ever tightening
federal blockade.

Letcher continued to push his plan without success. Late in the
year, he asked Secretary of War Seddon for help in transporting
a large shipment of cotton to England, but Seddon refused. The
Confederacy was having enough trouble meeting its own foreign
obligations without trying to handle a large shipment of Virginia
cotton. This ended the matter until 1864, when the new governor,
William "Extra Billy" Smith, followed North Carolina's example
and put the state in the blockade–running business—a move
Letcher had never advocated.[4]

In February, Letcher again protested Confederate impressment
practices. The very concept of impressment irritated the conservative governor, but he was outraged when a fair market—
and fully inflated—price was not paid for the impressed goods.
As usual, he did not force the issue and limited himself to a few
formal complaints as the Confederate impressment program accelerated. Later in the month, he protested a "gross outrage" in
Franklin County. Confederate troops had forcefully liberated several comrades jailed by the local sheriff and charged with a felony.
Letcher demanded an investigation, but he received no answer
from the War Department for two weeks. Prodded by the assembly, which was extremely sensitive to infringements upon the state's
traditional rights, Letcher continued to demand action. His letters disappeared in a maze of red tape. Letcher accepted this
bureaucratic run–around, contenting himself with his official protests; such was his standard procedure. He formally protested,
but spared the Confederates infinite arguments over trivial violations of Virginia's rights. In a sense, he served as a buffer between

the supersensitive assembly and the harassed central government, and he received criticism from both directions.[5]

The assembly, always eager to snipe at the harassed governor, began to investigate his policy of lending state weapons to the Confederates during emergencies. On February 9, General Dimmock warned Letcher that the legislators did not approve of his generosity with state property. Senator James M. Whittle of Pittsylvania County started an investigation and urged immediate Confederate payment for all arms borrowed from the state. Then, on February 18, Secretary of War Seddon asked Letcher to furnish Confederate troops with 1,500 small arms at once. Letcher agreed to furnish them, but before the transfer could be accomplished Seddon withdrew his request. Letcher had been quite willing to cooperate despite the assembly's obvious opposition. He believed that such loans to the Confederates were legal and logical, and he ignored the grumblings of the hostile assembly. This was typical. Letcher hesitated to use his full executive powers when he was unconvinced of the legality or need of an action, or when he feared that the people's traditional rights and privileges would be unduly abridged; but when it was solely a question of his own personal and political popularity, he acted instantly.[6]

The Confederacy needed this kind of selfless cooperation, for the fortunes of war were gradually shifting. The repulse at Antietam had been redeemed by a resounding victory at Fredericksburg, but the tide had turned. Antietam led to the Emancipation Proclamation. The proclamation was sharply criticized by many northerners, but gradually it transformed the Union war effort into an irresistible crusade for human freedom.

At the same time, the overwhelming manpower and industrial resources of the North were being marshaled. In the field, the Union armies were developing into first–class fighting machines. Competent leadership was finally emerging, as weak and inept generals were weeded out in the acid test of battle. Though the mighty Army of the Potomac still lurched and stumbled, it had the heart and muscle of a giant and would soon find the brain to lead it to victory. Early in 1863 nothing seemed certain, but, in reality, the South did not have the material and spiritual power to resist the rapidly growing might of the Union.[7]

In March and April, Lee's Army of Northern Virginia prepared for another clash with the Army of the Potomac under the command of "Fighting Joe" Hooker, an aggressive regular army officer of limited ability. Letcher confidently followed Lee's maneuvers, but he was primarily occupied with home front problems. The state penitentiary was dangerously overcrowded. In February, Letcher had been forced to reject Lee's personal request that the state place several of his court—martialed soldiers in the penitentiary. This was not a lack of cooperation by the governor. Since the beginning of the war, he had allowed convict labor to produce shoes and other equipment for the Confederates, and had also allowed work gangs from the penitentiary to build roads for the army. Certainly he would never have denied a personal appeal by Lee under ordinary circumstances, but the penitentiary was bulging with prisoners, and there was simply no more room. The governor repeatedly warned the assembly of this problem, but the lawmakers did nothing. Despite another spectacular, destructive fire in a state warehouse—probably sabotage by the Union underground—the assembly also continued to ignore his pleas for appropriations to fireproof the state's warehouses which were bulging with cotton and tobacco.[8]

The assembly's answer to the tobacco glut was a March act limiting for the duration the amount of tobacco a farmer could grow. On March 16, Letcher supplemented this act by urging the people of Virginia to reduce tobacco cultivation voluntarily and raise more livestock, grain, and other foodstuffs. Letcher assured the people that food was still available, and that this revolutionary shift in agricultural production was only a precautionary measure.[9]

Generally, the governor's duties and responsibilities diminished in 1863 because more and more of his functions were assumed by others. Early in the war, Lee had relieved him of some of the burden, and as the war progressed the Confederate government had assumed other responsibilities. Finally, the hostile General Assembly, eager to reestablish its normal, peacetime dominance over the executive department, relieved him of other duties. Letcher still had much to do, but his workload did noticeably lighten in the last year of his administration.

Plots and counter plots against the new state of West Virginia and the Pierpoint Virginia government occupied much of the governor's time, for he bitterly resented these new political entities created at the expense of the Old Dominion. The assembly passed a law opening up some state jobs to women—another striking innovation—and Letcher received many new applications for positions in the government. Never too busy to listen to a petitioner, he received more than his share of suggestions from the lunatic fringe.[10]

Always the coming battle lurked in the background, but the people on the home front could only wait and hope. In February, Letcher had accepted the resignation of his young military aide, Greenlee Davidson, son of his close friend in Lexington. Young Greenlee was like a son to the governor, but with the reduced executive workload and the severe shortage of soldiers, Letcher could not deny his demand for a combat command. Captain Davidson eagerly reported for duty as commander of the newly formed Letcher Artillery. The governor was proud but worried, for he knew that the inexperienced captain would soon face the holocaust of modern battle. Letcher knew that his own brother Sam and many of his friends and neighbors would be hurled into the same bloody chaos, and he realized that some, perhaps many, would never return. Thousands had already fallen, staining Virginia's fields with the South's best blood, and still the blue hordes came. What was to be the final price of victory?

Late in March, all melancholy was dispelled by the demands of the hour. Secretary of War Seddon's emergency request for 5,000 infantry arms was quickly granted, and on March 27 Letcher closed all state offices in accordance with President Davis' call for another day of prayer for victory. The stage was set for battle, but before the armies clashed, Letcher had to face an explosive threat on the home front.[11]

Uncontrolled inflation had continued to ravage the South, pushing prices higher and higher and crushing the common people under an intolerable economic burden. The cities suffered most, and overcrowded Richmond was hardest hit of all. By March, flour was selling for $100 a barrel; beef, $2 a pound; apples, $25 a bushel; coarse cotton, $2.25 a yard; molasses, $30 a gallon; boots, $50 a pair; wood, $30 a cord. People turned from currency to barter in this period of economic insanity.

Even on a salary of $5,000 a year, Letcher was pinched for funds. Too proud to appeal to the assembly for a higher salary, he tried to sell some property in Lexington. If Letcher was pinched, the poor of Richmond were crushed, and discontent rumbled through the city's crowded tenements. No longer the placid, genteel city of antebellum days, Richmond was now the wartime capital of the Confederacy, jammed with strangers and ever fearful of Yankee assault. A new class of government bureaucrats sprang up to rub shoulders with gamblers, criminals, and swarms of spirited soldiers, some only hours away from mutilation or death. A restless Negro population lurked in the background, and a small but active fifth column heightened the tension as mysterious fires continued to blaze in the night. Prostitutes were everywhere, and a host of greedy war profiteers swaggered through the streets, arrogant in their new riches. Everywhere masses of poor people, many of them newcomers, drifted aimlessly and restlessly. Richmond was a powder keg, awaiting only a spark to explode.

Letcher had watched the tension gradually build during his administration and was fully aware of the danger. On March 16, he appealed to Secretary of War Seddon to make the Confederates stop impressing cattle on the way to the Richmond market. He stressed the great public discontent caused by the severe shortage of meat. As usual, his plea was processed through normal Confederate channels and lost in a maze of red tape. A week later Letcher appealed to the assembly to stop inflation, another wasted plea. Like the governor, the assembly lacked the experience and the political philosophy necessary to solve this growing problem.[12]

Discontent continued to increase. The explosion finally came on April 2. The governor was breakfasting when a delegation of women came to appeal for more bread. He spoke briefly to the women and promised to see them later at his office. The women left, but then word came that a turbulent mob of several hundred women and children and a sprinkling of men had gathered on the west side of Capitol Square. At once Letcher ordered the bell in the old guard tower rung, a signal for the Public Guard to report for duty. In less than half an hour the Public Guard was assembled in Capitol Square, but meanwhile the mob had moved south down Ninth Street to the stores and shops on Main Street. Growing in numbers and boldness as it moved, the mob began to sack the Confederate commissary and several stores. A large crowd gathered to watch the looters, and onlookers began to join the mob as it plundered freely.

Then city, state, and Confederate officials arrived. Mayor Joseph Mayo begged the rioters to disperse, and President Davis eloquently appealed to the crowd's patriotism, but the riot grew in force. Letcher and the Public Guard and several fire engines reached the scene. A dousing by the firemen only angered the rioters, and the governor lost his patience. He warned the crowd that he would order the Public Guard to open fire in five minutes. The mob shouted defiance, and some of the women and boys brandished knives and hatchets. When the five minutes were up, Letcher calmly but loudly ordered the guard to load and prepare to fire, whereupon the mob began to disperse and the guard systematically herded its remnants out of the danger zone. By a strong show of force at the proper psychological moment, Letcher had smashed a dangerous riot before it could get out of control.[13]

The riot was smashed, but Letcher took no chances. The root cause of the trouble, inflation, remained, and the possibility of another upheaval was very real. Several leaders of the riot, such as pistol–packing Minerva Meredith and knife–wielding Mary Jackson, received short jail sentences, and other trials dragged on for another year. Letcher and Mayor Mayo kept a sharp lookout for more trouble, and on April 10 the governor alerted Confederate troops in the area for another possible riot. Unrest continued, and dissatisfaction showed itself in many acts of wanton vandalism, but open violence never flared up again. Letcher's

initial response to the riot and his subsequent vigilance contributed greatly to the maintenance of law and order in Richmond.[14]

Once the capital had calmed down again, Letcher turned briefly
to state politics. On April 6, he proclaimed that the state elections late in May for governor, lieutenant governor, attorney
general, delegates to the assembly, and Confederate congressmen
would be held as usual. Some had suggested suspending all elections at least until after the coming battle was over, but the governor was anxious to schedule normal elections. On April 22, he
formally announced his own candidacy for Congress from his district of the Valley.[15]

During the last half of April, General Jackson's wife visited
her old Lexington neighbors at the Governor's Mansion. She
planned to stay only long enough to obtain an escort to take her
to her husband's camp near Fredericksburg for a short visit.
Letcher invited Jackson to join them in Richmond, but the general was too busy preparing for combat to leave the field. His
wife got her escort and spent a few days with her husband, but
the mighty Jackson never saw the Letchers or Richmond again.[16]

On May 2, the great battle came. Lee's daring strategy worked
to perfection against the confused Hooker, and Jackson's brilliant
flanking movement broke the Union army's spirit. Letcher followed the battle as best he could from his office, but he was distracted by Union General George Stoneman's cavalry raid toward
Richmond. The raiders cut rail and telegraph lines running north
and came within sight of the capital, but the rout of the main
Union army and a spirited show of force by a motley force of
defenders stopped them. At the request of General Longstreet,
Letcher ordered the sheriffs of King William, New Kent, and
Henrico counties to block all roads and streams leading away
from Richmond, using impressed slave labor if necessary, but
Stoneman's cavalry was too fast and escaped without serious in-
jury.[17]

On May 5, the governor was notified that General Jackson had
lost his left arm but was recuperating. A few hours later he was
informed that his former aide, Captain Greenlee Davidson, had

been killed in action. Lee's victory was complete, but Letcher could not rejoice. Young Davidson and thousands of other southerners had fallen, thousands more were maimed, and the war continued. The Army of the Potomac, though beaten once again, was not yet destroyed.[18]

On May 10, Letcher's sadness deepened to gloom when he learned that Jackson had died. He proclaimed May 11 a day of mourning, "the great and good General Thomas J. Jackson having departed this life". That same day Jackson's body was brought to Richmond and placed in the Governor's Mansion. On May 12, an elaborate funeral service was held in the Capitol, and the next day the fallen hero was taken back to his beloved Lexington. Letcher and several of his aides accompanied Mrs. Jackson and her daughter all the way. Letcher attended the burial of Jackson in the local Presbyterian cemetery and then sadly returned to his duties in Richmond.[19]

Election day was only two weeks away, and friends in the Valley were busy championing the governor's candidacy. With the prestige of the governorship behind him, Letcher was confident, but he knew the contest would be close. The incumbent, John B. Baldwin of Augusta County, a prewar Whig, was a wily veteran of Valley politics. He was also a veteran of the proud Army of Northern Virginia, and he had briefly served in combat as colonel of the 52nd Virginia Regiment before entering Congress.

The election was held on May 28 as scheduled, but the excitement and enthusiasm of prewar days were lacking and the voting was light. Some counties were slow to report their vote, and the result in Letcher's eleventh district was uncertain for over a month. The governor held a thin edge in the army balloting, and late in June he held a slim over–all edge. However, Augusta County and some other Baldwin strongholds had not yet officially reported. It was obvious that Letcher had been beaten decisively. After three and a half years of selfless service, the governor was repudiated by his own people of the Valley. The opposition was strong, and Letcher, who had officially entered the contest at the last minute, had been unable to canvass the district. The real reason for his defeat, however, lay in his gubernatorial record.

He had subordinated himself and his state too much to the Confederate war effort. In his determination to do all he could for victory, he had infringed on the individual and property rights of the people and had diluted the sacrosanct rights of the state. Despite his caution and hesitation, he had offended a people completely unprepared for the demands of modern, total war. By twentieth–century standards his wartime leadership had been too weak, but by the standards of mid–nineteenth century Virginia it was far too strong. Letcher lost his political life, and the people soon lost their war.[20]

Letcher was stunned by defeat. Lieutenant Governor Montague, old congressional colleague Fayette McMullen, and the ancient William Cabell Rives had won seats in Congress, and Attorney General Tucker had retained his position. Yet Letcher had been repudiated by the same people who had sent him to the old federal Congress for a decade and then helped put him in the Governor's Mansion. Though disappointed, he retained his Jacksonian faith in democracy, and he accepted the will of the people without bitterness. The people's decision had a mystic, almost holy wisdom that he had always accepted, and which he would continue to trust for the rest of his life. The governor swallowed his disappointment, rejected self–pity, and plunged back into his executive duties.[21]

In June he received a complaint from kinsman J. E. B. Stuart about the Richmond press coverage of some of his latest cavalry exploits. Stuart felt that even the Yankee papers were giving him more credit. Letcher, hardly the darling of the local press himself, was unable to help his headline–hunting cousin.

Besides, the war was demanding all of his attention. In the west, the daring and relentless Grant was hammering away at Vicksburg, but every eye in Virginia was on Pennsylvania. Lee's army was on the offensive, seeking to end the war in the enemy's own territory. The oft–beaten but still powerful Army of the Potomac maneuvered to shield Washington, and slowly the two behemoths closed for another trial of strength near Gettysburg.[22]

Letcher watched hopefully. He had long favored taking the war to the enemy and was convinced that nothing could stop

Lee and his mighty legions. However, he had little time for speculation, for the absence of Lee's army left Virginia dangerously
exposed to cavalry raids and minor offensives by federal troops
in the west or on the tip of the peninsula. On June 13, he alerted
the state militia, and two weeks later he called on the citizens of
Richmond to prepare to repel a rumored cavalry raid. He also
mobilized the city's home guard units and threatened to treat
all slackers as deserters. Fearing a recurrence of the Bread Riot,
he temporarily closed the Richmond Theatre and kept a close
watch on the city's restless masses. Taking advantage of the Confederate's recent expulsion of the British consul from Richmond,
Letcher ordered all resident foreigners to join the home guard.
He also ordered the V. M. I. cadets to be ready to resist cavalry
attacks in the Valley.[23]

All possible preparations had been made, and everyone waited
for news from Pennsylvania, where two armies battled desperately
through the first three days of July. This was the showdown, and
a whole continent watched in awe. The rebel legions fought gal-
lantly, but Lee had temporarily lost his magic. The Army of the
Potomac had evolved into a great fighting machine, and at last
it was led by a capable commander, George G. Meade. Rebel
flank attacks were beaten back, Stuart's cavalry was chased from
the field by the rejuvenated Yankee horsemen, and the grand
assault on the Union center by Pickett's Virginians was cut to
pieces by confident veterans of a reborn army. Lee's mauled army
retreated slowly back to Virginia.

The crushing defeat at Gettysburg meant that Virginia would
soon be invaded in force again. And this time the bluecoats would
have not only their usual superiority in men and equipment but
also the confidence born of victory. Soon the Army of the Potomac
would find its brain—U. S. Grant, the conqueror of Vicksburg.
The Confederacy's days were numbered.[24]

Letcher prepared desperately for the coming trials. Broaden-
ing Confederate conscription had stripped Virginia of most of her
regular militia, men between the ages of 18 and 45. Only the
poorly organized home guard units in the cities remained in the
service of the state. Letcher resisted all Confederate efforts to

recruit his handful of home guardsmen, technically and optimistically designated second class militiamen. Only if a home guardsman volunteered would the governor consent to his transfer to Confederate service.

The governor faced many other difficulties. Inflation was still rampant. Virginians were rapidly losing the last shreds of their faith in the chaotic currency system, and Richmond still seethed with discontent. The state treasury was empty again, and immediate appropriations were needed to keep the government in operation. On the basis of all these needs, Letcher on August 10 called for a special session of the General Assembly to convene early in September.[25]

On August 20, Letcher cooperated with another of the president's frequent calls for a day of prayer by ordering all state offices closed the next day. On August 27, he closed all state offices again to commemorate the death of John B. Floyd, former commander of the Virginia State Line. A week later he gave his friend General Smith permission to use his V. M. I. cadets whenever the military situation in the west required it. The cadets had already participated in several skirmishes, but this decision gave Smith a free rein and prepared the way for the famous New Market charge almost a year later.[26]

On September 7, Letcher delivered his last formal speech to the assembly which had just reconvened. Beginning with his usual plea for southern unity, he recommended organizing all available males between the ages of 16 and 60 into military units patterned after the home guard, with strict rules against exemption, disobedience, or desertion. This was a total war measure, and the assembly hesitated to act. Only after additional prodding by the governor did the legislators on September 28 enact a weak substitute bill which empowered the governor to call for sixty–day volunteers in emergencies.

Letcher warned that a few defeats were inevitable, but he called on all southerners to fight on until independence was achieved. After a few words of praise for the women of the South, he suggested that Virginia cooperate with the central government in its efforts to improve the monetary situation. Specifically, he

recommended repeal of a law passed in March, 1863, which forbade the state to accept in payment of taxes any Confederate
money issued before April 6, 1863. A week later the assembly
followed this suggestion for increasing confidence in Confederate
money.

The governor asked for more appropriations to keep the government running, and the assembly quickly granted this request.
He asked for salary increases for state employees who were hard
hit by inflation. He discussed the inequalities which still existed
in the slave requisition program, and he repeated his familiar
and fruitless appeals for better railway maintenance and effective
action against speculators. Letcher's only concrete remedy for
speculation and inflation was the reenactment of a law of 1777,
with a few minor revisions. This "Act to prevent forestalling, re-
grading, etc." had been unenforceable during the Revolutionary
War, and it would have been totally ineffective in the advanced
economic era of the Civil War. Letcher and the other southern
leaders were unable to cope with the problem of inflation. They
were not even able to come to grips with it. The solution lay in the
future, not in the past, but the future belonged to the Union, not
to the Confederacy.

After a long emotional tribute to the fallen Jackson, Letcher
concluded his address with a review of Confederate and state
finances. He attacked Secretary of the Treasury Memminger's
policies—one of the few times he publicly criticized a high rebel
official—but he did some fancy statistical juggling to demonstrate
the soundness of Virginia's finances. This was somewhat difficult
to reconcile with a whopping debt of over $34,000,000, but the
governor had a solution. He recommended disposal of the state's
interests in state banks and railroad and canal companies. According to Letcher's calculations, this would bring in about $20,-
000,000 and fully reestablish the state's fiscal integrity. In prewar
days Letcher, as a westerner, had favored state support for
internal improvements, but under the pressure of wartime debt
he was willing to sell out. The assembly rejected this advice, however, and the state did not sell its internal improvement interests
until after the war.[27]

The governor continued to stay in close touch with the new assembly. After talking with Secretary of War Seddon late in September, he sent a gloomy military report to a secret session of the legislature, recommending the mustering of more troops to defend the exposed salt works in the southwestern section of the state. Alarmed, the assembly threw together a patchwork bill. On September 30, Lee wrote Letcher to the effect that the need for more troops was desperate. On the same day Letcher issued his first call for sixty–day volunteers to protect the salt works.

Saltville was clearly in danger, but veteran bureaucrats in Richmond correctly predicted that the governor's call would produce only a corporal's guard. Fortunately for the rebels, Union forces did not attack at this time; another year was to pass before Stoneman's raiders hit this vital region. Though Letcher cooperated to the extent of calling for troops, he refused to allow rebel forces to impress slaves to build fortifications. Impressment was one aspect of the war that the governor could never fully accept.[28]

Late in September, however, Letcher defended the use of Negro convicts in essential war industries. Occasional escapes by these skilled workers aroused concern in some quarters, and when twelve vanished from the Tredegar company criticism increased. Letcher admitted that the system had its dangers, but maintained that it was necessary for a time, and predicted that Virginia would return to the good old agrarian way after the war, when the Negro industrial workers could be sold for a handsome profit![29]

Early in October, the assembly had demanded a general accounting of Virginia's contributions to the Confederate military machine, and Letcher quickly submitted a detailed report to the House of Delegates. He calculated that the state had furnished over 130,000 men and vast quantities of supplies and equipment. The state still retained several thousand old muskets and a few obsolete cannons.[30]

Letcher was proud of Virginia's contributions to the rebellion, but he still resisted some Confederate encroachments on the state's traditional rights. Early in September, he had again refused to allow the Confederates to use the crowded penitentiary. On October 16, he successfully resisted two new proposals by the central government that he felt violated the "great doctrines of state rights". He vigorously denounced Secretary of the Treasury Memminger's plan to tax the state's bank deposit revenue as "most extraordinary and without parallel in the history of this Commonwealth". He also attacked the central government's attempts to force state tobacco inspectors to tabulate and actually pay with state funds a Confederate tax on the tobacco stored under their jurisdiction. Presumably the state was to pass the tax on to the owners of the tobacco. In these two matters Letcher simply refused to cooperate. His hair–splitting justification for resistance clearly illuminated the Confederacy's fatal flaw:

> The line of separation between Confederate and State authority is plain, distinct and well defined. The States are the sovereigns— the Confederate government is the creature called into existence by those sovereigns. The States retain all power, which has not been specifically delegated to the Confederate government, or which is not necessary to carry into effect the delegated powers. Every citizen owes *allegiance* to his State, and *fidelity* to the Confederate government.[31]

The last few months of Letcher's administration passed rapidly. The governor discontinued his detailed executive journal and concentrated on routine work. By this time the continuing inflation had brought Letcher to the verge of bankruptcy. The assembly had not raised his salary or increased his fringe benefits, though his annual pay of $5,000 was ridiculously inadequate. The rest of the state bureaucracy suffered even more as real income fell drastically.[32]

Late in October, Letcher sadly announced the death of General Dimmock, felled by a stroke at the age of sixty–three, and he quickly replaced him with Colonel Jacob Shriver. On November 11, Letcher ordered 100 home guardsmen in Richmond to patrol around prisoner–of–war compounds and suppress all disturbances by the captives. The elderly guardsmen complained at once about sentry duty on the bitter winter nights, and before Christmas Letcher had persuaded Secretary of War Seddon to relieve them.[33]

Tormented by a painful eye infection that threatened permanent blindness, frustrated by a paper shortage, worried about the safety of his beloved Valley, troubled by the suffering of his people in combat areas—Letcher again stormed into the delicate field of prisoner–of–war treatment. In June, 1862, a Botetourt County court had convicted two captured Union soldiers of trying to steal a slave and sentenced them to several years at hard labor in the state penitentiary. Letcher had approved and put the men in the penitentiary. Federal authorities did not learn of this affair for over a year, and formal inquiries were not sent to Letcher until November, 1863. The governor made short work of the whole affair by bluntly stating that the two men would remain in the penitentiary as long as he was in office.[34]

The governor also cleared up his personal affairs in Richmond. He settled his account on Pew 91 of St. Paul's Episcopal Church several months before his term ended. He remained skeptical of Christianity in general, and of its worldly officials in particular, but his wife was a devout Episcopalian, and Letcher attended St. Paul's with regularity if not enthusiasm.[35]

Not even his loudest critics doubted Letcher's devotion to the Confederate cause, and on December 15, a delegation from the assembly invited him to a complimentary dinner at the elite Ballard House on December 17. Though the assembly had been the center of opposition to the governor, the formal invitation included a glowing tribute to his official conduct. As the moment of retirement approached, old hostilities faded. Letcher genuinely appreciated this message from his old nemesis, and in his reply he promised to continue to back the war effort as a private citizen. However, owing to the death of a close relative in Lexington, he was unable to attend the dinner.[36]

Back from Lexington on December 19, Letcher sent a final, brief message to the assembly. He suggested a new naturalization law that would draw more resident "aliens" into the army. He opposed turning over the state's iron, lead, and coal mines to the Confederacy. And he opposed the policy of allowing captured Yankee officers to wander around freely on parole (he feared that some might encourage insurrection among the Negroes). On December 26, in one of his last official acts, the governor sent a new state flag to the Second Virginia Cavalry Regiment. On December 29, he gave a farewell banquet at the Governor's Mansion. Letcher, incoming Governor William Smith, and James D. Davidson gave speeches commemorating his arduous administration. The festivities lasted long into the night.[37]

On December 31, the final day of his administration, Letcher received yet another commendation, a well–deserved tribute from the city of Richmond. In a formal set of resolutions, the city council hailed his special efforts to protect the interests of the people of Richmond in their dual status as inhabitants of the Confederate capital and citizens of Virginia, and awarded Letcher a sword as a token of the city's gratitude and respect. The end had come. Letcher could now retire to private life.[38]

The final year of John Letcher's administration started with the Emancipation Proclamation, a turning point in the war. Despite continuing harassment by the General Assembly, he cooperated with the Confederates, and he finally paid the price for his support of the central government and his subordination of individual and property and state rights to the common cause: he was repudiated by his own people of the Valley. Letcher and many other political leaders were casualties in the spring congressional elections, indicating a growing public hostility to the Davis administration and the central government. Letcher ended his wartime administration as he had started it—championing southern harmony and unity as keys to victory. As determined as ever to carry on to the end, Letcher was still convinced that victory and independence lay at the end of the bloody trail. Virginia's first wartime governor was still full of fight—and vain hopes.[39]

CHAPTER 12

Catastrophe

The swift transition from a position of power and prestige to the role of ordinary citizen was not easy for a man who had devoted his adult life to the art of politics. However, with a large family to support, Letcher put aside all political ambition and returned to the practice of law. Wartime inflation had plunged him into debt, but worse was yet to come, for the war was far from over.

Letcher's administration had ended amidst general applause, and the bitter conflicts of his wartime leadership were temporarily forgotten in the mellowness of retirement. This retirement became official on January 1, 1864, when Governor William Smith and Lieutenant Governor Samuel Price took their oaths of office in the Capitol before a large crowd. The outgoing governor was present at this formal transfer of power and was loudly cheered by the audience. Later in the day, the city fathers of Richmond formally presented him the ceremonial sword honoring his wartime services to the capital.[1]

And now the Letchers returned to their beloved Valley. It was not easy to leave the Purcells, the Terrills, the Mayos, and their other friends in Richmond, but Lexington was their home, the natural center of their way of life. When Letcher left the capital, he abandoned the political ambition which had driven him relentlessly throughout his adult life, but old habits and instincts remained. He continued to be interested in politics, watching from the sidelines and occasionally offering advice and assistance.[2]

The new year was to be a time of rapid change. Smashing Union victories at Vicksburg, Gettysburg, and Chattanooga had changed the whole complexion of the war. Massive Union armies shook off the effects of repeated defeats and seized the initiative. Deep in the South, Sherman's army would strike into the vulnerable belly of the Confederacy, while in Virginia Grant would unleash the grinding, bloody offense of attrition that would end only at Appomattox. Operation Anaconda, the blockade, was steadily drawing its coils tighter and tighter around its victim. And all the while the North would continue to pour its overwhelming resources into a contest becoming more unequal with each passing day.[3]

Like most southerners, Letcher could not—or would not—see the impending doom of the Confederate experiment. On February 11, 1864, the birth of another healthy daughter, Fanny Wilson Letcher, further strengthened his instinctive optimism. He simply could not imagine defeat. But he did realize that an all—out effort by the whole South, civilian as well as military, would be needed for victory. He carried this message to the people of the Valley. In response to numerous requests, Letcher frequently delivered morale—building speeches, of which the one delivered at the Lexington Courthouse on March 19 was typical.[4]

Speaking for an hour and a half, he pointedly ignored such controversial topics as conscription, impressment, wartime taxes, and the suspension of the writ of habeas corpus, all of which he felt were unwise at the very least. He took a few minutes to defend himself from the old charge that he had not adequately prepared the state for war during his peacetime administration. This oft—repeated accusation was a holdover from the bitter prewar struggle between the seccessionists and the moderates, and many old radicals had never forgiven Letcher for his refusal to be stampeded into secession. Letcher had no apology to make for his prewar governorship, and he correctly pointed out that Virginia had been better prepared for war than any other southern state had been.

He then condemned the Yankees for destroying property—a practice of which Letcher was soon to learn at first hand—and for arming slaves. He singled out for special censure Colonel Ulric Dahlgren's unsuccessful attempt to raid Richmond. Then he channeled his denunciations toward President Lincoln and the hated Emancipation Proclamation. Characterizing the President as completely untrustworthy, Letcher predicted that he would retain the presidency after the November election either by legally winning the vote of the majority or by illegally using armed force.

Letcher declared that the South would eventually win the war, that the twin afflictions of desertion in the field and inflation at home would humble the Yankees. Ever optimistic, Letcher claimed that Confederate currency was becoming sounder—a sure sign that the South was solving the problem of inflation. Following his customary emotional tribute to his two heroes Jackson and Lee, the former governor concluded with an appeal for donations of food and clothing for Virginia troops in the field. He then yielded the rostrum to an old political competitor, Judge John W. Brockenbrough, who continued to bolster the audience's moral for another hour.[5]

The former governor did not sever all of his lines of communication with Confederate authorities in Richmond. Occasionally he wrote President Davis or Secretary of War Seddon, requesting routine military transfers, exemptions, discharges, and promotions, or suggesting a minor military tactic in the Valley. But he did not swamp the war leaders with a flood of trivial letters. His suggestions were few and often logical and useful, and he apparently was not offended when his ideas were ignored or rejected.[6]

Early in the spring, Letcher accepted an invitation to visit the city of Danville. The people there wanted to honor him for his wartime leadership, and they also wanted to get a good look at him. Throughout his administration rumors had drifted through the state hinting that Letcher was sometimes more devoted to bourbon than business. Such rumors—usually covert but occasionally stimulated by newspapers such as the Richmond *Examiner*—were grossly unfair. Like most Virginians, Letcher appreciated good whiskey, especially at social events, but he was certainly no drunkard. Nevertheless, the rumors persisted, and the people of Danville wanted to see for themselves.

After a formal reception by Mayor Roger P. Atkinson and the city council, the visiting celebrity was installed in the home of Robert E. Withers, another prominent local politician. Here Letcher received visitors for the next few days, delighting everyone with his friendliness, informality, and humor. Social drinking naturally accompanied the steady stream of callers. The congenial Lexingtonian mixed himself weak drinks and showed no signs of overindulgence, and only the dedicated scandal mongers still believed the rumors. Letcher and Mayor Atkinson, personal and political friends from the prewar era, spent pleasant hours discussing the good old days when the only fighting was done verbally between the Whigs and the Democrats. The citizens of Danville, including the children, were sorry to see the lively, entertaining former governor depart.[7]

But Letcher could not afford to spend much of his time visiting and making speeches. He was virtually penniless. Wartime inflation in Richmond had ruined him, and by 1864 even the Valley was feeling the effect of soaring prices. Luxuries were selling for staggering sums: a lady's plain crepe hat cost $75; enough silk for a dress, $500; tea, $40 a pound. Worse still, prices for food and other necessities had soared: molasses sold for $30 a gallon, coarse cotton was priced at $8 a yard, and flour ran as high as $250 a barrel.[8]

The former governor threw himself back into his law practice, working tirelessly to recoup some of his losses. He was a good lawyer, popular and experienced in the rural and small town environment of the Valley, but the practice of ordinary law in the confusion of wartime was difficult. Cases were scarce, and hard work brought only a meager income. Letcher and his wife both felt that the assembly should have increased his salary as governor and not allowed him to go into debt in the service of the state, but neither complained publicly. They were willing to sacrifice for the cause, and rejected offers of financial assistance from friends and well–wishers, while always retaining their happy

family environment and avoiding self–pity. They realized that
many—their friend Davidson was one—had lost more than money
in the war.[9]

The Letchers felt the war more personally in May, 1864, when
the entire cadet corps of V. M. I., 8 officers and 263 youths,
marched into battle. The corps' mission was to reinforce Confederate troops under General John C. Breckinridge who were
preparing to engage General Franz Sigel's Union army in the
northern part of the Valley. In September, 1863, Governor
Letcher had authorized the use of the cadets in emergencies, and
these eager young warriors—their average age was 17—suffered
10 killed and 48 wounded in the spirited assault that helped tip
the scales for the rebels at the battle of New Market. Among the
freshmen privates who emerged unscathed from this baptism of
fire was 16–year–old Samuel Houston Letcher, the former governor's eldest son.

This young warrior marched back to Lexington with the triumphant cadets, but he remained at V. M. I. only long enough
to finish his first session. He then volunteered for the army, served
with General Jubal Early's army in the Maryland and Valley
campaigns, and gained the rank of first lieutenant by the end of
1864. He spent the last months of the war with General William
Preston's brigade in southwestern Virginia. The war became far
more personal for John Letcher when his son went into combat.[10]

In June, 1864, the war became still more personal for Letcher.
The check administered to Union forces at New Market was only
temporary, and by June powerful Yankee formations under General David Hunter were smashing their way southward up the
Valley toward Lexington and the rail and canal center of Lynchburg. The strengthening of Richmond's defenses had left the
Valley temporarily exposed, and Hunter's 20,000–man army rolled
ahead swiftly. After crushing a small rebel force at the battle of
Piedmont on June 5, Hunter swept through Staunton. All that
stood between him and Lexington was Confederate General John
McCausland and fewer than 2,000 mounted troopers.

By June 7, the citizens of Lexington were preparing for the
onrushing Yankees. Refugees from the northern Valley poured

into town with their slaves, anxious to keep this particular type of "property" away from Hunter, who was known to be an ardent abolitionist. Lexingtonians hid their food and valuables and drove their cattle into the woods. V. M. I. was an obvious military objective; its vital equipment was sent down the North River by barge, and all its books were transferred to the Washington College library. By June 10, Union patrols were seen in Rockbridge County, and a last flurry of hiding valuables began. Letcher realized that he would have to flee, but he knew he could not take his whole family. On the evening of June 10 he rode alone into Bedford County, on his way to Richmond.[11]

General McCausland's troops could only harass Hunter's army, which was within ten miles of Lexington on the morning of June 11. The rebels destroyed the bridge across the North River, just north of town, and sniped at advanced elements of the Union army from the Lexington side of the river. The federals were delayed, but were soon fording the river a few miles upstream. At three in the afternoon the rebel forces, including the recently–returned V. M. I. cadets, evacuated the town under fire from Yankee artillery, and then retreated southward to avoid encirclement.

Federal artillery had opened fire soon after the sniping began. The first shells smashed into the V. M. I. barracks, where some of the snipers seemed to be stationed. Then the shell fire shifted to the town itself, through which rebel columns were retreating; this brief but intense barrage (one projectile dropped in front of the Letcher home) was lifted as soon as it became apparent that all rebel troops were gone. Before dusk Union troops were streaming into town.

Most of the Union army continued southward in pursuit of McCausland, but the commanding general, his staff, and several other detachments remained in Lexington. The zealous Hunter had intentionally wrought havoc all along his line of march and now, on Sunday, June 12, Lexington also felt his wrath. Many of his officers—including a Colonel Rutherford B. Hayes and a Captain William McKinley—opposed this style of fighting, but they obeyed their commander. Pillaging was widespread, but stronger medicine was dished out in some quarters. V. M. I. was put to the torch, as were the houses of all of its professors except that of General Smith, which Hunter used as his headquarters. The Washington College chemistry laboratory and library, reposi- tory of the institute's books, were also gutted. Several small iron mills, a flour mill, a brick factory, and all of the town's precious salt were destroyed. And, John Letcher's home was burned to the ground.

The single fact that Letcher had been such a vigorous supporter of the rebellion might have prompted General Hunter to destroy his home. In addition, however, the Yankees found a procla- mation by Letcher at V.M.I. urging the people of Virginia to wage guerilla warfare against the "invaders". Throughout his Valley offensive Hunter had been unmercifully harassed by John S. Mosby's famous raiders, and he had already issued an anti- guerrilla proclamation in May. Under the authority of this edict, Hunter ordered the destruction of Letcher's home.

As Union troops entered Lexington, Susan Letcher had nat- urally been worried. Her apprehension was not lessened by threats shouted by troops marching past the house, but at least one Union officer had reassured her. A Dr. Patton of the medical section had demanded lodging at the Letcher home on Saturday night, and early the next morning he gave the first reliable hint of trouble. In a half–serious, half–joking manner he remarked to 18– year–old Elizabeth Letcher that the meal they were eating would be their last in the house. Patton left after breakfast, and soon Captain Matthew Berry, Hunter's assistant provost marshal, rode up and informed Susan Letcher that the general had ordered her home destroyed.

Stunned, she asked to see the order, but Berry said it was oral. She asked for time to see Hunter but was refused. She asked for five minutes to rescue some clothing, but Berry gruffly rejected this request—the only thing he was interested in salvaging was Letcher's whiskey—and without further discussion stormed into the parlor and ignited highly combustible camphene on the floor. The house and its expensive furnishings were quickly consumed. Susan Letcher, her five children—the sixth, Sam, was with the

V. M. I. cadets—and her spinster sister, Mag Holt, stood in the street and watched the flames do their work.

Everything was either destroyed or stolen, and the adjoining house, belonging to Letcher's 78–year–old mother, was ransacked and only saved from the spreading flames by the efforts of a sympathetic Union officer and his men. A less sympathetic officer sought other possessions of the former governor, boasting that he would make certain that Letcher was reduced to abject poverty. Some equally unsympathetic troops denounced their absentee victim in coarse language, expressing a desire to have him as the guest of honor at a hanging party.[12]

By Tuesday, June 14, Hunter's command had moved on toward its ultimate objective, Lynchburg. The Union army penetrated to the outskirts of the city but was turned back by reinforced Confederate forces under General Jubal Early. Only after a rapid retreat westward by way of the Kanawha River did Hunter's army escape destruction. Though ultimately a failure, the Union offensive had dealt Lexington a stunning blow, with damage estimates running as high as $3,000,000. Nobody in town suffered more cruelly from Hunter's brief occupation than John Letcher.

The former governor soon returned to his razed home determined to overcome this new misfortune. Less than a month later, Early's army swept through the Valley into Maryland on its way to the very outskirts of Washington. Along the way the rebels burned Maryland Governor Augustus W. Bradford's home in retaliation for Hunter's conduct in Lexington. This may have soothed Letcher's outraged feelings, but it did not help him recoup his losses.[13]

Letcher's predicament was not ignored by his friends and admirers. Letters expressing indignation and sympathy poured into Lexington, and once again plans for financial aid were formulated. Familiar with the former governor's pride and independence, many channeled their relief funds through his friend Davidson, but a few sent contributions directly to Letcher. This help enabled the Letcher family to get through a difficult period, but the ex–governor soon refused to accept any more of it. He plunged back into his law practice and began to pull himself back up the economic ladder.[14]

Naturally, the war was not forgotten. In private discussions with close friends, Letcher did not hesitate to criticize Confederate policies—the inability of Secretary of the Treasury Memminger and the Congress to control inflation was a favorite lament. But, for the sake of unity and harmony, he remained silent publicly. Dissatisfaction with some of the Confederacy's programs did not rekindle political ambition in Letcher. On June 28, Secretary of War Seddon wrote him about the possibility of a position in the War Department, but Letcher was not interested. In Richmond, there were rumors that he was being groomed for the cabinet. The most persistent rumor, one that appeared in the columns of the Richmond *Daily Dispatch,* stated that Letcher would soon replace Seddon. Many of Letcher's old Richmond friends supported the idea enthusiastically, but he quickly informed his "non thinking friends" that he would under no circumstances accept any position in the Confederate cabinet. For the rest of the war, Letcher's political ambitions were dead.[15]

Throughout 1864 Letcher and most other southerners remained optimistic about the military situation. Pessimistic letters from old friend Colonel John Warren Grigsby, briefly sulking in Atlanta over his failure to be promoted, warned Letcher of danger in the South. This warning was soon fulfilled as the reckless John B. Hood led his army away from Atlanta on September 1, after having received a mauling from Sherman's forces. Hood's force drove into Tennessee, where it was virtually exterminated by superior Union forces under Virginian George H. Thomas—the officer Letcher had tried so hard to recruit for Virginia's armed forces before the war. Sherman's devastating march to the sea in Georgia climaxed the seemingly unending stream of rebel reverses in the south and west.

Letcher realized the seriousness of these defeats, but his attention was focused on the Virginia battleground. Here Lee still reigned supreme. In the bloody battles of May and June, he had inflicted terrible losses on Grant's forces, and then he had narrowly frustrated Grant's daring attempt to turn the rebel flank

and take Petersburg. Southerners failed to realize that these victories were actually defeats—that the grim attrition of combat
had sealed the doom of the Army of Northern Virginia. For every
Yankee cut down, another confidently filled the gap. For every
rebel who fell, there was only a void in the gaunt, tattered lines
of grey. In the peal of victory bells, there was the deeper rumble
of defeat.[16]

As far as Letcher was concerned, Virginia was the backbone
of the Confederacy—Richmond, the most vital city. Here was
the crucial area, and here too was the master strategist, Lee.
From the beginning of the war, Letcher had believed in Lee's
greatness, and by 1864 this confidence had become an impregnable
article of faith. He frequently warned the general to be careful,
for he was certain that victory would eventually come if Lee continued to lead the troops in Virginia. He yearned for another
Lee to restore the deteriorating situation in the deep South.[17]

Early in 1865, however, even Letcher's habitual optimism began
to waver a little in the face of reality. As wartime governor, he
had associated closely with the rebel hierarchy and had come to
be well aware of the deficiencies of the Confederate cabinet. He
had discussed these weaknesses privately with friends, but publicly
he had remained silent for the sake of unity. However, the vision
of incompetence in the highest councils of the Confederacy
haunted him. At last he decided to add his voice to the growing
chorus of criticism, hoping reform would come in time to save
the cause. He hurriedly wrote a rough draft of a letter to an un-
named newspaper, an open letter to the people of the Confederacy.

Years of pent–up frustration and dissatisfaction flowed through
his pen. Four pages of cheap, thin paper were filled back and
front as Letcher candidly appraised the state of affairs in the
Confederacy. As soon as he had finished this rough draft, Letcher
hesitated. Was it wise to attack rebel leadership at this crucial
time? Would this letter only encourage the rising tide of disaffection which was sweeping through the war–weary South? Letcher
thought for hours and finally made his decision. His letter would
do more harm than good. It would only further damage the fragile

unity of the Confederacy. Letcher filed the rough draft in his
personal papers and never mentioned it to anyone. This secret
letter tells more about the author and the Confederacy than
reams of official records:

Mr. Editor

I propose to make some reflections upon the state of our situation
of the Country. I think it would be inferred from the tone of the
press that recently that there is despondency in the Country and
that the people and even some of the states are beginning to falter.
I have regretted to see articles of that sort in some of our papers
who have always exhibited the greatest devotion to the cause of
Southern independence and these discouraging impressions are
made in the very appeals which they make to the country to stand
firm and rally to the support of our cause. Well is this a fact? Are
the people and some of the States beginning to falter? I hope not.
As far as my observations and information extends I think not. The
recent unexpected reverses in Tennessee and the almost unobstructed
transit of Sherman thru Georgia and the occupation of Savannah
and the base and servile expressions of the people of that City so unlike the conduct of every other Southern City to the insolent oppres-
sors has caused sadness, but I think, not despondency. Has it not, on
the contrary, aroused a spirit of higher resolve in every patriot bosom
never to submit. And may we not hope that it will cause every
freeman in our Broad Land to rally from mountain and plain to
overwhelm and crush our wicked foe? But it is not to be denied
nor should it be required, that the administration of our affairs
needs reforms and that there are abuses which have carried dissatisfaction and have tended to impair confidence in the public
agents if not alienate the minds of many of our people from the
Government, and that if these abuses are not reprimanded many
will be brought to the conclusion that we have gained nothing by
a successful revolution, that our Government is no better than the
Yankees and that all the losses we have sustained, and above all
our precious blood has been poured out in vain. I wish to speak
plainly Sir and I tell you that there is danger of this feeling pre-
vailing. There is an impression that there is a want of wisdom and
capacity from the station assigned them in all departments. I will
except the Treasury since the appointment of the present incumbent [George A. Trenholm]. He has made a favorable impression
and it is believed he will restore the currency if any man can. But
there was no confidence in the capacity of his Predecessor [Mem-
minger] tho' recognized as a good and patriotic man. And there
is but little if any more confidence now in the management of all

the other departments, than there was in the Treasury—And the people judge of men by their results which is after all a very good way. By their fruits ye shall know them. Will they judge of the capacity of the General Post Master [John H. Reagan] by the facilities afforded by him for the prompt and safe communication of intelligence when letters and papers are usually from six to 10 days & sometimes as high as twenty days in their transmission, which ought to be received two days from the time they are deposited in the receiving offices, and this continued year after year, people are apt to think that there is a screw loose some where. There is some faithless agent concerned in the transmission either as post Master or as Courier. And because the Head Man of the department don't fetch him out and hold him to account—dispatch him—put him in the army in conscript, and put a better man in his place, one who will have a faithful regard to the obligations of his office, people are apt to think that he don't understand his business—or is not fit for his place. And I think not without reason. Some allowance must be made for the condition of the railroads. Occasionally a car is thrown off the track, & the connection is not made. Well that would delay the mail one day. It ought to come on the next day —and that would not excuse its detention for 10 days—or from 4 to 10 days beyond the time it should be delivered almost every mail. There is a great tendency especially among officials, to attribute all the evils which we experience to the war and the war is often made the scapegoat for the evils of our public agents who wilfully neglect their duty to the public. And it is just this negligence & faithlessness of public agents, this want of official responsibility which causes confusion and uncertainty in the affairs of daily life in War Times. And much of it would be corrected and the people saved from many annoyances to which they are now subjected if all men holding public office were made to feel that it was a trust reposed in them for the public good, & held to a strict responsibility and because . . . it is more important in war than in . . . peace times that there should be a rigid enforcement of official responsibility—and because these abuses exist in the administration of the post office department & this faithlessness are not found out & held to strict account that the people have concluded that the head of that department is unfit for his place and ought to be replaced. I think they are right.

I omit to pass any criticism on the State Department. Mr. Benjamin is said to be a smart man. But does not seem to have much to do, as our foreign relations are not very extensive as yet. But I promised to let him pass.

Well what shall we say of the great war department. Perhaps the most important department of the government at this time, not excepting the Treasury. The administration of this department which requires I should think a man of large and comprehensive vision who is familiar with the Geography and topography of the country and its military resources in their various and extensive complications. He should be also well acquainted with the Enemy's country & its military resources and if not a trained military man, which I think would be better, he ought to be well versed in the history of wars and what has given one belligerent the advantage over the other. He ought to be a man of sound judgement & of great practical knowledge. He ought to be a man of decision of will & force of character. He ought to be systematic and habituated to business and with all he ought to be what is called a working man Well how does the present incumbent in this great office compare with these requisitions. The public will judge. By their fruits ye shall know them. Mr. Seddon is a Gentleman of refinement & literary taste if not attainment. He wishes to do right, if he allways had the nerve to do it. But it is said he leans upon his chiefs of Bureaus. He was a pretty good lawyer it is said—Some years ago. He is a man of wealth, had retired from the practice if I am not misinformed some time before the war. Let him be judged by his fruits. I would not take a feather from his cap.

With his administration may be dated the introduction of the impressment system. There had been occasional impressments before perhaps. But to him is due the Credit or the obloquy of saddling it upon the country as a system and so far as it has been modified or restricted by legislation it is believed it was not by his advice but in spite of every influence he could exert to prevent it. He boasted that he was no politician—he had no favors to ask of the people, tho' he had just before his appointment been defeated to a seat in Congress to which he aspired. And he was therefore the very man to introduce and carry through this odious system of impressments, which I believe has done our Cause all most as much harm as the Yankees have done. Nothing in my opinion has so irritated our people, & dampened their ardour, or has paralysed the productive resources of the Country as has this odious system. I do not remember to have read of a single instance, in the history of war, when the system of impressment was relied upon by a Government, against its own subjects or citizens to provision an army and keep it supplied. It is my impression that the power has only been exercised in case of emergency, by the commanding general when the stores which had been provided in a regular and legitimate mode, had failed or were inaccessible. But tell me, has there ever been an instance in the history of any Country, when one of the Departments of impressing agents intruding into the homes of private Citizens, property of the Citizens against their consent to feed & cloth the armies and to furnish their trains and equipments. And when was there a Country been flooded as has been this State with an army of impressing agents intruding into the homes of private Citizens, & searching them from top to bottom, to wrest from the proprietors the products of his labour? Is there an example anywhere to be found, where such means have been resorted to to supply and replenish the Army stores to feed and clothe the department officials and their subordinates and to stock the Government work shops. If there is such an example I ask for it. Mr. Editor this movement was the greatest blunder of the war. There was no necessity for it. To say there was is to libell the patriotism of a people who have shown themselves to be as noble & patriotic a race of men as ever trod the Earth. A people who have sustained a revolution more gigantic in its opposition than any that has ever occurred on earth— and have manfully stood up in its black as well as its bright days regardless of all the blunders that have been made by their trusted agents, and not withstanding the injustice which has been done them by the Authorities constituted by themselves. It is Mr. Seddons misfortune to have his name identified with this system. He is regarded as the Father of it—tho' in my opinion he is only the Adopted Father. It is the base thing of one who fills a much smaller space in the public eye—very small indeed [probably Gorgas]. And it is a wonder that a man of Mr. Seddons position & grade could have been induced to follow his lead.[18]

Despite his misgivings about the Confederate cabinet, Letcher still found it possible to believe in an eventual rebel victory. The new year would mark the end of the old order in the South, the only way of life Letcher had ever known. The first quarter of this fateful year was blurred in turmoil as the Confederate nation disintegrated. Letcher served on a Lexington citizens committee seeking food for the troops, and later he assisted the Confederate evacuation of Richmond, but most of his actions were obscured in the general chaos. The crisis in the deep South turned to catastrophe. Sherman's blue legions left humble Savannah on February 1 and drove up the Atlantic coast, passing through South Carolina like avenging angels, and mauling General Joseph Johnston's deteriorating army in North Carolina. Even the mighty Army of Northern Virginia tottered. Beseiged at Petersburg by the relentless Grant, Lee's genius finally succumbed to the overwhelming power of the enemy. The fatal breach in the rebels' defenses came on April 1, and Lee's desperate attempt to escape to Lynchburg was thwarted by hordes of blue coats. The inevitable surrender came at Appomattox on April 9. The war was over; the Confederacy was dead.[19]

For the last 15 months of the Confederate experiment Letcher was a private citizen, but he had continued to support the war wholeheartedly. However, his and the whole South's efforts and sacrifices were in vain. The cause was lost, and now southerners had to face the new challenge of reconciliation and reunion.

CHAPTER 13

Peace Again

Letcher calmly accepted the Union's victory and turned to face the problems of defeat. The realization of failure sank into the hearts and minds of the people of Virginia; yet it was hard to comprehend that the old, traditional way of life was gone forever, that the bright dreams of the future had been no more than mirages. Four years of sacrifice and suffering had reaped a bitter harvest. The war had devastated Virginia. Material damage had been extensive, and many of her finest sons had fallen in battle. Many who survived left their spirit and vitality with their dead comrades, and many others, soldiers and civilians alike, were unable to adjust fully to the new world of peace and reunion.

Letcher was certainly no stranger to the rigors of war but, like most southerners, he tried to return to as normal a life as the times —and the conquerors—would allow. The moderateness so characteristic of his prewar career flowered again with the coming of peace. Bitterness, self–pity, and hatred were rejected by the former governor, who wrote to his hero Lee less than five weeks after Appomattox:

> . . . my confidence in you as a gentleman, a christian, and an unrivalled military leader is unshaken. . . . If when the struggle commenced, we could have convinced the leading men, and the administration, that the war would be a long and bloody one, and most fiercely contested, I feel persuaded, the result would have been

different. All however is now over, and it is useless to complain of the past.[1]

Letcher refused to become obsessed with the past, with what might have been. He looked to the future, convinced that his generation had the obligation to begin the work of restoring a nation torn and sundered by the war, but it was not easy to escape the past. As the former war governor of one of the most powerful states of the Confederacy, as a vigorous, enthusiastic rebel leader, he was remembered by friend and foe. The war was over, but many people on both sides of the Potomac were bitter and vengeful. The assassination of Lincoln aroused the North to fever pitch. On May 4, a telegram from Grant to the commander of the military district of the James River decided Letcher's immediate future: ". . . I wish you would have efforts made to arrest [William] Smith, [R.M.T.] Hunter, Letcher and all other particularly obnoxious political leaders in the State."[2]

Grant's order filtered down the chain of command, and on May 17 a detachment of Union cavalry under Major Alexander Moore left Winchester and rode through the Valley toward Lexington. Three days later the cavalrymen entered Lexington before dawn and quietly surrounded Letcher's home. Major Moore knocked loudly, and Letcher sleepily arose to investigate. As soon as he opened the door, Moore arrested him. Letcher hurriedly packed a few clothes, wrote Davidson a short note about business affairs, said his goodbyes, and climbed into the troop's ambulance wagon. As the first rays of dawn came over the horizon, the cavalrymen and their prisoner headed back toward Winchester.[3]

News of the former governor's arrest preceded the cavalry troop. Along the way people gathered at every crossroad and village to cheer him and give him flowers and food. He was treated courteously by his guards, but the all–day ride over the rough road to Staunton tired the 52–year–old prisoner. The troop arrived in Staunton just after dark, and Letcher was allowed to send a note back to his wife. As usual, he accepted his fate calmly, assuring his wife that there was nothing to worry about.

The next morning the cavalry detachment resumed its journey, which proceeded uneventfully until early on May 23. Then, at a point just north of Woodstock and only 20 miles from Winchester, the rear of the column was ambushed by four armed horsemen. By the time order was restored among the confused cavalrymen, the raiders had disappeared with six mounted Yankee prisoners. Major Moore naturally assumed that the raid was an attempt to liberate Letcher; he increased the guard around the wagon and double–timed the rest of the way to Winchester. Letcher bounced around in the speeding wagon, unaware of the daring attack.

The mysterious raiders were Captain George Summers and three troopers of the Seventh Virginia Cavalry Regiment who could not resist the temptation to hit the rear of the column and capture some loot. They inflicted no casualties and quickly released their embarrassed captives, disappearing into the nearby mountains with six Yankee horses as their prize. Summers soon realized the rashness of his little game with the conquerors, and late in the month he returned the six horses to federal authorities. The Union army was in no mood for such antics. In June, Summers and one of his companions were arrested and executed summarily.

Meanwhile, Letcher arrived in Winchester late on the morning of May 23. He remained there for a day, and again he was treated well by his captors. On the morning of May 24 he was sent on to Washington. Arriving in the nation's capital around midnight, Letcher was kept in an army arsenal overnight. The next morning he was taken to Carroll Prison, his home for the next 47 days.[4]

Carroll Prison was an annex to the better known Old Capitol Prison. During the war this entire prison complex had housed at various times rebel prisoners of war, smugglers, blockade runners, contraband southern Negroes, court–martialed Union officers, spies, and a mass of suspects of all kinds interned under the broad powers of the Lincoln administration. The Old Capitol section, located just across First Street from the Capitol, was built in 1815 to house Congress temporarily following the destructive British raid in 1814. Later it became a boarding house, and here died John C. Calhoun, the real father of the Confederacy. The adjoining Carroll annex was originally a closely packed row of residences named Duff Green Row. During the war, the Old Capitol alone could not handle the masses of assorted prisoners, and this row of homes was hastily converted into a wing of the main prison.[5]

Letcher was treated well during his imprisonment. Responsible army officers and prison officials showed him every possible consideration. After a month in a private cell, Letcher was transferred to a larger cell with ex–Governor Vance of North Carolina, ex–Governor Brown of Georgia, banker Gazeway B. Lamar of Savannah, General Edward Johnson of Chesterfield County, Virginia, and a Doctor Stewart of King George County, Virginia. A close comradeship developed between these political prisoners, and Letcher and Vance forgot their wartime clashes and became particularly close friends. Both were gregarious and optimistic, refusing to yield to despondency, while the others, particularly Brown, became melancholy and moody. The energetic Letcher chaffed under enforced idleness, but he knew his friends and neighbors would look after his interests until he returned. He occasionally received money from banker Purcell in Richmond, and his family received food and funds from Rockbridge neighbors who quietly took up collections whenever the Letcher family needed help.

The withering heat of summertime Washington forced the prisoners to strip down to their underclothes, but prison life was not unbearable. Many hours were spent playing cards and conversing on every imaginable subject. Old politicians Brown, Vance, and Letcher were never at a loss for words. Occasionally the prisoners could watch outside events from their windows, such as the gigantic Fourth of July celebration staged less than three months after the Union had overcome its greatest menace. Good food from nearby restaurants and large supplies of whiskey and brandy were available as long as the prisoners had money. Letcher and his fellow rebels were not maltreated by the government they had fought for four years.[6]

Letcher had known Washington well as a congressman in the 1850's, and he had never drawn a sectional line in his social and business activities there. Now some of his old Yankee friends came to his assistance. Radical Congressman Elihu B. Washburne offered to help, and Abel R. Corbin, the Virginian's partner in prewar speculation in Washington real estate, visited him several times. Corbin verified the fate of Letcher's Washington property: the land had been confiscated for non—payment of taxes and sold for $200. Corbin estimated its real value at over $20,000, and erroneously claimed that it would revert to Letcher's heirs after his death. Further assistance came from former Maryland Governor Philip Francis Thomas, Colonel John A. Bridgeland, and the powerful financier Commodore Cornelius Vanderbilt.

The most useful help came from Horatio G. Wright. At the beginning of the war, Captain Wright had been captured while attempting to destroy the facilities at the Gosport naval base. Before being returned to the North, he had spent several days as a paroled prisoner of war at the Governor's Mansion in Richmond, and he had never forgotten the governor's kindness in a time of rising passion and hatred. The chaos of war had swallowed up Captain Wright, but his unspectacular yet solid abilities had rocketed him upward. In 1865 he was no longer an obscure captain of engineers but Major General Wright, Commander, VI Corps, Army of the Potomac. One of Grant's ablest lieutenants, he was an influential figure in Washington. He made certain that Letcher was well treated. He told Secretary of War Stanton the whole story of his encounter with the wartime governor of Virginia, and vigorously pressed for Letcher's release.[7]

But kind treatment was no substitute for freedom. Letcher and his cellmates, anxious to be released, all applied for pardons or paroles. On June 4, Letcher officially asked President Johnson for a pardon, but he received no answer and assumed that Secretary of War Stanton had intercepted his application. Later he applied directly to Stanton for a pardon, but this petition was flatly rejected. Lawyer Letcher was doubly frustrated because he had never been formally charged with any crime.[8]

The depressed Brown was the first to be released, and he was soon followed by Dr. Stewart and then by Vance on July 6. Letcher became more and more restless as his comrades departed, but he retained his optimism. He particularly missed his new friend Vance, an enjoyable fellow under any circumstances, but he was determined to wait patiently without further appeals to federal authorities. His thoughts were constantly of his wife and children whom he instructed to conceal their sorrow and depression.[9]

On July 5, Letcher's old friend Davidson acted. He persuaded Virginia Governor Francis H. Pierpoint, Letcher's wartime rival, to write the President requesting a pardon. Just how effective this letter and the efforts of Letcher's other friends were is uncertain, but on July 10 the former governor successfully applied for a parole. Under its strict terms, he had to return to Lexington, remain in his home county, and send periodic reports on his activities to Washington.[10]

Before leaving for home, Letcher had a half hour interview with President Johnson. The two men were not strangers. Both had been in Congress in the 1850's, Letcher in the House and Johnson in the Senate. Both had been southern Democrats, and both retained a streak of Jacksonianism. The interview went smoothly, and a week later Letcher enthusiastically described the meeting to his friend Vance:

> I had quite a pleasant and satisfactory conversation with the President. He received me cordially, was courteous, polite, frank and every way agreeable. He spoke kindly in regard to our troubles, and expressed an anxious desire to see all our troubles speedily settled, and upon mutually satisfactory terms to all parties interested. I passed a pleasant half hour with him, and I think if the Southern people, will meet him in a proper spirit (as I have no doubt they will,) we will get out of our difficulties upon far better terms, than I had anticipated.[11]

The day after the interview, Letcher started home, retracing the route of his less pleasant journey in May. He passed through most of his old congressional district and everywhere people welcomed him back. These were the same people who had sent him to Congress for a decade and then rejected him in 1863. Letcher was pleased at the warmth of his reception, and his journey almost became a triumphant procession. His arrival in Lexington surprised his family and friends, who had not been notified of his release. Tired but happy, he spent the next few days relaxing at home.

Letcher considered his imprisonment unjust, but he was not bitter, and consoled himself with the notion that his ordeal proved that the North recognized the effectiveness of his and Virginia's war effort. He counseled patience, moderation, and reconciliation, always emphasizing the future rather than the past. Over and over he told his friends that normal relations had to be reestablished as quickly as possible. He felt that the best way to get rid of the military occupation and reconstruct normal governmental machinery was to cooperate fully with Johnson's reconstruction program. Letcher believed that Johnson could be trusted to treat the South fairly, and he felt that the budget–conscious President was anxious to demobilize the huge federal army of occupation quickly. A political realist, Letcher knew that Johnson's mild Reconstruction was a real bargain for the South. He knew that Johnson's enemies, the Radical Republicans, would impose a much harsher Reconstruction if they gained power. Johnson was the South's best hope in Washington. A letter early in September to a friend in Richmond summarized Letcher's position:

> We must however accept the present condition of affairs, and make the best of it. We must pursue the line of policy, in effecting the re-organization, which has been marked out for us by the authorities at Washington. The President has adopted his policy, after mature consideration, and it is folly to cavil or complain, or suggest wherein it can be changed to advantage. We must take it as it is . . . I have confidence in President Johnson . . . His feelings toward the South are kind. . . . We must therefore give him our confidence, and cheerful and cordial cooperation in the efforts he is making to restore the reign of civil law. If we do this we will have no reason to complain of him.[12]

Letcher discussed reconstruction with Davidson, Dorman, Munford, Lee, and other friends, but he did not address his opinions to the general public. He did not feel free to speak publicly while on parole, and also he feared that his pro–Johnson stand would be interpreted as cynical, craven boot licking. Despite the urging of many, particularly former Adjutant General Richardson, Letcher adamantly refused to reenter the political whirl; but politics was still in his blood. Almost instinctively he followed the rapidly unfolding political events of the postwar period. However, his legal status as a parolee, his financial difficulties, and his shaky health all contributed to his decision to remain on the sidelines.

Tired physically and mentally, Letcher spent the last two weeks of August at Rockbridge Springs, resting and receiving treatments for inflamed eyes. Then he returned to Lexington and plunged back into his legal work. A large backlog of wartime litigation increased his optimism about the future. He spent most of the fall reading law and handling minor cases. Several times he attempted to take lucrative cases in other counties, but each time he sought permission to leave Rockbridge, the request became entangled in government red tape; permission to leave the county was always granted, but too late to do any good. For the moment, while waiting for his presidential pardon, Letcher had to make do on the slim legal pickings of his home county.[13]

Lexington and Rockbridge County were hard hit by the war, but the economy, based primarily on small–scale farming and local business enterprises, revived quickly. The wheat crop failed in 1865, and the large farms were disrupted by the loss of their slave labor, but there were bountiful harvests of corn, rye, and oats. This gave the community the economic boost it needed to begin the long journey back to prosperity. The two schools that were so important to the economic and cultural life of Lexington, Washington College and V.M.I., both reopened during the year, and the people of Rockbridge returned to their peacetime occupations.[14]

Letcher contributed to the revival of both schools. He encouraged the board of trustees of Washington College to offer the presidency of the school to Lee, and he encouraged the former general to accept the board's offer. Everyone in Lexington was delighted by Lee's acceptance, but none more than Letcher, who still idolized the distinguished, aristocratic hero of the Confederacy. These two men, so dissimilar in background and personality, were close friends in the last years of Lee's life. Each in his own way worked to heal the wounds of the war and to reunite the nation. The general indulged the whims of his only goddaughter, as a friendship that had begun in the high noon of war matured in the twilight of peace.[15]

Letcher contributed even more to the reestablishment of V.M.I.

In 1866, he was appointed to the board of visitors by Governor Pierpoint. Letcher worked hard to restore the shattered institute, and the next year he was elevated to the presidency of the board. He retained this post until 1881, when failing health forced his retirement. In October, 1865, 16 cadets reported for the first postwar term, but the enrollment increased to 55 at the end of the academic year. Working closely with his old friend, Superintendent Francis H. Smith, Letcher faced many problems: debt reduction, physical reconstruction, and recruitment of outstanding professors and students. The first years were difficult, but by 1869 the worst was over. A fine faculty, including General G. W. C. Lee and Commodore Matthew Fontaine Maury, was assembled, and the student body was first—rate. The physical plant was rebuilt, and the debt was almost completely eliminated. V.M.I., the school Letcher had adopted as his own, was flourishing once again.[16]

Despite his many services to the institute, Letcher continued to concentrate primarily on rebuilding his shattered finances through his law practice, but he was still severely handicapped by his parole restrictions. Once again former political enemies came to his rescue. Unpredictable John Minor Botts made the first move. A prewar Whig, Botts had opposed secession, and during the war he had been a pacifist and a Unionist, spending several months in jail for his convictions. Now he was a Republican, one of the leaders of an emerging political force in Virginia. In 1867 Botts would fall from favor with the increasingly radical Virginia Republicans, but late in 1865 he was on the rise in Virginia and not without influence in Washington. On November 10, he asked President Johnson to grant Letcher a full pardon.

Another rising Republican, farmer John F. Lewis of Rockingham County, spoke up for his old friend Letcher. Lewis was another prewar Whig who had opposed secession, remaining strictly neutral during the war. Lewis would become lieutenant governor in 1869, and he already spoke with some authority about state politics. On November 15, he conferred with Johnson and strongly recommended a full pardon for Letcher. R. A. Gray, a Rockingham Unionist, also suggested a pardon for his friend from Lexington. The pardon did not come for almost two years, but lesser results were immediate. On November 15, President Johnson broadened the terms of Letcher's parole to allow him to travel freely on business. This was a real breakthrough in Letcher's postwar law practice, and his financial situation gradually began to improve.[17]

Letcher buried himself even more deeply in his expanding practice. He concentrated on Rockbridge, Botetourt, and Bath Counties, but he made known his availability anywhere in the state and frequently journeyed to Richmond. In Rockbridge, he collected most of his fees in the form of flour, bacon, beef, potatoes, or corn—and just enough cash to pay taxes and purchase a few essential items for his bare home. The failure of the 1865 wheat crop killed hope for a spectacular recovery, but steady progress continued in Rockbridge. The Letchers lived comfortably in the old Tutwiler House, and once again their home was alive with laughter, song, and activity.[18]

Letcher watched the political tides carefully, noting with sorrow the rise of the Radical Republicans in Washington and their cohorts in Virginia. He foresaw dark days. In April, 1866, he discussed his own situation with an old friend who had marched with him in the Jacksonian crusade, millionaire industrialist Cyrus Hall McCormick. "The war has swept from me all my property", he wrote,

> and I am now commencing life anew. I have health, energy and industry, and I feel confident of success. I am however still under parole, and likely to remain so, from present indications. I have not cast a vote since May, 1860, nor do I expect either as a voter or otherwise, to meddle in politics. I have no desire to do so, and even if I had, it would in my present condition be little short of absolute madness. I served the country faithfully in the better days of the Republic, I have no desire to serve in these days of its decline.[19]

In the midst of his law practice Letcher did not entirely ignore the railroad construction craze which swept through the nation as soon as the war ended. Every region had its own grandiose dreams, and the Valley of Virginia was no exception. Here the pet project was a line connecting Harper's Ferry on the Baltimore & Ohio Railroad with Salem on the Virginia & Tennessee Railway. Two great wartime railroads, one Union and one Confederate, would be joined in the newly reunited nation! This profitable and symbolic—very definitely in that order—connection would run through the heart of the Valley from Harper's Ferry to Winchester to Staunton to Lexington and on to Salem.

The idea kindled the imagination of many a Lexingtonian, and Colonel Samuel Houston Letcher, the former governor's brother, was one of its most enthusiastic supporters. In March he became editor of the Lexington *Gazette and Banner,* and until his death in 1868 he used the columns of his journal to promote the project. In April, 1866, John W. Brockenbrough, Samuel McDowell Moore, and many other prominent citizens of Rockbridge trooped off to an eight-county convention in Staunton which formally organized the Valley Railroad.

Letcher supported this effort to improve the Valley's access to outside markets, just as he had backed the extension of the James River and Kanawha Canal before the war. During the war, he had been one of the few Confederate leaders to appreciate fully the importance of railroads as transportation arteries, and now he backed the Valley Railroad cautiously. He had no excess capital to invest, and thus he was not one of the local investors who lost heavily when the venture eventually failed. Tracks were laid; the line reached Staunton in 1874 and, finally, Lexington in 1883. But here the project collapsed, still 50 miles from Salem. The powerful B. & O. assumed control of the bankrupt line and operated it until 1942. However, for lack of the Salem linkup the road never became the economic panacea its supporters had envisioned.[20]

During this same period, Monsieur Ernest Bellot des Minières came to Virginia to reinvestigate the possibility of buying the James River and Kanawha Canal from the state and extending it over the mountains to the Ohio River system. Letcher had attempted to close this same deal with the French capitalist early in 1861, but the war had terminated negotiations. Now the Frenchman was back again, and the people of Rockbridge gave him a warm welcome. This time Letcher was not involved in the negotiations, and the canny capitalist soon realized that railroads had rendered his old plan impractical. Much to the disappointment of the debt—conscious assembly and the people along the route of the obsolete canal, the negotiations came to nothing.[21]

Spectacular business dreams did not distract Letcher from his routine legal work. He handled more and more cases involving claims against the federal government, part of the bonanza bequeathed to lawyers by the war. His financial status improved somewhat, but his large family quickly absorbed his earnings. He was forced to rent some rooms in his home to students at Washington College. He also tried to sell a plot of land to the college, but the trustees would not meet his price.[22]

Only V.M.I. could lure the former governor from his law practice for long. He agreed to make his first postwar speech at the institute on September 10 at the rededication of William J. Hubard's statue of Washington, a copy of Houdon's original at the Capitol in Richmond. The assembly had first placed this statue at V.M.I. in 1856, but Hunter's troops had carried the Union's father away from rebel land in 1864. The return of the statue to its proper pedestal, the erasing of another scar of the war, was a festive occasion in Lexington, and over 1,500 people gathered for the ceremony.

For Letcher it was more than a celebration. It was his first formal address to the public since the end of the war, his first open appraisal of the new order in the South and the nation. He made up for his long silence with a lengthy, rambling speech. Letcher looked far back into the nation's past, seeking fundamental causes of the Civil War. Primarily he blamed the "politicians and political parsons of New England". Then he launched into a detailed justification of secession and an even more involved discussion of the sacrosanct rights of the states, still the foundation of his political credo. He condemned Congress for refusing to seat southern delegations in December, 1865, but he predicted that patience and forbearance would correct that injustice—Radical Reconstruction was only a few months away! He reminded his audience that slavery, the main cause of contention between the North and the South, was gone forever and best forgotten.

This led the former war governor to his main theme: reconciliation. This was his message, the doctrine he had been advocating privately ever since the end of the war. He challenged the victors to be magnanimous, and he appealed to both sides to forgive and forget. In conclusion he stepped back, unveiled the statue of Washington, and shouted, "God bless America".[23]

Returning to his law practice, Letcher was soon involved in a case destined to create widespread repercussions and hinder the reconstruction policy he had just championed. On November 13, 1866, Dr. James L. Watson and his family were on their way to church in Rockbridge County. Suddenly their carriage was passed and slightly bumped by another carriage driven by William Medley, a freedman. Enraged, Doctor Watson returned to his home, got a pistol, sought out the unarmed freedman, and shot him dead as he tried to flee. A county court of five magistrates voted three to two not to turn the case over to a jury. General John M. Schofield, military commander in Virginia, considered the court's action a clear threat to the rights and welfare of all freedmen, and early in December he ordered Watson's arrest. The doctor was brought to Richmond and tried before a military commission.

Letcher and his friend Dorman journeyed to the capital to assist in the defense. Working with several outstanding Richmond lawyers, they challenged the commission's right to try a civilian, but General Schofield, convinced that a recent act of Congress condoned this procedure, rejected their protests. Letcher appealed directly to President Johnson, citing the recent Supreme Court decision in the Milligan case forbidding such a procedure, even in wartime, if the civil courts were functioning. After conferring with his attorney general, the president ordered the release of Watson.

This legal victory was a costly political defeat. The Watson case had been covered thoroughly by the press, and it helped convince many northerners that the South would never voluntarily grant justice to Negroes. The Radicals had already decisively defeated Johnson (and the South) in the congressional elections in November, but the Watson case and similar incidents throughout the South added more fuel to the roaring flames of Radical Re-

construction. The black codes, rejection of the Fourteenth Amendment, widespread terror and violence, prejudiced court decisions,
and other rebel reflexes had finally brought down upon the South
the pent—up wrath of the victors. Like Letcher, most southerners
sincerely desired reconciliation but, instinctively conservative and
incredibly insensitive to northern public opinion, they did not
fully realize the need for change in their traditional way of life.
The same inflexibility that had doomed the Confederacy now
plunged the South into Radical Reconstruction.[24]

During the early months of the postwar period, Letcher had
stayed on the political sidelines, concentrating on his law practice.
His instinctive moderation had flowered in peacetime despite
severe hardships, but the times were not ripe for moderation. The
South resented and resisted federal control, and the people of the
North came to believe that the fruits of their victory were in
danger. Thus Virginia entered an agonizing period of political
and psychological readjustment. In the twilight of his life, Letcher
still faced perplexing problems. Politically he again had to choose
between moderation and extremism, and he also faced personal
and financial difficulties. His last years were not to be easy ones.

CHAPTER 14

Twilight

The year 1867 began well for John Letcher. On January 15, President Johnson granted him a full pardon. His law practice, embracing everything from debt collections to the defense of accused murderers, was flourishing. In March, he was offered a directorship of the old James River and Kanawha Canal Company, but had to refuse the position: he was too busy for any more outside chores.[1]

Rockbridge County was continuing to recover from the ravages of war, but the pace was agonizingly slow and everyone was short of cash. Despite his booming law practice, Letcher's financial status improved rather slowly, and, like almost everyone else, he was unable to accumulate capital. And now Radical Reconstruction threw a shadow over the whole state. Led by Thaddeus Stevens, the Radical Republicans were in control in Washington, and they were determined to give the freedmen every traditional American civil right, including suffrage, the key to practical power.

In March, Congress transformed Virginia into Military District Number One under General John M. Schofield. By April, the restless Negroes had been tightly organized under the leadership of James W. Hunnicutt, a white clergyman and editor from Fredericksburg. Botts, Pierpoint, and other moderate Republicans were soon downgraded. Compromise efforts failed, and the Republican Party of Virginia swung sharply toward radicalism.[2]

The white southern reaction to this turn of events was slow to come, but Letcher, an instinctive moderate, saw danger and acted quickly. He decided to go to the source of the new policies, Washington, where he could talk frankly with some of his old congressional colleagues and learn exactly what they wanted from the South. He also hoped to convince some of the error of their "radical" ways. As a congressman Letcher had never allowed politics to interfere with personal relations, and some leading postwar Radicals were old friends. Letcher, Davidson, and another friend, Dolph White, arrived in the nation's capital late in July. Congress was still in session, and Letcher was able to see old associates. However, his conversations with leading Radicals produced more heat than light.

First he talked with Thaddeus Stevens. In prewar days these two practical, bourgeois congressmen had not allowed the widening sectional schism to destroy their personal respect for each other. The war had severely strained their relationship, but "Old Thad" greeted Letcher without hostility and they talked for over an hour. Stevens suggested that Letcher return to Congress as a spokesman for the sound, conservative people of the South, and he offered to run through Congress a special bill removing all of Letcher's political disabilities. He wrote out a petition for Letcher to sign, but this petition contained a clause expressing regret and sorrow for the rebellion. When Letcher read this he exploded, declared that his only regret was the rebellion's failure, and stalked away.[3]

Letcher next encountered Schuyler Colfax of Indiana, speaker of the house. He and his friends met Colfax in his hotel room one evening, and Letcher, still fuming from his clash with Stevens, immediately assailed the Republican program of Radical Reconstruction. He suggested that the whole problem be turned over to Lee and Grant. Colfax sharply rejected this naïve proposal, and the conversation grew still more heated. Whiskey and cigars loosened restraints, and finally Letcher shouted that he would gladly renew the war if he could and stormed from the room, followed by Davidson and White. Davidson secretly slipped back to Colfax's room and asked the Hoosier congressman not to repeat

Letcher's emotional pronouncements. Colfax agreed to forget the incident, and Davidson rejoined Letcher and White without having been missed.

Letcher also talked with old friend Elihu B. Washburne and other Radicals. These talks were not so heated, but were no more productive of any tangible results in Letcher's favor. Letcher realized that the Radicals were in earnest about their reconstruction program, and that nothing he might say could dampen their ardor and determination.[4] The former governor returned to his law practice in Lexington, wary of the political future.

Opposition to the Radical Republican surge in Virginia evolved slowly but surely. Only after the disciplined Republicans won the October election for delegates to the new constitutional convention did opponents of black suffrage belatedly begin to organize. The conservative white folk of Virginia held county rallies all over the state to mobilize their strength. In Rockbridge, political veterans such as Samuel McDowell Moore, J. H. and William Paxton, James W. Massie, Dorman, and Brockenbrough led the new movement. Letcher supported them but remained in the background.[5]

When a convention was called to organize a new Conservative Party, Letcher became more active. In December, he joined Moore and four others on the Rockbridge delegation to the convention in Richmond. The Radical—dominated constitutional convention was meeting in Richmond at the same time, but for a few days the budding Conservatives had the center of the stage. Letcher was delighted to be back in the whirl of politics, the only life he really loved. He was appointed to the business committee that organized the convention proceedings. His parliamentary experience and political prestige helped nurture the nascent Conservative Party.

Letcher was also appointed to one of the permanent district committees that directed the development of the party on the local level. He was certainly active in the birth of this new party, but was not a member of the high command. The real power rested with his friend "Sandy" Stuart, a very shrewd political operator, and a few others including John B. Baldwin, Thomas

S. Bocock, James L. Kemper, James R. Branch, and R. T. Daniel.
As usual, many prewar Whigs were in key positions as the cur-
rents of postwar Virginia politics shifted again. The Conservatives formally launched their new movement with a manifesto
that recognized the abolition of slavery but demanded a quick,
complete restoration of Virginia to the Union, and insisted on
white rule in the state. Letcher returned to Lexington and supported the new party, but continued to put his law practice ahead
of politics. He was never to join the upper echelons of the movement.[6]

Legally he was still ineligible for federal or state office, and
early in 1868 an indictment by a federal grand jury in Richmond
further handicapped his political activities. This was the government's fourth and final legal assault on Jefferson Davis, and the
broad indictment was a virtual who's who of the Confederacy:

> . . . the Grand Jurors . . . find and present, that the said Jefferson
> Davis . . . did at Richmond . . . on the twenty-fifth day of May, in
> the year one thousand eight hundred and sixty-one, conspire and
> unite with Robert E. Lee, Judah P. Benjamin, John C. Breckin-
> ridge, William Mahone, Henry A. Wise, John Letcher, William
> Smith, Jubal A. Early, James Longstreet, Daniel H. Hill, Ambrose
> P. Hill, Gustave T. Beauregard, William H. C. Whiting, Edward
> Sparrow, Samuel Cooper, Joseph E. Johnston, John B. Gordon, Clai-
> borne F. Jackson, and F. O. Moore, and with other persons whose
> names are to the Grand Jurors unknown, to the number of one hun-
> dred thousand, to levy war against the said United States.[7]

The Johnson administration did not push this long–delayed
trial. Public opinion now resisted the idea of executing Davis or
any other rebel for treason, and the Davis case had become something of a legal and political hot potato. The trial was repeatedly
delayed until the President's general amnesty on Christmas, 1868,
disposed of the matter. The indictment was officially dropped
early in 1869, but for a year the threat of being tried for treason
had hung over Letcher's head. His friend Munford had stood
his bond of $1,000—Letcher simply did not have this much liquid
capital—and he had to go to Richmond several times to report
to the court. In the summer of 1868 his bail had been raised to

$5,000. When the indictment was dropped a great mental and financial burden was taken from Letcher's shoulders.[8]

He continued to watch Washington closely, and in November, 1868, he wrote his Radical friend Washburne asking about the significance of Grant's election to the presidency. Letcher still wanted Grant and Lee, "representative men of the two sections", to work out reconstruction by themselves so that economic prosperity would return. He insisted that he still had no political ambitions of his own. Washburne assured Letcher that Grant meant well for the South, and he urged the former governor and other southern moderates to resume leadership. Letcher was pleased with Washburne's letter, and the vision of a return to political prominence was far from repugnant to him. However, he continued to concentrate on his law practice, and remained only moderately active in the Conservative party.[9]

The Conservatives were led by "Sandy" Stuart, who had the courage and the foresight to champion a compromise that would accept the Negro suffrage section of the new state constitution in return for deletion of sections disfranchising ex–Confederates. First, he persuaded the reluctant Conservatives to take their half of the loaf. Then he helped persuade Congress to accept the other half. The Virginia electorate gave this compromise its stamp of approval by ratifying the liberal Underwood Constitution minus the disfranchising sections.

The concurrent gubernatorial election was another triumph for the Conservatives. The wily railroader and politician William Mahone—always maneuvering to combat rival B. & O. interests in the state—split the Republicans by swinging moderates behind Gilbert C. Walker, a carpetbagger from New York. The Conservatives quickly dropped their own candidate, Robert E. Withers of Danville, and supported their former enemy (Walker). After a bitter struggle, this unstable coalition defeated the Radical Republican candidate, acting–Governor Henry H. Wells.

Governor Walker was inaugurated in September, 1869, and the Conservative–dominated assembly swiftly ratified the Fourteenth and Fifteenth Amendments. By the end of January, 1870, Radical Reconstruction was finished in Virginia—over before it had really begun. Letcher was sorry to see his friend Withers sacrificed in the complex, Machiavellian maneuvering, and he was cool to the "carpetbagger" Walker, but he was pleased to see his friend and benefactor John F. Lewis gain the lieutenant governorship. Letcher did not campaign extensively but rejoiced in the Conservative triumph.[10]

Letcher's growing law practice, which on occasion included defending freedmen, allowed little time for politics. Much of his leisure was spent with Davidson, Dorman, General Smith, and other friends, reminiscing about the good old days. He spent many hours carrying out his duties as president of the board of visitors of V.M.I. And he enjoyed a happy family life, living simply and frugally in the rented Tutwiler House. The furnishings were plain, and Susan Letcher still took in Washington College students as boarders to augment the family finances, but the atmosphere was as gay, friendly, and informal as ever. They entertained frequently, still drawing most of their many friends from the ranks of the middle class. The war had not dampened the Letchers' zest for life, and the former governor spent many a pleasant evening with family and friends, liberally mixing whiskey, tobacco, and conversation.[11]

Letcher made several unsuccessful attempts to obtain immediate and full payment for his former real estate holdings in Washington. In December, 1870, he asked his friend Cornelius Vanderbilt for help. Vanderbilt tried to talk the problem over with Abel R. Corbin, one of Letcher's partners in the speculation, but this sly brother–in–law of President Grant was "unavailable". He had been implicated in Jay Gould and Jim Fisk's scandalous attempt to corner the gold market in 1869, and, when the story broke, Corbin had run for cover. In January, 1871, Vanderbilt wrote and apologized for not being able to help—and enclosed a check made out to Letcher for $1,000. This money was certainly a godsend to Letcher, who had been unable to accumulate much capital, despite strenuous efforts. At last he had enough cash–in–hand to be able to accept the complex, lengthy cases that enriched lawyers who could afford to wait months for their fees.[12]

Meanwhile, political fortunes were changing rapidly in Vir-

ginia, and Letcher watched intently. Governor Walker's administration was full of conflict. The sale of most of the state's railroad stock, a move Letcher had suggested in 1863, had reduced
Virginia's huge $45,000,000 debt, but there were those who felt
the state had sold its stocks too cheaply. The refunding of the debt
with new bonds paying a lucrative 6 per cent interest stirred
further discontent. Opposition to these policies rumbled through
the state, previewing a later upheaval.[13]

Following the General Amnesty Act of June, 1872, Letcher
continued to restrict his political activities. He was often mentioned as a possible candidate for high public office, but he was
quick to reject these suggestions. His own candidate for the governorship was John Randolph Tucker, his former attorney general, and his second choice was James L. Kemper, one of the
legion of former brigadiers active in postwar politics throughout
the country. The gubernatorial showdown with the fading Republicans came in 1873. A nationwide panic had created economic
chaos, but the Conservatives' power in Virginia was not shaken.
The Yankee Walker had been a useful tool during the party's
infancy, but now the Conservatives felt strong enough to dump
him. Most Conservatives agreed with Letcher that only a native
son should be in the Governor's Mansion. Kemper, a war hero,
was picked to replace the "alien" Walker, and Letcher's friend
Withers was nominated for the lieutenant governorship.

Though he still took a lively interest in political affairs, Letcher
was not particularly active in the effort to elect Kemper, whose
campaign was a repetitious slaying of the dragon of Negro rule
under federal control, but he did appear with the candidate at
political rallies in the Valley, and was delighted when Kemper
won a resounding victory over the rapidly disintegrating Republican state organization.[14]

Inauguration day, January 1, 1874, symbolized the end of the
last vestiges of outside control. Virginia was herself again. William H. Richardson congratulated Kemper, and predicted a
return to the good old days of the Letcher administration:

> . . . the chair of State [will be] filled by one of her own true sons
> gloriously chosen by her own people—and who will be indeed and

in truth their own Governor—one who like brave, true & honest
John Letcher, who in all his trying course, never did, or said or
even thought of anything for the personal or political advancement
of himself.[15]

Pleased as he was by Kemper's victory, Letcher could not resist
recommending a few appointments to the new governor. Politics
were in Letcher's blood, and he was getting more and more
anxious to plunge back into the thick of the fray. It was only a
matter of time.

The Kemper administration faced hard times. The Panic of
1873 was followed by a severe depression, and the new governor's
austerity program very soon gave rise to serious discontent
throughout the state. Kemper drastically reduced the state budget,
including funds for the new and increasingly popular public school
system. He also increased taxes and strictly honored the burden-
some state debt. Letcher, ever an advocate of economy in government and of fiscal integrity, supported Kemper's unpopular
program. In 1874, Kemper vetoed a blatant attempt by the assembly to gerrymander the powerful Negro vote in Petersburg into
oblivion. Many Conservatives were angered by this veto. Letcher
was not. His broad faith in democracy was stronger than his
racism, and he publicly denounced the assembly's action.[16]

The practice of law still came first with Letcher, and as energetic as ever, he gradually expanded his practice all over the
Valley. Vanderbilt's gift had been a big help, and the formation
of a law partnership with his eldest son, Samuel Houston Letcher,
helped further. In 1874 Letcher was sidelined by a serious illness,
one of the numerous maladies that had plagued him throughout
his life, but this time his son handled his duties until he recovered
several weeks later. At last he was able to accumulate some sav-
ings, over $2,000 in the Bank of Lexington. His experience as
wartime governor brought him many cases involving claims against
the federal government. Some southerners resented his handling
such cases for former Union soldiers, but for Letcher the war was
over, and he took any case he could get.[17]

He still devoted most of his leisure time to his family and friends
and his V.M.I. duties. The death of General Lee in 1870 had

cost him one friend, but the arrival of Matthew Fontaine Maury at V.M.I. had briefly added a new one. William Mahone was another close friend. Letcher could not approve of Mahone's postwar political manipulations, and he would soon oppose Mahone's deviation from Conservative gospel, but he drew a sharp line between politics and personalities. Except during the war years, Letcher was always too moderate, friendly, and gregarious a man to allow politics to ruin a friendship.[18]

The former governor still idolized Lee and Jackson and was active in campaigns to raise funds for monuments to these heroes of the rebellion. He was chairman of the Jackson Statue Committee, which eventually collected the $25,000 needed for an equestrian statue of the fallen hero of V.M.I. He was also active in the nationwide campaign to raise funds for the mausoleum and reclining statue of Lee. His devotion to the "Lost Cause" made him an enthusiastic member of the Virginia chapter of the Southern Historical Society, an organization then primarily devoted to the preservation of Confederate history. He presided over the society's convention at White Sulphur Springs in the summer of 1873, but in spite of his enthusiasm, Letcher never became a very active member.[19]

Despite his conservative respect for the past, Letcher always looked to the future, and now his renascent political instincts took command. All of his adult life he had been enchanted by the art of politics, and in 1874 he plunged again into the political whirl. Just as in his early days in the Jacksonian crusade, he became a candidate for one of Rockbridge County's two seats in the House of Delegates. This time he won an easy victory, and in December, 1875, he took his seat in the General Assembly.[20]

After eight years in Congress, the Virginia House of Delegates was no technical challenge, and Letcher enjoyed his political renaissance immensely. The younger delegates showed him great respect, for his was a famous name from the golden past. The older members rejoiced to see the old warhorse from the Valley back in harness.[21]

Letcher was now sixty–two years old but as energetic as ever. Characteristically, he took an active part in the proceedings.

He retained his mastery of parliamentary procedure, and, still the legalist, insisted that everything be done strictly according to the rules. He was assigned to the Federal Relations and Resolutions Committee, where his moderation and desire for reconciliation had free play. He still did his legislative homework conscientiously and kept abreast of the house's activities.

Just as in his congressional career, he sponsored no major legislation, but he did succeed in getting an annual appropriation of $10,000 for V.M.I.—no mean trick at a time when the state budget was so limited. He also pushed through a bill taxing all dogs in Rockbridge County. This was not primarily a financial measure but a reasonably effective effort to eliminate the menace of wild dogs that were decimating the county's herds of sheep, thereby threatening a new and profitable economic activity in the Valley.

On December 17, Letcher suggested a special committee of the assembly to study ways of further reducing the state budget. Thus he retained his traditional insistence on economy in government, and his policy was in perfect harmony with Governor Kemper's penny–pinching Conservative administration. Letcher's opposition to Virginia's participation in the Philadelphia Centennial Exhibition in 1876 was not an abandonment of his postwar policy of reconciliation, but rather another manifestation of his older and stronger dedication to cutting government expenses to the bone.

He also resisted demands for partial or complete repudiation of the state debt. This call for a lightening of Virginia's crushing obligation to the holders of state bonds was not new, but it was becoming more and more insistent, and increasing popular discontent seemed almost certain to influence the next state elections. Letcher's conservative, bourgeois mentality rejected the concept of readjusting a valid debt, of repudiating the state's financial obligations. As he had fought free spending in Congress, now he fought readjustment in the House of Delegates. At the same time an older, almost contradictory policy reappeared as westerner Letcher once again favored extension of the James River and Kanawha Canal further inland. He insisted on a preliminary audit of assets and expenses, while still favoring state expenditures for the development of western Virginia.

Another of his basic principles reasserted itself when he successfully opposed a bill requiring the disfranchisement of anyone convicted of petty larceny. This measure was aimed primarily at the Negro. Letcher was certainly no crusader for the black man —even his brief flirtation with emancipation in 1847 had had other basic motives. However, he was and always had been a crusader for democracy, and refused to support a restriction of the suffrage. There was still a streak of Jacksonian Democracy in the old gentleman that nothing could erase. He had fought the good fight at the Reform Convention of 1850–51, and not even the insanity of the Civil War and a stunning defeat at the polls in 1863 could shake his faith in democracy. He would go to his death firm in his belief in the ultimate wisdom of the people.[22]

The other basic tenet of his political creed, states' rights, was also as strong as ever. Letcher was perfectly content to conclude his long political career in the General Assembly, serving the state he had always held before all other political entities. During his lifetime the United States had evolved from a shaky confederation into a unified, centralized nation, but Letcher's devotion to states' rights had changed very little since he had first hailed this Virginia doctrine on the masthead of the *Valley Star* in 1839.

The former governor had hardly settled into the comfortable routine of the House of Delegates when, on March 1, 1876, the whole fabric of his life was torn asunder again. Letcher was attending the assembly as usual, but he was bothered by a sore shoulder. He was no stranger to aches and pains, for he had suffered from a wide variety of maladies throughout his adult life. He assumed the pain was just another touch of rheumatism and remained at his desk all day. That night, he retired early to his room at the Exchange Hotel, for he felt unusually tired and the pain had grown worse.

The next morning he was found paralyzed in his bed, the victim of a severe cerebral stroke. His whole right side was paralyzed, and he was in a mild stupor. He was hastily examined by several doctors, who gave him little chance to survive and even less chance to recover from the paralysis. The next day Susan Letcher arrived, and the battle for life and health continued, quietly and undramatically. Letcher had always been a fighter, and he faced this greatest battle with his usual optimism and stolid courage. Slowly the animation returned to his face, and the paralysis began to fade. In a few weeks his nimble mind was normal again. On March 28, he declined the assembly's offer to pay his medical expenses. The proud, conservative Lexingtonian knew of no precedent for this and feared it would set a bad example.

Letcher slowly regained control of most of his body, but his right leg never recovered completely, and he was to limp along on a cane for the rest of his life. His right arm improved rapidly, and by September he was able to write again. He returned to Lexington and simply refused to become an invalid. Late in 1876, he resumed his law practice on a part time basis and returned to his interrupted political renaissance. He wrote Governor Kemper regularly and decided to return to the second session of the assembly.[23]

The legislature reassembled on December 6. In Washington, the bitter dispute over the Hayes–Tilden presidential election was raging, while the nation waited uneasily for a decision. In Virginia, the demand for a scaling down of the state debt was still the most dynamic political movement. Letcher was at his desk in the house on opening day. This time his wife accompanied him to Richmond, for now he needed her assistance. He limped badly on his right leg. The rest of his body seemed to have recovered, but the damage to his never robust health had been severe, and he had lost some of his boundless energy. Though he attended the assembly's sessions regularly, he was much less active than usual, watching others carry his dog law through to final passage and speaking publicly on only a few occasions.

He still opposed a downward readjustment of the state debt but remained a good friend of Mahone, the wily politico who would ride the popular demand for readjustment to power. Letcher tried to do a few legal chores while in Richmond, but his weakened body revolted against the strain. Swollen ankles and sharp pains gave the warning, and the former governor slackened his pace. He would remain a semi–invalid for the rest of his life.[24]

Letcher returned to Lexington in the spring of 1877. All of his adult life he had worked hard, drawing on a limitless supply of energy and ambition. The ambition was still there, but the energy was fading rapidly. He drastically limited his political activities and his law practice. The political instinct died hard, and the old campaigner refused to retire from the House of Delegates. The Conservatives of Rockbridge dutifully renominated him, but he was decisively defeated at the polls after a rough, bitter canvass. Letcher's physical disability was an obvious handicap, but this was not the main reason for his defeat. The growing demand for readjustment had become a tidal wave of discontent that swept through the state late in 1877, and this movement was particularly strong in the Valley, where it crushed all opposition.

Letcher was too experienced to be caught unaware by this new crusade, but he refused to yield his conservative principles to the demands of the hour. To him readjustment was simply repudiation of a valid debt, a rejection of fiscal integrity. The whole complex question of the state debt seemed quite simple to Letcher when it was put in personal terms: "every honest man is bound by the moral law, to pay *what he owes*".[25]

He had always had confidence in Governor's Kemper's ability to withstand the popular pressure for readjustment, but he had doubts about his Conservative successor, Colonel Frederick W. M. Holliday. This native of the Valley had slipped into the governorship just before the readjuster movement solidified and separated its friends from its enemies, and Letcher did not think the governor could resist the growing pressure. He encouraged Holliday with a stream of letters congratulating him for every veto he threw in the path of the nascent Readjuster Party and exhorting him to fight on.

Letcher's philosophical opposition to the Readjusters was bolstered by an important practical consideration. V.M.I., Washington and Lee College, the University of Virginia, Hampton Institute, and the Virginia Agricultural and Mechanical Institute all had most of their assets in state bonds. A downward adjustment of the value of these bonds would be a severe financial blow that might even bankrupt these schools. Thus, while some favored readjustment as a means of diverting more state tax money into education, particularly the public school system, one reason for Letcher's opposition was his fear that readjustment would cripple or destroy the state's institutions of higher learning. Letcher had not completely abandoned his early support of public education, but he was convinced that readjustment was not the panacea.[26]

When the Readjusters won control of the General Assembly in 1879, he was not dismayed. He accepted the verdict of the people, certain that the genius of democracy would soon correct their mistake. Not only the political tides flowed against Letcher in 1879. In the spring, his wife suffered a stroke similar to the one that had crippled him three years earlier. Like her husband, Susan Letcher slowly recovered but remained paralyzed in one leg. Letcher's health continued to deteriorate, and by 1880 he was bedridden most of the time. He was still mentally alert, and still followed politics. He championed Tilden for president in a letter to the Lexington *Gazette* in April, for he liked the New Yorker's hard money stand—a Jacksonian reflex—and felt that Tilden had been robbed of victory in 1876 just as "Old Hickory" had been cheated in the election of 1824. Letcher's political opinions were no longer influential. A new generation was in control, and the former governor was just another honored but ignored voice from the past.[27]

The final years of Letcher's life were dominated by sickness and pain. By 1882, paralysis had spread to his right arm, and he could no longer write. As death approached, he remained cool to the possible consolations of Christianity. He was too honest to flee to the church at the last minute while still a skeptic at heart. His stoic courage, not religion, prepared him for death. In 1883, the 70–year–old former governor was under the constant medical care of his old friend Dr. James McDowell Taylor, and by the end of the year he was unable to leave his bed. At 2 A.M., on

Saturday, January 26, 1884, John Letcher died peacefully, surrounded by his family. The long, eventful journey was over.[28]

The state paused briefly in its march toward the twentieth
century to acknowledge the death of another old rebel leader.
The assembly adjourned early on January 26 in honor of the
former governor, and a committee of two senators and three
delegates came to Lexington to represent the state at the funeral.
Tributes poured in from all over Virginia as Letcher was laid to
rest in the Presbyterian cemetery. He was in congenial company.
Nearby lay James McDowell, the hardy western Democrat who
had given young Letcher his start in politics. General "Stonewall"
Jackson was also buried here, along with some 400 other Confederate soldiers. Letcher could sleep well beside these men, for
he too had served the Lost Cause faithfully. Here John Letcher
could rest in peace.[29]

Letcher had lived a full life. His marriage was happy and
fruitful. He had a host of loyal friends. His law practice was
rewarding financially and personally, and he had more than a
little success in his best-loved profession—politics.

The years of greatest historical significance in Letcher's political
career were those of the Civil War. As governor of Virginia, John
Letcher was no more prepared for the demands of war than were
the other political leaders of the time, but during the early, confused months of the war he did exercise the kind of strong, calm,
confident leadership that enabled Virginia to become part of the
Confederacy without excessive friction.

Then came the long years in which the Confederacy's survival
power was put to the test. These years also tested Letcher's qualities as a man and as a statesman. Generally, Letcher subordinated
his sense of traditional states' rights and his strict construction of
constitutional principles to the demands of the hour. He usually
cooperated wholeheartedly with Confederate officials, willingly
throwing Virginia's human and material resources into the desperate fight for survival. Yet he could not completely forsake his
lifelong beliefs. The exaggerated concepts of personal, property,

and states' rights, and the elaborate, picayune legalism that had long flourished in the South could not be completely abandoned overnight. Letcher's bourgeois pragmatism allowed him to support many Confederate policies that he considered illegal or unconstitutional, but his flexibility was limited. When popular resistance to infringements on traditional rights and privileges developed, the governor sometimes wavered.

The people of Virginia were philosophically and psychologically unprepared for the demands of war, and Letcher, a lifelong champion of democracy, was not prepared to ignore entirely the will of the people. He could seek to persuade them to modify principle to meet the harsh realities of the moment, but he neither ignored nor denied their final sovereignty. Occasionally, at crucial moments, he hesitated to employ his extraordinary wartime powers to the fullest. This hesitancy sometimes delayed or disrupted vital programs, but his failures of leadership were as often the result of inept administration as of obsolete political principles.

At times Letcher's devotion to states' rights dominated his thinking and he directly opposed some program of the central government. Invariably such opposition gave way under pressure and became troublesome but not crippling harassment. Common sense and realism, rather than weakness, led the governor to yield to Confederate persuasion. By comparison to all but a very few rebel governors, Letcher was a model of cooperativeness, a pillar of strength for the Confederacy.

By today's standards, certainly, his leadership was lacking in imagination, strength, and vigor. He failed to inspire his people. And yet in the context of mid–nineteenth century southern politics he was a comparatively forceful and effective leader. His wartime administration was basically a success. It directed the power and spirit of one of the key southern states into the mainstream of the rebel war effort. His cooperation with the central government was generally effective—so much so, indeed, that his own people of the Valley repudiated him in the congressional election of 1863. This electoral defeat is one of the clearest indications of the wisdom of his administration. The historian must surely reverse the 1863 judgment of the voters of the Valley.

Governor Letcher was a credit to Virginia and to the Confederacy. He was usually the right man in the right place at the right time. He was a man of force and character, a key figure in the Confederate experiment. One of the main reasons for the failure of that experiment was a lack of coordination and cooperation between the central and the state governments. The political climate of the South made this almost inevitable. However, a few state leaders were able to rise above the narrow, negative political doctrines of Dixie and exercise the pragmatic flexibility so necessary in modern war. John Letcher was such a leader— one of the few southern governors with the foresight and courage needed to lead effectively in the face of fierce popular resistance. He was, on balance, a strong rebel war governor.

Historians have ignored Letcher in favor of such men as Brown and Vance, colorful war governors who endlessly frustrated the Confederate war effort on the home front. That these men were obstructionists may seem to have been inevitable—until one remembers that Letcher was heir to the same political heritage. He demonstrated that a rebel governor *could* realistically accept new solutions for the new problems that war created. His ability to replace hoary doctrine with common sense and flexibility was the principal source of Letcher's strength, the basic ingredient of his wartime leadership.

Yet Letcher the politician was only a reflection of Letcher the man. The key to his character lies beyond politics and geography. Basically he was a middle class American. In some respects he was the archetypical "bourgeois man": ambitious, acquisitive, industrious, thorough, thrifty, strongly attached to home and family, moderate, cautious, conservative. But he was something more than this. Independent and courageous, idealistic and optimistic, Letcher was a man of better than average ability, character, and integrity. Unpolished, he spoke his mind frankly and often very bluntly. He was a religious skeptic in the pious Valley, a Democrat in a Whig county, and briefly an emancipationist in slave country. He never hesitated to follow his conscience and to oppose popular movements, such as secession and readjustment, but he was flexible enough to accept defeat gracefully and, as the successful politician he was, he sometimes bent with the wind.

He was very much a human being—not the stern, stuffy official of his formal portraits, but rather a warm, friendly, genial, gregarious man who led a lively social life. His large, happy family and his legion of friends were his pride. Stoical in the face of tragedy or danger, Letcher was a plain, unpretentious lawyer–politician who came from the people and remained one of them. He neither aped the aristocrat nor shunned the commoner.

Informal gatherings and songfests, anecdotes and conversation, cigars and whiskey, visits to friends and relatives—these were his entertainments. Shouting flocks of children, dusty, tree–lined streets, small towns nestled in rolling farmland, lively discussions at the court house, quiet Sunday afternoons—this was his environment. This was mid-nineteenth century America, on both sides of the Mason-Dixon line. Even the Civil War did not destroy this basic pattern.

Notes

CHAPTER 1

1. John Letcher's Notebook, Letcher Papers, Lexington, Va. (hereafter referred to as Letcher Notebook/Lexington). The notebook is only one item in an extensive collection of John Letcher records and correspondence that remains in the possession of the family in Lexington (hereafter referred to as Letcher Papers/Lexington). There are smaller collections of John Letcher papers at the Library of Congress, Duke University, the Virginia Military Institute, the Virginia Historical Society, and the Rockbridge County Historical Society.

2. George W. Diehl, "The Saga of an Old Field School", *Proceedings of the Rockbridge Historical Society,* V (1954-1960), 29; Letcher Papers/Lexington; *County News* (Rockbridge), Feb. 21, 1951, p. 3.

3. Colonel William Couper, *One Hundred Years at V. M. I.* (Richmond: Garrett and Massie, 1939), I, 13, 17; Oron F. Morton, *A History of Rockbridge County, Virginia* (Staunton: The McClure Co., 1920), p. 261; F. N. Boney, "Un Américain à Bordeaux, 1841-1849", *Revue historique de Bordeaux et du département de la Gironde,* XIII (1964), no. 1, p. 2.

4. Letcher Papers/Lexington; Thomas C. Wilson (ed.), *Washington and Lee University Alumni Directory: 1749-1949* (Lexington: W. & L. Alumni, Inc., 1949), p. 161; *Staunton Spectator,* June 12, 1877, p. 1; Clement Eaton, *Freedom of Thought in the Old South* (Durham: Duke University Press, 1940), p. 264.

5. Letcher Notebook/Lexington; Henry H. Simms, *The Rise of the Whigs in Virginia: 1824-1840* (Richmond: William Byrd Press, 1929), pp. 24-86; Charles Henry Ambler, *Thomas Ritchie: A Study in Virginia Politics* (Richmond: Bell Book & Stationery Co., 1913), pp. 118-169.

6. *Gazette* (Lexington), Mar. 4, 1836, p. 2; Richard Hofstadter, *The American Political Tradition and the Men Who Made It* (New York: Alfred A. Knopf, 1949), pp. 65-66.

7. Letcher Papers/Lexington; Francis Pendleton Gaines, Jr., "The Political Career of James McDowell, 1830-1851" (unpublished thesis, 1947, University of Virginia), *passim.*

8. Simms, *op. cit.,* pp. 12-13, 167-192; Arthur Charles Cole, *The Whig Party in the South* (Washington: American Historical Association, 1913), pp. 4, 38.

9. Letcher Papers/Lexington; *Biographical Directory of the American Congress: 1774-1949: The Continental Congress; September 5, 1774, to October 21, 1778 and the Congress of the United States from the First to the Eightieth Congress, March 4, 1789, to March 3, 1949, Inclusive* (U. S. Government Printing Office, Washington, 1950), p. 1902.

10. Letcher Papers/Lexington; Van Buren to Letcher, others, Aug. 31, 1838, Van Buren Papers, Library of Congress; John P. Frank, *Justice Daniel Dissenting: A Biography of Peter V. Daniel, 1784-1860* (Cambridge: Harvard University Press, 1964), pp. 137-138. Daniel served as a justice of the United States Supreme Court from 1841 until his death in 1860.

11. Letcher Papers/Lexington; *Daily Dispatch* (Richmond), Jan. 27, 1884, p. 3.

12. Series of letters from Grigsby to Letcher, 1841-1849, Smith to Mrs. Letcher, Feb. 1, 1884, Letcher Papers/Lexington; William Henry Ruffner, "History of Washington College", *Washington and Lee Historical Papers* (Lexington, 1893), no. 3, p. 153, and no. 4, pp. 132, 135, 138, 183.

13. Charles Henry Ambler, *Sectionalism in Virginia From 1776 to 1861* (Chicago: University of Chicago Press, 1910), pp. 229-230; Ambler, *Ritchie,* pp. 187-210; Simms, *op. cit.,* pp. 127-129; McDowell to Letcher, Mar. 1 and 19, 1838, Letcher Papers/Lexington; *Gazette* (Lexington), Apr. 6, 1838, p. 2 and Apr. 27, 1838, p. 2. In Rockbridge the official count was: Leyburn, 407; Dorman, 400; McDowell, 291; Letcher, 271.

14. Simms, *op. cit.,* pp. 129-130; Gaines, *op. cit.,* p. 56; *Gazette* (Lexington), Mar. 17, 1840, p. 2; *Staunton Spectator,* June 12, 1877, p. 1.

15. *Valley Star* (Lexington), 1839-1840, and Sept. 30, 1858, p. 1; *Gazette* (Lexington), 1839-1840; E. B. Prettyman, "John Letcher", *John P. Branch Historical Papers of Randolph-Macon College,* III (1912), 316; Simms, *op. cit.,* p. 142; Ritchie to Letcher, July 18, 1839, and McDowell to Letcher, June 16, 1839, Letcher Papers/Lexington; Gaines, *op. cit.,* pp. 50-52, 58, 71-72.

16. McDowell to Letcher, June 11 and 16, 1839, Letcher Papers/Lexington.

17. *Gazette* (Lexington), June 15, 1839, p. 2 and Dec. 17, 1839, pp. 2-3.

18. McDowell to Letcher, June 11, 1839; Ritchie to Letcher, July 18, 1839; H. A. Garland to Letcher, May 24, 1839; Fayette McMullan to Letcher, Dec. 16, 1839; Robert Craig to Letcher, Dec. 5, 1839, Letcher Papers/Lexington.

CHAPTER 2

1. Henry H. Simms, *The Rise of the Whigs in Virginia: 1824-1840* (Richmond: William Byrd Press, 1929), p. 143; Charles Henry Ambler, *Thomas Ritchie: A Study in Virginia Politics* (Richmond: Bell Book & Stationery Co., 1913), p. 214.

2. *Gazette* (Lexington), March and April, 1840; John Letcher, *To the Freemen of Rockbridge County* (Lexington, 1840), *passim;* handbill pasted on inside cover of 1840 bound edition of *The Yeoman* (Richmond), Alderman Library, University of Virginia.

3. *Gazette* (Lexington), Apr. 28, 1840, p. 3.

4. Craig to Letcher, Apr. 27, 1840, Letcher Papers/Lexington; Simms, *op. cit.,* p. 144; *Gazette* (Lexington), Apr. 28, 1840, p. 2. The final count in Rockbridge was: Dorman, 568; Leyburn, 566; Letcher, 490; Brockenbrough, 488.

5. Letcher Papers/Lexington; *Gazette* (Lexington), January-July, 1840; Francis Pendleton Gaines, Jr., "The Political Career of James McDowell, 1830-1851" (unpublished thesis, 1947, University of Virginia), pp. 60-62.

6. *Gazette* (Lexington), Sept. 1, 1840, p. 2; *Staunton Spectator,* June 12, 1877, p. 1; Simms, *op. cit.,* p. 149; Jos. A. Waddell to S. H. Letcher, May 2, 1905, Letcher Papers/Lexington. The Letcher Papers contain many references to the campaign of this period.

7. John K. Anderson to Wm. C. Rives, Sept. 18, 1840, William Cabell Rives Papers, Library of Congress; Letcher Papers/Lexington.

8. Simms, *op. cit.,* pp. 143-158; William T. Hutchinson, *Cyrus Hall McCormick: Seed Time, 1809-1856* (New York: The Century Company, 1930), I, 464; *Gazette* (Lexington), May 5, 1840, p. 2 and Nov. 5, 1840, p. 2; Letcher Papers/Lexington; James McDowell Reid to W. C. Rives, Oct. 5, 1840, Rives Papers, Library of Congress.

9. Alg. S. Gray to Susan Holt, Apr. 30, 1843, and a series of letters from Grigsby to Letcher, 1841-1842, Letcher Papers/Lexington.

10. Alexander F. Robertson, *Alexander Hugh Holmes Stuart: 1807-1891: A Biography* (Richmond: William Byrd Press, 1925), pp. 26-27; Gaines, *op. cit.,* pp. 161-163; *Gazette* (Lexington), Feb. 25, 1841, pp. 2-3; Letcher Papers/Lexington.

11. *Valley Star* (Lexington), Sept. 30, 1858, p. 2; Grigsby to Letcher, Mar. 31 and Aug. 27, 1841, and brief autobiographical sketch

by John Letcher, Letcher Papers/Lexington; *Gazette* (Lexington), 1839-1841.

12. Grigsby to Letcher, June 7, 1842, and series of letters from Benton to Letcher, 1842, Letcher Papers/Lexington.

13. Ambler, *op. cit.,* pp. 223-229; *Gazette* (Lexington), Apr. 29, 1841, p. 2 and May 5, 1842, p. 2; Letcher to Benton, Dec. 15, 1842, Letcher Papers/Lexington.

14. Letcher to McDowell, Dec. 22, 1843, James McDowell Papers, Duke University; Letcher to Benton, Dec. 15, 1842, Van Buren Papers, Library of Congress; Calhoun to Letcher, May 20, 1842, Letcher Papers/Lexington; *Valley Star* (Lexington), Sept. 30, 1858, p. 20.

15. Oscar Doane Lambert, *Presidential Politics in the United States: 1841-1844* (Durham: Duke University Press, 1936), pp. 121-142; Ambler, *op. cit.,* pp. 226-243; Letcher to Ritchie, Sept. 23, 1843 and William H. Roane to Van Buren, Oct. 17, 1843, Van Buren Papers, Library of Congress; Letcher to McDowell, Dec. 22, 1843, McDowell Papers, Duke University; Benton to Letcher, June 21, 1844, Letcher Papers/Lexington; *Valley Star* (Lexington), Sept. 30, 1858, p. 2. Benton blamed the "disunionists of the South" for dumping Van Buren.

16. *Richmond Enquirer,* Jan. 10, 1843, p. 3; Letcher to McDowell, Jan. 19, 1843, Letcher Papers/Lexington.

17. McDowell to Letcher, Feb. 16, 1843, Letcher Papers/Lexington; Letcher to McDowell, Mar. 9, 1843, McDowell Papers, Duke University; Ambler, *op. cit.,* pp. 297-298.

18. Letcher to McDowell, Mar. 9, 1843; McDowell to Letcher, Feb. 16, 1843; William Smith to Letcher, Mar. 27, 1843, Letcher Papers/Lexington; Robertson, *op. cit.,* pp. 27, 42. Stuart claimed that he resigned for financial reasons.

19. Letcher Notebook/Lexington; Letcher to wife, May 14, 1852, Letcher Papers/Lexington; Robert C. Glass and Carter Glass, Jr., *Virginia Democracy: A History of the Achievements of the Party and Its Leaders in the Mother of Commonwealths, the Old Dominion* (Springfield, Ill.: Democratic Historical Association, 1937), II, 18-19.

20. Letcher to McDowell, Dec. 22, 1843, McDowell Papers, Duke University; Letcher to McDowell, Apr. 9, 1844, McDowell Papers, University of Virginia; series of letters to Letcher, April-September, 1844, and R. E. Withers to S. H. Letcher, Mar. 19, 1905, Letcher Papers/Lexington; David P. Curry to W. C. Rives, Dec. 10, 1844, Rives Papers, Library of Congress; *Gazette* (Lexington), Mar. 28, 1884, p. 3, May 2, 1844, p. 2, Nov. 7, 1844, p. 2; Ambler, *op. cit.,* pp. 243-253; Poll Book, Rockbridge County, Virginia Historical Society, Richmond. In Rockbridge, the count was Clay 697, Polk 543, a Whig gain of 42 votes over the last presidential election. Letcher had expected the Democrats to do better, not worse in Rockbridge.

21. Letcher Notebook/Lexington; Mr. and Mrs. J. C. Blackwell

to Letcher, Apr. 7, 1845; John Echols to Letcher, Dec. 8, 1849, Letcher Papers/Lexington. Echols said that the millennium would truly have arrived when Letcher and his friend James D. Davidson joined the church. Mrs. Blackwell was Letcher's sister Mary.

22. Ambler, *Ritchie*, pp. 250-253; *Gazette* (Lexington), July 3, 1845, p. 3; Taylor to Letcher, Dec. 23, 1844; Grigsby to Letcher, Apr. 13, 1845; letter written by Letcher on June 29, 1858 (unsigned and evidently never mailed), Letcher Papers/Lexington.

23. Letcher Notebook/Lexington; Jacob Shafer to Letcher, Feb. 9, 1846; Sam Houston to William H. Letcher, Nov. 25, 1845, Letcher Papers/Lexington; Gaines, *op. cit.*, p. 79; Dr. Graham to McDowell, Mar. 4, 1846, James McDowell Papers, University of North Carolina. For the complete text of Houston's letter see F. N. Boney, "The Raven Tamed: An 1845 Sam Houston Letter", *Southwestern Historical Quarterly*, LXVIII (1964), 90-92.

CHAPTER 3

1. Francis Pendleton Gaines, Jr., "The Virginia Constitutional Convention of 1850-1851: A Study in Sectionalism" (unpublished dissertation, 1950, University of Virginia), pp. 5-15, 68-70; Charles Henry Ambler, *Sectionalism in Virginia From 1776 to 1861* (Chicago: University of Chicago Press, 1910), pp. 140-169, 273-275; *Richmond Enquirer*, Feb. 4, 1851, p. 2.

2. William Gleason Bean, "The Ruffner Pamphlet of 1847: An Antislavery Aspect of Virginia Sectionalism", *Virginia Magazine of History and Biography*, LXI (1953), 263-264; Bean, "John Letcher and the Slavery Issue in Virginia's Gubernatorial Contest of 1858-1859", *Journal of Southern History*, XX (1954), 23; *Gazette* (Lexington), Aug. 7, 1845, p. 3.

3. Bean, "Letcher", *JSH*, XX, 23; Bean, "Ruffner Pamphlet", *Virginia Magazine*, LXI, 266-268; *Gazette* (Lexington), Aug. 7, 1845; Robert J. Jones, "The Movement Leading to the Virginia State Convention of 1850-51 and the Work of this Convention" (unpublished thesis, 1930, University of Virginia), pp. 33-34.

4. Bean, "Ruffner Pamphlet", *Virginia Magazine*, LXI, 268-269; Bean, "Letcher", *JSH*, XX, 23-25; *Richmond Whig and Daily Advertiser*, May 17, 1859, p. 4. Brockenbrough was a district judge appointed by President Polk.

5. Henry Ruffner, *Address to the People of West Virginia: Shewing That Slavery Is Injurious to the Public Welfare, and That It May Be Gradually Abolished, Without Detriment to the Rights and Interests of Slaveholders* (Lexington, 1847), *passim;* Bean, "Ruffner Pamphlet", *Virginia Magazine*, LXI, 270-277.

6. S. Bassett French Notes, no date, S. Bassett French Papers, Virginia State Library, Richmond, Virginia; Letcher Notebook/Lex-

ington. French planned to write a study of Virginia's outstanding sons in this general period, but never completed this ambitious project. His notes contain only superficial information in most cases.

7. Letcher Papers/Lexington. Echols was an officer in the Confederate army and later became a prominent official in the Chesapeake and Ohio Railroad.

8. Paxton to Letcher, May 18, 1848, and Buchanan to Letcher, Apr. 24, 1848, Letcher Papers/Lexington; Letcher to John Rutherford, Aug. 19, 1848, John Rutherford Papers, Duke University; *Richmond Enquirer,* May 12, 1848, p. 1; *Gazette* (Lexington), Apr. 30, 1848, p. 1.

9. J. W. Paine to W. C. Rives, Oct. 31, 1848, Rives Papers, Library of Congress.

10. Ambler, *op. cit.,* p. 237; Henry T. Shanks, *The Secession Movement in Virginia: 1847-1861* (Richmond: Garrett and Massie, 1934), pp. 14-15; Paine to Rives, Oct. 31, 1848, Rives Papers, Library of Congress; *Gazette* (Lexington), Apr. 30, 1848. Cass' majority in Virginia was only 1,473.

11. Letcher to Stuart, Jan. 21, 1849, Letcher Papers/Lexington.

12. Letcher to Curry, May 5, 1849, Letcher Papers/Lexington; Francis Pendleton Gaines, Jr., "The Political Career of James McDowell, 1830-1851" (unpublished thesis, 1947, University of Virginia), p. 98.

13. Letcher Papers/Lexington. For the Negro man, Patrick, the price was $750—$125 in cash and $625 in a two year note.

14. Shanks, *op. cit.,* p. 27; R. Toombs to Wm. B. Preston, May 18, 1849, William B. Preston Papers, Virginia Historical Society, Richmond; [?] to Letcher, Dec. 13, 1849, Letcher Papers/Lexington; *Valley Star* (Lexington), Aug. 16, 1849, p. 2, and Feb. 28, 1850, p. 3.

15. Joseph Bell to Letcher, Aug. 4, 1849, Letcher Papers/Lexington; Gaines, "Convention", pp. 89-90. The Valley was not as underrepresented in the assembly as the Trans-Allegheny.

16. Gaines, "Convention", p. 90; *Gazette* (Lexington), July 18, 1850, p. 3; Letcher Papers/Lexington.

17. Letcher to John Bird, June 8,1850, Letcher Papers/Lexington.

18. Letcher Papers/Lexington. "Sandy" Stuart was a skillful adversary who remained on good personal terms with almost all of his legal and political opponents.

19. McDowell to Ritchie and Stuart, July 12, 1850, McDowell Papers, University of North Carolina; Letcher to [?], Apr. 16, 1850, Letcher Papers, Duke University; Letcher Papers/Lexington; *Richmond Enquirer,* Sept. 3, 1850, p. 2; Bean, "Ruffner Pamphlet", *Virginia Magazine,* LXI, 278.

20. Letcher to McCue, Aug. 24, 1850, McCue Family Papers, University of Virginia; McDowell to Letcher, Oct. 9, 1850, Letcher Papers/Lexington.

JOHN LETCHER OF VIRGINIA

21. *Richmond Enquirer,* Oct. 15, 1850, p. 2; Gaines, "Convention", pp. 106-112; George W. Munford to Letcher, Sept. 28, 1850, Letcher Papers/Lexington. Westerners particularly favored adjournment because the census of 1850 was certain to indicate a growing white majority in the west.

22. Letcher Papers/Lexington; *Valley Star* (Lexington), Feb. 28, 1850, p. 3.

23. Dorman to Letcher, Dec. 13, 1850, and Curry to Letcher, Dec. 13, 1850, Letcher Papers/Lexington.

24. Letcher Papers/Lexington. The brief quotation is taken from a letter from Letcher to his brother Sam, dated Jan. 7, 1851.

25. Letcher to Curry, Feb. 21, 1851, Letcher Papers/Lexington; Gaines, "Convention", pp. 252-253; *Richmond Enquirer,* Jan. 31, 1851, p. 1. Letcher frequently wrote his friend Curry about the proceedings at the convention.

26. Letcher to Curry, Feb. 21, 1851, Letcher Papers/Lexington.

27. Letcher to Curry Jan. 9, 1851, Letcher Papers/Lexington.

28. John Letcher, *et al., Memorial of Members of the Virginia Reform Convention,* Feb. 11, 1851, *passim;* Letcher Papers/Lexington; *Richmond Enquirer,* May 2, 1851, p. 3, and Aug. 1, 1851, p. 1.

29. *Gazette* (Lexington), Mar. 27, 1851, p. 2, and Apr. 24, 1851, pp. 1-2, and May 1, 1851, pp. 1-2; Letcher to Curry, Mar. 22, 1851, Letcher Papers/Lexington. Letcher's speech was such a torrent of facts and figures that reporters were unable to record it accurately. Letcher later wrote it out for publication.

30. Gaines, "Convention", pp. 172-200; Letcher to Curry, May 21, 1851, Letcher Papers/Lexington; James Whittle to Langhorne Scruggs, Apr. 16, 1851, Langhorne Scruggs Papers, Duke University; R. G. Scott to W. C. Rives, Mar. 7, 1851, Rives Papers, Library of Congress; *Richmond Enquirer,* May 16, 1851, p. 2.

31 Gaines, "Convention", pp. 200-213; Ambler *op. cit.,* pp. 261-268; Letcher to Curry, July 5, 1851, Letcher Papers/Lexington.

32. Cocke to Charles Ellis, June 10, 1851, Ellis-Munford Papers, Duke University.

33. Bean, "Letcher", *JSH,* XX, 25; Ambler, *op. cit.,* p. 271; *Gazette* (Lexington), Jan. 9, 1851, p. 2; Gaines, "Convention", pp. 280-281; Letcher to Imboden, Jan. 29, 1852, John D. Imboden Papers, University of Virginia.

34. Letcher to Curry, Mar. 22, 1851, Letcher Papers/Lexington.

35. Letcher to Curry, Mar. 22, 1851, Letcher Papers/Lexington; Letcher to McCue, Aug. 29, 1851, McCue Family Papers, University of Virginia; Francis Pendleton Gaines, Jr., "The Political Career of James McDowell, 1830-1851" (unpublished thesis, 1947, University of Virginia), pp. 103-104. McDowell died on Aug. 24, 1851, after an extended illness.

36. James H. Skinner to Letcher, Oct. 22, 1851, Letcher Papers/ Lexington.

37. George W. Hopkins to Letcher, Oct. 28, 1851, Letcher Papers/ Lexington; Bean, "Letcher", *JSH*, XX, 26; *Richmond Enquirer,* Oct. 28, 1851, p. 2.

CHAPTER 4

1. Letcher to Curry, Dec. 21, 1851, and presidential invitation with note on back, Dec. 19, 1851, Letcher Papers/Lexington; Letcher to James D. Davidson, Jan. 13, 1852, James D. Davidson Papers, Mc-Cormick Collection, State Historical Society of Wisconsin, Madison.

2. Letcher to Davidson, Mar. 21, 1852, Davidson Papers, Mc-Cormick Collection.

3. Letcher to Davidson, Feb. 25, 1852, Davidson Papers, McCor-mick Collection; *The Congressional Globe: New Series: Contains the Debates, Proceedings, and Laws, of the First Session of the Thirty-Second Congress* (Washington, 1852), XXIV, part I, 96, 601, part II, 1545, 1625-1630, and part III, 1813, 1893; Allan Nevins, *Ordeal of the Union* (New York: Charles Scribner's Sons, 1947), I, 548.

4. Amelia W. Williams and Eugene C. Barker (eds.), *The Writings of Sam Houston: 1813-1863* (Austin: University of Texas Press, 1941), V, 261-267. See page 267 for a brief biographical sketch of Letcher.

5. Letcher to Davidson, Mar. 21, 1852, Davidson Papers, McCor-mick Collection; Letcher to Curry, Dec. 21, 1851, and Letcher to Sam Letcher, Jan. 23, 1852, Letcher Papers/Lexington; Nevins, *op. cit.,* II, 6-15.

6. Letcher to Pierce, July 13, 1852, Franklin Pierce Papers, Library of Congress; Letcher to Davidson, May 31 and July 9, 1852, Davidson Papers, McCormick Collection. See Nevins, *op. cit.,* II, 39, for this same quotation.

7. Letcher to wife, May 14, 1852, Letcher Papers/Lexington.

8. Series of letters from Letcher to Davidson, Davidson Papers, McCormick Collection; Letcher to Sam Letcher, Jan. 23, 1852, Letcher Papers/Lexington; Wayland Fuller Dunaway, *History of the James River and Kanawha Company* (New York: Columbia University, 1922), pp. 161-162.

9. Letcher to Davidson, July 20, 1852, Davidson Papers, Mc-Cormick Collection. See also Henry T. Shanks, *The Secession Movement in Virginia: 1847-1861* (Richmond: Garrett and Massie, 1934), p. 14.

10. Letcher to wife, May 14, 1852, Letcher Papers/ Lexington.

11. Letcher to Davidson, Feb. 16, 1852, Davidson Papers, Mc-Cormick Collection.

12. Nevins, *op. cit.*, II, 36; *Richmond Enquirer,* Nov. 30, 1852, p. 2.

13. Series of letters seeking favors, 1851-1859, Letcher Papers/ Lexington; Letcher to Grigsby, Feb. 28, 1853, John Warren Grigsby Papers, Filson Club, Louisville, Kentucky.

14. Letcher to Grigsby, Feb. 28, 1853, Grigsby Papers; *Congressional Globe,* XXVI, *passim;* Letcher to Davidson, Mar. 21, 1852, Davidson Papers, McCormick Collection.

15. *Congressional Globe,* XXVI, 829, 865; Alexander F. Robertson, *Alexander Hugh Holmes Stuart: 1807-1891: A Biography* (Richmond: William Byrd Press, 1925), p. 55.

16. Letcher to Grigsby, Feb. 28, 1853, Grigsby Papers.

17. Rockbridge County Deed Books, 1850-1860; Letcher Papers/ Lexington; draft of speech delivered by Davidson on Dec. 29, 1863, Davidson Papers, McCormick Collection.

18. Letcher to [?], June 3, 1853, Miscellaneous Personal Papers File, Library of Congress; B. J. Bogan to Letcher, July 21, 1853, Letcher Papers/Lexington; Letcher Notebook/Lexington.

19. Nevins, *op. cit.,* II, 93-145.

20. Letcher to Grigsby, Apr. 7, 1854, Grigsby Papers.

21. Letcher to wife, May 14, 1854, and H. Stevenson to Letcher, May 8, 1854, Letcher Papers/Lexington. Some observers erroneously interpreted Letcher's reluctance to be actual opposition.

22. *Congressional Globe: First Session of Thirty-Third Congress* (1855), XXVIII, 1254-1255; Nevins, *op. cit.,* II, 154-157.

23. *Congressional Globe,* XXVIII, *passim,* 309-310, 506 (the quotation) and 916.

24. *Congressional Globe,* XVIII, 2103-2104 and XXX, 8, 263, 550, 553, 572-579; *Reports of Committees of the House of Representatives, Made During the First Session of the Thirty-Third Congress* (Washington, 1854), III, 1-92. Letcher's old friend Cyrus Hall McCormick also came under attack for his lobbying activities.

25. J. Marshall McCue Manuscript, no date, J. M. McCue Papers, Virginia Historical Society, Richmond; Stevenson to Letcher, May 8, 1854, Letcher Papers/Lexington, *Congressional Globe Appendix,* XXIX, 874.

26. James P. Hambleton, *A Biographical Sketch of Henry A. Wise With A History of the Political Campaign in Virginia in 1855* (Richmond, 1856), p. 30; Shanks, *op. cit.,* pp. 46-59.

27. Charles Henry Ambler, *Sectionalism in Virginia From 1776 to 1861* (Chicago: University of Chicago Press, 1910), p. 306; Shanks, *op cit.,* pp. 48, 55-57, 257; Hambleton, *op. cit.,* p. 116; *Richmond Enquirer,* Nov. 12, 1858, p. 1; Letcher to Paulus Powell, Sept. 25, 1854, Paulus Powell Papers, Virginia Historical Society; R. P. Letcher to Letcher, Mar. 29, 1855, Letcher Papers/Lexington; Philip Morrison

Rice, "The Know-Nothing Party in Virginia, 1854-1856", *Virginia Magazine of History and Biography,* LV (1947), 66. William Smith soon became a staunch Know-Nothing. In his case, nativism may have been the main reason for opposing Wise.

28. *Appendix to Congressional Globe,* XXXI, 317-320; *Congressional Globe,* XXX, 11, 12, 15, 144, 288, 485, 756, 843, 913, 1074; Letcher to Powell, Feb. 25, 1854, Powell Papers, Virginia Historical Society.

29. Supreme Court document signed by chief clerk Wm. Thos. Caroll, Mar. 1, 1855, Letcher Papers/Lexington; Letcher Notebook/Lexington. Letcher never actually practiced before the Supreme Court.

30. *Valley Star* (Lexington), May 31, 1855, p. 2; Shanks, *op. cit.,* p. 48; Nevins, *op. cit.,* II, 397; Wise to Jas. Kemper, July 23, 1855, James L. Kemper Papers, University of Virginia; Letcher to John Brooks, May 25, 1855, Letcher Papers/Lexington.

31. Letcher to Davidson, Dec. 11, 1855, Letcher Papers/Lexington; Nevins, *op. cit.,* II, 412-414.

32. *Appendix to Congressional Globe: First Session, Thirty-Fourth Congress,* pp. 230-233; *Congressional Globe: First and Second Sessions, Thirty-Fourth Congress, passim;* Nevins, *op. cit.,* II, 415-420.

33. C. R. Harris to James L. Kemper, Apr. 28 and Aug. 28, 1856, Kemper Papers, University of Virginia; Letcher to [?], May 28, 1856, Letcher Papers, Duke University; Shanks, *op. cit.,* p. 52. Harris coveted Letcher's seat in Congress, but he realized that Letcher would be able to retain it indefinitely.

34. *Appendix to Congressional Globe: First Session, Thirty-Fourth Congress,* pp. 922-923; Letcher to Davidson, May 29, 1856, Davidson Papers, McCormick Collection.

35. *Congressional Globe Appendix,* pp. 1121-1126.

36. Letcher to Davidson, Aug. 24, 1856, Davidson Papers, McCormick Collection.

37. John Lewis Peyton, *The American Crisis; or Pages from the Note-Book of a State Agent During the Civil War* (London: Saunders & Otley, & Co., 1867), II, 152-157; *Congressional Globe: First Session, Thirty-Fourth Congress,* pp. 2160-2161; Harris to Kemper, Dec. 20, 1856, Kemper Papers, University of Virginia; McCue Manuscript, no date, McCue Papers, Virginia Historical Society; *Staunton Spectator,* Sept. 24, 1856, p. 2. Peyton, a highly critical and rather cynical observer, said of Letcher: "I had always regarded Mr. L. as an honest man, as the world goes."

38. Nevins, *op. cit.,* II, 495; Roy Franklin Nichols, *The Disruption of American Democracy* (New York: The Macmillan Company, 1948), pp. 14-18, 41-47; Bogan to Letcher, Nov. 8 and 11, 1856, and Nov. 7, 1857, Letcher Papers/Lexington; Letcher to Grigsby, Sept. 26, 1856, Grigsby Papers.

39. Nichols, *op. cit.,* p. 48; Nevins, *op. cit.,* II, 510-514; *Richmond*

Enquirer, Nov. 18, 1856, p. 2; Brown's Hotel bills, November, 1856, Letcher Papers/Lexington.

40. *Congressional Globe: Third Session, Thirty-Fourth Congress,* p. 69; Letcher to Davidson, Dec. 10, 1856, Davidson Papers, McCormick Collection.

41. Letcher to James Dorman, Dec. 10 and 21, 1856, Davidson Papers, McCormick Collection; Nichols, *op. cit.,* p. 57.

42. Letcher to Dorman, Dec. 10 and 21, 1856, Davidson Papers, McCormick Collection; Harris to Kemper, Dec. 19, 1856, Kemper Papers, University of Virginia; series of letters to Letcher in December, 1856, Letcher Papers/Lexington.

43. *Appendix to the Congressional Globe: Third Session, Thirty-Fourth Congress,* pp. 188-192; Nichols, op. cit., pp. 68-69. As always, Letcher employed masses of statistics in his talk. He put much of the blame for tight money and depreciating state bonds on the federal treasury surplus.

44. Letcher to Imboden, Aug. 7, 1852, John D. Imboden Papers, University of Virginia; Letcher Papers/Lexington.

45. Nichols, *op. cit.,* p. 190; Letcher handwritten memo, 1857, Strain to Letcher, Jan. 24, 1861, and Thompson to Letcher, Mar. 7, 1861, Letcher Papers/Lexington; *Richmond Whig and Public Advertiser,* May 10, 1859, p. 1.

46. Nichols, *op. cit.,* p. 113; Shanks, *op. cit.,* pp. 55-57; Charles Henry Ambler (ed.), "John Letcher to R. M. T. Hunter, August 1, 1857", *Correspondence of Robert M. T. Hunter, 1826-1876: Annual Report of the American Historical Association for the Year 1916* (Washington: Government Printing Office, 1918), II, 215; Hiram Martz to Letcher, Oct. 29, 1857, and D. H. Wood to Letcher, Nov. 11, 1857, Letcher Papers/Lexington; Henry Harrison Simms, *Life of Robert M. T. Hunter; A Study in Sectionalism and Secession* (Richmond: William Byrd Press, 1935), pp. 138-139.

47. Letcher to Grigsby, June 15, 1857, Grigsby Papers; series of letters to Letcher in 1857, Letcher Papers/Lexington. An Indiana admirer predicted that Letcher would someday be President of the United States.

48. *Valley Star* (Lexington), June 4, 1857, p. 2; Harris to Kemper, Dec. 31, 1857, Kemper Papers, University of Virginia; Letcher Notebook/Lexington; Letcher and Curry business correspondence, Rockbridge County Historical Society, Lexington, Va. The official count in the congressional race was: Letcher 7,494; Imboden, 2,463.

49. Nichols, *op. cit.,* pp. 132-140, 150-151; Ambler (ed.), "D. H. Wood to R. M. T. Hunter", *Correspondence of Hunter,* II, 253-254; Bogan to Letcher, Oct. 31, 1857, and Sherrard Clemens to Letcher, Nov. 12, 1857, Letcher Papers/Lexington.

50. *Appendix to the Congressional Globe: First Session, Thirty-*

Fifth Congress, pp. 329-331; George F. Milton, *The Eve of Conflict: Stephen A. Douglas and the Needless War* (Boston: Houghton Mifflin, 1934), pp. 290-291.

51. Nichols, *op. cit.,* pp. 179-180; Letcher to Davidson, Jan. 25 and Apr. 11 and 25, 1858, Letcher Papers/Lexington.

52. Nichols, *op. cit.,* pp. 187-189; *Congressional Globe: First Session, Thirty-Fifth Congress, passim.* The printing bill was only reduced temporarily.

53. *Congressional Globe: First Session, Thirty-Fifth Congress,* pp. 660-663. This bill provided for regulation of intrastate steamboats under very special, limited circumstances.

54. Letcher to Davidson, Jan. 2, 1858, Davidson Papers, McCormick Collection.

CHAPTER 5

1. Series of letters to Letcher, 1857-1858, Letcher Papers/Lexington; Harris to Kemper, July 2, 1857, Kemper Papers, University of Virginia; W. G. Bean, "John Letcher and the Slavery Issue in Virginia's Gubernatorial Contest of 1858-1859", *Journal of Southern History,* XX (1954), 26-27; Henry T. Shanks, *The Secession Movement in Virginia: 1847-1861* (Richmond: Garrett and Massie, 1934), 56-57.

2. Hiram Martz to Letcher, Nov. 3, 1857, Letcher Papers/Lexington; Shanks, *op. cit.,* p. 57.

3. Bean, *op. cit.,* pp. 27-28, 31; Charles Henry Ambler, *Sectionalism in Virginia From 1776 to 1861* (Chicago: University of Chicago, 1910), p. 320.

4. Shanks, *op. cit.,* pp. 57-58; Bean, *op. cit.,* p. 29; *Richmond Enquirer,* July 2, 1858, p. 4; Harris to Letcher, June 29, 1858, Letcher Papers/Lexington.

5. Howell Cobb to Letcher, July 10, 1858, Letcher Papers/Lexington.

6. J. M. Johnson to Letcher, July 14, 1858; J. E. S. to Letcher, Aug. 17, 1858; Dr. Arch. Graham to Letcher, July 4, 1858, Letcher Papers/Lexington. Johnson labeled his cousin Faulkner a "deceitful hypocrite" who would take advantage of Letcher if he could.

7. Bean, *op. cit.,* pp. 29-30; *Richmond Enquirer,* Aug. 6, 1858, p. 2; Echols to Letcher, July 9, 1858, and J. E. S. to Letcher, Aug. 17, 1858, Letcher Papers/Lexington; *Valley Star* (Lexington), July 15, 1858, p. 2. The letter requesting Ruffner to publish his speech stated that the signers (Letcher and others) did not expect Ruffner to remember his speech word for word. It also said that the signers did not desire that he limit himself strictly to the views expressed in the speech. They simply wanted the anti-slavery argument presented in an effective form. Thus Ruffner may have honestly added new material, and the signers

may have honestly been shocked by additions which seemed minor to a zealot like Ruffner. Probably both Letcher and Ruffner were partially correct, and they both may have been wholly sincere.

8. *Richmond Enquirer,* Nov. 5, 1859, p. 1; Shanks, *op cit.,* p. 58.

9. Letcher to Dr. Graham, July 9, 1858, Graham Manuscripts, Duke University; Faulkner to Letcher, June 21, 1858, Letcher Papers/ Lexington.

10. Porterfield to Kemper, June 22, 1858, Kemper Papers, University of Virginia; series of letters to Letcher in July and August, 1858, Letcher Papers/Lexington; Letcher to Davidson, July 17, 1858, Davidson Papers, McCormick Collection; Edmund Pendleton Tompkins, *Rockbridge County, Virginia: An Informal History* (Richmond: Whittet & Shepperson, 1952), pp. 118-125; John J. Moorman, *The Virginia Springs and Springs of the South and West* (Philadelphia: J. B. Lippincott & Co., 1859), pp. 262-264. Next to White Sulphur Springs, Rockbridge Alum Springs was the most popular resort in Virginia. Its bitter and supposedly medicinal waters drew a steady stream of well-to-do sick people and vacationers.

11. Letcher to Buchanan, July 24, 1858, James Buchanan Papers, The Historical Society of Pennsylvania, Philadelphia. Less than two weeks later, the voters of Kansas rejected the Lecompton Constitution in a fair election.

12. Letcher to Orr, Aug. 12, 1858, James L. Orr Papers, University of North Carolina.

13. Series of letters to Letcher in 1857 and 1858, Letcher Papers/ Lexington.

14. Davidson to J. J. Moorman, Aug. 6, 1858, Davidson Papers, McCormick Collection.

15. Corbin to Letcher, Aug. 17, 1858, and Jno. Seddon to Letcher, Aug. 31, 1858, Letcher Papers/Lexington.

16. Sam Letcher to Letcher, Aug. 31, 1858; Clemens to Letcher, Aug. 14 and 24, 1858; several other letters to Letcher, August-October, 1858, Letcher Papers/Lexington; Wm. H. Richardson to Davidson, Nov. 18, 1858, Davidson Papers, McCormick Collection.

17. Ambler, *op. cit.,* pp. 321-323; Bogan to Letcher, Oct. 27, 1858, Letcher Papers/Lexington; Letcher to Howell Cobb, Oct. 22, 1858, Howell Cobb Papers, University of Georgia.

18. Series of letters to Letcher, September-December, 1858, Letcher Papers/Lexington.

19. Bean, *op. cit.,* pp. 33-35; Shanks, *op. cit.,* p. 58; Earl G. Swem and John W. Williams (eds.), *A Register of the General Assembly of Virginia: 1776-1918: and of the Constitutional Conventions* (Richmond, 1918), p. 408; Davidson to Moorman, Dec. 11, 1858, Davidson Papers, McCormick Collection.

20. Roy Franklin Nichols, *The Disruption of American Democracy* (New York: The MacMillan Company, 1948), pp. 218-242.

21. Letcher to Davidson, Jan. 3 and Feb. 7, 1859, Davidson Papers, McCormick Collection; *Valley Star* (Lexington), Feb. 3, 1859, p. 2.

22. *The Congressional Globe: Containing the Debates and Proceedings of the Second Session of the Thirty-Fifth Congress: Also the Special Session of the Senate* (Washington, 1859), p. 637; Nichols, *op. cit.*, pp. 230-242; Letcher to Davidson, Feb. 7, 1859, Davidson Papers, McCormick Collection.

23. *Congressional Globe: Second Session of the Thirty-Fifth Congress,* p. 1100 and *passim;* Bean, *op. cit.*, p. 26.

24. Letcher to Davidson, Feb. 18, 1859, Davidson Papers, McCormick Collection; Bean, *op. cit.*, pp. 38-40; Shanks, *op. cit.*, p. 59.

25. Alex. Rives to Wm. Ballard Preston, Dec. 9, 1858, William B. Preston Papers, Virginia Historical Society, Richmond; Nichols, *op. cit.*, p. 250; Bean, *op. cit.*, p. 45; N. Sargent to Stuart, Feb. 27, 1859, A. H. H. Stuart Papers, Library of Congress. Preston had suffered politically for his support of emancipation in 1831. He apparently did not answer Rives' letter.

26. Clement Eaton, *Freedom of Thought in the Old South* (Durham: Duke University Press, 1940), p. 264; Bean, *op. cit.*, p. 37; Shanks, *op. cit.*, p. 59; *Richmond Whig and Daily Advertiser,* March-May, 1859.

27. Bean, *op. cit.*, pp. 40-41; *Staunton Spectator,* Mar. 15, 1859, p. 2.

28. State Central Committee of the Whig Party, *To the People of Virginia! John Letcher and His Antecedents* (Richmond, 1859), *passim;* Shanks, *op. cit.*, p. 59.

29. *Gazette* (Lexington), July 22, 1858, p. 2; Shanks, *op. cit.*, pp. 59, 117; Bean, *op. cit.*, pp. 41-44; Ambler, *op. cit.*, pp. 323-324.

30. Bean, *op. cit.*, pp. 43-45; E. B. Prettyman, "John Letcher", *John P. Branch Historical Papers of Randolph-Macon College,* III (1912), 334.

31. Bean, *op. cit.*, p. 44; William C. Pendleton, *Political History of Appalachian Virginia: 1776-1927* (Dayton, Va.: The Shenandoah Press, 1927), pp. 227-228; *Richmond Whig and Daily Advertiser,* March and April, 1859; William E. Glenn to Henry St. George Harris, Mar. 8, 1859, Henry St. George Harris Papers, Duke University; Leggett to S. H. Letcher, Feb. 14, 1905, and R. E. Withers' account, Mar. 19, 1906, Letcher Papers/Lexington; *Staunton Spectator,* Apr. 19, 1859, p. 1. There were a few charges that Letcher fled to Washington to escape debates with Goggin, but no responsible Whig accused Letcher of faking illness. He was obviously very sick at this time.

32. James E. Stewart to Letcher, May 16, 1859, Letcher Papers/ Lexington; Conway to Scruggs, May 23, 1859, and Tunstall to Scruggs, May 31 and Dec. 24, 1859, Langhorne Scruggs Papers, Duke University;

Richmond Whig and Daily Advertiser, Apr. 12, 1859, p. 4. James Gordon Bennett of the flamboyant New York *Herald* had a reporter covering the campaign, and Mississippians watched closely too. In general, Mississippians felt Letcher was "soft" on abolitionism.

33. J. R. Pole, "Representation and Authority in Virginia from the Revolution to Reform", *Journal of Southern History,* XXIV (1924), 49; Shanks, *op. cit.,* p. 117; Bean, *op. cit.,* pp. 45-46.

34. Shanks, *op. cit.,* p. 61; Ambler, *op. cit.,* pp. 324-325; Bean, *op. cit.,* pp. 46-47; *Richmond Whig and Public Advertiser,* June 3, 1859, p. 2; series of letters to Letcher in May and June, 1859, Letcher Papers/Lexington; Daniel Lee Powell to Alfred Harrison Powell, June 3, 1859, Daniel Lee Powell Papers, Virginia Historical Society, Richmond.

35. Nichols, *op. cit.,* pp. 243-263; Letcher Notebook/Lexington.

36. C. Vann Woodward, *The Burden of Southern History* (Baton Rouge: Louisiana State University Press, 1960), pp. 61-68; J. R. Tucker to J. H. Sherrard, Nov. 17, 1859, J. R. Tucker Letterbook, Tucker Papers, University of North Carolina; Dorman to Letcher, Jan. 2, 1860, Davidson Papers, McCormick Collection.

37. Charles Henry Ambler (ed.), "John Letcher to R. M. T. Hunter, December 9, 1859", *Correspondence of Robert M. T. Hunter, 1826-1876: Annual Report of the American Historical Association for the Year 1916* (Washington: Government Printing Office, 1918), II, 274-275.

38. *Ibid.;* Nichols, *op. cit.,* pp. 270-281; Davidson to [?], Dec. 17-18, 1859, Davidson Papers, McCormick Collection.

CHAPTER 6

1. Certificate of Qualification, Jan. 2, 1860, Executive Papers, Virginia State Library, Richmond. (hereafter designated EP); Executive Journal, Jan. 2, 1860, p. 1, Virginia State Library (hereafter designated EJ); *Richmond Enquirer,* Jan. 3, 1860, p. 1; H. Greeley (ed.), *The Tribune Almanac and Political Register for 1860* (New York, 1860), p. 64; Letcher to Davidson, Jan. 8, 1860, Davidson Papers, McCormick Collection. Only golden California topped Virginia with a governor's salary of $10,000 a year.

2. Terrill to Letcher, Mar. 15, 1864, and S. Bassett French to S. H. Letcher, Feb. 28, 1891, Letcher Papers/Lexington.

3. Henry T. Shanks, *The Secession Movement in Virginia: 1847-1861* (Richmond: Garrett and Massie, 1934), pp. 85-96; Charles Henry Ambler (ed.), "William Old Jr. to R. M. T. Hunter, January 1, 1860", *Correspondence of Robert M. T. Hunter, 1826-1876: Annual Report of the American Historical Association for the Year 1916* (Washington: Government Printing Office, 1918), II, 278-279 and 285-287; James C.

NOTES 263

McGregor, *The Disruption of Virginia* (New York: The MacMillan Company, 1922), pp. 87-88; Tucker to Kemper, Nov. 19, 1860, James L. Kemper Papers, University of Virginia. Old was fairly accurate in guessing what Letcher would say in his inaugural address.

4. Shanks, *op. cit.*, pp. 96-99; McGregor, *op. cit.*, pp. 103-104; *Richmond Enquirer,* Jan. 10, 1860, p. 4; Ollinger Crenshaw, *The Slave States in the Presidential Election of 1860* (Baltimore: The Johns Hopkins Press, 1945), p. 128.

5. Robert R. Jones, "Forgotten Virginian: The Early Life and Career of James Lawson Kemper: 1823-1865" (unpublished thesis, 1961, University of Virginia), p. 231; *Calendar of State Papers and Other Manuscripts from January 1, 1836 to April 15, 1869: Preserved in the Capitol in Richmond* (Richmond, 1893), XI, 157-158; *Acts of the General Assembly of the State of Virginia, Passed in 1859-1860, in the Eighty-Fourth Year of the Commonwealth* (Richmond, 1860), pp. 86-104, 126-127; *The War of the Rebellion: A Compilation of the Official Records of the Union and Confederate Armies* (Washington, 1880-1902), Series 4, I, 389 (hereafter designated *O.R.*); appointments, Jan. 30 and Feb. 2, 1860, EP; EJ, Jan. 30, 1860, p. 33 and Feb. 11, 1860, p. 43. In March the assembly also appropriated $20,000 to expand V. M. I. The militia laws were also streamlined. The contract with Anderson called for all machinery to be installed by Dec. 1, 1861 —a little late it turned out.

6. Ollinger Crenshaw, "Christopher G. Memminger's Mission to Virginia, 1860", *Journal of Southern History,* VIII (1942), 339-348; Shanks, *op. cit.,* pp. 97-99; Letcher to assembly, Jan. 16, 1860, and Governor Gist to Letcher, January, 1860, EP; Sallie R. Munford to Ellis Munford, Jan. 26, 1860, Ellis-Munford Papers, Duke University; Dwight Lowell Dumond, *The Secession Movement: 1860-1861* (New York: The Macmillan Company, 1931), pp. 29-32. Governor Gist of South Carolina and Governor Pettus of Mississippi were both avid secessionists.

7. Oswald Garrison Villard, *John Brown: 1800-1859: A Biography Fifty Years After* (New York: Houghton Mifflin Company, 1910), p. 578; EJ, Jan. 28, 1860, pp. 32-33; Andrew Hunter, "John Brown's Raid", *Publications of the Southern Historical Association,* I (1897), 188-190; *Calendar of State Papers,* XI, 100; Letcher to citizens of Norwich, Conn., Feb. 24, 1860, EP. The Brown raid eventually cost the state the sum of $250,000.

8. Shanks, *op. cit.,* pp. 91-92; EJ, Mar. 17, 1860, p. 78; Thomas Teakle, "The Rendition of Barclay Coppac", *Iowa Journal of History and Politics,* X (1912), 522-535. Letcher never favored a southern convention. His call for "a united South", made in the wake of the refusal of northern governors to extradite the fugitives, referred to a vague, general unity.

9. *Calendar of State Papers,* XI, 98-99; executive papers in gen-

eral for 1860; Tucker to Strother, June 19, 1860, John R. Tucker Letter Book, 1859-1864, University of North Carolina; Ellis to Letcher, Mar. 1, 1860, John W. Ellis Papers, Duke University.

10. Letcher to Jones, Apr. 8, 1860, Henry E. Huntington Library, San Marino, Calif.; Shanks, op. cit., p. 103.

11. Letcher to [?], Apr. 29, 1860, Henry E. Huntington Library, San Marino, Calif. The last two quotations appeared in F. N. Boney, "Governor Letcher's Candid Correspondence", Civil War History, X, Number 2 (1964), 169-170. Several other quotations in this work previously appeared in the same article.

12. Shanks, op. cit., pp. 103-109; J. G. Randall and David Donald, The Civil War and Reconstruction (Boston: D. C. Heath and Company, 1961), pp. 128-129; Dumond, op. cit., pp. 34-91; Letcher to Davidson, Feb. 18, 1860, Davidson Papers, McCormick Collection.

13. Shanks, op. cit., p. 142; Richmond Daily Whig, Feb. 5, 1860, p. 1; Wayland Fuller Dunaway, History of the James River and Kanawha Company (New York; Columbia University, 1922), pp. 200-204.

14. Richmond Daily Whig, Aug. 22, 1860, p. 1; Crenshaw, op cit., p. 141; Shanks, op. cit., pp. 108-119; Letcher to Davidson, July 25, 1860, Davidson Papers, McCormick Collection; Ollinger Crenshaw, "Rockbridge County and the Secession Convention of 1861", Proceedings: Rockbridge County Historical Society, III (1949), 7-8; Perceval Reniers, The Springs of Virginia: Life, Love and Death at the Waters: 1775-1900 (Chapel Hill: University of North Carolina Press, 1941), p. 202; Ambler, op. cit., pp. 317-318, 330-332. The governor lived in one of Company F's tents during his vacation but otherwise took no part in military drills. Company F did not expose itself to many rigorous maneuvers, and generally a good time was had by all.

15. Richmond Daily Whig, Aug. 22, 1860, p. 1; A. H. H. Stuart to Blanton Duncan, Aug. 23, 1860, John Bell Papers, Library of Congress; Munford to Ellis Munford, Dec. 9, 1860, Ellis-Munford Papers, Duke University; Charles Talcott, III, typewritten manuscript, Duke University; J. B. Dorman to Letcher, Nov. 18 and 27, 1860, Davidson Papers, McCormick Collection. After the election Dorman claimed that the Constitutional Unionists tricked some Douglas men into voting their ticket by spreading the rumor that Douglas had withdrawn from contention. Such strategems may have been decisive in this very close election.

16. Letcher to "Gentlemen", Oct. 19, 1860, Letcher Papers/Lexington.

17. Shanks, op. cit., pp. 111-119; Charles Henry Ambler, Sectionalism in Virginia from 1776 to 1861 (Chicago: University of Chicago Press, 1910), pp. 335-336.

18. EJ, June 28, 1860, p. 153; Thomas H. Ellis to Letcher, Jan. 1, 1861, EP; Richmond Enquirer, Sept. 18, 1860, p. 1 and Oct. 9, 1860,

p. 2; Lord Lyons to Letcher, Oct. 5, 1860, Letcher Papers/Lexington; W. Asbury Christian, *Richmond: Her Past and Present* (Richmond: L. H. Jenkins, 1912), p. 209. During this period, Letcher received several letters from the Frenchmen discussing terms of sale of the canal. The key clause of the proposed contract obligated the buyer to complete the canal. Some Virginians feared that French capital might come to dominate Virginia politics, but the deal seemed to be going through —until the threat of civil war discouraged the French entrepreneurs.

19. *O.R.*, Series III, I, 1-3; Shanks, *op. cit.*, pp. 120-129; *Richmond Enquirer*, Nov. 16, 1860, p. 3; John L. Carlile to Letcher, Nov. 19, 1860, and Dorman to Letcher, Nov. 18 and 27, 1860, Letcher Papers/Lexington. In Lexington, the Franklin Society debated the question: Should Virginia secede if the cotton states secede? Dorman assured Letcher that the majority in Lexington was still for the Union.

20. Letcher to L. P. Clover, Nov. 30, 1860, Clover to Letcher, Dec. 20, 1860, and Clover to Mrs. Letcher, Aug. 29, 1884, Letcher Papers/Lexington; Shanks, *op. cit.*, pp. 129-130; *Richmond Enquirer*, Nov. 30, 1860, p. 1; W. C. Rives to W. C. Rives, Jr., Nov. 29, 1860, William Cabell Rives Papers, Library of Congress; Dorman to Letcher, Nov. 27, 1860, Letcher Papers/Lexington. Virginia's gradual drift into secession is a striking example of the ability of a well-organized, vocal minority to sway the majority. Clover and Letcher had been friends when Clover was the rector of the Episcopal Church in Lexington. Clover said he showed Letcher's correspondence to Lincoln, who was a neighbor in Springfield.

21. Letcher to [?], Nov. 29, 1860, Executive Letter Book, EP; EJ, Nov. 15, 1860, p. 261; Alfred Hoyt Bill, *The Beleaguered City: Richmond, 1861-1865* (New York: A. A. Knopf, 1946), p. 33.

22. Letcher to Clover, Dec. 25, 1860, Letcher Papers/Lexington; *Richmond Enquirer*, Dec. 28, 1860, p. 1; R. I. Ellis to Charles Ellis, Jan. 8, 1861, Ellis-Munford Papers, Duke University; Davidson to Letcher, Jan. 3, 1861, Davidson Papers, McCormick Collection; Shanks, *op. cit.*, pp 131-141. According to Ellis, some planned "to burn Letcher in effigy on the Court House Green [at Afton] if he takes ground in his message against secession or a Convention".

23. *Message of the Governor of Virginia and Accompanying Documents* (Richmond; January, 1861), *passim; Richmond Enquirer,* Jan. 8, 1861, p. 3; William H. Richardson to Francis H. Smith, Jan. 3 and 12, 1861, William H. Richardson File, Virginia Military Institute. Like most of Letcher's speeches, this one was poorly organized. The summary in the text is rearranged for the sake of concise condensation.

24. [?] to Angus R. Blakey, Mar. 1, 1861, and G. D. Gray to Angus R. Blakey, Dec. 31, 1860, Angus R. Blakey Papers, Duke University; Dorman to Letcher, Jan. 13, 1861, Davidson Papers, McCormick Collection; Moorman to Letcher, Jan. 10, 1861, and R. W. Thomp-

son to Letcher, Jan. 11, 1861, Letcher Papers/Lexington; Shanks, *op. cit.*, pp. 143-144. Gray stated: "The strongest indignation is felt here [Culpeper County] against Letcher and anybody else who talks about a Border Confederacy or even a Border Convention."

25. John Tyler, William Cabell Rives, George W. Summers, John W. Brockenbrough, and James A. Seddon were Virginia's delegates to the Peace Convention.

26. Letcher to Davidson, Feb. 11, 1861, Letcher Papers/Lexington; *O.R.*, Series IV, I, 90-91.

27. EJ, Jan. 15, 1861, p. 16; Shanks, *op. cit.*, p. 150; M. G. Harman to John D. Imboden, Feb. 16, 1861, John D. Imboden Papers, University of Virginia. Some moderates feared that the convention would depose Letcher and reinstate the radical Wise as governor.

28. *O.R.*, Series IV, I, 204, 389; *Calendar of State Papers*, XI, 107, 158, 164; EJ, Mar. 26, 1861, p. 85 and Apr. 2, 1861, p. 94; Shanks, *op. cit.*, pp. 147-148; S. Adams to Edward Manigault, Apr. 24, 1861, C.S.A. Papers, miscellaneous, Library of Congress. Dimmock sent Master Armorer S. Adams north to buy weapons soon after his confirmation on April 2. Adams bought 500,000 percussion caps, a bullet machine, and a cap machine, but had only begun to ship these items when Virginia seceded and the federal government clamped an embargo on such shipments. Adams himself had to slip back to Virginia under disguise on April 23. The $1,000,000 appropriated on January 29 was issued in Virginia treasury notes after seven months' delay (see Chapter VIII, p. 142).

29. *O.R.*, Series III, I, 33-34; Edward McPherson, *The Political History of the U. S. of A. during the Great Rebellion* (Washington: Philip and Solomons, 1865), p. 36.

30. John Herbert Claiborne, *Seventy-Five Years in Old Virginia* (New York: The Neale Publishing Company, 1904), pp. 145-156; McPherson, *op. cit.*, p. 28; *Message of the Governor and Accompanying Documents* (Richmond, Dec. 2, 1861), p. vii; series of letters to Letcher in January, 1861, Letcher Papers/Lexington.

31. Series of letters to Letcher late in 1860 and early in 1861, EP; Thomas to Letcher, Mar. 12, 1861, EP; Bruce Catton, *This Hallowed Ground: The Story of the Union Side of the Civil War* (Garden City, N. Y.: Doubleday, 1956), p. 75; Douglas Southall Freeman, *Lee's Lieutenants: A Study in Command* (New York: Charles Scribner's Sons, 1942), I, 713-715; *O.R.*, Series I, LI, part 1, 317; William Mahone to Letcher, Feb. 6, 1861, and Letcher to Fitzhugh Lee, June 20, 1870, Letcher Papers/Lexington. Letcher's attempt to recruit all available military talent partially explains his delay in appointing a colonel of Virginia ordnance. He tried to get Thomas and several others before finally selecting Dimmock, but still he was quite slow to fill this key position. After the war a bitter dispute raged about Thomas' proper

place in Virginia history. Fitzhugh Lee defended Thomas as a sincere, kind man who followed his conscience.

32. EJ, Feb. 20, 1861, p. 51; J. S. Calvert to Letcher, Jan. 7, 1861, and order by Letcher, Jan. 14, 1861, and Letcher to Dr. A. Jones, Jan. 10, 1861, EP; Letcher to Davidson, Feb. 1, 1861, Letcher Papers/Lexington.

33. Letcher to Davidson, Feb. 1 and 4, 1861, and Davidson to Letcher, Jan. 31 and Feb. 4, 1861, Letcher Papers/Lexington; John B. Floyd to Senator Wigfall, Feb. 3, 1861, Lewis T. Wigfall Papers, Library of Congress; Shanks, *op. cit.*, pp. 158-160. George W. Summers and "Sandy" Stuart led the Unionists, and Lewis E. Harvie, Henry A. Wise, and John B. Floyd were in the forefront of the radicals. The heterogeneous moderates were led by R. Y. Conrad, William B. Preston, James Barbour, R. E. Scott, and others. Rockbridge County sent moderates James B. Dorman and Samuel McDowell Moore to the convention.

34. Davidson to Letcher, Feb. 7, 1861, Davidson Papers, McCormick Collection; Shanks, *op. cit.*, pp. 158-161; Letcher to Davidson, Feb. 11, 1861, and S. H. Letcher typewritten manuscript, no date, Letcher Papers/Lexington; J. William Jones, "The Secession of Virginia", *Southern Historical Society Papers*, XIII (1885), 360.

35. Davidson to Letcher, Feb. 7, 1861, Davidson Papers, McCormick Collection; Letcher to Davidson, Feb. 12, 1861, Letcher Papers/Lexington. This was not the last time Letcher was accused of excessive drinking. These charges were unfair, persistent, and very much in the tradition of American politics.

36. Davidson to Letcher, Mar. 2, 1861, Davidson to Dorman, Mar. 6, 1861, Davidson Papers, McCormick Collection; Shanks, *op. cit.*, p. 175; Herbert A. Kellar, "A Journey Through the South in 1836: Diary of James D. Davidson", *Journal of Southern History*, I (1935), 345-348. Davidson was not the only border slave stater in Washington at this time trying to fathom Lincoln. During the war, Davidson carried out other confidential missions for the governor.

37. Letcher to Davidson, Mar. 9, 1861, Davidson Papers, McCormick Collection; Randall and Donald, *op. cit.*, pp. 180-181; Shanks, *op. cit.*, pp. 175-177; Moorman to Letcher, Feb. 21, 1861, and Powell to Letcher, Mar. 4, 1861, Letcher Papers/Lexington; J. W. Pegram to Ellis Munford, Feb. 21, 1861, Ellis-Munford Papers, Duke University; Davidson to Letcher, Mar. 6 and 9, 1861, and Dorman to Davidson, Mar. 8 and Apr. 1, 1861, Davidson Papers, McCormick Collection.

38. Letcher to Davidson, Mar. 24, 1861, Dorman to Davidson, Mar. 8 and Apr. 1, 1861, Davidson to Letcher, Mar. 14, 1861, Davidson Papers, McCormick Collection; F. H. Hill to [?], Mar. 8, 1861, Francis H. Hill Papers, Duke University. Letcher also praised old Whig

John Baldwin of Augusta County for his attack on the radicals in the convention.

39. Shanks, *op. cit.,* pp. 182-192; *O.R.,* Series I, LI, part 1, 319; and Series IV, I, 203-204; Joint Resolution of the General Assembly, Apr. 1, 1861, EP; J. B. Jones, *A Rebel War Clerk's Diary at the Confederates States Capitol* (New York: J. B. Lippincott & Co., 1935), I, 20, 23; Joseph Segar, *Letter of Hon. Joseph Segar to a Friend in Virginia* (1862), pp. 37-39; Davidson to Dorman, Mar. 6, 1861, and Davidson to Letcher, Mar. 9, 1861, Davidson Papers, McCormick Collection. The only Richmond newspaper to retain even a semblance of moderation was the *Whig,* Letcher's enemy in 1859.

40. Dorman to Davidson, Apr. 1, 9, 12, 14, 1861, Davidson Papers, McCormick Collection; Shanks, *op. cit.,* pp. 190-199, 268; E. Merton Coulter, *The Confederate States of America: 1861-1865* (Baton Rouge: Louisiana State University Press, 1950), pp. 40-41; Bill, *op. cit.,* pp. 39-41; *Richmond Enquirer,* Apr. 16, 1861, p. 1; Benj. B. Weisiger to S. Bassett French, Apr. 5, 1892, Letcher Papers/Lexington. When the crowd first fired the cannon, one rabid secessionist cried, "would to God that one of those guns were loaded with shot and pointed at the Gubernatorial Mansion". The crowd had little use for moderation. A few Unionists in the crowd greatly admired Letcher's calm yet firm speech to a hostile audience.

41. Letcher to Simon Cameron, Apr. 16, 1861, Papers of the U. S. Secretary of War, letters received 1861, National Archives, Washington, D. C.; Beverley B. Munford, *Virginia's Attitude toward Slavery and Secession* (New York: Longmans, Green, and Company, 1909), p. 282; Shanks, *op. cit.,* pp. 199-206; Randall and Donald, *op. cit.,* pp. 180-182; Robert M. Hughes, "Civil War and/or War Between the States", *William and Mary College Quarterly Historical Magazine,* XV (2) (1935), 44. President Lincoln's call for troops on April 15 probably caused a greater shock in Virginia than the opening cannonade at Fort Sumter. These two incidents are difficult to separate in the rapid flow of events; each helped eliminate opposition to secession.

42. Segar, *op. cit.,* pp. 37-39; Barton H. Wise, *The Life of Henry A. Wise of Virginia: 1806-1876* (New York: The Macmillan Company, 1899), pp. 275-278; John M. Payne, "University of Virginia Companies", *Confederate Veteran,* XL (1932), 256-258; *Richmond Daily Whig,* Nov. 3, 1860, p. 2; unidentified newspaper clipping dated Nov. 4, 1959, J. M. McCue Papers, Virginia Historical Society.

CHAPTER 7

1. *Richmond Enquirer,* Apr. 18, 1861, p. 2; Dunbar Rowland (ed.), *Jefferson Davis: Constitutionalist: His Letters, Papers and Speeches* (New York: J. J. Little & Ives Company, 1923), V, 63; series of orders,

letters, and telegrams, April, 1861, EP; J. William Jones, "Virginia's Armed Forces", *Southern Historical Society Papers,* XIII (1885), 179-181; EJ, Apr. 18, 1861, p. 112; *O.R.,* Series I, LI, part 2, 16-22, 213 and II, 940 and Series IV, I, 413; General Josiah Gorgas, "Notes on the Ordnance Department of the Confederate Government", *Southern Historical Society Papers,* XII (1884), 65-67; Richardson to Smith, Apr. 12, 1861, William H. Richardson File, Virginia Military Institute.

2. S. Bassett French to Letcher, Apr. 17, 1861, and French, Newton, others to Letcher, Apr. 18, 1861, Letcher Papers/Lexington; Donald B. Webster, Jr., "The Last Days of Harpers Ferry Armory", *Civil War History,* V (1959), 30-31; John Sherman Long, "The Gosport Affair, 1861", *Journal of Southern History,* XXIII (1957), 159-160; series of dispatches and telegrams, Apr. 17, 1861, EP; *O.R.,* Series I, II, 771; *Official Records of the Union and Confederate Navies in the War of the Rebellion* (Washington, 1896), Series I, IV, 301 (hereafter designated *O.R.N.*); EJ, Apr. 17, 1861, p. 111; Henry T. Shanks, *The Secession Movement in Virginia: 1847-1861* (Richmond: Garrett and Massie, 1934), pp. 203-204.

3. Douglas Southall Freeman, *R. E. Lee: A Biography* (New York: Charles Scribner's Sons, 1934), I, 481-483; Gorgas, *op. cit.,* pp. 67-71; *O.R.N.,* Series I, V, 803; Jones, *op. cit.,* pp. 179-181; S. A. Cunningham, "How the Confederacy Armed Its Soldiers", *Confederate Veteran,* XXX (1922), number 1, 11, Long, *op. cit.,* pp. 159-169; Webster, *op. cit.,* pp. 30-40; Margaret L. Von Der Au, "Virginia's Contribution to the Confederacy", *Confederate Veteran,* XXIII (1915), number 2, 65. This 300,000 pounds of gunpowder was the Confederacy's main source for many months.

4. *O.R.,* Series I, LI, part 2, 18-19, and Series IV, I, 242; Shanks, *op. cit.,* p. 204.

5. James C. McGregor, *The Disruption of Virginia* (New York: The Macmillan Company, 1922), p. 252; Shanks, *op. cit.,* p. 211; Richard Orr Curry, *A House Divided: A Study of Statehood Politics and the Copperhead Movement in West Virginia* (Pittsburgh: University of Pittsburgh Press, 1964), p. 34, *passim.* The detention of a few leading Unionists might have changed the course of events in western Virginia.

6. Virgil Carrington Jones, *Grey Ghosts and Rebel Raiders* (New York: Holt, 1956), pp. 11-12; Festus P. Summers, *The Baltimore and Ohio in the Civil War* (New York: G. P. Putnam's Sons, 1939), p. 56; Thos. M. Keese to Letcher, Apr. 18, 1861, and Letcher's notation on back, EP; *O.R.,* Series I, LI, part 2, 21. Garrett was pro-Southern but under heavy pressure from Secretary of War Simon Cameron in Washington. Eventually the Baltimore and Ohio performed vital service for the Union armies.

7. *O.R.,* Series I, II, 771 and LI, part 2, 27-30, 60, and Series

IV, I, 390 and Series II, II, 21; *O.R.N.,* Series I, V, 797; *Calendar of State Papers,* XI, 113; EJ, May 15, 1861, p. 174; French to H. B. Tomlin, May 15 and 18, 1861, and Letcher to Tomlin, May 16, 1861, Harrison Ball Tomlin Papers, Virginia Historical Society, Richmond; note by Letcher, Apr. 23, 1861, and proclamation by Letcher, Apr. 24, 1861, EP. Several ships including the steamer *Yorktown* were held and fitted out for war service.

8. Freeman, *op. cit.,* p. 494; Letcher to Harman, Apr. 20, 1861, and Letcher to convention, Apr. 20, 1861, E.P.; *O.R.,* Series IV, I, 390; *Calendar of State Papers,* XI, 158. At this time Virginia bonds were selling 20 per cent below face value. Therefore the inflationary expedient of issuing treasury notes was used instead of trying to sell state bonds. A shortage of engraving plates caused a delay, and the first notes were not issued until August.

9. Clifford Dowdey, *The Land They Fought For: The Story of the South As the Confederacy: 1832-1865* (Garden City, N.Y.: Doubleday and Company, 1955), p. 94; S. H. Letcher typewritten manuscript, Letcher Papers/Lexington; Frank L. Owsley, *King Cotton Diplomacy: Foreign Relations of the Confederate States of America* (Chicago: University of Chicago Press, 1931), pp. 5-49; Allan Nevins, *The War for the Union: The Improvised War: 1861-1862* (New York: Charles Scribner's Sons, 1959), I, 97-99. The concept of "King Cotton" was strongest in the deep South. In the upper South, Letcher was by no means the only skeptic. Secretary of the Treasury Christopher G. Memminger believed in a short war won by "King Cotton", and his economic policies reflected this myth. The Confederate treasury was unprepared for a long war, and Letcher was very critical of Memminger's performance.

10. Clifford Dowdey, *Experiment in Rebellion* (Garden City: Doubleday and Company, 1946), p. 27; W. Asbury Christian, *Richmond: Her Past and Present* (Richmond: L. H. Jenkins, 1912), p. 217; Freeman, *op. cit.,* p. 462; proclamation by the governor, Apr. 21, 1861, EP. This proclamation was simply an alert. Primarily because of the shortage of weapons, Letcher refrained from calling up large numbers of volunteers for some time.

11. *O.R.,* Series I, LI, part 2, 21, 28-29; EJ, Apr. 21, 1861, p. 115; Freeman, *op. cit.,* p. 463, 486-487; *Calendar of State Papers,* XI, 110. One of the main functions of the council was to advise Letcher on the appointment of field grade officers for Virginia forces. The convention had provided that company officers should be elected by the troops. Competent officers were scarce and militia officers were usually local politicians. Previously the volunteer forces had no officers above the rank of captain.

12. Munford to Gayle, Apr. 21, 1861, EP; EJ, Apr. 21, 1861, p. 115, and Apr. 22, 1861, p. 117.

13. Crump to Letcher, May 5, 1861, J. M. McCue Papers, Virginia Historical Society; Dowdey, *Experiment,* p. 30; C. E. Stuart to Letcher, Apr. 22, 1861 (telegram), and Letcher's answer on back, EP; *O.R.,* Series I, LI, part 2, 24, and 34, and Series II, I, 626, 675, 772-774; Davis to Letcher, Apr. 22, 1861 (telegram), Jefferson Davis Papers, National Archives; Steuart to "Willy", Apr. 24, 1861, George Hume Steuart Papers, Duke University; *Message of the Governor of Virginia and Accompanying Documents* (December, 1861), pp. xi-xii; E. H. McDonald, "How Virginia Supplied Maryland With Arms", *Southern Historical Society Papers,* XXIX (1901), 163-166; Edward McPherson, *The Political History of the U. S. of A. during the Great Rebellion* (Washington: Philip and Solomons, 1865), p. 394. Maj. E. H. McDonald delivered the Harper's Ferry weapons, and Baltimorean T. Parkin Scott brought in about 2,000 arms from Lexington. Muskets, not rifles, were risked in such gambles. Virginia general Kenton Harper almost ordered 1,000 of his troops to march on Baltimore from Harper's Ferry on April 23 when he was unable to contact Letcher. Only Steuart's message to wait stopped him. General Lee opposed sending troops into Maryland. The pro-southern Baltimore police board stored the Virginia weapons that were not immediately distributed. When the board was arrested on July 1, eight cannons, more than 300 muskets, and many other arms were seized.

14. Freeman, *op. cit.,* pp. 444-448, 462-464, 637-638; *O.R.,* Series I, II, 775-776; Scott to Letcher, Oct. 29, 1860, John Kenney to Letcher, Apr. 22, 1861, and Letcher handwritten manuscript, no date, Letcher Papers/Lexington; Letcher to convention, Apr. 20, 1861, EP; William G. Stanard, "Some Virginia Portraits", *Virginia Magazine of History and Biography,* XXX (1922), 108; J. William Jones, "R. E. Lee to Reverdy Johnson, February 25, 1868", *Southern Historical Society Papers,* XI (1883), 421; J. William Jones, "Official Correspondence of Governor Letcher", *SHSP,* XII (1884), 455-456; Bruce Catton, *This Hallowed Ground: The Story of the Union Side of the Civil War* (Garden City: Doubleday and Company, 1956), pp. 16-17. On April 19 the council advised Letcher to appoint Lee commander of all Virginia forces. Despite every effort, almost one-third of the state's West Point graduates remained in federal service. The deep South had a better recruiting record.

15. Letcher to convention, Apr. 23, 1861, EP.

16. Letcher to sheriffs, etc., Apr. 23, 1861; a proclamation, Apr. 24, 1861; Susan E. Wash to Letcher, May 7, 1861; J. R. Anderson to Letcher, Apr. 27, 1861 and May 6, 1861; George B. Sloat to Letcher, May 8, 1861, EP; *Acts of the General Assembly of the State of Virginia, Passed in 1861, in the Eighty-Fifth Year of the Commonwealth* (Richmond, 1961), pp. 27, 58 (Appendix); *O.R.,* Series I, LI, part 2, 36-37;

also EP in general. Anderson's Tredegar Iron Works had great difficulty keeping its skilled labor from volunteering for army service.

17. A proclamation, Apr. 24, 1861, and M. A. Sullivan to Letcher, Apr. 22, 1861, EP. Most volunteer units offering their services were inadequately armed and equipped. The executive papers for April and May are full of such tenders of service.

18. *O.R.N.,* Series I, IV, 297; Wright to Letcher, Apr. 26, 1861, Letcher Papers/Lexington; Wright to E. M. Stanton, Apr. 25, 1865, Union Provost Marshal File, entry 465, National Archives. Richmonders were angry at Wright and Rodgers for trying to destroy "Virginia's property".

19. Shanks, *op. cit.,* p. 204; *O.R.,* Series I, LI, part 2, 29; *Richmond Enquirer,* Apr. 25, 1861, p. 2; EJ, Apr. 25, 1861, p. 126. The convention agreed to join the Confederacy on April 24, and the alliance was completed on April 25. Thus the plebiscite on May 23 was only the popular stamp of approval for what the convention had already done on April 17-25.

20. Jas. P. Holcombe to William B. Preston, May 9, 1861, William B. Preston Papers, Virginia Historical Society; account by R. E. Withers, Mar. 19, 1905, and Letcher to Wm. K. Heiskell, May 10, 1861, Letcher Papers/Lexington; executive papers in general for this period; *Staunton Vindicator,* Apr. 26, 1861, p. 1; William Nelson Pendleton to Letcher, May 20, 1861, and Letcher to Pendleton, May 24, 1861, William Nelson Pendleton Papers, University of North Carolina. Pendleton, a West Pointer and future chief of Lee's artillery, was unhappy about some of Letcher's military appointments. Letcher was unimpressed with Pendleton and most other "military Parsons". He remained skeptical of Pendleton's ability throughout the war.

21. W. C. Rives to Letcher, Apr. 25, 1861, William Cabell Rives Papers, Library of Congress; A. F. Roller, "Lack of Equipment in '61", *Confederate Veteran,* XVII (1908), number 2, 123; L. P. Walker to Letcher, Apr. 27, 1861 (telegram), and series of other telegrams to Letcher late in April, 1861, EP; EJ, May 1, 1861, p. 142; *O.R.,* Series I, LI, part 2, 37; *Message of Governor* (Richmond, December, 1861), pp. vi-viii.

22. Dowdey, *Experiment,* p. 34; Freeman, *op. cit.,* pp. 491-502, 514-515; Douglas Southall Freeman, *Lee's Lieutenants: A Study in Command* (New York: Charles Scribner's Sons, 1942), I, 721-724; *O.R.,* Series I, II, 783, 792, and Series I, LI, part 2, 74. In this period arguments over rank were endless.

23. Freeman, *Lee,* I, 501, 515; *O.R.,* Series I, II, 805, 813, and Series I, LI, part 2, 65-66, 70-71, 74. The Confederates continued to direct some troops in Virginia despite the May 10 order. On May 14, Lee was commissioned a Confederate brigadier general, the highest rank then existing.

24. EJ, Apr. 25, 1861, p. 127, and Apr. 27, 1861, p. 135; *O.R.N.*, Series I, IV, 312; Joshua Carhart to governor, Apr. 26, 1861, EP. Letcher finally released the paymaster early in May.

25. *O.R.*, Series I, LI, part 2, 50, 65; J. R. Pendleton to R. Y. Conrad, Apr. 26, 1861 (telegram), and James H. Carson to Letcher, Apr. 26, 1861 (telegram), EP. General Lee was also active in this unsuccessful recruiting effort.

26. Freeman, *Lee,* I, 484; Freeman, *Lee's Lieutenants,* I, 706-707; *O.R.*, Series I, II, 784, and Series I, LI, part 2, 47-48; R. A. Brock, "The Career of General Jackson", *Southern Historical Society Papers,* XXXV (1907), 79; Dowdey, *Experiment,* pp. 27-28.

27. *O.R.*, Series I, LI, part 2, 54-55, 73, and Series I, II, 797; Freeman, *Lee,* I, 493; EJ, May 3, 1861, p. 147; series of letters in May, 1861, R. E. Lee Papers, National Archives. The Lee Papers in the National Archives reveal a conspicuous scarcity of Letcher letters. Lee endured considerable harassment, but none of it came from Letcher. Lee issued local volunteer calls and May 3, 6, 7, and 9, as mobilization swung into high gear.

28. *O.R.*, Series I, II, 804, 814, 849, and LI, part 2, 69; O.R.N., Series I, IV, 307-312.

29. John S. Burton to Letcher, Apr. 21, 1861, Letcher Papers/Lexington.

30. A. W. Spies to Letcher, Apr. 28, 1861, with enclosed newspaper article, Letcher Papers/Lexington.

31. A. G. Hicks to Letcher, May 8, 1861, Letcher Papers/Lexington. The Letcher Papers contain other similar letters, the last voices from the North before the cannons began to speak in earnest. These letters were first published in the *Lincoln Herald* (Winter, 1963), pp. 190-193.

32. EJ, May 2, 1861, p. 144, May 7, 1861, p. 153, and May 9, 1861, p. 160; John W. Ellis to Letcher, May 6, 1861, Letcher Papers/Lexington; Capt. John Weems to Letcher May 7, 1861, and Letcher to Weems, May 8, 1861 (both telegrams), EP; R. Thompson to Army of N. Va., May 22, 1861, R. E. Lee Papers, National Archives; Fred A. Olds, "North Carolina Troops", *Southern Historical Society Papers,* XXIX (1901), 151; Douglas Southall Freeman, *A Calendar of Confederate Papers, With a Bibliography of Some Confederate Publications: Preliminary Report of the Southern Historical Manuscripts Commission* (Richmond: Confederate Museum, 1908), pp. 266, 329. When Letcher did not want a band of unarmed outside volunteers, he referred their tender of service to Confederate officials, a convenient way to pass the buck. For a partial accounting of aid sent to other states, see *O.R.N.*, Series I, V, 806.

33. EJ, May 7, 1861, p. 153; *O.R.*, Series I, LI, part 2, 90-91; Letcher to M. G. Harman, May 18, 1861, and Letcher to Brockenbrough

and Staples, May 12, 1861, EP. A complaint about Letcher's appointment of Walter Gwynn as commander at Norfolk caused Letcher to complain about the lack of Confederate support. Gwynn was one of Letcher's worst appointments. The convention invited the Confederate government to move to Richmond on April 27.

34. Jones, "Official Correspondence of Governor Letcher", *Southern Historical Society Papers,* I, 457-458; A. J. Grigsby to Letcher, Apr. 25, 1861, C.S.A. Papers, miscellaneous, Library of Congress; H. T. Martin to Col. F. M. Boykins, Jr., May 1, 1861, and Col. J. McCausland and to Letcher, May 28, 1861, Letcher Papers/Lexington; Alex Rives to W. C. Rives, May 13, 1861, Rives Papers, Library of Congress; *O.R.,* Series I, II, 630; *Message of Governor* (Richmond: December, 1861), pp. xiii-xiv. Rives condemned the radicals, "those conspirators, who commenced this revolution to supply themselves with offices they were losing in the old government".

35. *Message of Governor* (Richmond: December, 1861), pp. xiii-xiv; Jones, "Correspondence of Letcher", *SHSP,* I, 457-458; Curry, *op. cit.,* pp. 38-45.

36. EJ, May 11, 1861, pp. 165-166; *Message of Governor* (Richmond: December, 1861), p. iii. "Beef, pork, bacon, flour & general provisions" was the way it was phrased in the proclamation.

37. EJ, May 30, 1861, p. 204; Letcher to Governor Ellis of North Carolina, May 11, 1861, and Letcher to J. Gorgas, May 15, 1861 (telegram), EP. Many scarce items were temporarily misplaced in shipment, causing more confusion.

38. *Calendar of State Papers,* XI, 143, 155-156; Geo. W. Munford to H. B. Tomlin, May 18, 1861, Tomlin Papers, Virginia Historical Society; *O.R.,* Series I, II, 872, and Series IV, I, 354; Shanks, *op. cit.,* 204, 213. On June 14, Letcher announced the official results of the plebiscite as 125,950 to 20,373 for secession. He had to estimate the figures for some areas under federal control.

CHAPTER 8

1. W. Asbury Christian, *Richmond: Her Past and Present* (Richmond: L. H. Jenkins, 1912), p. 222; Clifford Dowdey, *The Land They Fought For: The Story of the South As the Confederacy: 1832-1865* (Garden City: Doubleday and Company, 1955), p. 114; Clifford Dowdey, *Experiment in Rebellion* (Garden City: Doubleday and Company, 1946), pp. 37-38. Virginia was admitted to the Confederacy on May 7, almost two weeks before the plebiscite on secession.

2. Dunbar Rowland (ed.), *Jefferson Davis: Constitutionalist: His Letters, Papers and Speeches* (New York: J. J. Little & Ives Company, 1923), V, 101-102; *Calendar of State Papers,* XI, 142; *O.R.,* Series I, LI, part 2, 124, 133, and Series IV, I, 364; Jeffn. Davis to Letcher, June

2, 1861, Jefferson Davis Papers, National Archives; transcript of council journal, May 21, 1861, EP. Letcher conferred with Davis on May 31 and June 1.

3. EJ, June 4, 1861, pp. 215-218; *Calendar of State Papers*, XI, 146; *O.R.*, Series I, LI, part 2, 124-135; Alice Maury Parmelee (ed.), *The Confederate Diary of Betty Herndon Maury, Daughter of Lieut. Commander M. F. Maury, "The Pathfinder of the Seas": 1861-1863* (Washington, D.C.: 1938), p. 5; Douglas Southall Freeman, *R. E. Lee: A Biography* (New York: Charles Scribner's Sons, 1934), I, 510, 519. Maury was worried about how Davis and his "clique" would perform under pressure.

4. *O.R.*, Series I, II, 911-912, and LI, part 2, 122, and Series IV, I, 358; *Calendar of State Papers*, XI, 172-173; EJ, May 30, 1861, p. 205, and June 12, 1861, pp. 229-230; General Josiah Gorgas, "Notes on the Ordnance Department of the Confederate Government", *Southern Historical Society Papers*, XII (1884), 67-94; S. Adams to Edward Manigault, Apr. 24, 1861, C.S.A. Papers, miscellaneous, Library of Congress. Letcher's proclamation was first dated June 6 but issued on June 8.

5. Convention to Letcher, June 29, 1861, Walker to Letcher, July 20, 1861, Munford to Davis, July 12, 1861, Dimmock to Letcher, July 31, 1861, EP; EJ, July 13, 1861, pp. 272-273; *O.R.*, Series IV, I, 468-473, 476, 488-489, 491-492, 504-505; Frank Lawrence Owsley, *State Rights in the Confederacy* (Chicago: University of Chicago Press, 1925), pp. 14-15; Frank E. Vandiver (ed.), *The Civil War Diary of General Josiah Gorgas* (Tuscaloosa: University of Alabama Press, 1947), p. 80. In one of the many letters exchanged in this controversy, Walker sarcastically asked Letcher if Virginia intended to operate a separate ordnance department. He was closer to the mark than he realized.

6. *O.R.*, Series IV, I, 530, 534; EJ, July 25, 1861, p. 284, Aug. 2, 1861, p. 292, Aug. 6, 1861, p. 295, Aug. 21, 1861, p. 308, and Sept. 2, 1861, p. 356; Walker to Letcher, Aug. 1, 1861, Letcher to Tucker, Aug. 16, 1861, Gorgas to Letcher, Aug. 21, 1861, Deed of Transfer, Sept. 2, 1861, all EP. Appropriately enough, the final deed covered many pages in very fine print.

7. Letcher to Maj. H. B. Tomlin, May 30, 1861, and French to Tomlin, June 3, 1861, Harrison Ball Tomlin Papers, Virginia Historical Society; order of the governor, June 4, 1861, J. L. Morron to Letcher, June 4, 1861 (telegram), W. W. Townes to Letcher, June 6, 1861 (telegram with Letcher's answer on back), C. Pate to Letcher, June 4, 1861, Letcher memo, June 10, 1861, EP.

8. Col. Jas. C. Wilson to Letcher, May 31, 1861, R. E. Lee Papers, National Archives.

9. Freeman, *op. cit.*, pp. 502, 580; Rowland, *op. cit.*, V, 105;

O.R., Series IV, I, 374; J. William Jones, "Official Correspondence of Governor Letcher, of Virginia", *Southern Historical Society Papers*, I (1876), 458-459. This Confederate brigade also harassed Lee, the commander in that area.

10. Charles W. Turner, "The Virginia Central Railroad at War, 1861-1865", *Journal of Southern History*, XII (1946), 516-517; Samson and Poe to Dimmock, June 7, 1861, Dimmock to Letcher, June 7, 1861, W. T. Joynes to Letcher, June 8, 1861 (telegram), Henry Daingerfield to Davis to Letcher, June 16, 1861, EP; EJ, June 10, 1861, pp. 224-225; Robert C. Black, III, *The Railroads of the Confederacy* (Chapel Hill: University of North Carolina Press, 1952), 3-4, 8-9.

11. Davis to Letcher, no date (telegram), Davis Papers, National Archives; *Richmond Enquirer*, June 4, 1861, p. 2. Lee had been in charge of mobilizing volunteers since May 3. He had gradually mustered the volunteers as soon as they could be effectively integrated into combat units. This proclamation on June 3 scooped up the last pool of available volunteers. The overconfident convention had set the term of service for volunteers at one year. Lee had recommended swearing them in for the duration of the war.

12. *O.R.*, Series I, II, 951, and LI, part 2, 124; council to Letcher, June 1, 1861, EP; Freeman, *op. cit.*, pp. 519-521. All of this action took place abut the time of the transfer of forces on June 6. The counties included in the militia callup were Bath, Pendleton, Pocahontas, Highland, Randolph, Barbour, and Tucker. All but Bath and Highland eventually became part of the new state of West Virginia.

13. *Calendar of State Papers*, XI, 150; *O.R.*, Series I, II, 951-952; proclamation, June 14, 1861, EP; French to Lee, June 10, 1861, Lee Papers, National Archives; E. T. Munford to Charles Ellis Munford, June 12, 1861, Ellis-Munford Papers, Duke University. The special tax reform amendment was an attempt to pacify the northwest, but it came at least a decade too late.

14. Parmelee (ed.), *Diary of Betty Herndon Maury*, pp. 7, 18; *O.R.N.*, Series I, II, 926-929; Freeman, *op. cit.*, p. 524; EJ, June 15, 1861, p. 235; Munford to Letcher, June 14, 1861, EP; *Message of Governor* (Richmond: December, 1861), *passim*.

15. *O.R.*, Series IV, I, 388-393; *Calendar of State Papers, XI*, 157-163; Lee A. Wallace, Jr., *A Guide to Virginia Military Organizations: 1861-1865* (Richmond: Virginia Civil War Commission, 1964), p. 205. Technically, the provisional army was not disbanded; but, in reality, it ceased to exist as an effective military command.

16. *O.R.*, Series IV, I, 396; Dorman to Davidson, June 19, 1861, Davidson Papers, McCormick Collection; Francis H. Smith to Lee, June 3, 1861, Lee Papers, National Archives. This action by the convention was as much a sign of confidence in Lee as in Letcher. The

council's activities had decreased noticeably since the transfer of forces on June 6. Smith returned to V.M.I. as superintendent.

17. Fred J. Cridland to Letcher, June 28, 1861, Munford to Cridland, June 29, 1861, Cridland to Letcher, July 10 and Aug. 13, 1861, and Mar. 22, 1862, Cridland to William M. Brown to Letcher, Mar. 20, 1862, Cridland to Munford, Jan. 24, 1862, Geo. Moore to Letcher, Jan. 8 and 15, 1863, and Letcher to Moore, Jan. 20, 1863, all EP; EJ, June 20, 1861, p. 245; *Calendar of State Papers*, XI, 203; *O.R.*, Series II, III, 687-688; J. G. Randall and David Donald, *The Civil War and Reconstruction* (Boston: D. C. Heath and Company, 1961), pp. 506-507. Moore was the consul actually expelled. The rest of the British consuls were expelled in October, 1863.

18. E.J, June 25, 1861, p. 251; memo to all RR presidents, June 27, 1861, EP. In the South, the only effective security measures were directed against the Negroes, but this was a traditional policy, not an innovation.

19. Letcher to executive department, July 1, 1861, Letcher to Walker, July 3, and Walker to Letcher, July 13, 1861, C.S.A. Secretary of War, letters received, National Archives; Walker to Letcher, June 30, 1861, Letcher to convention, July 3, 1861, Munford to Walker, July 11, 1861, EP; *Calendar of State Papers,* XI, 179-180; *O.R.*, Series IV, I, 419-420.

20. Dorman to Davidson, July 1 and 8, 1861, Davidson Papers, McCormick Collection; *O.R.*, Series I, LI, part 2, 158, 168-169, and Series I, II, 260, 263; EJ, July 13, 1861, p. 273; proclamation, July 15, 1861, EP; John B. Baldwin to Letcher, July 5, 1861, Letcher Papers/Lexington; Freeman, *op. cit.*, pp. 527-535. Garnett's army suffered about 20 per cent casualties in the battle.

21. Proclamation, July 15, 1861, EP; French to Lee, July 17, 1861, Lee Papers, National Archives; Charles Talcott, III, typewritten manuscript, p. 257, Duke University. Letcher was limited to three aides by the convention. He could have used more.

22. *O.R.*, Series I, V, 810, 816-821; Parmelee, *Diary of Betty Herndon Maury*, p. 19; Randall and Donald, *op. cit.,* pp. 197-199. If Union General Robert Patterson had exerted more pressure on Johnston at Winchester, the rebels probably could not have slipped away to Manassas despite militia reinforcements, which were few and untrained anyway.

23. H. D. Whitcomb to Letcher, July 16, Walker to Letcher, July 16, order by Letcher, July 16, John M. Daniel to Letcher, July 17, M. J. Michelbacher to Letcher, with Letcher's answer on back, July 18, and proclamation signed by William H. Richardson, Aug. 23, 1861, all EP; EJ, July 19, 1861, p. 278, and Aug. 23, 1861, p. 311; *O.R.*, Series I, LI, part 2, 263. In February, 1862, the General Assembly created permanent exemption boards in the counties. The Shenandoah

County and Winchester areas responded poorly to the July militia calls.

24. Maj. H. B. Tomlin to Letcher, July 17, 1861, French to Tomlin, July 19, 1861, Letcher to Tomlin, July 25, 1861, Harrison Ball Tomlin Papers, Virginia Historical Society; Letcher to L. P. Clover, Dec. 25, 1860, Letcher Papers/Lexington.

25. William H. Richardson to Francis H. Smith, July 31, 1861, William H. Richardson File, Virginia Military Institute.

26. EJ, July 19, 1861, p. 278; Bennett to Letcher, July 30, 1861, EP; *O.R.,* Series IV, I, 389-390. The assembly appropriated $1,000,000 on Jan. 29, 1861. Since state bonds had depreciated 20 per cent, the convention on March 14 ordered the issuance of Virginia treasury notes to cover this amount. On April 30, the convention appropriated another $2,000,000 in state treasury notes. (See footnote 8, chapter 7.) The convention also ordered the issuance of $4,000,000 in certificates bearing interest at 6 per cent. Certificates were actually issued in the amount of $4,279,000. Now Bennett wanted to issue $7,000,000 in state treasury notes, part of the amount to cover the $279,000 excess in certificates, part to cover the authorized $4,000,000 in certificates as they matured, part to cover current operating expenses, and the balance to create the $3,000,000 authorized earlier but delayed by a shortage of printing equipment.

27. Munford to Dimmock, July 17, H. L. Clay to Dimmock, July 20, Gorgas to Munford, July 22, Munford to Gorgas, July 23, 1861, Gorgas to J. P. Benjamin, Feb. 18, 1862, Gorgas to H. L. Clay, no date, all EP. Secretary of the Commonwealth Munford handled most of this controversy, but he acted under orders from the governor. Occasionally, Letcher referred to this incident when similar clashes occurred later.

28. Letcher to Walker, Aug. 14, 17, 24, and 26, and Sept. 6, 1861, C.S.A. Secretary of War, letters received, National Archives; John Tyler, Jr., to Letcher, Sept. 10, 1861, Letcher Papers, Duke University; *Calendar of State Papers,* XI, 189-190, 193; *O.R.,* Series IV, I, 354; EJ, Sept. 6, 1861, p. 330. As early as May 24, Letcher had agreed to arm 5,000 Confederate troops with muskets.

29. Freeman, *op. cit.,* pp. 541-574, 588-604

30. *O.R.,* Series IV, I, 601-611; *Calendar of State Papers,* XI, 193-197; Rowland, *op. cit.,* 131-132; Jeffn. Davis to Letcher, Sept. 25, 1861, Letcher Papers/Lexington. Hunter's attempt to create a dispute was typical of his overall contribution to the Confederate cause.

31. Letcher to Davidson, Sept. 14, 1861, Letcher Papers/Lexington.

32. Letcher to Davidson, Sept. 14, 1861, Letcher Papers/Lexington; William C. Harris, *Leroy Pope Walker: Confederate Secretary of War* (Tuscaloosa: Confederate Publishing Company, 1962), pp. 112-114. Most modern scholars agree with Letcher's general evaluation.

33. EJ, Sept. 21, 1861, p. 326; Allan Nevins, *The War for the Union: The Improvised War: 1861-1862* (New York: Charles Scribner's Sons, 1959), I, 268.

34. E. Bellot des Minières to Letcher, no date on this letter from Paris which was received on Oct. 4, 1861, Letcher to Benjamin, October 11, and Benjamin to Letcher, Oct. 16, 1861, EP.

35. John Lewis Peyton, *The American Crisis; or, Pages from the Note-Book of a State Agent During the Civil War* (London: Saunders, Otley and Company, 1867), I, 148-151. As Peyton never eulogized the characters mentioned in his books, this is probably a rather realistic description of Letcher.

CHAPTER 9

1. *O.R.*, Series I, IV, 665; Letcher to Munford, Mar. 30, 1875, Fannie Ellis Munford Papers, Virginia Historical Society; Douglas Southall Freeman, *Lee's Lieutenants: A Study in Command* (New York: Charles Scribner's Sons, 1942), I, 209; Edward Younger (ed.), *Inside the Confederate Government: The Diary of Robert Garlick Hill Kean, Head of the Bureau of War* (New York: Oxford University Press, 1957), pp. 14-15; Frank E. Vandiver (ed.), *Narrative of Military Operations Directed, During the Late War Between the States, By Joseph E. Johnston, General, C.S.A.* (Bloomington: Indiana University Press, 1959), p. 602. The *Examiner* virtually existed to criticize, and one of its favorite themes was drunkenness.

2. Mrs. Jefferson Davis' calling card, December, 1861, John Echols to Letcher, Dec. 7, 1861, Letcher Papers/Lexington; Letcher Notebook/Lexington; *Calendar of State Papers*, XI, 198; Wm. H. Richardson to Francis H. Smith, Nov. 29, 1861, William H. Richardson File, Virginia Military Institute. By this time, four of eight children had died at birth or in childhood.

3. *O.R.*, Series IV, I, 738-739; *O.R.N.*, Series II, II, 107-112. Letcher enclosed records of Virginia's ordnance activities since June 14, and records of the Gosport navy yard loot were sent to the convention on November 30. The convention held its last session on Dec. 6, 1861.

4. *O.R.*, Series I, VI, 334; J. William Jones, "Official Correspondence of Governor Letcher, of Virginia", *Southern Historical Society Papers*, I (1876), 455-462; Letcher to Benjamin, Nov. 27, 1861, C.S.A. Secretary of War, letters received, National Archives.

5. Harrison A. Trexler, "The Opposition of Planters to the Employment of Slaves as Laborers by the Confederacy", *Mississippi Valley Historical Review: A Journal of American History*, XXVII (1940), 211: *O.R.*, Series I, LI, part 2, 431-432, and Series I, II, 988, and Series I, IV, 674, 707-710, 713; [?] to Letcher, Nov. 29, 1861, EP; Howell

Cobb to wife, Jan. 10, 1862, Howell Cobb Papers, University of Georgia. In the summer of 1861, Magruder obtained slaves for building fortifications against the same imagined Yankee host. This was the actual beginning of Confederate slave requisitions, and the planters resisted from the very beginning.

6. Series of letters by Letcher, Benjamin, Gorgas, Baldwin, Dimmock, and Turner Ashby in a folder marked February, 1862, EP; *O.R.,* Series I, V, 1051-1052; Letcher to Benjamin, Dec. 3 and 27, 1861, C.S.A. Secretary of War, letters received, National Archives. Part of this argument was over ownership of the weapons seized at Harper's Ferry arsenal by Virginia troops. The entire dispute was another hair splitting contest which contributed to administrative chaos within the Confederacy. Briscoe G. Baldwin eventually became a lieutenant colonel and chief of ordnance, Army of Northern Virginia. His brother John B. Baldwin would also clash with Letcher before the war ended.

7. *Message of the Governor* (Richmond, December, 1861), *passim; Acts of the General Assembly of the State of Virginia, Passed in 1861-2, in the Eighty-Sixth Year of the Commonwealth* (Richmond, 1862), pp. 82-84; D. Zirkle to Letcher, Dec. 3, 1861, EP; Dorman to Davidson, Nov. 24, 1861, Davidson Papers, McCormick Collection; Letcher to William Weaver, Nov. 28, 1961, William Weaver Papers, Duke University. Letcher estimated that more than $1,000,000 in small note currency, some as small as five cents, was in circulation in Virginia. Richmond alone had issued almost $300,000 worth, he said. By March, 1862, the legislature enacted some weak laws along the lines Letcher had suggested, but inflation continued to undermine the economy. Dorman listened to Letcher's speech in advance and rated it very effective.

8. Letcher to Davis, Dec. 2, 1861, and Letcher to assembly, Dec. 20, 1861, EP; Letcher to Davis, Dec. 29, 1861, C.S.A. Secretary of War, letters received, National Archives; Letcher to Smith, Dec. 24, 1861, Letcher File, Virginia Military Institute; *Calendar of State Papers,* XI, 201-202; *O.R.,* Series I, LI, part 2, 424, and Series IV, I, 775; Colonel William Couper, *One Hundred Years at V.M.I.* (Richmond: Garrett and Massie, 1939), II, 122, 137.

9. Dorman to Davidson, Nov. 24 and Dec. 1, 11, 1861, Davidson Papers, McCormick Collection; Davidson to Letcher, Dec. 4, 1861, Letcher Papers/Lexington. In the Valley Letcher was more and more frequently mentioned as a candidate for the confederate senate.

10. Dorman to Davidson, Nov. 24 and Dec. 1, 1861, Dorman to Letcher, Dec. 11, 1861, Letcher to Davidson Dec. 9, and Davidson to Letcher, Dec. 13, 28, 1861, Davidson Papers, McCormick Collection; Davidson to Letcher, Dec. 4, 1861, Letcher Papers/Lexington. At first Davidson opposed the withdrawal of any troops from the northwest because he felt this would hurt the morale of loyalists in the area, but

by December 28 he favored giving up what was left of the northwest and concentrating all defenses in the exposed Valley. Both Letcher and Davidson feared that V.M.I. would tempt Union forces to smash into Rockbridge County.

11. Charles Lee Lewis, *Matthew Fontaine Maury: The Pathfinder of the Seas* (Annapolis: U. S. Naval Institute, 1927), pp. 157-160; Frances Leigh Williams, *Matthew Fontaine Maury: Scientist of the Sea* (New Brunswick, N. J.: Rutgers University Press, 1963), pp. 379-389; *O.R.,* Series I, LI, part 2, 416-423; Letcher to assembly, Dec. 14, 1861, and Mar. 12, 1862, EP. The R. F. and P. Railroad and the Orange and Alexandria Railroad were eventually connected as he desired, but otherwise he got little action from the assembly on his suggestions. The R.F. and P.-O. and A. hookup required more than the simple crosstown connection mentioned in the previous chapter. Letcher also supported Maury's work with torpedoes (mines).

12. *O.R.,* Series IV, I, 847-852; Letcher to assembly, Jan. 6, 1861, EP. Letcher's concluding remarks were an endorsement of a recent resolution by the Georgia legislature opposing any reconstruction of the old Union.

13. *O.R.,* Series I, V, 1051-1052; Letcher to assembly, Jan. 7, 1862, and executive memo of Jan. 18, 1862, EP; T. Conn Bryan, *Confederate Georgia* (Athens: University of Georgia Press, 1953), pp. 60-62. Johnston denied any knowledge of the missing muskets, and Letcher dropped the matter.

14. Jackson to Letcher, Nov. 30, 1861, EP; G. G. Vest to S. H. Letcher, Apr. 3, 1903, and French to S. H. Letcher, Apr. 5, 1893, Letcher Papers/Lexington; Clifford Dowdey, *The Land They Fought For: The Story of the South As the Confederacy: 1832-1865* (Garden City: Doubleday & Company, 1955), pp. 132-134; Elizabeth Preston Allan, *The Life and Letters of Margaret Preston Junkin* (Boston: Houghton Mifflin Company, 1903), pp. 127-128; Hudson Strode, *Jefferson Davis: Confederate President* (New York: Harcourt Brace, 1955), II, 194-196; Robert Douthat Meade, *Judah P. Benjamin: Confederate Statesman* (New York: Oxford University Press, 1943), pp. 215-218; George Cary Eggleston, *The History of the Confederate War: Its Causes and Its Conduct: A Narrative and Critical History* (London: Sturgis and Walton, 1910), I, 366-371; *Calendar of State Papers,* XI, 200-201; Freeman, *op. cit.,* pp. 122-130; *O.R.,* Series I, V, 389-390, 1060-1067, and Series I, LI, part 2, 339. Letcher never saw Davis in this feud, but Davis openly backed Benjamin. French's and Vest's accounts contain colorful sidelights of the dispute, but they were written decades after the event and hence may not be entirely accurate.

15. Letcher to Weaver, Feb. 4, 1862, William Weaver Papers, Duke University.

16. Letcher to Smith, Feb. 8, 1862, Letcher File, Virginia Military Institute.

17. The Diary of Thomas Bragg, Feb. 10, 1862, p. 140, University of North Carolina; Dorman to Letcher, Feb. 7, 1862, Davidson Papers, McCormick Collection; Letcher to assembly, Feb. 5 and 17, and Letcher to Davis, Feb. 17, 1862, EP; Davis to Letcher, Dec. 20, 1861, Letcher Papers/Lexington; EJ, Feb. 17, 1862, p. 42; Douglas Southall Freeman, *R. E. Lee: A Biography* (New York: Charles Scribner's Sons, 1934), II, 27; Dunbar Rowland (ed.), *Jefferson Davis, Constitutionalist: His Letters, Papers and Speeches* (New York: J. J. Little & Ives Company, 1923), V, 191-192; *Acts of the Assembly, 1861-2,* pp. 41-46, 147; *O.R.,* Series IV, I, 923-925, 931, 967-969, 1011, 1114-1115; Alvin Arthur Fahrner, "The Public Career of William 'Extra Billy' Smith" (unpublished dissertation, 1953, University of North Carolina), pp. 254-255. Many southern towns already had home guard units. By March 3, Letcher was seeking more power to draft troops, claiming that the law of February 10 was imperfect. The Confederate conscription act in April removed the necessity for further state action.

18. Benjamin to Letcher, Feb. 14, 1862, and Letcher to assembly, Feb. 17 and 24, 1862, EP; *O.R.,* Series IV, I, 944; EJ, Feb. 17, 1862, p. 46.

19. Letcher to assembly, Feb. 17, 1862, EP; Bragg Diary, Feb. 10, 1862, p. 140; general order, Mar. 7, 1862, John R. Tucker Letter Book, 1859-1864, University of North Carolina; proclamation, Feb. 24, 1862, and Letcher to assembly, Feb. 25, 1862, EP. Bragg was particularly suspicious of Richmond's Germans and of John Minor Botts, who was jailed a month later.

20. Letcher to Smith, Mar. 3, 1862, Letcher File, Virginia Military Institute; Bragg Diary, Feb. 22, 1862, p. 160.

21. *Acts of the Assembly, 1861-2,* pp. 51-52; *O.R.,* Series I, XII, part 1, 4, 5, 423, and part 3, 62, 72-75, Series I, LI, part 2, 526, 531, and Series IV, I, 1030, 1094; EJ, Mar. 18, 1862, p. 72; *Message of the Governor of Virginia, and Accompanying Documents* (Richmond, Jan. 7, 1863), p. xxvii; Jno. W. Younger to Letcher, Feb. 2, Lee to Letcher, Apr. 9, and Tucker to Letcher, Apr. 11, 1862, EP; G. W. Berlin to Letcher, July 4 and 13, 1862, Letcher Papers/Lexington.

22. *O.R.,* Series I, LI, part 2, 495, 513-514, 534, 546, and Series I, V, 1097, and Series I, X, part 2, 322-324, 450, and Series IV, I, 1011-1012; Vandiver, *op. cit.,* p. 108; EJ, Mar. 10, p. 63, Mar. 11, p. 65, and Mar. 24, 1862, p. 80; G.W.C. Lee to Letcher, Apr. 1, 1862, Davis Papers, National Archives; Letcher to House of Delegates, Jan. 27, 1862, and Letcher to assembly, Mar. 25, 1862, EP; Lt. Col. John Withers' Diary, National Archives; Frances H. Smith to Benjamin, Feb. 3, 1862, C.S.A. Secretary of War, letters received, National Archives. This

mobilization was confused, and for months no one knew how many patriots had answered the call. Botts was held in jail for eight weeks.

23. Letcher to senate, Feb. 4, 1862, and proclamation, Apr. 1, 1862, EP; Dorman to Davidson, Mar. 10, 1862, McDowell Papers, University of Virginia; Richardson to Smith, Apr. 1, 1862, Richardson File, Virginia Military Institute. Some legislators were simply out to get the governor, and Letcher became increasingly cautious in exercising his authority in borderline cases. On March 27, the assembly authorized yearly sessions of the legislature. The prolonged session lasted from April 1 to May 19, but the real work was done after May 5.

24. *O.R.*, Series I, XI, part 3, 683, and Series I, LI, part 2, 534; Tucker to Letcher, Apr. 15, 1862, Munford to Richardson, Apr. 23, 1862, and Munford to Wise, Apr. 29, 1862, EP.

25. Douglas Freeman, "The Confederate Tradition of Richmond", *Civil War History,* III (1957), number 1, 369; Strode, *op. cit.,* 247-249; French to S. H. Letcher, Apr. 5, 1893, Letcher Papers/Lexington; *Acts of the Assembly, 1861-2,* extra session section, pp. 5-8, 14, 24; EJ, May 15, p. 132, and July 26, 1862, p. 181; proclamations, May 15, 26, and 29, 1862, joint resolution of the assembly, May 15, 1862, Letcher to assembly, May 6, 1862, Letcher to Senate, May 7, 1862, EP; H. S. Foote, *War of the Rebellion; or, Scylla and Charybdis, Consisting of Observations Upon the Causes, Course, and Consequences of the Late Civil War in the United States* (New York: Harper and Brothers, 1866), p. 352; W. Asbury Christian, *Richmond: Her Past and Present* (Richmond: L. H. Jenkins, 1912), p. 231.

26. Davis to Letcher, Dec. 20, 1862, Letcher Papers/Lexington; *O.R.*, Series IV, I, 1095-1097, 1114-1115, II, 123-124, and III, 723; Letcher to F. W. Pickens, Apr. 28, 1862, Letcher to John Gill Shorter, Aug. 11, 1862, Letcher to Davis, Dec. 2, 1862, Letcher to Senate, Feb. 14, 1863, all EP; E. Merton Coulter, *The Confederate States of America: 1861-1865* (Baton Rouge: Louisiana State University Press, 1950), p. 391. The quotation is from the letter to Governor Shorter of Alabama. By February 1863, Letcher was complaining that the draft was hampering state (but not Confederate) railroad maintenance.

27. Dorman to Davidson, May 30, 1862, Davidson Papers, McCormick Collection; EJ, May 16, 1862, p. 133; French to S. R. Mallory, June 3, 1862, EP; Freeman, *Lee's Lieutenants,* I, 300-301; *O.R.,* Series IV, I, 1151, and II, 7; J. G. Randall and David Donald, *The Civil War and Reconstruction* (Boston: D. C. Heath and Company, 1961), pp. 208-216. Some southern governors would not cooperate with Confederate attempts to round up deserters and stragglers.

28. George W. Randolph to Letcher, July 2, 1862, and Letcher to assembly, Oct. 17, 1863, EP; *O.R.*, Series I, LI, part 2, 584.

29. *O.R.*, Series I, LI, part 2, 581-584, 620-621, 655-657, 686, XII, part 3, 924, 947, XVI, part 2, 765, XIX, part 2, 617, 624, 628,

671, and XXI, 1065-1066; EJ, Aug. 15, 1862, p. 197, and Nov. 26, 1862, p. 280; *Message of the Governor and Accompanying Documents* (Richmond, Jan. 7, 1863), p. viii; Letcher to Pickens, Apr. 28, 1862, proclamations on Aug. 4 and 30, 1862, act of the assembly, Feb. 28, 1863, Letcher to assembly, Jan. 9 and Mar. 19, 1863, and Floyd to Col. John T. Anderson, Feb. 16, 1863, all EP; L. R. Smoot to Letcher, July 20, 1862, Floyd to Letcher, Sept. 25, 1862, series of applications for positions in the Line, Letcher Papers/Lexington; Letcher to Seddon, Dec. 10, 1862, C.S.A. Secretary of War, letters received, National Archives; Floyd to Letcher, Jan. 4, 1863, and Floyd to Isaac H. Carrington, Jan. 28, 1863, Isaac H. Carrington Papers, Duke University; R. L. Beale to Letcher, Jan. 7, 1863, Letcher Papers, Duke University; Letcher to Smith, Sept. 31, 1862, Letchei File, Virginia Military Institute. The executive papers contain much additional information on the Line. Letcher's clashes with the Confederates over the Line were sometimes heated, and he was particularly angry with Gorgas' assistant, Col. Albert T. Bledsoe, "that Prince of Blatherskites".

30. J. T. Patton to Letcher, July 5, 1862, Letcher Papers/Lexington; Letcher to Munford, July 11, 1862, EP; Richardson to Smith, July 14, 1862, Richardson File, Virginia Military Institute.

31. *O.R.*, Series II, III, 885, Series II, IV, 691, 828-829, 849-850, 855, 874-876, 885, 905, and Series II, V, 212; C. D. Bennett to Letcher, Oct. 19 and Nov. 2, 1863, Letcher to Randolph, July 28, Randolph to Letcher, Sept. 11, Letcher to Randolph, Sept. 12, 1862, Tucker to Letcher, Oct. 20 and Dec. 20, 1862, and Sept. 11, 1863, all EP; EJ, Oct. 19 and 20, 1863, p. 519. Dr. William Rucker was the man turned over to state justice. He was charged with treason, murder, and horse stealing. Fortunately for the doctor, the legalistic approach which got him into trouble also saved him. Legal technicalities caused several postponements of the trial, and the defendant finally settled the whole matter by escaping from jail in October, 1863.

CHAPTER 10

1. Wm. G. Rodgers, others to Seddon, October, 1862, C.S.A. Secretary of War, letters received, National Archives; G.W.C. Lee to Letcher, Aug. 25, 1862, J. R. Anderson to Letcher, Aug. 6 and 13, 1862, Letcher Papers/Lexington; contract signed by Anderson, Sept. 3, 1862, and contract signed by Letcher, Jan. 13, 1862, EP. Anderson first offered to pay $50 per convict per year, but finally he raised his offer to $94, and Letcher accepted. See the executive papers for August, 1862, for numerous examples of petitions for exemption or discharge from military service.

2. Bennett to Letcher, Aug. 16, 1862, EP; EJ., Aug. 18, 1862, p. 220; Thomas L. Bayne, "Life in Virginia", *Confederate Veteran*, XXX

(1922), number 3, 100; Letcher to Weaver, Aug. 27, 1862, William Weaver Papers, Duke University; Davidson to Letcher, Feb. 1-2 and 19, 1862, Davidson Papers, McCormick Collection. The Franklin Society in Lexington discussed the problem of inflation but found no solution. Davidson, Weaver, and Letcher's mother sent most of the food from Lexington to the governor.

3. Letcher to Weaver, Aug. 27, 1862, Weaver Papers, Duke University.

4. Letcher to Smith, Sept. 13, 1862, Letcher File, Virginia Military Institute.

5. Davis to Letcher, Sept. 2, 1862, Letcher Papers/Lexington; Letcher to Weaver, Aug. 27, 1862, Weaver Papers, Duke University.

6. Munford to wife, Oct. 20, 1862, Ellis-Munford Papers, Duke University; John S. Preston to Letcher, Aug. 16, 1862, Preston Papers, Virginia Historical Society; Letcher to [?], Aug. 16, 1862, Letcher Papers/Lexington; Tucker to Letcher, June 20, 1862, proclamations, Aug. 19 and Oct. 10, 1862, Letcher to assembly, Sept. 15, 1862, act of assembly, Oct. 1, 1862, all EP; EJ, Oct. 7, 1862, p. 242. Some of the salt-producing companies were owned by Yankees before the war, and many Virginians believed that Yankees still controlled these companies and deliberately tried to wreck the southern economy. Such companies were ripe for seizure by the state.

7. Ella Lonn, *Salt As a Factor in the Confederacy* (University, Ala.: University of Alabama Press, 1965), pp. 82, 137-141; Mrs. Virginia G. Mosby to Letcher, Nov. 2, 1862, Letcher Papers/Lexington; S. McDowell Moore to Letcher, Oct. 8, 1862, C.S.A. Secretary of War, letters received, National Archives; Letcher to Munford and Munford to Letcher, October 14 (telegrams); Jas. Barbour, others, to Letcher, Nov. 6, 1862, all EP; *Message of the Governor of Virginia, and Accompanying Documents* (Richmond: Jan. 7, 1863), p. ix; EJ, Oct. 14, 1862, p. 248.

8. Lonn, *op. cit.*, pp. 137-154, 210-211; *Acts of the General Assembly of the State of Virginia, Passed at the Called Session, 1862* (Richmond, 1863), pp. 52-56; *Message of the Governor* (January, 1863), pp. ix-xii; Letcher to assembly, Sept. 22, 1862, and Letcher to Senate, Feb. 14, 1863, and series of letters to and from Letcher, October, 1862-August, 1863, EP; J. R. Wikle to Gov. Joseph E. Brown, October 8 and 18, 1862, Telamon Cuyler Collection, University of Georgia; Letcher to Vance, Dec. 10, 1862, Vance Papers, North Carolina State Department of Archives and History, Raleigh, N. C.; Letcher to Howell Cobb, Oct. 31, 1862, Howell Cobb Papers, University of Georgia; EJ, Oct. 25, 1862, p. 253; series of letters to Letcher in October and November, 1862, Letcher Papers/Lexington. Late in 1862, the governor's correspondence was full of complaints about the scarcity of salt and applications for the position of local salt agent. The Confederacy made

vigorous efforts to find new salt deposits; the state of Virginia did not.

   9. Letcher to Smith, Sept. 26, 1862, Letcher File, Virginia Military Institute; Letcher to Governor Pickens, Apr. 28, 1862, EP; Letcher to Weaver, Nov. 25, 1862, Weaver Papers, Duke University; EJ, Sept. 10, p. 216, Sept. 17, p. 222, and Sept. 25, 1862, p. 228; *O.R.*, Series I, XIX, part 2, 590.

   10. A. Sinclair to Letcher, Sept. 3, 1862, Letcher Papers/Lexington; Letcher to Randolph, Sept. 4, 1862, C.S.A. Secretary of War, letters received, National Archives. Randolph promised that the Virginia general would not be arrested again.

   11. House of Delegates to Letcher, September 27, and Letcher to House of Delegates, Sept. 30, 1862, EP. This sort of harassment partially explains the governor's unwillingness to mobilize troops to seize uncooperative salt works or impress needed salt. The assembly crippled the governor more and more at the very time strong executive leadership was essential.

   12. An act of the assembly, Oct. 3, 1862, Munford to Mayor Mayo, Oct. 21, 1862, Col. J. F. Gilman to Letcher, Nov. 24, 1862, Letcher to Davis, Oct. 11, 1862, EP; *O.R.*, Series I, LI, part 2, 634, 651; Letcher to Secretary of War James A. Seddon, Dec. 1, 1862, C.S.A. Secretary of War, letters received, National Archives; EJ, Oct. 11, 1862, p. 245. The counties involved in this first requisition were Amherst, Albemarle, Appomattox, Buckingham, Bedford, Campbell, Cumberland, Charlotte, Fluvanna, Halifax, Louisa, Nelson, Pittsylvania, and Prince Edward. Some (e.g. Prince Edward, Cumberland, and Fluvanna) almost filled their quotas; others (e.g. Bedford and Campbell) did less well, and Albemarle County failed to furnish any of its 540-man quota.

   13. Dunbar Rowland (ed.), *Jefferson Davis: Constitutionalist: His Letters, Papers and Speeches* (New York: J. J. Little & Ives Company, 1923), V, 420, 427, 431-432, 437, 446-448, 597, and VI, 91; Col. Gilman to Seddon, Mar. 4, 1863; C. R. McDonald to Col. Stevens, Sept. 29, 1863, Stevens to Letcher, Oct. 30, Nov. 25, and Dec. 12, 1862, all EP; *O.R.*, Series I, XXIX, part 2, 702 and LI, part 2, 690, and Series IV, II, 426; EJ, Dec. 5, 1862, p. 288, February 9, p. 343, March 13, p. 373, Aug. 31, 1863, p. 478; Munford to Seddon, Sept. 7, 1863, C.S.A. Secretary of War, letters received, National Archives; Allan Nevins, *The Statesmanship of the Civil War* (New York: The Macmillan Company, 1953), p. 53.

   14. *Message of the Governor* (Richmond, Jan. 7, 1863), pp. viii-x; Robert C. Dabney to Letcher, Feb. 2, 1863, and John B. Baldwin to Letcher, Nov. 30, 1863, EP; French to Davidson, Dec. 11, 1863, Davidson Papers, McCormick Collection; EJ, Feb. 7, 1863, p. 342; W. K. Heiskell to Letcher, Mar. 11, 1863, C.S.A. Secretary of War, letters received, National Archives; P. Saunders, Jr., to Letcher, Dec. 13, 1862, Letcher Papers, Duke University; Carter W. Wormeley to

Letcher, Mar. 1, 1863, Letcher Papers/Lexington. The Confederates had no adequate system of compensation for lost or injured slaves.

15. Letcher to assembly, Sept. 14, 1863, and Colonel Stevens to Letcher, Oct. 30 and Nov. 25, 1863, EP.

16. M. F. Maury to Letcher, Oct. 4, 1862, and Roger A. Pryor to Letcher, Jan. 19, 1863, Letcher Papers/Lexington; Letcher Notebook/Lexington.

17. Letcher to assembly, Sept. 15, 1862, and Letcher to Randolph, Oct. 28, 1862, EP; Letcher to Randolph, Oct. 27, 1862, C.S.A. Secretary of war, letters received, National Archives; Letcher to Weaver Oct. 26 and Nov. 25, 1862, and Jan. 12 and Feb. 4, 1863, Weaver Papers, Duke University.

18. D. J. Whipple to Letcher, Dec. 2, 1862, and Taylor to Letcher, Dec. 29, 1862, C.S.A. Secretary of War, letters received, National Archives; Letcher to governor of N. C., Dec. 12, 1862, Battle Family Papers, North Carolina University; Mrs. Page to Letcher, Nov. 17, 1862, Dr. F. T. Stribling to Letcher, Jan. 9, 1863, and Stuart to Letcher, Feb. 16, 1863, EP. Mayor Roger P. Atkinson of Danville telegramed his complaint to Letcher on Jan. 7, 1863. Letcher simply passed this telegram on to the secretary of war without comment. Rebel troops in the area continued to be unruly.

19. *O.R.*, Series IV, II, 240; EJ, Nov. 14, p. 269, and Nov. 17, 1862, p. 272, and Dec. 4, 1862, p. 286. Letcher organized, commissioned and armed the Tredegar workers into a home guard battalion in June, 1861. This unit, numbering roughly 300 men, drilled regularly and was exempt from the Confederate draft.

20. Letcher to Weaver, Nov. 25, 1862, Weaver Papers, Duke University; Richardson to Smith, Dec. 11 and 15, 1862, Richardson File, Virginia Military Institute. Letcher continued to visit Lee's army frequently.

21. Letcher to Weaver, Nov. 25, 1862, Weaver Papers, Duke University.

22. James D. Armstrong to A. H. H. Stuart, Dec. 3, 1862, A. H. H. Stuart Papers, Library of Congress.

23. *Message of the Governor* (Richmond, Jan. 7, 1863), *passim; Acts of the General Assembly of the State of Virginia, Passed at Adjourned Session, 1863, in the Eighty-Seventh Year of the Commonwealth* (Richmond, 1863), pp. 3-34, 39-47. By modern standards Virginia's taxes were quite low. About 10 per cent of an individual's income was taken by the tax collector in a few cases, but taxes were generally much lower.

24. *O.R.*, Series I, II, 738, and IV, 553-555, and Series II, II, 379-415, and IV, 774-781, and V, 147-148, 222-223; *O.R.N.*, Series I, IV, 553-555; EJ, July 1, p. 256, July 2, p. 259, July 5, 1861, p. 263, Dec. 29, 1862, pp. 307-308, Jan. 3, p. 310, Jan 7, p. 320, May 7, p. 406,

July 1-2, p. 443, and July 5, 1863, p. 445; *Calendar of State Papers,*
XI, 222-223; Mary Jane Solomon's Scrapbook, Duke University; Virgil
Carrington Jones, *Grey Ghosts and Rebel Raiders* (New York: Holt,
1956), pp. 90, 139-140; series of letters, memos, orders and other com-
munications, July, 1861—July, 1863, EP; *Message of the Governor*
(Richmond, Jan. 7, 1863), p. xxvii; Frances Leigh Williams, *Matthew
Fontaine Maury: Scientist of the Sea* (New Brunswick: Rutgers Uni-
versity Press, 1963), pp. 375-376. The hostages for Zarvona were Capt.
Thomas Damron, Lt. Wilson Damron, and Privates John W. Howe,
Isaac Goble, David V. Auxier, Samuel Pack, and William S. Dills.
Dusky's hostage was Capt. William Gramm, and Vanner's hostage was
Lt. Isaac A. Wade. Most of the hostages wrote Washington urging an
exchange to get them out of the state penitentiary.

25. *O.R.,* Series I, XVIII, 827, 834-835; EJ, Jan. 8, pp. 315-316,
and Jan. 10, 1863, p. 318; Seddon to Letcher, Jan. 7, 1863, and Letcher
to assembly, Jan. 12, 1863, EP; Letcher to Weaver, Jan. 12, 1863,
Weaver Papers, Duke University. The counties included in the call
were Greenville, Dinwiddie, Brunswick, Lunenburg, Mecklenburg, Halifax, Charlotte, Pittsylvania, Henry, Patrick, Nottoway, Prince Edward,
Franklin, and Campbell. Simultaneous militia calls in North Carolina
were even less effective.

CHAPTER 11

1. Letcher to assembly, Jan. 19, 1863, EP; J. G. Randall and
David Donald, *The Civil War and Reconstruction* (Boston: D. C.
Heath and Company, 1961), pp. 387-388. The assembly did not follow
the governor's advice. In this speech Letcher called President Lincoln
a witch and declared that the proclamation only served to further unite
the South.

2. Letcher to Bocock, Jan. 21, 1863, EP; Wilfred Buck Yearns,
The Confederate Congress (Athens: University of Georgia Press, 1960),
p. 14; E. Merton Coulter, *The Confederate States of America: 1861-
1865* (Baton Rouge: Louisiana State University Press, 1950), pp. 134-
148. Bocock was one of the more useful members of Congress. R. M. T.
Hunter served continuously, as wordy and ambitious as ever.

3. Letcher to Assembly, Jan. 26 and 30, and Mar. 11, 1863, EP;
Angus James Johnston, II, *Virginia Railroads in the Civil War* (Chapel
Hill: University of North Carolina Press, 1961), pp. 65, 69, 118;
Coulter, *op. cit.,* pp. 270-271; EJ, Jan. 26, p. 333, Feb. 3, p. 339, Feb.
18, p. 351, Feb. 19, p. 353, and Feb. 20, 1863, p. 354. Often Letcher
did get essential slaves out of labor drafts. Virginia iron continued to
be confiscated for the Danville-Greensboro railroad, which proved its
value in the last year of the war.

4. Letcher to assembly, Jan. 28, 1863, and Seddon to Munford

and Bennett, Dec. 2, 1863, EP; Alvin Arthur Fahrner, "The Public Career of William 'Extra Billy' Smith" (unpublished dissertation, 1953, University of North Carolina), p. 260; J. A. Seawell to Letcher, Jan. 12, 1863, Letcher Papers/Lexington.

5. Letcher to Seddon, Feb. 12 and Mar. 4, 1863, and Thomas H. Ellis to Seddon, Feb. 16, 1863, C.S.A. Secretary of War, letters received, National Archives; Letcher to [?], Feb. 21, 1863, register of letters received, Adjutant and Inspector General Office, chap. I, vol. 54, p. 52, National Archives. Letcher also failed in his efforts to have four skilled boat builders discharged from the army and returned to their essential work with the James River and Kanawha Canal Company.

6. Dimmock to Letcher, Feb. 9, 1863, Letcher Papers/Lexington; Seddon to Letcher, Feb. 18, 1863, EP.

7. Randall and Donald, *op. cit.*, pp. 221, 224-225, 384; Bruce Catton, *This Hallowed Ground: The Story of the Union Side of the Civil War* (Garden City: Doubleday, 1956), pp. 169-172, 177.

8. Letcher to assembly, Mar. 9 and 12, 1863, EP; *O.R.,* Series IV, II, 96; Lee to Letcher, Feb. 17, and Letcher to Lee, Feb. 20, 1863, Letcher Papers/Lexington; Letcher to Benjamin, Dec. 4, 1861, C.S.A. Secretary of War, letters received, National Archives; EJ, Aug. 27, 1861, p. 313.

9. Proclamation, Mar. 16, 1863, EP; *Acts of the General Assembly of the State of Virginia, Passed at the Adjourned Session, 1863, in the Eighty-Seventh Year of the Commonwealth* (Richmond, 1863), pp. 70-71; EJ, Mar. 16, 1863, p. 375. The assembly's law was mandatory, not voluntary.

10. *O.R.,* Series I, XXV, part 2, 193; proclamation by Pierpoint, Jan. 12, 1863, R. O. Davidson to Letcher, Mar. 21, 1863, and Letcher to Munford, Apr. 17, 1863, EP; O. P. Baldwin to Letcher, Mar. 19, 1863, Letcher Papers/Lexington; EJ, Mar. 12, 1863, p. 321.

11. EJ, Feb. 15, 1862, p. 45; executive order, Mar. 26, 1863, and Seddon to Letcher, Mar. 25, 1863, EP; Letcher to Seddon, Mar. 23, 1863, C.S.A. Secretary of War, letters received, National Archives.

12. Joseph F. White, "Social Conditions in the South During the War", *Confederate Veteran,* XXX (1922), number 4, 142-144; W. Asbury Christian, *Richmond: Her Past and Present* (Richmond: L. H. Jenkins, 1912), pp. 240, 244; Robert Douthat Meade, *Judah P. Benjamin: Confederate Statesman* (New York: Oxford University Press, 1943), pp. 192, 230; Coulter, *op. cit.,* p. 422; Elizabeth Preston Allan, *The Life and Letters of Margaret Preston Junkin* (Boston: Houghton Mifflin Company, 1903), pp. 166-167, 172; Letcher to Seddon, Mar. 16, 1863, C.S.A. Secretary of War, letters received, National Archives; Letcher to Smith, Jan. 28, 1863, Letcher Papers/Lexington;

Letcher to assembly, Mar. 23, 1863, EP. Prices were approximately twice as high in Richmond as in Lexington.

13. Coulter, *op. cit.*, pp. 422-423; Christian, *op. cit.*, pp. 240-241; John Damerel, "100 Years Ago in Richmond", *The Reb: Richmond Employees Bulletin*, IX (1963), number 10, 4; Mrs. Jefferson Davis, *Jefferson Davis: Ex-President of the Confederate States of America: A Memoir* (New York: Bedford Company, 1890), II, 374-376; Hudson Strode, *Jefferson Davis: Confederate President* (New York: Harcourt Brace, 1955), II, 381-382; J. B. Jones, *A Rebel War Clerk's Diary at the Confederate States Capital* (New York: J. B. Lippincott & Co., 1935), I, 284; French to Letcher, Apr. 17, 1878, Herbert Kerr to Letcher, May 18, 1878, and G. G. Vest to S. H. Letcher, Apr. 3, 1903, Letcher Papers/Lexington. There are many accounts of the Bread Riot, all differing in details and many differing in substance. Strode and Mrs. Davis portray Davis as the one and only hero of the affair.

14. *O.R.*, Series I, XVIII, 977-978; Coulter, *op. cit.*, p. 423; P. G. Coghlan to Letcher, Apr. 4, 1863, EP; EJ, Apr. 21, 1863, p. 398.

15. Proclamation, Apr. 6, 1863, EP; Fahrner, *op. cit.*, p. 248; *Richmond Whig and Public Advertiser*, Apr. 22, 1863, p. 3. Letcher's eleventh congressional district was composed of Augusta, Rockingham, Rockbridge, Pendleton, Highland, Bath, Pocahontas, and Allegheny Counties.

16. Mrs. Jackson to Mrs. Letcher, Apr. 16, 1863, Letcher Papers/Lexington; Jackson to Letcher, Apr. 20, 1863, Letters to Letcher, Library of Congress.

17. Letcher to sheriff of King William County, May 5, 1863, EP; Randall and Donald, *op. cit.*, pp. 399-400; Douglas Southall Freeman, *R. E. Lee: A Biography* (New York: Charles Scribner's Sons, 1934), II, 508-559. Stoneman finally reached Richmond after the war and served as military commander of the Virginia district during the early period of Reconstruction.

18. James B. Smith to Letcher, May 5, 1863, and C. H. Exall to Letcher, May 5, 1863, EP. Jackson was wounded on the evening of May 2, and Davidson was killed on May 3. Both messages were telegrams.

19. EJ, May 11, 1863, p. 410; Mrs. Davis, *op. cit.*, p. 382; Christian, *op. cit.*, pp. 242-243; Belle Boyd to Letcher, May 11, 1863, EP; Douglas Southall Freeman, *Lee's Lieutenants: A Study in Command* (New York: Charles Scribner's Sons, 1945), II, 684-687.

20. William McLaughlin to Letcher, May 10, 1863, Letcher Papers/Lexington; Yearns, *op. cit.,* pp. 157, 237; *Gazette* (Lexington), Apr. 29, 1863, p. 1, June 3, p. 2, and June 17, 1863, p. 3; *Richmond Enquirer,* May 1, 1863, p. 3, and June 26, 1863, p. 1. Letcher's contest was hardly mentioned in the Richmond papers. The people were too

concerned about the war to get enthusiastic about the state elections. Letcher's gubernatorial record was the main reason for his defeat, but there were other, lesser factors. Many could not forget their old Whig allegiance. Some opposed Letcher for minor actions completely unrelated to his cooperation with the Confederates. A few felt he was too dependent on Munford, French, Tucker, and other aides, and a few others thought he drank too much whiskey. The final count was Baldwin 3,019 and Letcher 2,048, with Baldwin carrying his home county by an overwhelming 1,352 to 162 margin. These congressional elections generally went against the Davis administration.

21. *Richmond Enquirer,* June 30, 1863, p. 1.

22. Stuart to Letcher, June 15, 1863, Letcher Papers/Lexington; Randall and Donald, *op. cit.,* pp. 401, 411.

23. *O.R.,* Series I, XXVII, part 3, 883-884; Edward Younger (ed.), *Inside the Confederate Government: The Diary of Robert Garlick Hill Kean, Head of the Bureau of War* (New York: Oxford University Press, 1957), pp. 76-77; proclamation, June 13, 1863, T. H. Watts to Seddon, June 29, Tucker to Letcher June 30, and R. D'Assey Ogden to Letcher, July 1, 1863, EP; Henry A. Wise, "The Cadets at New Market, Va.", *Confederate Veteran,* XX (1912), number 8, 360-361.

24. Randall and Donald, *op. cit.,* pp. 401-405.

25. *O.R.,* Series I, XXVII, part 3, 972, and Series IV, II, 643; Mrs. Davis, *op. cit.,* p. 496; proclamation, Aug. 10, 1863, EP.

26. *O.R.,* Series I, LI, part 2, 762; EJ, Aug. 20, 1863, p. 470 and Aug. 27, 1863, p. 474; Colonel William Couper, *One Hundred Years at V.M.I.* (Richmond: Garrett and Massie, 1939), II, 216-217. Floyd died peacefully at the home of his daughter near Abingdon, Virginia.

27. Letcher to assembly, Sept. 7, 1863, EP; Harvey Mitchell Rice, *The Life of Jonathan M. Bennett: A Study of the Virginias in Transition* (Chapel Hill: University of North Carolina Press, 1943), p. 137; *Acts of the General Assembly of the State of Virginia, Passed at the Called Session, 1863, in the Eighty-Eighth Year of the Commonwealth* (Richmond, 1863), pp. 3-6. A detailed outline of the governor's financial calculations gives a more complete picture of his solution for the state debt of $34,399,680.30:

$ 8,500,000.00	war debt to be refunded by Confederate government after the war
2,730,891.61	debt owed to the United States government
2,662,691.38	debt owed to the state Literary Fund
16,543,055.34	value of company stocks easily sold
3,019,125.00	value of bank stocks easily sold

$33,455,763.33 total

Subtracting this total from the state debt of $34,399,680.30 would leave a negligible debt of less than $1,000,000. Thus Letcher was willing not only to sell the state's various business stocks but also repudiate its debt to the U. S. government and cripple the Literary Fund. This was a harbinger of Redeemer policy in the postwar period.

28. Letcher to assembly, Sept. 21, 1863, Lee to Letcher, Sept. 30, 1863, and proclamation, Sept. 30, 1863, EP; Younger, *op. cit.*, p. 111; EJ, Sept. 22, 1863, p. 494; Ella Lonn, *Salt As a Factor in the Confederacy* (University, Ala.: University of Alabama Press, 1965), pp. 197-203.

29. Letcher to assembly, Sept. 28, 1863, EP.

30. EJ, Oct. 8, 1863, p. 506; S. Cooper to French, no date, and Dimmock to Richardson, Oct. 6, 1863, EP; Lyon G. Tyler, "Confederate Forces in the War for Southern Independence", *Tyler's Quarterly Historical and Genealogical Magazine*, VIII (1926), 158; R. A. Brock, "Virginia's Contribution to the Confederate States Army", *Southern Historical Society Papers*, XXXII (1904), 43-45. According to Dimmock, Virginia contributed 399 cannons, 103,840 muskets, 6,428 rifles, 795 carbines, 446 musketoons, 4,438 pistols, and 7,863 sabers.

31. Letcher to assembly, Oct. 16 and Sept. 8, 1863, EP. All quotations are taken from the October 16 message.

32. Letcher to Seddon, Oct. 20 and Nov. 14, 1863, C.S.A. Secretary of War, letters received, National Archives; Davidson to Letcher, Nov. 1 and Dec. 17, 1863, Davidson Papers, McCormick Collection; P. G. Coghlan to Letcher, Sept. 23, 1863, Letcher Papers/Lexington. In Rockbridge County, a campaign began to raise enough money to get the governor out of debt. Letcher was unable to sell any of his real estate in Lexington.

33. Letcher to assembly, Oct. 28, 1863, and Letcher to the Senate, Dec. 7, 1863, EP; J. B. Danforth to Letcher, Nov. 24, and Danforth to Richardson, Dec. 11 and 28, 1863, J. B. Danforth Letterbook, Duke University.

34. Letcher to Smith, June 9, 1863, Letcher File, V.M.I.; EJ, Sept. 16, 1863, p. 489; *O.R.*, Series I, XXIX, part 2, 823-824, and Series II, VI, 539-541, 557, 597; Davidson to Letcher, Nov. 6 and Dec. 17, 1863, Davidson Papers, McCormick Collection. Letcher made a half-hearted effort to purchase paper independently in Europe.

35. Letcher to Smith, Oct. 3, 1862, Letcher File, V.M.I.; treasurer of St. Paul's to Letcher, June 1, 1863, Letcher Papers/Lexington. A good pew in fashionable St. Paul's cost $3.67 per month, a trivial sum in inflation-ridden Richmond. Letcher continued to lack confidence in the former Episcopalian minister in Lexington, General William Nelson Pendleton, commander of Lee's artillery.

36. Letcher to B. B. Douglas, Dec. 16, 1863, Letcher Papers/Lexington; *Gazette* (Lexington), Jan. 6, 1864, p. 1.

37. Letcher to assembly, Dec. 19, 1863, EP; Colonel T. T. Mun-

ford to Letcher, Dec. 30, 1863, Letcher Papers/Lexington; Davidson's speech, Dec. 29, 1863, Davidson Papers, McCormick Collection. As usual, Davidson's speech was lengthy and elaborate. He characterized Letcher eloquently: "the stone which was rejected by the builders [secessionists], is become the head of the corner".

38. Copy of minutes of the city clerk, Dec. 31, 1863, and Letcher to A. W. Morton, Jan. 1, 1864, Letcher Papers/Lexington.

39. Letcher to Col. T. T. Munford, Dec. 26, 1863, Ellis-Munford Papers, Duke University. T. T. Munford was the son of Secretary of the Commonwealth George W. Munford.

CHAPTER 12

1. W. Asbury Christian, *Richmond: Her Past and Present* (Richmond: L. H. Jenkins, 1912), p. 245; *Richmond Enquirer,* Jan. 1, 1864, p. 4.

2. Terrill to Letcher, June 22, 1864, Letcher Papers/Lexington; E. G. Swem and J. A. C. Chandler, "Letters of John Letcher to J. Hierholzer, 1864-1865", *William and Mary College Quarterly Historical Magazine,* VIII (2) (1928), 137-140.

3. J. G. Randall and David Donald, *The Civil War and Reconstruction* (Boston: D. C. Heath and Company, 1961), pp. 399-453; William Ranulf Brock, *The Character of American History* (London: The Macmillan Company, 1960), pp. 141-151.

4. Letcher Notebook/Lexington; Richard Crenshaw and others to Letcher, Jan. 29, 1864, Letcher Papers/Lexington.

5. *Gazette* (Lexington), Mar. 23, 1864, p. 2; C. W. Purcell to Letcher July 18, 1864, Letcher Papers/Lexington. If a hard-headed banker like Purcell could foresee economic chaos, class warfare, and bread riots in the North, it is not surprising that a practical politician like Letcher could also be unrealistically optimistic. Southern mythology seriously handicapped the Confederacy.

6. M. S. Thompson, "Colonel Elijah V. White", *Confederate Veteran,* XV (1907), number 4, 159-160; petition to Davis signed by many and endorsed by Letcher, Mar. 3, 1864, Davidson Papers, McCormick Collection; Letcher and Davidson to "Colonel", Oct. 13, 1864, C.S.A. Adjutant & Inspector General Office, letters received, National Archives. The secretary of war's incoming mail for the last 15 months of the war reveals only a few letters from Letcher. These letters were all polite requests or suggestions, not blustering demands.

7. Robert Eunoch Withers, *Autobiography of an Octogenarian* (Roanoke: The Stone Printing Company, 1907), pp. 207-208, Letcher's visit was almost a holiday for the city, which furnished the solid and liquid nourishment for the former governor.

8. Elizabeth Preston Allan, *The Life and Letters of Margaret*

Preston Junkin (Boston: Houghton Mifflin Company, 1903), pp. 166-177.

9. Mrs. John Letcher to Davidson, June 1864, Davidson Papers, McCormick Collection; Swem and Chandler, *op. cit.*, p. 138. Davidson lost three sons in the war.

10. Jennings C. Wise, *The Military History of the Virginia Military Institute from 1839 to 1865, With Appendix, Maps, and Illustrations* (Lynchburg: J. P. Bell Company, 1915), pp. 425-431; Wm. Couper, *The V.M.I. New Market Cadets: Biographical Sketches of All Members of the Virginia Military Institute Corps of Cadets Who Fought in the Battle of New Market, May 15, 1864* (Charlottesville: The Michie Company, 1933), pp. 120-121, 253-255; Col. William Couper, *One Hundred Years at V.M.I.* (Richmond: Garrett and Massie, 1939), II, 305-345, and III, 1-17. After New Market, the cadets were sent to Richmond to help repel a Yankee offensive. After the victory at Cold Harbor on June 3, they returned to Lexington to resume their studies. The cadets arrived in Lexington just in time for some more fireworks.

11. Couper, *V.M.I.*, III, 14-24; Randall and Donald, *op. cit.*, pp. 435-436; Allan, *op cit.*, pp. 183-185; typewritten manuscript by S. H. Letcher, no date, Letcher Papers/Lexington; S. H. Letcher to Davidson, June 15, 1864, and Letcher to Purcell, June 16, 1864, Davidson Papers, McCormick Collection.

12. Mrs. Cornelia McDonald, *A Diary With Reminiscences of the War and Refuge Life in the Shenandoah Valley: 1860-1865* (Nashville: Collom and Ghertner Company, 1935), pp. 316-339; David Donald, *Divided We Fought: A Pictorial History of the War; 1861-1865* (New York: The Macmillan Company, 1953), p. 352; *Gazette* (Lexington), July 15, 1864, p. 2; Oron F. Morton, *A History of Rockbridge County, Virginia* (Staunton: The McClure Co., 1920), p. 129; Allan, *op. cit.*, pp. 186-196; Julia Davis, *The Shenandoah* (New York: Farrar and Rinehart Inc., 1945), pp. 248-249; Susan P. Lee, *Memoirs of William Nelson Pendleton, DD: Rector of Latimer Parish, Lexington, Virginia: Brigadier-General C.S.A.; Chief of Artillery, Army of Northern Virginia* (Philadelphia: J. B. Lippincott Co., 1893), p. 349; Wise, *op. cit.*, p. 471; Couper, *V.M.I.*, III, 25-43; *O.R.*, Series I, XXXVII, part 2, 96-97; J. William Jones, "Ex-Governor Letcher's Home", *Southern Historical Society Papers,* XVIII (1890), 393-395; Letcher to Gen. John D. Imboden, Apr. 20, 1877, John D. Imboden Papers, University of Virginia; S. H. Letcher to T. T. Munford, Aug. 31, 1910, Ellis-Munford Papers, Duke University. The accounts of this particular atrocity vary greatly. Pro-southern accounts scoff at Hunter's claim that he found a proclamation by Letcher inciting guerrilla warfare. Actually, such a proclamation would have been typical of Letcher, who had vigorously backed such tactics all through his administration.

It is possible that the disputed proclamation was nothing more than Letcher's proclamation of June 14, 1861, beseeching the people of western Virginia to reman loyal to the state. A zealot like Hunter might even interpret this as an incitement to guerrilla warfare. It could also have been Letcher's proclamation of June 27, 1862, seeking recruits for the State Line from Union-held areas of the northwest.

13. Allan, *op. cit.,* p. 196; Randall and Donald, *op. cit.,* p. 436; *O.R.,* Series I, XXXVII, part 2, 212; Typewritten manuscript by S. H. Letcher, no date, Letcher Papers/Lexington.

14. R. E. Lee to Letcher, July 4, 1864, and series of other letters to Letcher mainly in July, 1864, Letcher Papers/Lexington; Letcher to Seddon, July 2, 1864, C.S.A. Secretary of War, letters received, National Archives. Only scattered fragments of Letcher's financial records in this period are available. Lee consoled Letcher by advising him to "pity those who wrought this wrong in the satisfaction of your own course".

15. Swem and Chandler, *op. cit.,* VIII, 137-138; Letcher to Seddon, July 2, 1864, C.S.A. Secretary of War, letters received, National Archives; William Terrill to Letcher, June 22, 1864, and G. W. Purcell to Letcher, July 18, 1864, Letcher Papers/Lexington. In the March, 1865, election for the House of Delegates, Letcher received 82 votes, but he was not running for office. These were complimentary, unsolicited ballots by a few of the former governor's staunchest admirers in Rockbridge County. Even so, he was fourth in a field of six.

16. Randall and Donald, *op. cit.,* pp. 417-433, 523; Bruce Catton, *This Hallowed Ground: The Story of the Union Side of the Civil War* (Garden City: Doubleday, 1956), pp. 320-334.

17. Swem and Chandler, *op. cit.,* VIII, 139-140; Lee to Letcher, July 4, 1864, Letcher Papers/Lexington. Lee frequently assured Letcher that he was not in danger while leading the army.

18. Letcher to "Mr. Editor", no date, Letcher Papers/Lexington. The obvious errors in this rough draft are not indicated in the text. This letter was first published in *The Virginia Magazine of History and Biography* (July, 1964), vol. 72, no. 3, pp. 348-355.

19. Rembert W. Patrick, *The Fall of Richmond* (Baton Rouge: Louisiana State University Press, 1960), pp. 9, 19; *Gazette* (Lexington), Mar. 31, 1865, p. 2; Douglas Southall Freeman, *Lee's Lieutenants: A Study in Command* (New York: Charles Scribner's Sons, 1944), III, 658-672, 726-752; Randall and Donald, *op. cit.,* pp. 523-532.

CHAPTER 13

1. Letcher to Lee, May 15, 1865, R. E. Lee Papers, Virginia Historical Society.

2. E. G. Swem and J. A. C. Chandler, "Letters of John Letcher to J. Hierholzer, 1864-1865", *William and Mary College Quarterly Historical Magazine,* VIII (1928), 139-140; *O.R.,* Series I, XLVI, part 3, 1082. Mosby's Rangers and some other diehards were still under arms in Virginia. Lincoln's assassination increased fears that the war might be prolonged, and the arrest of the South's top political leaders was a logical precaution. Union officials evidently rated Letcher rather high on their "most wanted" list of rebel politicians.

3. *O.R.,* Series I, XLVI, part 3, 1202, and Series II, VIII, 534; Brief account of his own arrest by Letcher, no date, and Letcher to Davidson, May 20, 1865, Letcher Papers/Lexington.

4. Typewritten manuscript by S. H. Letcher, no date, brief account of his own arrest by Letcher, no date, Letcher to wife, May 20, 1865, Letcher Papers/Lexington; S. H. Letcher to T. T. Munford, July 17 and Aug. 31, 1910, Ellis-Munford Papers, Duke University; *Staunton Spectator,* June 12, 1877, p. 1. The arsenal where Letcher spent the night was probably the combination arsenal and penitentiary at Greenleaf's Point at the extreme southern tip of the city.

5. Margaret Leech, *Reveille in Washington: 1860-1865* (New York: Harper & Brothers, 1941), pp. 133-135, 148, 249, and map on inside cover; C. P. Smith, "Famous War Prisons and Escapes", *Confederate Veteran,* XXXI (1923), 411; Stanley Kimmel, *Mr. Lincoln's Washington* (New York: Coward-McCann, 1957), p. 71.

6. Letcher to W. G. Paine, July 30, 1865, Purcell to Letcher, June 8, 1865, Letcher to wife, July 4, 1865, and account by Letcher, no date, Letcher Papers/Lexington; lists of persons contributing funds and provisions to Letcher family, June, 1865, Davidson Papers, McCormick Collection; Clement Dowd, *Life of Zebulon Vance* (Charlotte: Observer Printing and Publishing House, 1897), p. 97; Richard E. Yates, *The Confederacy and Zeb Vance* (Tuscaloosa: Confederate Publishing Company, 1958), p. 122. Purcell said Richmonders were well treated by federal authorities. He said he was beginning to suspect that the late war was the politicians', not the people's war.

7. Letcher to Munford, Aug. 2, 1865, Ellis-Munford Papers, Duke University; typewritten manuscript by S. H. Letcher, no date, and Letcher to wife, July 4, 1865, Letcher Papers/Lexington; *O.R.,* Series I, LII, part 1, 316, and Series II, I, 811; *O.R.N.,* Series I, IV, 297; Bruce Catton, *This Hallowed Ground: The Story of the Union Side of the Civil War* (Garden City: Doubleday, 1956), pp. 332-333; F. N. Boney, "Turn About and Fair Play", *The Connecticut Historical Society Bulletin,* XXXI (April, 1966), 33-39. Wright's VI Corps was a crack unit. It stopped Early's 1864 assault on Washington, and in April, 1865, it broke Lee's thin line at Petersburg by direct assault.

8. Brief account of his own arrest by Letcher, no date, Letcher Papers/Lexington.

9. Letcher to wife, July 6, 1865, Letcher Papers/Lexington.

10. Davidson to [?], July 5, 1865, Letcher to Paine, July 30, 1865, typewritten manuscript by S. H. Letcher, no date, and Letcher's pardon papers, Letcher Papers/Lexington; asst. adj. gen. to C. C. Augur, July 10, and Augur to William P. Wood, July 10, 1865, Union Provost Marshal File, National Archives.

11. Letcher to Vance, July 19, 1865, Vance Papers, State Department of Archives and History, Raleigh, N. C.

12. Swem and Chandler, *op. cit.,* IX (2) (1929), 123; Letcher to Vance, July 19, Letcher to Paine, July 30, Letcher to Munford, Aug. 2, and Letcher to Vance, Oct. 16, 1865, Letcher Papers/Lexington; Richardson to Davidson, Aug. 7, 1865, Davidson Papers, McCormick Collection.

13. Letcher to [?], Sept. 7, 1865, Letcher to Vance, Sept. 7 and Oct. 16, 1865, and Letcher's pardon papers, Letcher Papers/Lexington; *Staunton Spectator,* June 12, 1877, p. 1; Swem and Chandler, *op. cit.,* IX, 123; Letcher to Munford, August 30, 1865, Ellis-Munford Papers, Duke University; Richardson to Davidson, Aug. 7, 1865, Davidson Papers, McCormick Collection. Richardson felt that the state legislature had lacked strong leadership for some time, and he recommended Letcher to fill this void.

14. David Starr Jordan and Henry Ernest Jordan, *War's Aftermath: A Preliminary Study of the Eugenics of War As Illustrated by the Civil War of the United States and the Late Wars in the Balkans* (Boston: Houghton Mifflin Company, 1914), pp. 10, 73; Letcher to Vance, Sept. 7 and Oct. 16, 1865, Letcher Papers/Lexington; Letcher to Munford, Aug. 30, 1865, Ellis-Munford Papers, Duke University.

15. Letcher to Vance, Sept. 7, 1865, Letcher Papers/Lexington; Lee to Letcher, Aug. 28, 1865, Letters to Letcher, Library of Congress; J. William Jones, *Personal Reminiscences, Anecdotes, and Letters of Gen. Robert E. Lee* (New York: D. Appleton and Company, 1874), p. 203; typewritten manuscript by S. H. Letcher, no date, Letcher Papers/Lexington; Douglas Southall Freeman, *R. E. Lee: A Biography* (New York: Charles Scribner's Sons, 1935), IV, 215--216; Franklin L. Riley, *General Robert E. Lee After Appomattox* (New York: The McMillan Company, 1930), pp. 44-45.

16. Francis H. Smith, *The Virginia Military Institute: Its Building and Rebuilding* (Lynchburg: J. P. Bell Company, 1912), pp. 268-272; Col. William Couper, *One Hundred Years at V.M.I.* (Richmond: Garrett and Massie, 1939), III, 103-113, 121, 133, 152; John Letcher, *Report of the Board of Visitors of the Virginia Military Institute with Accompanying Documents* (Richmond, 1867), *passim*. These annual reports examine in detail virtually every activity at V.M.I.

17. Letcher to Vance, Sept. 7 and Oct. 16, 1865, Letcher's par-

don papers, and typewritten manuscript by S. H. Letcher, no date, Letcher Papers/Lexington; Hamilton James Eckenrode, *The Political History of Virginia during the Reconstruction* (Baltimore: The Johns Hopkins Press, 1904), pp. 66-68, 120; William Edwin Hemphill, Marvin Wilson Schegel, and Sadie Ethel Engelberg, *Cavalier Commonwealth: History and Government of Virginia* (New York: McGraw-Hill, 1957), p. 354.

18. Letcher to Vance, Sept. 7, 1865 and May 4, 1866, Letcher Papers/Lexington; *Price Current Letter Sheet* (Richmond), Jan. 20, 1866, p. 1; Letcher to William L. Mitchell, Aug. 13, 1866, William Letcher Mitchell Papers, University of North Carolina.

19. Letcher to McCormick, Apr. 23, 1866, Davidson Papers, McCormick Collection; Letcher to Vance, May 4, 1866, Letcher Papers/Lexington. Letcher's letter to Vance repeats the same general sentiments.

20. Papers relating to the Valley Railroad, Letcher Papers/Lexington; M. G. Harman to James L. Kemper, Dec. 26, 1865, James L. Kemper Papers, University of Virginia; William Couper, *A History of the Shenandoah Valley* (New York: Lewis Historical Publishing Company, 1952), II, 975, 991, 1032-1036, 1341-1342. Actually, the Staunton convention discussed only a line from Harrisonburg to Salem. The overall plan included a line all the way from Harper's Ferry to Salem, but a spur already ran part of the way from Harper's Ferry to Harrisonburg. The big obstacle was the new construction necessary to link Harrisonburg and Salem.

21. *Gazette* (Lexington), Feb. 7, 1866, p. 2. Col. S. H. Letcher took over the *Gazette* the following month, added the word *Banner* to the title, and placed Stonewall Jackson's picture on the masthead.

22. Legal and tax receipts from the town of Lexington, 1866, and Lee to Letcher, June 6, 1866, Letcher Papers/Lexington; Letcher to M. Woods, June 15, 1866, William James Rucker Papers, University of Virginia.

23. *Gazette and Banner* (Lexington), Sept. 5, p. 2, and Sept. 12, 1866, pp. 1-2.

24. Eckenrode, *op. cit.*, pp. 50-51; *Gazette and Banner* (Lexington), Dec. 19, 1866, p. 2; Letcher to Davidson, Dec. 18, 1866, Davidson Papers, McCormick Collection; Robert McCulloch, "Reminiscence of Reconstruction", *Confederate Veteran*, XII (1904), number 9, 427-428; Kenneth M. Stampp, *The Era of Reconstruction, 1865-1877* (New York: Alfred A. Knopf, 1965), pp. 83-118; Eric L. McKitrick, *Andrew Johnson and Reconstruction* (Chicago: University of Chicago Press, 1960), pp. 458-459.

CHAPTER 14

1. Johnson to Letcher, Jan. 15, 1867, Letcher Papers/Lexington;

Gazette and Banner (Lexington), Jan. 30, 1867, p. 2, Apr. 3, p. 3, Apr. 24, p. 3, and May 1, 1867 p. 3. One of the most publicized postwar trials in Rockbridge involved a Georgian named J. L. Ellis, who had shot down a prominent young Lexingtonian on Main Street in broad daylight. Defense lawyers Letcher and Brockenbrough got Ellis off the legal hook with a plea of insanity and self-defense. Letcher won much popular attention in this spectacular case.

2. Hamilton James Eckenrode, *The Political History of Virginia during the Reconstruction* (Baltimore: The Johns Hopkins Press, 1904), pp. 49-80; typewritten manuscript by S. H. Letcher, no date, Letcher Papers/Lexington; Wm. S. Keen to Davidson, June 17, 1867, Davidson Papers, McCormick Collection.

3. Typewritten manuscript by S. H. Letcher, no date, Letcher Papers/Lexington; Letcher Notebook/Lexington; S. Bassett French notes, no date, S. Bassett French Papers, Virginia State Library; *Gazette and Banner* (Lexington), July 24, 1867, p. 2; James Albert Woodburn, *The Life of Thaddeus Stevens: A Study in American Political History, Especially in the Period of the Civil War and Reconstruction* (Indianapolis: Bobbs-Merrill Company, 1913), pp. 223-224. During the war, Stevens had labeled Letcher "a traitorous Governor of a traitorous state". Another son, Greenlee Davidson Letcher, was born just before the trip to Washington.

4. Colfax to Letcher, Jan. 20, 1869, Schuyler Colfax Papers, Library of Congress; Letcher to Colfax, Jan. 18 and 25, 1869, Letcher Papers/Lexington. This Letcher-Colfax correspondence is a complicated argument over exactly what was said during their conversation in Washington. Letcher denied having said that he wanted to renew the war, claiming that he had said only that he was not repentant, that he had done what he thought was right at the time, and that he would do it again under the same circumstances. Exactly what the two men did say is uncertain, but both became angry, and both probably said things they later regretted. Reports of the argument spread. Letcher never considered the affair confidential, and he told many people his side of the story. The Republican ticket of Grant and Colfax won the presidential election of 1868, but, of course, the usual political passions were aroused in the process. The Louisville *Democrat* printed a version of the Letcher-Colfax dispute quoting Colfax to the effect that Grant "was no statesman". Colfax blamed Letcher for this quotation, and this accusation started the exchange of letters.

5. Eckenrode, *op. cit.,* pp. 80-85; *Gazette and Banner* (Lexington), Dec. 4, 1867, p. 2. In the October balloting, 93,145 Negroes voted, but only 76,084 of more than 116,000 eligible whites went to the polls. The obvious remedy for such apathy was an effective political organization, a new political party.

6. *Gazette and Banner* (Lexington), Dec. 18, 1867, p. 2; *Daily*

Dispatch (Richmond), Dec. 12-14, 1867, all p. 2; Eckenrode, *op. cit.,* pp. 9-86; Charles Chilton Pearson, *The Readjuster Movement in Virginia* (New Haven: Yale University Press, 1917), pp. 19-20. Letcher's district committee was composed of himself, Kemper, and Baldwin. Many veteran politicians attended the convention. Among the delegates were R. M. T. Hunter, John D. Imboden, R. E. Withers, James Lyons, Thomas S. Flournoy, John R. Tucker, William W. Crump, and J. M. McCue.

7. Dunbar Rowland (ed.), *Jefferson Davis: Constitutionalist: His Letters, Papers and Speeches* (New York: J. J. Little & Ives Company, 1923), VII, 182; Jonathan Truman Dorris, *Pardon and Amnesty Under Lincoln and Johnson: The Restoration of the Confederates to Their Rights and Privileges, 1861-1898* (Chapel Hill: University of North Carolina Press, 1953), pp. 294-296, 421; Letcher to Elihu B. Washburne, November 17, 1868, Elihu B. Washburne Papers, Library of Congress. Davis was first indicted for treason in Norfolk in May, 1865, then in Washington, and then again in Norfolk in May, 1866. The Fourteenth Amendment, officially ratified on July 28, 1868, rendered Letcher ineligible for political office; he never petitioned Congress to remove this disability.

8. Dorris, *op. cit.,* pp. 301-311, 321-323, 376; Rowland, *op. cit.,* pp. 226-227; Elizabeth Cutting, *Jefferson Davis: Political Soldier* (New York: Dodd Mead & Company, 1930), p. 304; typewritten manuscript by S. H. Letcher, no date, and note written by Letcher, no date, Letcher Papers/Lexington; S. H. Letcher to T. T. Munford, July 17 and Aug. 31, 1910, Ellis-Munford Papers, Duke University; *Gazette* (Lexington), Jan. 31, 1884, p. 3. Despite his difficulties, Letcher visited New York City for a week in June, 1868.

9. Letcher to Washburne, Nov. 17, and Washburne to Letcher, Nov. 24, 1868, Washburne Papers, Library of Congress.

10. E. Merton Coulter, *The South During Reconstruction: 1865-1877* (Baton Rouge: Louisiana State University Press, 1947), p. 349; Eckenrode, *op. cit.,* pp. 41, 106-128; Pearson, *op. cit.,* pp. 21-23; Alex. H. H. Stuart, *A Narrative of the Leading Incidents of the Organization of the First Popular Movement in Virginia in 1865 to Re-establish Peaceful Relations Between the Northern and Southern States, and of the Subsequent Efforts of the "Committee of Nine", in 1869 to Secure the Restoration of Virginia to the Union* (Richmond, 1948), *passim;* Audrey Marie Cahill, "Gilbert C. Walker: Virginia's Redeemer Governor" (unpublished thesis, 1956, University of Virginia), pp. 43-45, 75-77; Letcher to William Mahone, June 9, 1870, William Mahone Papers, Duke University; John Hope Franklin, *Reconstruction: After the Civil War* (Chicago: University of Chicago Press, 1961), pp. 195-197. Of all the former Confederate states, only Tennessee escaped Radical Reconstruction more completely than Virginia.

11. Letcher to Mahone, June 9, 1870, Mahone Papers, Duke University; Letcher to Prof. J. B. Minor, June 28, 1871, Davidson Papers, McCormick Collection; Richardson to Letcher, May 3, 1871, Letcher Papers/Lexington; John Letcher, *Annual Report of the Board of Visitors and Superintendent of the Virginia Military Institute for the Year Ending July 1, 1872* (Richmond, 1872), *passim; Gazette and Banner* (Lexington), May 13 and Sept. 16, 1868, p. 1.

12. C. Vanderbilt to Letcher, Jan. 12, 1871, Letcher Papers/Lexington; Letcher to Davidson, May 5, 1871, Davidson Papers, McCormick Collection.

13. Pearson, *op. cit.,* pp. 24-34; C. Vann Woodward, *Origins of the New South: 1877-1913* (Baton Rouge: Louisiana State University Press, 1851), pp. 4-5. The railroads retained their old privileges but escaped most state control, and their influence on the legislature increased dangerously.

14. Pearson, *op. cit.,* pp. 47-50; *Daily Dispatch* (Richmond), November 5, 1873, p. 1; Gilman to N. B. Meade, June 12, 1873, Letcher to Kemper, Nov. 24, 1873, and Chas. A. Davidson to Kemper, Dec. 8, 1873, James L. Kemper Papers, University of Virginia; French to Mrs. Letcher, June 18, 1872, Letcher Papers/Lexington.

15. Richardson to Kemper, Nov. 26, 1873, Kemper Papers, University of Virginia; Kemper to Purcell, Dec. 10, 1870, James L. Kemper Papers, Virginia Historical Society. Kemper told Purcell that Letcher "has my very high and warm regard".

16. Chas. A. Davidson to Kemper, Dec. 8, 1873, and Letcher to Kemper, Nov. 24, 1873 and Mar. 17, 1874, Kemper Papers, University of Virginia; Pearson, *op. cit.,* pp. 47-67. After the veto, Governor Kemper was hanged in effigy in Petersburg. Letcher condemned this mob action and congratulated Kemper on his stand.

17. Jubal Early to Letcher, Mar. 14, 1874, and Letcher's financial records, 1872-1874, Letcher Papers/Lexington; Letcher & Letcher to Jno. K. Mitchell, Sept. 11, and Mitchell to Letcher & Letcher, Sept. 18, 1874, John Kirkwood Mitchell Papers, Virginia Historical Society Mitchell condemned Letcher for assisting former Union officers attempting to gain prize money for rebel ships they destroyed when Richmond fell. Mitchell said this only meant higher taxes for the southern people, who were already deeply in debt.

18. Mary H. Maury to Mrs. Letcher, Oct. 2, 1873, Letcher Papers/Lexington; Kemper to Letcher, Dec. 11, 1874, Kemper Papers, University of Virginia; Letcher to Mahone, June 9, 1870, Mahone Papers, Duke University. Maury died in 1873 and was buried in Hollywood Cemetery, Richmond. His son Richard practiced law with Letcher & Letcher for a short time.

19. Early to Letcher, July 21, 1873, and typewritten manuscript by S. H. Letcher, no date, Letcher Papers/Lexington; John Letcher,

To the Descendants, in the great North-West, of the Scotch-Irish Settlers of the Valley of Virginia (printed letter, Lexington, July 21, 1873), *passim; Gazette* (Lexington), May 21, 1863, p. 1; Henry Harrison Simms, *Life of Robert M. T. Hunter: A Study in Sectionalism and Secession* (Richmond: William Byrd Press, 1935), pp. 155-156; *The Proceedings of the Southern Historical Convention and of the Southern Historical Society As Reorganized* (Baltimore: Turnbull Brothers, 1873), pp. 1-14; "Recumbent Figure of Gen. R. E. Lee", *Confederate Veteran,* VII (1899), number 10, 513. An association was formed in 1863 to procure "a Colossal Equestrian Statue" of Jackson, and a contract was signed with A. Frederic Volck of Nuremberg, Bavaria. The statue was completed, but Herr Volck refused to ship it until he received his fee of $25,000. This stimulated the fund raising campaign. At the White Sulphur Springs convention Jefferson Davis in private conversations hailed Letcher's selfless devotion to the cause.

20. Early to Letcher, Sept. 14, 1874, and typewritten manuscript by S. H. Letcher, no date, Letcher Papers/Lexington; *Staunton Spectator,* June 12, 1877, p. 1.

21. A. W. Wallace to S. H. Letcher, no date, Letcher Papers/Lexington; *Daily Dispatch* (Richmond), Mar. 3, 1876, p. 1.

22. Pearson, *op. cit.,* pp. 65-66; *Daily Dispatch* (Richmond), December, 1875–March, 1876, p. 2. For special mention of Letcher see issues of Dec. 10, 18, and 20, 1875, and Jan. 14, 29, 31, Feb. 3, 18, 22, 26, and Mar. 21, 28, 29, 1876.

23. G. W. Jones to Letcher, Feb. 21, 1877, Letcher Papers/Lexington; Letcher to Kemper, Aug. 9, Oct. 20, and Nov. 24, 1876, Kemper Papers, University of Virginia; Letcher to Wm. L. Mitchell, Apr. 16, 1878, Mitchell Papers, University of North Carolina; *Daily Dispatch* (Richmond), Mar. 4, 1876, p. 1; *Gazette* (Lexington), Jan. 31, 1884, p. 3. The main treatment administered to the stricken Letcher was the application of leeches and other fluid absorbing medications along the spine and on the neck. Letcher was strong enough to survive the cure as well as the illness.

24. Letcher to Judge Welford, Feb. 4, 1877, Isaac H. Carrington Papers Duke University; Letcher to S. H. Letcher, Feb. 6, 1877, and A. R. Corbin to Letcher, Nov. 30, 1876 and Jan. 31, 1877, Letcher Papers/Lexington; Pearson, *op cit.,* p. 65; C. Vann Woodward, *Reunion and Reaction: The Compromise of 1877 and the End of Reconstruction* (Boston: Little, Brown and Company, 1951), pp. 1-50. The *Daily Dispatch* (Richmond) furnished thorough coverage of this second session of the legislature. Corbin, a seasoned financial manipulator, advised Letcher to support partial repudiation of the state debt. He pointed out that Alabama, Indiana, and other states had already experimented successfully with this policy.

25. Letcher to Gov. F. W. M. Holliday, Mar. 5 and 12, 1878,

W. M. Holliday Papers, Duke University; clipping from a Lexington newspaper, no date, John R. Tucker Scrapbook, University of North Carolina; typewritten manuscript by S. H. Letcher, no date, Letcher Papers/Lexington; *Richmond Weekly Whig*, Aug. 3, 1877, p. 2; *Gazette* (Lexington), Oct. 19, p. 2, Nov. 2, p. 2, and Nov. 9, 1877, p. 2. Letcher's Conservative running mate was Colonel John C. Shields, former editor of the *Richmond Whig*. Shields was vigorous and healthy, but he also lost. Two political unknowns, James A. Frazier and John B. Lady, were the victors.

26. Letcher to Holliday, Jan. 8, Mar. 12, and Dec. 11, 1878, and May 20 and Dec. 20, 1879, Holliday Papers, Duke University; Letcher to Kemper, Nov. 13, 1877, Kemper Papers, University of Virginia; Pearson, *op. cit.*, pp. 62, 68-80.

27. Letcher to Holliday, May 20, 1879, Holliday Papers, Duke University; *Gazette and Citizen* (Lexington), April 1, 1880, p. 3; Pearson, *op. cit.*, pp. 95-131.

28. Mary Letcher Blackwell to Letcher (her brother), Mar. 29, 1882, Letcher Papers/Lexington; newspaper clipping, 1883, R. A. Lancaster, Jr., Scrapbook, Virginia Historical Society; ledger of Dr. J. McDowell Taylor, 1883-1884, Rockbridge County Historical Society, Lexington; *Daily Dispatch* (Richmond), Jan. 27, 1884, p. 3. Sister Mary advised Letcher to "dispel the mists of doubt and unbelief which becloud the understanding of the unregenerate man".

29. General Assembly Resolution, Jan. 26, 1884, Letcher Papers/Lexington; *Daily Dispatch* (Richmond), Jan. 27, 1884, p. 3; Writers' Program of the Work Projects Administration in the State of Virginia, *Virginia: A Guide to the Old Dominion* (New York: Oxford University Press, 1941), p. 429.

Selected Bibliography

This biography is based largely on primary sources. Two manuscript depositories have been particularly vital: John Letcher's private records and correspondence, still in the possession of the family (Letcher Papers/Lexington); and the Executive Papers, 1860–1863, at the Virginia State Library (EP). The first of these collections has never before been systematically exploited; the second, though frequently examined by scholars, has never before formed the basis for a thorough study of Letcher's administration.

These sources were reinforced by materials in manuscript collections at Duke University, the University of North Carolina, the University of Georgia, the University of Virginia, Virginia Military Institute, the Library of Congress, the National Archives, the State Historical Society of Wisconsin, the Historical Society of Pennsylvania, the Virginia Historical Society, the Rockbridge County Historical Society, the Henry E. Huntington Library, the Filson Club, and other depositories. State newspapers, particularly the Richmond and Lexington journals, were also used extensively, as were the *Congressional Globe, Acts of the General Assembly, Official Records of the Union and Confederate Navies in the War of the Rebellion, The War of the Rebellion: A Compilation of the Official Records of the Union and Confederate Armies,* and other essential printed sources.

Unpublished theses and dissertations, journal articles, and a host of books, old and new, were also consulted, and have been cited fully in the Notes. The most important are the following:

BOOKS

Allan, Elizabeth Preston, *The Life and Letters of Margaret Junkin Preston.* See chapter 9, note 14.

304

Ambler, Charles Henry, editor, *Correspondence of R. M. T. Hunter, 1826—1876.* See chapter 5, note 37.

Ambler, Charles Henry, *Sectionalism in Virginia from 1776 to 1861.* See chapter 1, note 13.

Ambler, Charles Henry, *Thomas Ritchie: A Study in Virginia Politics.* See chapter 1, note 5.

Bryan, T. Conn, *Confederate Georgia.* See chapter 9, note 13.

Catton, Bruce, *This Hallowed Ground: The Story of the Union Side of the Civil War.* See chapter 6, note 31.

Christian, W. Asbury, *Richmond: Her Past and Present.* See chapter 6, note 18.

Claiborne, John Herbert, *Seventy-Five Years in Old Virginia,* See chapter 6, note 30.

Coulter, E. Merton, *The Confederate States of America: 1861—1865.* See chapter 6, note 40.

Couper, Colonel William, *One Hundred Years at V. M. I.* See chapter 1, note 3.

Crenshaw, Ollinger, *The Slave States in the Presidential Election of 1860.* See chapter 6, note 4.

Dorris, Jonathan Truman, *Pardon and Amnesty Under Lincoln and Johnson: The Restoration of the Confederates to Their Rights and Privileges, 1861—1898.* See chapter 14, note 7.

Dowdey, Clifford, *Experiment in Rebellion.* See chapter 7, note 10.

Dowdey, Clifford, *The Land They Fought For: The Story of the South As the Confederacy: 1832—1865.* See chapter 7, note 9.

Dunaway, Wayland Fuller, *History of the James River and Kanawha Company.* See chapter 4, note 8.

Eaton, Clement, *Freedom of Thought in the Old South.* See chapter 1, note 4.

Eckenrode, Hamilton James, *The Political History of Virginia during the Reconstruction.* See chapter 13, note 17.

Freeman, Douglas Southall, *Lee's Lieutenants: A Study in Command.* See chapter 6, note 31.

Freeman, Douglas Southall, *R. E. Lee: A Biography.* See chapter 7, note 3.

Hambleton, James P., *A Biographical Sketch of Henry A. Wise With A History of the Political Campaign in Virginia in 1855.* See chapter 4, note 26.

Johnston, Angus James II, *Virginia Railroads in the Civil War.* See chapter 11, note 3.

Jones, J. B., *A Rebel War Clerk's Diary at the Confederate States Capitol.* See chapter 6, note 39.

Leech, Margaret, *Reveille in Washington: 1860—1865.* See chapter 13, note 5.

Lonn, Ella, *Salt As a Factor in the Confederacy*. See chapter 10, note 7.

McDonald, Mrs. Cornelia, *A Diary With Reminiscences of the War and Refuge Life in the Shenandoah Valley: 1860—1865*. See chapter 12, note 12.

McGregor, James C., *The Disruption of Virginia*. See chapter 6, note 3.

McPherson, Edward, *The Political History of the U. S. of A. during the Great Rebellion*. See chapter 6, note 29.

Meade, Robert Douthat, *Judah P. Benjamin: Confederate Statesman*. See chapter 9, note 14.

Morton, Oron F., *A History of Rockbridge County, Virginia*. See chapter 1, note 3.

Nevins, Allan, *Ordeal of the Union* (2 vols.). See chapter 4, note 3.

Nevins, Allan, *The Statesmanship of the Civil War*. See chapter 10, note 13.

Nevins, Allan, *The War for the Union: The Improvised War: 1861—1862*. See chapter 7, note 9.

Nichols, Roy Franklin, *The Disruption of American Democracy*. See chapter 4, note 38.

Owsley, Frank Lawrence, *King Cotton Diplomacy: Foreign Relations of the Confederate States of America*. See chapter 7, note 9.

Owsley, Frank Lawrence, *State Rights in the Confederacy*. See chapter 8, note 5.

Parmelee, Alice Maury, editor, *The Confederate Diary of Betty Herndon Maury, Daughter of Lieut. Commander M. F. Maury, "The Pathfinder of the Seas": 1861—1863*. See chapter 8, note 3.

Pearson, Charles Chilton, *The Readjuster Movement in Virginia*. See chapter 14, note 6.

Peyton, John Lewis, *The American Crisis; or Pages from the Note-Book of a State Agent During the Civil War*. See chapter 4, note 37.

Randall, J. G., and Donald, David, *The Civil War and Reconstruction*. See chapter 6, note 12.

Roland, Dunbar, editor, *Jefferson Davis; Constitutionalist: His Letters, Papers and Speeches* (10 vols.). See chapter 7, note 1.

Shanks, Henry T., *The Secession Movement in Virginia: 1847—1861*. See chapter 3, note 10.

Simms, Henry H., *The Rise of the Whigs in Virginia: 1824—1840*. See chapter 1, note 5.

Smith, Francis H., *The Virginia Military Institute: Its Building and Rebuilding*. See chapter 13, note 16.

Stampp, Kenneth M., *The Era of Reconstruction, 1865—1877*. See chapter 13, note 24.

Stuart, Alex. H. H., *A Narrative of the Leading Incidents of the Organization of the First Popular Movement in Virginia in 1865 to Re-Establish Peaceful Relations Between the Northern and Southern*

States, and of the Subsequent Efforts of the "Committee of Nine", *in 1869 to Secure the Restoration of Virginia to the Union*. See chapter 14, note 10.

Summers, Festus P., *The Baltimore and Ohio in the Civil War*. See chapter 7, note 6.

Vandiver, Frank E., editor, *The Civil War Diary of General Josiah Gorgas*. See chapter 8, note 5.

Villard, Oswald Garrison, *John Brown: 1800—1859: A Biography Fifty Years After*. See chapter 6, note 7.

Williams, Frances Leigh, *Matthew Fontaine Maury: Scientist of the Sea*. See chapter 9, note 11.

Withers, Robert Eunoch, *Autobiography of an Octogenarian*. See chapter 12, note 7.

Woodward, C. Vann, *Origins of the New South: 1877—1913*. See chapter 14, note 13.

Yearns, Wilfred Buck, *The Confederate Congress*. See chapter 11, note 2.

Younger, Edward, editor, *Inside the Confederate Government: The Diary of Robert Garlick Hill Kean, Head of the Bureau of War*. See chapter 9, note 1.

ARTICLES

Bean, William Gleason, "John Letcher and the Slavery Issue in Virginia's Gubernatorial Contest of 1858—1859". See chapter 3, note 2.

Bean, William Gleason, "The Ruffner Pamphlet of 1847: An Antislavery Aspect of Virginia's Sectionalism". See chapter 3, note 2.

Boney, F. N., "Governor Letcher's Candid Correspondence". See chapter 6, note 11.

Boney, F. N., "John Letcher's Secret Criticism of the Confederate Cabinet", *Virginia Magazine* . . . (July, 1964). See chapter 12, note 18.

Crenshaw, Ollinger, "Christopher G. Memminger's Mission to Virginia, 1860". See chapter 6, note 6.

Jones, J. William, "Official Correspondence of Governor Letcher". See chapter 7, notes 14 and 34.

Kellar, Herbert A., editor, "A Journey Through the South in 1836: Diary of James D. Davidson". See chapter 6, note 36.

Long, John Sherman, "The Gosport Affair, 1861". See chapter 7, note 2.

McDonald, E. H., "How Virginia Supplied Maryland With Arms". See chapter 7, note 13.

Prettyman, E. B., "John Letcher". See chapter 1, note 15.

Rice, Philip Morrison, "The Know—Nothing Party in Virginia, 1854—1856". See chapter 4, note 27.

Ruffner, William Henry, "History of Washington College". See chapter 1, note 12.

Swem, E. G., and Chandler, J. A. C., "Letters of John Letcher to J.

Hierholzer, 1864—1865". See chapter 12, note 2, and chapter 13, note 2.

Teakle, Thomas, "The Rendition of Barclay Coppac". See chapter 6, note 8.

Trexler, Harrison A., "The Opposition of Planters to the Employment of Slaves as Laborers by the Confederacy". See chapter 9, note 5.

Webster, Donald B. Jr., "The Last Days of Harpers Ferry Armory". See chapter 7, note 2.

PAMPHLETS

Letcher, John, *To the Freemen of Rockbridge County*. See chapter 2, note 2.

Letcher, John, *Report of the Board of Visitors of the Virginia Military Institute with Accompanying Documents*. See chapter 13, note 16.

Letcher, John, *Annual Report of the Board of Visitors and Superintendent of the Virginia Military Institute for the Year Ending July 1, 1872*. See chapter 14, note 11.

Letcher, John, and others, *Memorial of Members of the Virginia Reform Convention*. See chapter 3, note 28.

Ruffner, Henry, *Address to the People of West Virginia: Shewing That Slavery Is Injurious to the Public Welfare, and That It May Be Gradually Abolished, Without Detriment to the Rights and Interests of Slaveholders*. See chapter 3, note 5.

Segar, Joseph, *Letter of Hon. Joseph Segar to a Friend in Virginia*. See chapter 6, note 39.

State Central Committee of the Whig Party, *To the People of Virginia! John Letcher and His Antecedents*. See chapter 5, note 28.

THESES AND DISSERTATIONS

Cahill, Audrey Marie, "Gilbert C. Walker: Virginia's Redeemer Governor". See chapter 14, note 10.

Fahrner, Alvin Arthur, "The Public Career of William 'Extra Billy' Smith". See chapter 9, note 17.

Gaines, Francis Pendleton Jr., "The Political Career of James McDowell, 1830—1851". See chapter 1, note 7.

Gaines, Francis Pendleton Jr., "The Virginia Constitutional Convention of 1850—1851: A Study in Sectionalism". See chapter 3, note 1.

Jones, Robert R., "Forgotten Virginian: The Early Life and Career of James Lawson Kemper: 1823—1865". See chapter 6, note 5.

Index

316 JOHN LETCHER OF VIRGINIA